THE HISTORY
OF
THE LIBERAL PARTY
1895-1970

The History of the
LIBERAL PARTY
1895–1970

Roy Douglas

with a Foreword by the
Rt. Hon. Jeremy Thorpe, M.P.

FAIRLEIGH DICKINSON UNIVERSITY PRESS

Madison · Rutherford · Teaneck

First American Edition 1971

Associated University Presses
Cranbury, N.J. 08512

Copyright © Roy Douglas 1971

Library of Congress Catalogue Card Number: 70-169814
ISBN: 0—8386—1056—0

Printed in Great Britain

To
MY WIFE AND CHILDREN

Contents

	List of Plates	ix
	Foreword by the Rt. Hon. Jeremy Thorpe, M.P.	xi
	Acknowledgements	xix
1	The Background	1
2	The Long Road Back	18
3	The Top of the Hill	36
4	The New Radicalism	52
5	Lib-Lab Politics	64
6	The Lamps Go Out	91
7	The Coupon Election	108
8	The Hard-faced Men	132
9	Nemesis	154
10	Switchback	166
11	St Martin's Summer	188
12	Disruption	208
13	Between the Millstones	233
14	New Directions	265
15	Retrospect and Prospect	287
	Biographical Notes	303
	Short Bibliography	315
	Index	319

List of Plates

William Ewart Gladstone and granddaughter	*between pages* 62–3
Sir Henry Campbell-Bannerman	62–3
Herbert Henry Asquith	62–3
Viscount (Sir Herbert) Samuel	62–3
Viscount (Sir John) Simon	62–3
The Last Great Bid for Power	156–7
David Lloyd George 1st Earl Lloyd-George	156–7
Lloyd George with the Prince of Wales	156–7
Sir Archibald Sinclair, Viscount Thurso	156–7
Clement Davies	248–9
'The Orpington Man'	248–9
Jeremy Thorpe	248–9

Foreword

by the

RT. HON. JEREMY THORPE, M.P.

LEADER OF THE LIBERAL PARTY

Dr Douglas's book makes fascinating but frustrating reading for Liberals. We are reminded not only of lost opportunities for the Party, but of how tantalizingly unnecessary the loss of these opportunities was. The disaster for British radicalism when the Labour Party replaced the Liberals as the larger opponent of Conservatism can be seen clearly enough in electoral terms. In the half-century from 1868 (the first general election with a mass electorate) to 1918 the Tories or Tory-dominated coalitions were in office for only twenty-two years. In the subsequent fifty years, with Labour as the main opposition to them, the Tories were at the head of affairs, or much the largest force in coalitions, for three-quarters of the time. Mr Harold Wilson's determination to make the Labour Party the natural party of Government was cruelly disappointed for him in 1970. Although Tory dominance has accompanied half a century of British decline there seems small ground for supposing that the long period of Conservative electoral success is at an end.

Nor was the failure of British radicalism after 1918 merely quantitative. Reading Dr Douglas's account of the decline of the Liberal Party is the more distressing when the inventiveness of Liberals and the sheer ineptitude of their Socialist supplanters is remembered. It was Keynes who saw the way out of the slump while Snowden was screwing down the meagre reliefs for the unemployed. It was Sinclair who saw that standing up to the dictators required military preparedness, while the Socialists were still drifting in dreams of disarmament.

It was Beveridge who provided the ideas for the great extension of welfare while the Labour leadership was still obsessed with nationalization. It was Clement Davies and not Clement Attlee who had the vision to see the significance of the Schuman Plan and who urged – with, I fear, Dr Douglas's disapproval – British participation in the emerging European Community.

The record of Liberal percipience and of Labour myopia is as evident as it is disastrous. Before 1939 it marred the hopes of the world. Today, in Britain's shrunken state, it does not perhaps do more than inhibit national recovery and reinforce the tendencies of decline. But that is bad enough.

Dr Douglas shows how much the fall of Liberalism was due to the muddles and confusions of the Liberal Whips before the First World War. The very British virtue of the early Labour movement, its moderation or lack of dogmatism, was a great misfortune. It meant that the Liberals could look on the Labour M.P.s as allies rather than rivals. It encouraged the forward-thinking in the Liberal Party to see politics too much in simple Left–Right terms rather than as a struggle between Liberalism and illiberalism, and so disarmed them for the post-1917 world of the totalitarians. It allowed organized labour, once overwhelmingly sympathetic to the great party of reform, to drift gradually into forming a party so dependent on class feeling that even now many of the most progressive minds in Britain can find no place on the official Left.

The Liberals were to blame for giving room to the Socialist cuckoo in the radical nest. The Herbert Gladstone/Ramsay MacDonald arrangement, which relieved thirty-one Labour candidates of Liberal competition in 1906 without extracting any advantage for the Liberals, was an act of uncalled-for electoral generosity unforgivable in a Chief Whip. At the very moment when the Liberals needed no support from outside to win a smashing victory, they gratuitously admitted to Westminster, and even encouraged the entry of, a group of M.P.s whose only opportunity for expansion lay in replac-ing the Liberal Party. The warnings of constituency loyalists were ignored. The miners, for long regarded as archetypal Labour supporters, were at that time still well inclined to Liberalism. But in some seats the miners were actually put under pressure by Liberals to accept Labour candidates! Dr Douglas does well to quote Euripides at the beginning of the chapter recounting in fascinating if morbid detail, these lamentable blunders.

These self-inflicted wounds might not have proved so grievous, but for the great disaster of 1914.

Dr Douglas wisely eschews any attempt at a recapitulation of the world crisis. He concentrates on the internal agonies of Liberalism. That the Chief Whip, Percy Illingworth, recognized the mortal danger to the values of Liberalism as the war began in a mood of national solidarity and not a little euphoria, is remarkable. It is a comment not only on his personal sensitivity, but on the strains within the Party and Government of which, by virtue of his office, he must have been particularly well-informed.

Dr Douglas inclines to sympathize with those who argued against British commitment to the war. But I have always felt that one of the most remarkable achievements of Asquith's leadership was the way he was able, although beset by the Irish Crisis which threatened civil war, to understand and to get the nation to understand, that the attack on Belgium left Britain with no honourable option.

That Asquith assessed the public will accurately may be seen by the acceptance by Lloyd George, the Unionists, the Labour Party, and the Irish Nationalists of the Government's decision. Under his leadership – reinforced by the patent integrity of Sir Edward Grey – the Government, which a few days before was threatened by unconstitutional challenge from the official, putatively loyal, Opposition and which contained among its own supporters many who were for peace at almost any price, was able to unite the nation against aggression.

Dr Douglas's sympathy with Morley's position leads him, I think, to underrate the harm done to peace by those who, in the years before 1914, made an absolutely clear commitment by the Liberal Government to a full scale Anglo-French alliance impossible. Their motives were impeccable, but their policy was irresponsible. It is one of the curiosities of the time that those who, like Grey and Churchill, understood best how obsolete was the theory of splendid isolation in both its imperialist and pacific forms, showed so little anger against the Liberals who clung to its illusions. In *Great Contemporaries* Churchill gives a moving salute to Morley. In the highest quarters there seems to have been almost no recrimination. It would be interesting to know if any traces of it can be found in the records of constituency Liberal associations and in the memories of back-benchers.

Dr Douglas has produced none and he has been so thorough in his researches that one can only presume that in this the Liberal rank and file followed their leaders' example. It is not, after all, as though they lacked other material for mutual acrimony after 1916!

As one who was fortunate enough to enjoy the friendship of both Lady Asquith of Yarnbury and Lady Megan Lloyd George I can appreciate the more Dr Douglas's fairness to their fathers. To avoid partisanship while giving weight to the passions on both sides is a notable achievement. It is easy to appear Olympian by casting generalized scorn, but very difficult to be objective when caring deeply about the issues as Dr Douglas clearly does.

The quarrel – or rather quarrels, for the book brings out well the multiplicity of divisions – between Asquith and Lloyd George make very sad reading. But in this account it is brought home to us that they were not merely exchanges of personal bitterness. Irish policy, as in the 1880s, was the great question which kept the venom in the disputes between Liberals. By the time that the Free State and Partition were established facts and the Black and Tans only an evil memory, Asquith had lost his seat at Paisley, Lloyd George had lost his tenure of No. 10, and Churchill and Haldane were only the most prominent of those who had abandoned the Party in despair at its divisions.

Although the Party was to fight a brilliant campaign in 1929 on a Keynesian programme it had lost the aura of authority which only a real reconciliation of Asquith and Lloyd George could have provided for its followers and for the nation at large. It had become a progressive pressure group rather than a Party of Government.

In the Waste Land of British politics between the wars, when the Tories acquiesced in the Slump and then grovelled before Hitler, while the Socialists wrung their hands about unemployment and appeasement but refused to take any constructive action about either, the need for such a pressure group was immense. It failed. But its failure was not total. Roosevelt was able to borrow from the Liberal Yellow Book many ideas for the New Deal. Churchill acknowledged on the floor of the Commons the role of the Liberals in supporting his lonely stand against appeasement. It is important for our national self respect that there were others besides the great warrior, in an organized, democratic, political body, who recognized the folly and the shame of the Chamberlain years. Mr Ian Colvin's researches have recently confirmed that the critics of Chamberlain were guilty only of leniency.

Still, in their main objectives, the Liberals failed in the thirties and the fact that the Conservative and Labour failures were more abject is cold comfort.

One cause so far as economic questions are concerned, to which I would give more weight than Dr Douglas allows, is that traditional free trade policies inevitably seemed inadequate in the age of the dole queue. In fact they *were* insufficient, although not erroneous. The absurdities of protectionism and their disastrous consequences between the wars are now generally agreed – if not always publicly acknowledged. But free trade on its own was not enough. It is greatly to the credit of the Liberal Party that it understood this and welcomed so radical an innovator as Keynes. But it is hardly surprising, if regrettable, that many of the general public, seeing the Slump all round them, were unimpressed by the achievements of traditional economics. It was inevitable that they associated the suffering and failures of the depression with the economic system then obtaining. The tradition of Free Trade had defeated Baldwin in the 1923 election. By 1932 it was a tradition which reduced the chances of its advocates. It was associated with the depression and deemed obsolete. However deplorable, that was not unnatural. The Liberal ministers who resigned over Ottawa, while acting honourably if belatedly, appeared as the upholders of a vanished age rather than as radical critics. Samuel and his colleagues were right, but it was surely to be expected that given the failure of free trade to remedy the situation in the twenties, the thirties should regard them as irrelevant.

Dr Douglas writes most interestingly of the war years. Party politics were necessarily and properly a side-show between 1939 and 1945, but beneath the surface great shifts of opinion were taking place, and that they went largely in a positive direction was greatly due to the constructive proposals for social and economic reorganization which will always be associated with the names of Beveridge and Keynes. It was the misfortune of the Party, if the gain of the allied cause, that its leader was at the Air Ministry, prevented from devoting his energies to the rebuilding of Liberalism, and unable to exploit the huge reputation as a far-sighted opponent of Hitlerism which he had acquired before the War.

For all its ups and downs since 1945 the Liberal Party has shown plenty of vitality. It has pioneered policies of industrial co-partnership, constitutional reform, and, above all, Western European unity, which are beginning to find a wider acceptance. In the 1940s it was vigilant in protesting against Socialist indifference to the rights of the individual. In the 1960s it has led the fight against racialism, being the only Party which stood solidly against the devaluation of the passport of East African Asians who had opted for British citizenship. It has proved that if it did not continue to exist it would have to be invented. In spite of the vast handicaps imposed by an electoral system and Parliamentary procedure heavily weighted against third parties; in spite of the lack of automatic financial assistance from trade unions and big business; in spite of a Press which is overwhelmingly Conservative or Labour in sympathy, the Liberal Party has proved its durability and demonstrated its potential. It has outlived all the Tory-sponsored splinters with 'Liberal' as part of their misleading description, who confused and distorted the electoral scene for so many years. Even in bad years like 1950 and 1970, well over two million people have voted Liberal. At moments like Orpington, many times that number were near to committing themselves to the cause.

Dr Douglas rightly emphasizes that the Liberal struggle is a continuing one. For a Party which declares in its constitution that 'in everything it puts freedom first', 'eternal vigilance' is a duty. 'Freedom's battle' which springs, Liberals believe, from the nature of individual man, and not from vast anonymous forces, 'is never lost and never won'.

But the severity of the struggle varies greatly. The British people may hope that both the Labour and Conservative Parties have been sufficiently schooled in Liberalism for essential freedoms to be safe. They may hope, but they would be unwise to count on it. British reaction and British Marxism have always so far had to face an organized and articulate Liberal opposition which has helped the small 'l' liberals in both the Tory and Labour Parties to withstand the excesses of extremism. As Dr Douglas points out in his concluding chapter, today great divisions of opinion run within Parties. On almost every emotionally charged and morally important issue there are gulfs between the Liberals and illiberals which are much deeper than the gap in the orthodox party positions.

This gives Liberals grounds for hope. But it is also a warning that the security of the gains won by Liberals in the past cannot be assumed. Dr Douglas puts us all in his debt because, by the clarity and honesty of his narrative, he shows how heavy is the responsibility of those who form the Liberal core, and how much has been lost to this country, and so to civilization, since Liberalism lost the commanding heights of power and responsibility.

3 February 1971

B

Acknowledgements

A book of this kind can never be the exclusive work of one person, and I am indebted to many people for help of one kind or another. First I wish to thank my wife, who has read and criticized all the manuscript, and typed a large part of it. I have been peculiarly fortunate in receiving careful and detailed criticism of the operative parts of the book from officials who between them have held senior professional posts in the Liberal Party throughout nearly all of the three-quarters of the century which the book covers: Mr R. Humphrey Davies, c.b., who started to work at Liberal Headquarters in 1895, became Private Secretary to the Chief Liberal Whip in 1899, and was later Secretary of the Liberal Central Association until his retirement in 1926; Mr W. R. Davies, o.b.e., who was Secretary first of the National Liberal Federation and then of the Liberal Party Organization from 1931 until 1955, but who had worked at Liberal Party Headquarters from 1908; and Mr T. D. Nudds, o.b.e., who commenced work for the Liberal Party in 1920 and was for over twenty years Secretary of the Liberal Central Association until his retirement a couple of years ago. In addition to these people I would like to thank others who have read and criticized part or all of the manuscript: Mr Ronald Banks, Miss Barbara Bliss, Mr V. H. Blundell and Dr K. Watkins.

I wish to acknowledge the gracious permission of Her Majesty the Queen to publish extracts from documents addressed by or to past Sovereigns or Royal Secretaries. I wish also to thank others who have allowed me access to original material, or have permitted me to quote from documents in which they have the copyright: Sir Richard Acland, The Bodleian Library, Oxford, Mr Mark Bonham-Carter, the First Beaverbrook Foundation, the British Museum, Sir William Gladstone, Helen Lady Graves, the Haldane family, Viscount Harcourt, Lord Harmsworth, Mr David McKenna, Mr A. D. Maclean, the National Library of Scotland, Lord Pentland,

Viscount and Sir Steven Runciman, Mr Godfrey Samuel, Mr Laurence P. Scott, Viscount St Davids, Earl Spencer, Mr A. J. P. Taylor, Viscount Thurso, *The Times*, Sir George Trevelyan, Mrs R. Wilson-Walker (quotations from Vivian Phillipps' book), Viscount Wimborne, Lord Wrottesley. In a few cases I have been unable to determine, or unable to contact, the owners of copyrights; and I hope that these people will forgive me for quoting from documents.

I have had much assistance in tracking down source material from Mr George Awdry, Librarian of the Gladstone Library at the National Liberal Club (where I have been able to consult, *inter alia*, the Club's impressive collection of election addresses) Mr Pat Cavanaugh of the Labour Party and Mr Geoffrey Block, o.b.e., of the Conservative Party. I have had helpful discussions with, or received useful correspondence from, many people who have been able to throw light on aspects of the story which I am trying to tell. Some of them, alas, are now dead: Lady Asquith of Yarnbury, C. R. Dudgeon, H. J. Glanville Jr., David Goldblatt, Lady Megan Lloyd-George, Viscount Tenby and F. C. Thornborough. Among the others who have helped in this way I would gratefully mention Mr Desmond Banks, Miss Barbara Bliss, Lord Boothby, Mr William Glanville Brown, Mrs K. Cossar, Lord Drumalbyn, Mr J. Edgar Hardy, Mr Derek Hudson, Mr Barry McGill, Mr Andrew McLaren, Mrs Lucy Masterman, Mr Richard Moore, Mrs Doris Norris, Mr Frank Owen, Lord Rea, Sir Steven Runciman, Sir Geoffrey Shakespeare, Lady Simon of Wythenshawe, Mr Reginald Smith, Mr Lancelot Spicer, Mr A. J. Sylvester, Sir Ronald Walker.

I also wish to thank Mr Chris Cook for allowing me a preview of *Lloyd George: Twelve Essays* (edited by A. J. P. Taylor), and the University of Surrey for the grant which has been made from the Faculty IV research fund to assist this work.

One matter concerns all the kind people who in various ways have helped, advised, criticized or suggested. It is I, and not they, who must take the blame for the errors, both of fact and of judgement, which have doubtless crept into the book. Without the help of these people the errors would have been a great deal more numerous than they are.

University of Surrey   April 1971   ROY DOUGLAS

1

The Background

The democracy must depend upon organization much more than the aristocracy. – DAVID LLOYD GEORGE at Liverpool, 15 February 1889. Quoted in *Slings and Arrows – sayings of Lloyd George,* edited by Philip Guedalla.

In 1914, a Liberal Government was in office. Ten years later, the Liberal Party was reduced to about forty M.P.s, and the great majority of those M.P.s evidently owed their election to the fact that they had had straight fights with one or other of the opposing Parties. What was the cause of this remarkably rapid decline? Was it the result of circumstances which already existed in 1914, but whose effects were not visible until a later date? Or was it the result of some event or events which occurred during that particular decade?

This problem has attracted a good deal of attention and comment. But there is another problem no less puzzling: the continued survival of the Liberal Party. For fifty years, it has been neither the Government nor the official Opposition. For most of that period, no one can have regarded the Liberal Party as a serious aspirant for early office; yet at all times Liberal candidates could reasonably expect to poll thousands of votes in most kinds of constituencies. Only seven of the Liberal M.P.s of 1924 had been returned in three-cornered contests. Since then, the number of M.P.s has been down to five. It rose during the 1960s to reach a peak of thirteen in 1969, and all of those M.P.s had both Conservative and Labour opponents; but in 1970 it returned to six. Although the seats remaining to the Liberals in 1970 look like what the ecologists call a 'relict fauna' in areas of traditional Liberal strength, yet not one of the present Liberal seats has been consistently Liberal since 1939, and one was held in 1969–70 in the town of Birmingham, which last returned a Liberal in 1885. Political commentators in the late 1920s may have expected the Liberal Party to revive as one of the great Parties of the State, or they may have expected it to disappear; but it is doubtful whether anyone, friend or foe, would have anticipated the course which events have taken. There seems to be no wholly satisfactory explanation of this remarkable survival, but a few tentative suggestions will be attempted.

The near-destruction of the Liberal Party and the establishment of the Labour Party as a major force in British politics are evidently related in some way. To understand this relationship, it is necessary to look at the story of the Liberal Party throughout this century. Different explanatory theories have started off from different dates, and we are less likely to go wrong if we begin at an early stage, so that the first possible symptoms of the disease may be investigated.

Perhaps the commonest theory is 'inevitability'. According to this view, the establishment of the Labour Representation Committee, forerunner of the Labour Party, in 1900, made the eventual destruction of the Liberal Party at the hands of the champion of the emerging working class inevitable. To test the validity of this theory, it is necessary to study in some detail the behaviour of the Liberals at the turn of the century, and in particular the relationship between the Liberal Party and the incipient Labour Party.

The second theory admits that the Liberal Party was suffering from troubles of various kinds in 1914, but contends that there is no proof that these troubles were insuperable. It argues that the tensions of the First World War actually encompassed the ruin of the Liberal Party – the need to do thoroughly illiberal things if that war was to be prosecuted to victory, and the different reactions of different Liberals to these requirements.

There is a third theory, the 'personality' theory. This seeks to attribute the whole process, or most of it, to some particular individual or group of individuals. The man who is usually blamed is Lloyd George; but some would argue that the fault lay with Asquith, or with Asquith's principal associates.

In this book, it will be contended that the Liberal Party was essentially in good health down to 1914, although certain actions which it had taken before that date – not through obligation but by choice – were to prove a great source of weakness in the years which followed. The effect of the First World War was not so much to disrupt the Liberal Party as to set in motion a train of events which led to this disruption. There is much of the atmosphere of a Greek tragedy. One character commits a sin or blunder. Another person reacts naturally to this act by a greater wrong, and the process leads to a grim sequel of destruction and disaster – not through the particular depravity of some individual, but because of the way in which people naturally act towards each other in retaliation. Nevertheless, it will be argued that there were several occasions when this process could reasonably have been arrested. The decline of the Liberal Party was not due to the inescapable logic of history, or the inapplicability of Liberal remedies to the issues of the day, but to avoidable mistakes made by Liberals themselves. What failed was not Liberalism but Liberals.

*   *   *

The role of the Liberal Party at the turn of the nineteenth and twentieth centuries can only be properly understood in the context of social conditions at the time. The social divisions of late-Victorian Britain bore the same names as they do today, but the distinctions between them were profoundly more marked. Whether the purely financial disparities were greater is a matter of continuing dispute; but the differences in behaviour, dress, and the whole way of life were incomparably greater; and for most people the idea that they or their children should be able to pass from one class to another remained unthinkable well into our own century.

In the 1870s, Britain's industrial ascendancy began to be challenged by other countries, particularly by Germany and the United States. Agriculture was shaken by a series of abominable harvests at the end of the decade. This resulted in a substantial diminution of farm rents, and it is arguable that the 'great slump in dukes', to which Lloyd George was to refer a third of a century later, had its origin in the relatively straitened circumstances in which the great landowners found themselves about this time.

In the early 1880s, the American land reformer, Henry George, exerted an enormous influence on opinion, not only in the actual remedies which he offered for existing social disparities, but even in suggesting that the problem could be treated at all. The operative part of George's doctrine was that the root of social inequality lay in restrictions on access to land, and his remedy was a tax on land values. This began to influence Liberal opinion to a great extent, and the various resolutions passed by the National Liberal Federation from 1889 onwards bear the strong imprint of Georgeist ideas. Furthermore, many people who called themselves socialists had been influenced at first by George, and later deviated from the path which he had prescribed.

Until the middle 1880s, Liberals were to be found in all classes. There were even Liberal dukes. But in 1886 the Liberal Party split over the Irish question. The Liberal Government which Gladstone led proposed to grant 'Home Rule' – which meant simply the establishment of an Irish Parliament to deal with purely Irish affairs, which would be subordinate to the Parliament at Westminster. Nearly all of the Liberal aristocracy departed from the main body of the Party, to become Liberal Unionists, and many Liberals who were by no means aristocrats (including Joseph Chamberlain) departed with them. For a time, they maintained that they were still Liberals, although they differed from the rest of the Party on the Irish question. By the 1890s, however, they were Conservatives for all practical purposes. The word 'Unionist' was extensively used as a generic term for Conservatives and Liberal Unionists. For convenience, 'Unionists' will mostly be used in that sense in this book in describing events from 1886 to 1922, while the work 'Conservative' will be used for events before and after that time.

Although the aristocracy went Unionist almost to a man, many wealthy industrialists were Liberals down to the First World War, and in some parts of the country most of this class were Liberals. Conversely, although most working-class votes were probably cast for the Liberals, yet there were many working-class districts where the Unionists predominated. As late as the 1900 General Election, for example, ten of the thirteen constituencies of the East End of London[1] were Unionist, and two of them remained Unionist even in the Liberal landslide of 1906. At that memorable election, when Chelsea went Liberal, Stepney remained Unionist. In Liverpool and many of the smaller towns of industrial Lancashire, the workers of Irish origin voted Liberal, but the others mostly voted Unionist. In Birmingham the situation was even more extreme, for every single constituency returned the Unionists and their allies right from the Home Rule split of 1886 until King's Norton went Labour with a

[1] Here taken to comprise the Parliamentary Boroughs of Shoreditch, Bethnal Green, Tower Hamlets, and West Ham.

tiny majority in 1924. But in spite of these numerous and important exceptions, the people who might have reason to challenge the existing social order were mostly to be found in the Liberal Party by the late 1880s.

While the Liberals were concerning themselves increasingly with social problems, other people began to ask very different questions. From the middle of the nineteenth century, it had seemed almost axiomatic that the best possible economic order was one pivoting on Free Trade. During the 1880s, some Unionists began seriously to challenge the Free Trade position, and in 1887 the conference of the National Union of Conservative Associations passed a resolution in favour of a policy of tariffs against foreign imports, to grant 'Protection' to home manufacturers. The issue, however, was not really brought into the cockpit of politics, and although the Unionists were in office for all but three of the years from 1886 until the end of the century, no assault was made on Free Trade.

The late 1880s and the 1890s also saw the growth of a new imperialism. This imperialism tended, on the whole, to exert most influence on the young and forward-looking people of the time, and it was extremely popular among the working classes of most of the large towns. At its best, imperialism was characterized by a real sense of responsibility and duty to the subject peoples, and the idea of 'developing our estate' for the good of the native people as well as the good of Britain. At its worst, it was rapacious, arrogant, and jingoistic. Imperialism in all its forms was most marked among the Unionists, but it also had a great influence on the minds of some Liberals.

In any study of politics at the turn of the century, it is vital to remember the effect which religion exerted on political attitudes and behaviour. Of course there was plenty of unctuous hypocrisy, but there was also a great measure of genuine religious feeling among people for whom, as one distinguished historian has put it,[1] 'hell and heaven seemed as certain . . . as tomorrow's sunrise, and the Last Judgement as real as the week's balance sheet'. The influence of religion was less at the end of the century than it had been a few decades earlier, but the churches were full, and the various denominations exercised a massive influence on political life and political attitudes, which was partly unifying and partly divisive.

[1] R. C. K. Ensor, *England 1870–1914*, p. 138.

To a great extent, attitudes on religion and on politics coincided. The Church of England has sometimes been described cynically as 'the Conservative Party at prayer', and it was equally noticeable that Liberals tended to be Nonconformists. There was some difference between the attitudes of members of different Nonconformist denominations; Primitive Methodists, Congregationalists, and Baptists probably contained a higher proportion of Liberals than did the Wesleyan Methodists. The leaderships of the Parties were sometimes anomalous; Liberals like Gladstone and Cobden were Anglicans, and the Unionist Joseph Chamberlain was a Unitarian. Nevertheless, the distinction was broadly valid, and attitudes characteristic of religious groups often corresponded with attitudes in politics. Liberal Nonconformists were often temperance workers, anxious to see restrictions on the sale of alcohol; hence publicans were usually Unionists. Liberals were also very watchful about the influence of the Church of England in secular affairs, notably in education. Church schools operated by Anglicans were more common than Nonconformist schools, and Nonconformist parents were anxious to ensure that their children should not be exposed to the corrupting influence of the Anglican catechism.

Education was much more of a live public issue in the late nineteenth century than it is today. Universal compulsory elementary education dates only from 1880, and many people were beginning to face completely new vistas. This eventually exerted a great effect on the Press, although that influence was not yet visible in the early 1890s. The Press in its turn was exerting a great influence on opinion, since for most people their daily newspaper was almost the only source of information about the world outside their own experience. Until the appearance of the *Daily Mail* in 1896, the newspapers were, to modern tastes, extremely stodgy; but they were also authoritative and reliable. Journalists then knew what many have now forgotten – how to separate news from comment.

*　　*　　*

In the year 1892, Gladstone, then eighty-two years of age, formed his fourth and last Ministry. The great issue of politics was Irish Home Rule. In 1893, Gladstone's second Home Rule Bill passed the Commons, but was rejected by a two to one majority in the Lords. Gladstone desired an immediate appeal to the country, but his associates opposed the idea. Gladstone lingered in office for several months more, and finally resigned in March 1894 because he opposed increases in naval expenditure.

Gladstone had very largely formed the Liberal Party in his own image, or, to change the metaphor, we may regard him as the big tree in whose shadow nothing could grow to its potential height. To appreciate the magnitude of his stature, it is not necessary to consider the tributes of his supporters. Lord Morley's biography of Gladstone relates[1] how the Unionist Prime Minister, Lord Salisbury, later described him as 'a great example, to which history hardly furnishes a parallel, of a great Christian man'. Salisbury's eventual successor, A. J. Balfour, went even further, calling Gladstone, 'the greatest member of the greatest deliberative assembly that the world has seen'.

At the time of Gladstone's retirement, there was no obvious Liberal successor for the office of Prime Minister. Gladstone himself proposed to advise Queen Victoria to call the First Lord of the Admiralty, Earl Spencer. The Liberals in the Commons would probably have selected the Chancellor of the Exchequer, Sir William Harcourt. The Queen, on her own initiative, invited the Foreign Secretary, the Earl of Rosebery, to form an administration. None of these men towered over his rivals, and there were several other Liberals whose claims were not much less than these three.

Lord Spencer does not seem to have had strong ambitions for the highest office; but relations between the new Prime Minister and Harcourt were not good, and later became worse. As Harcourt was both Liberal leader in the Commons and Chancellor of the Exchequer, this made the position peculiarly difficult.

Rosebery was one of the few members of the old Whig aristocracy who had not deserted Gladstone at the time of the Home Rule split of 1886. He was conscious of the difficulties confronting a peer as Prime Minister – particularly as a Liberal Prime Minister. His ability as Foreign Secretary in the old Government, and his remarkable skill as an orator, were not in doubt; but his temperament was really unsuitable for the Premiership – not least because he seemed to lack any consistent enthusiasm for politics, or a strong sense of loyalty to his own supporters. Furthermore, at forty-seven he was

[1] John (later Viscount) Morley, *The Life of William Ewart Gladstone* (1908 edn), ii, 577.

remarkably young for the office, and it was almost inevitable that Harcourt, twenty years his senior, should feel a measure of resentment. To make Rosebery's position even worse, he was well known as the owner of racehorses, which did not endear him to the Nonconformists. Nor were his general political attitudes close to those radical policies which were becoming increasingly popular among Liberals active at the constituency level.

Sir William Harcourt was not noticeably more fitted for the first office. His character has been described as 'Falstaffian'. Certainly there was something clumsy and irascible about his manner which contrived to alienate his potential supporters. Moreover, his political attitudes, notably but not exclusively on the imperial question, were almost diametrically opposed to those of Rosebery. Sir William's devoted son Lewis (generally known as 'Loulou') acted almost as his father's 'business manager' in politics, and was noted for his talent at political intrigue – a skill which his father completely lacked.

Thus Rosebery could not count on the support of his principal associate in the House of Commons; while in the House of Lords the Liberals formed a very tiny minority. Nor was the political situation in which Rosebery and Harcourt found themselves a happy one. The Liberals had no overall majority in the Commons, and were dependent for survival on the continued support of the Irish Party, which was itself split into two hostile groups. This composite majority was only forty at the preceding General Election, and had been whittled down further by adverse by-elections.

What work remained for the Government to do? Liberals in the country, and Liberals in the Commons, were anxious for a long list of social reforms, many of which were distasteful to the new Prime Minister. With some skill, Harcourt contrived to secure an important modification of death duties; but there was little more to report in terms of positive achievement after Gladstone retired.

The House of Lords was immensely more powerful in the 1890s than it is today, and the Unionist majority was overwhelming. It would freely throw out Bills from the Commons which it did not like. There was some talk among Liberals of 'filling the cup' – that is, passing a series of measures through the Commons in anticipation that the Lords would reject them, and then appealing to the country on the issue of 'Peers versus People', as a preliminary to a major reform of the House of Lords.

Without plan or purpose, and without any real need, the Government took the occasion of a rather bad Parliamentary week in June 1895 to resign office. Obviously relieved, the Queen invited the previous Unionist Prime Minister, the Marquis of Salisbury, to form another administration. His Government included the principal Liberal Unionist figures as well as Conservatives. A General Election was necessary to secure a majority in the House of Commons, and polling was held in the latter part of July 1895.

The Liberals showed little sign of co-ordination, and the principal figures campaigned more or less independently on issues which happened to interest themselves or their electors. Of the leading Liberals, both Sir William Harcourt and John Morley (Chief Secretary for Ireland in the old Government) suffered the indignity of being defeated in their own constituencies. Both, however, soon managed to return to the House of Commons representing other places.[1]

The Conservative element of the Government received a small majority in the House of Commons over all other Parties combined; when the Liberal Unionists were added, the Government had a lead of 152.

Not only was the Liberal Party weak and disunited, but the pattern of its Parliamentary representation was ominous. Nearly three-quarters of the Welsh seats were still Liberal, and just over half of the Scottish seats; but in England they held less than a quarter. The Liberal Party seemed to be retreating from the centre to the 'Celtic fringe', and a few districts, like the West Riding, and Tyneside, where the Nonconformists were particularly strong. It is not difficult to understand why men were saying in 1895 that Liberalism had been exterminated.[2]

The actions of the leading Liberal politicians might seem to have been designed to prove that these prophets of doom were right. As we shall later see, the Liberal troubles were very far from over, and another seven years of savage and bitter acerbity were to elapse before any great issue arose on which the Liberals could speak with a united voice. Yet the Liberal Party contrived to survive. To under-

[1] Harcourt, defeated at Derby, was returned for West Monmouthshire, which polled later in the same election. Morley, defeated at Newcastle, was returned at a by-election in Montrose at February 1896.

[2] R. Spence Watson, *The National Liberal Federation 1877–1906* (London 1907), p. 180.

stand this remarkable survival, it is necessary to look at the organization of the Liberal Party.

*   *   *

The organizational structure of both Liberal and Unionist Parties was broadly similar in the 1890s to that which exists today. But it is important to remember that features of the political order which today are so familiar that they seem natural and inevitable were still novelties in the middle 1890s. The franchise had only become general to male householders in 1884. Both the franchise and the political parties had changed beyond recognition well within living memory. Therefore there was an element of instability in politics, and the political axioms of our own time were often by no means axioms then. This bore on the behaviour of both electors and statesmen. Party loyalty was much less strong. M.P.s, *pace* Gilbert and Sullivan, were less willing to 'do what their leaders tell 'em'. On issues which we should regard now as major questions of confidence, M.P.s were often to be found voting in the 'wrong' division lobby – and neither the officials of the Party nor the M.P.s' own electors were necessarily inclined to remonstrate with them. Party notables retained a freedom to criticize each other in public which they do not possess today. These features existed among Unionists as well as the Liberal Party, and they are important to our study, for if we do not allow for them we shall pass some unwarranted judgements on the Liberals at the turn of the century. It is extremely tempting to try to interpret actions and standards of the past by criteria with which we are familiar; but even when we are considering a period within living memory, the result of so doing is often very bad history.

In certain towns, constituency Liberal Associations had already reached a very high degree of organization as early as the 1830s.[1] The 1867 Reform Act enfranchised many working men, and in a large number of places they formed the majority of the electorate. In some constituencies, Liberal organizations were rapidly remodelled to incorporate this new mass of voters, while others were much more lax, and in some places there was nothing which could properly be called a Liberal Association. Whether the Association was strong or weak, however, it was very seldom financially self-supporting, and usually relied on the M.P. or candidate, or a few

[1] *Ibid.*, p. 3.

wealthy supporters, or on substantial donations from the political funds raised by Chief Whips. Voluntary work, however devoted, tends to be spasmodic, and by the latter part of the nineteenth century it was common for constituencies to employ full-time salaried Agents.

*   *   *

The need for constituencies to co-ordinate their activities was first brought home through the special problem of outvoters, that is, people who had votes in constituencies where they did not reside.[1] In the 1850s, outvoters amounted to some 15 per cent of the electorate, and the task of getting them on the electoral register and persuading them to vote necessitated co-operation between different constituencies. A small staff was employed by the Liberal M.P.s to co-ordinate this work.

The need to deal with outvoters seems to have led to a more general co-operation of Liberal M.P.s on matters relating to organization in the constituencies. On 21 February 1860,[2] twenty Liberal M.P.s resolved to form a body known as the Liberal Registration Association (L.R.A.). This soon secured a substantial membership of past and present M.P.s, who each subscribed four guineas a year.[3] The L.R.A. did not confine its activities to the registration of voters; it organized conferences in various parts of the country in order to stimulate and strengthen constituency organizations. By 1862 it had no fewer than 566 local correspondents, and had made inquiries concerning close on ten thousand outvoters.

Changes in electoral law and the increased need for communication between constituencies led the L.R.A. to remodel itself in 1874 as 'the central medium of communication with and between the Party throughout the whole Kingdom in aid of and in connection with local organization'.[4] At the same meeting, the title was changed to the Liberal Central Association (L.C.A.), under which name it persists to this day. The Chairman of the L.C.A. was originally the

[1] Information about the early history of the Liberal Central Association is largely based on an unpublished memorandum by Mr R. Humphrey Davies, c.b., former secretary of the L.C.A.

[2] Many authors state the date of origin wrongly as 1861.

[3] *Liberal Magazine*, 1925, p. 78.

[4] Minutes of meeting 19 May 1874.

Leader of the M.P.s, but by the later years of the nineteenth century it was the Chief Whip, and remained so down to 1950.

Long before the end of the nineteenth century, the L.C.A., although nominally a members' association, was for all practical purposes the Liberal Whips' Office, and the finance needed for its work was raised by the Chief Whip in that capacity, rather than in his capacity as L.C.A. Chairman. The L.C.A. was often able to put constituency Liberal Associations in touch with potential candidates. It also made grants of money for Party purposes, especially to help candidates in elections, and generally served the requirements of the Parliamentary Liberal Party. Nevertheless, there always remained the possibility that the L.C.A. might revert to its old structure, perhaps to the considerable embarrassment of the Party Whips. Thus, during the dissensions over imperialism – which will be discussed later – it seemed for a time likely that the imperialists might capture the L.C.A., which could cause a great deal of trouble for the Party leadership.[1]

* * *

The General Election of 1874 resulted in a heavy defeat for the Liberals, but it also played the major part in stimulating a new nationwide Liberal organization. The Liberal showing had been poor, not only in the sense that they had been defeated in the country as a whole, but also because no fewer than 142 seats in Great Britain had not been contested by Liberals at all.[2] But the Liberals noted one light amid the gloom. In spite of a determined Conservative attack, the three M.P.s for Birmingham were still all Liberals. This victory was generally attributed to the remarkable political organization which had been established by Joseph Chamberlain, who at that time was the great Liberal luminary, and also mayor, of the town.

On 31 May 1877, a great meeting was held in Birmingham to establish a body known as the National Liberal Federation (N.L.F.).[3] The chief sponsor was Joseph Chamberlain. Gladstone visited

[1] Herbert Gladstone to Campbell-Bannerman, 23 February 1902. Campbell-Bannerman papers, 41,216, fol. 195–6.

[2] Barry McGill, 'Francis Schnadhorst and the Liberal Party Organisation', *J. Mod. Hist.* xxxiv, i (1962), at p. 23.

[3] A general account of the origin and history of the N.L.F. is given in R. Spence Watson, *op. cit.* p. 9.

Birmingham during the Federation meeting, and received a hero's welcome.

The Officers and Committee were charged with the task of forming 'new Liberal Associations based on popular representation', and of submitting political questions to the Council. This was a large body, to which all affiliated Liberal Associations were entitled to send representatives. The Council met annually, and was comparable with the Assembly of Conference of a modern political party. The Executive Committee, which also made pronouncements on political questions, was a body of considerable size as well.

The political declarations of the N.L.F. raised the rather difficult question of how far the electors could justly expect a Liberal government to attempt to put these policies into operation. Although the N.L.F. insisted at its inception, and repeatedly reaffirmed, that its resolutions were never intended to be binding on the Liberals in Parliament, yet they gave the leadership a pretty accurate idea of what active Liberals were thinking, and any leader could only ignore such information at his peril. The most famous and comprehensive of these N.L.F. policy statements was the so-called 'Newcastle Programme' of 1891. It did not differ in kind from earlier and later pronouncements, but it attracted a great deal more public attention, and caused much embarrassment later to Lord Rosebery, when he sought to strike out in a very different direction. Measures advocated in the 'Newcastle Programme' included Irish Home Rule, the disestablishment of the Church of Wales, steps to 'mend or end' the House of Lords, free schools within easy reach of every home; public control over all schools subsidized by public money, a 'popular veto' on the liquor trade wherever a majority of the people favoured this, the taxation of land values and mining royalties, leasehold enfranchisement, compensation for evicted tenants, the abolition of entails, power for local authorities to acquire land compulsorily for allotments, smallholdings and labourers' dwellings, and the removal of all remaining taxes on food.

The danger of a head-on clash between the L.C.A. and the N.L.F. was always present, but this was greatly reduced after the Liberal Unionist secession of 1886. Birmingham had been the N.L.F. headquarters, and Birmingham was prepared to follow Chamberlain into Liberal Unionism. But the overwhelming majority of Liberal activists in the constituencies were Gladstonians, and so was the N.L.F.

c

It was therefore decided to transfer the N.L.F. headquarters from Birmingham to London. The professional secretary, Francis Schnadhorst, who had a massive reputation as a political organizer, became also secretary of the L.C.A. He remained in office until 1893, by which time his powers had much declined. Mr R. Humphrey Davies, who joined the staff of the Liberal Party a couple of years after Schnadhorst's retirement, has written to the present author: 'I never saw him, but I was very disappointed to find no trace of his craftsmanship when I joined the L.C.A. in 1895. ... My firm impression is that Schnadhorst was more interested in policy than organisation and letters of his which I saw confirm that impression.'

Schnadhorst's handling of the Liberal finances appears to have been most unsatisfactory. Not long after his death, a statement in *The Spectator* prompted some inquiries by Liberal officials concerning a donation of £5,000 said to have been given by Cecil Rhodes to the Liberal Party in 1891. Arnold Morley, who had been Chief Whip at the time, had no knowledge of this donation, and a search of the books indicated that it had not been passed into the accounts of either the L.C.A. or the N.L.F. While Liberal officials were disinclined to believe that – in Campbell-Bannerman's word – Schnadhorst had 'trousered' the money, it was clear that he had disbursed it at his own discretion.[1] The fact that a paid official could control such large sums of money is an indication of the great power which such men exercised.

Schnadhorst's successor was the twenty-nine-year-old Robert (later Sir Robert) Hudson, whose abilities, at their zenith, were probably even greater.[2] He was destined to remain at the centre of the organization of the Liberal Party until the beginning of 1927, and he survived by less than a year the unhappy circumstances of his eventual departure. Although it is difficult at times to determine at just what points Hudson's personal influence was crucial, he was a man who would meet the leading political figures of the day on a footing of equality rather than in the capacity of a hired official. His biographer describes him[3] as 'a man of deep religious convictions and sensitive honour, to whom meanness, corruption and intrigue were

---

[1] Campbell-Bannerman papers 41,216, fol. 135–45; various letters.
[2] J. A. Spender, *Sir Robert Hudson*, pp. 197, 210.
[3] *Ibid.*, p. 189.

an abomination'. His social standing is indicated by the fact that his second wife was the widow of Lord Northcliffe.

*   *   *

It was often necessary for constituencies in geographical proximity to take counsel together on matters of mutual concern. By the early 1890s,[1] local Federation organizations had been formed in the Home Counties, the Northern area, and in Devon and Cornwall. They grew naturally from the work of political organization, and were not imposed from above. The modern practice of dividing the whole country into Area Federations under the aegis of some central body (originally the Whips' Office) was a later development.

Quite early in its history, the N.L.F. produced some political literature,[2] but in 1887 the N.L.F. and the L.C.A. co-operated to establish the Liberal Publications Department (L.P.D.). The L.C.A. representatives included James Bryce, the distinguished historian and future Cabinet Minister.

In 1893, the L.P.D. appointed a new Secretary. He was Charles Geake, who later became Hudson's brother-in-law, but was very much a personality in his own right. His accuracy and productivity were almost unbelievable, and for the remainder of his life he poured out a stream of publications and information for men at all levels in the Party, from the Cabinet downwards.[3]

Charles Geake's greatest monument was the *Liberal Magazine* which he edited from very soon after its inauguration in 1893 until his death in 1919. It was a publication which maintained standards of accuracy of which any scholar might feel proud. The hand of Geake is also seen in the *Liberal Year Books* which commenced publication in 1905, and in a service (known to contemporaries as 'The Recording Angel') by which detailed information was supplied to Liberals concerning the voting record of any Unionist M.P. whom they might wish to embarrass.

There were other professional workers of the highest calibre who were working for Liberal Headquarters in the 1890s, and two of them, Jesse (later Sir Jesse) Herbert and R. Humphrey Davies, will

[1] W. Finnemore, *The Liberal Agent*, September 1930.
[2] R. Spence Watson, *op. cit.*, p. 9.
[3] J. A. Spender, *op. cit.*, p. 189, etc.

call for frequent reference in this book. Presiding over them all was the Chief Whip, Thomas Edward Ellis, a man who, by common consent of those who knew him, was a Whip of quite exceptional calibre.

Ellis's preferment began towards the end of the long reign of Gladstone, when he became Junior Whip to the new Ministry in 1892, at the age of thirty-three. He was, as Wyn Griffiths puts it,[1] 'the only member [of the Government] who could say that he was the son of a tenant farmer, related to four farmers who had been evicted for refusing to vote for the Tory candidate, and whose father had been harshly treated by his landlord'.

Lord Rosebery advanced Ellis further, and he was appointed Chief Liberal Whip and Patronage[2] Secretary to the Treasury when the Government was reconstituted in March 1894.

These men of quite exceptional ability played an absolutely vital role in keeping the Liberal Party together, and men who preserve an institution from destruction are not less worthy of mention than those who encompass its ruin. Yet the headquarters from which they operated were tiny and quite unpretentious. Mr R. Humphrey Davies has thus described how they existed in the middle 1890s:

'The N.L.F. occupied the four ground floor rooms at the back of 41, Parliament Street. Geake and his staff had the two front rooms, the L.C.A. had rooms on the first floor. . . .

'For the first year or two I worked in the N.L.F. – in a room adjoining Hudson's. The staff of the N.L.F. consisted of Hudson (the secretary), Frank Baxter (the assistant secretary) and one clerk.

'At this time the L.C.A. was almost derelict. The four rooms which it occupied on the first floor at Parliament Street looked forlorn. The carpets were in holes. I had heard much of Mr Schnadhorst's genius as an organizer, but there was hardly any office equipment in the L.C.A. The staff consisted of one very inefficient clerk (who was eventually pensioned off by Mr Herbert Gladstone) and an office boy. There was no telephone. . . .

'When Lord Rosebery's Government was defeated in 1895, Mr

---

[1] Wyn Griffiths, *Thomas Edward Ellis, 1859–1899* (Llandybie, 1959), p. 30.
[2] *Sic.* The official title of the Government Chief Whip was only changed to Parliamentary Secretary to the Treasury in the twentieth century.

Ellis came to the L.C.A., and the arrangements of the General Election of 1895 were conducted by him and Mr Hudson without engaging any extra help. . . . After the election, Mr Ellis, having ceased to be Patronage Secretary to the Treasury, took up his official quarters at the L.C.A., and the offices wore an altogether different aspect. . . . Financially we lived from hand to mouth, and had to cut our coat according to our cloth.'

Thus, the central 'machine', including the N.L.F., the L.C.A., and L.P.D. together, consisted of about ten employees at the most, plus a few packers at the L.P.D.; but the L.P.D. was not a great burden financially. The small, precarious and fluctuating income of the Liberal Party was not spent on ostentation and large staffs, but on a small and devoted team who would work to the limit for Liberalism because they were Liberals themselves.

*   *   *

A very important role was played by the numerous Liberal Clubs which were scattered throughout the land, although it is extremely difficult to assess this role in detail. Most of these clubs required some sort of declaration from aspirant members that they were Liberals in politics, and it was made clear that the clubs would have no compunction in expelling any member who gave public support to a Unionist. The fact that a member spent much of his leisure among Liberal friends no doubt deterred him from weakening in his Liberalism. The chief of these clubs, the National Liberal Club in London, has been throughout its existence the social centre of Liberalism, and the venue of a large number of Liberal meetings. It owes its existence to the initiative of the L.C.A., which perceived the importance of such an institution.[1] The fine Club House in Whitehall Place was opened in 1887. The whole venture was not only dependent on L.C.A. initiative, but was rendered possible through debentures to the amount of £52,400 raised under the auspices of the L.C.A.

---

[1] Information about the early history of the National Liberal Club is based mainly on an unpublished account compiled by Mr R. Humphrey Davies.

2

The Long Road Back

'Tariff Reform' means work for all!
Work for all! Work for all!
'Tariff Reform' means work for all
— Chopping up wood in the workhouse!
(Tune: 'Here we go round the mulberry bush')

Just after the crushing defeat of 1895, Tom Ellis, the Chief Liberal Whip, wrote to Robert Hudson with almost uncanny accuracy: 'The disease of the Party is deep-seated. Time alone can eradicate it, and Time will take ten good years of its own self to do the job.'[1]

How matters stood between Lord Rosebery and his former Chancellor of the Exchequer is indicated by a letter which the ex-Prime Minister wrote to Lord Spencer shortly after the Government fell: 'My political connection with Harcourt was entirely official and terminated with the late government. In no shape and form can it be renewed. One plain lesson at any rate we have learned from experience which is that that connection was essentially unreal and injurious to our party and irksome (to say the least of it) to each other. . . .'[2]

In a similar vein, Rosebery told Gladstone that 'the firm of Rosebery and Harcourt was a fraud upon the public',[3] and the older man declared that 'these difficulties really go down to the very base of character' — saying of Harcourt that 'I have never known anyone else approaching his powers of self-deception.'[4]

Harcourt was, or persuaded himself that he was, not averse to the

---

[1] J. A. Spender, *Sir Robert Hudson*, p. 53.

[2] Rosebery to Spencer, 12 August 1895 (copy?). Rosebery papers 49.

[3] Rosebery to W. E. Gladstone, 25 August 1895. W. E. Gladstone papers 44,290, fol. 264–5.

[4] W. E. Gladstone to Rosebery, 25 August 1895. Gladstone papers 44,290, fol. 262–3.

idea of a reconciliation,[1] but it is difficult to believe that any real *modus vivendi* was possible. Both men had their devoted admirers, and both were of high ability; but both were to prove disloyal to their followers and colleagues, and neither could speak with authority for the Party as a whole. At best they were sectional leaders, who antagonized as many Liberals as they fired with enthusiasm.

Although Gladstone retired from the House of Commons at the 1895 General Election, he continued to issue pronouncements on public affairs; pronouncements which had enormous weight because of the prestige of his name and career, and because of the evident lack of leadership from anybody else. On 24 September 1896, these statements culminated in a long speech at Liverpool, during which he inveighed against the Turkish atrocities in Armenia, and by implication called for British intervention. This speech was delivered in a manner which made it evident that his mental vigour was unabated, even though he was approaching the end of his eighty-seventh year.

This precipitated an event which had really been inevitable for a long time. On 6 October 1896, Lord Rosebery wrote to Tom Ellis, resigning the leadership of the Liberal Party – having given virtually no warning to anyone that this step was impending. Gladstone had neither desired nor intended Rosebery's resignation,[2] but Sir Edward Grey, a young Liberal politician who was among Rosebery's most enthusiastic supporters, rejoiced in the new freedom of action which this independent position provided.[3]

So massive was the authority of Rosebery's predecessor that voices were even raised for the recall of Gladstone to the leadership, in spite of the fact that he would have been over ninety if he had lived to the next General Election. In fact, no decision was taken about the overall leadership of the Party. Harcourt, as Leader of the M.P.s, was usually regarded as more authoritative than Lord Kimberley, who returned after Rosebery's resignation to the post of Leader of the Liberal Peers; but Harcourt's enemies, who were many, were ready to remind him that he was by no means the inevitable choice for Prime Minister if the Liberals again formed the Government.

Although it was Gladstone's action which had finally precipitated

[1] Asquith to Rosebery, 15 January 1896. Rosebery papers 1.
[2] W. E. Gladstone to Rosebery, 8 October 1896. Rosebery papers 22.
[3] Grey to Rosebery, 13 October 1896. Rosebery papers 23.

Rosebery's resignation, it is evident that the younger man bore no resentment,[1] yet he declared of Gladstone that, 'as to his "policy", I disagree with it *in toto*, and must say so'.[2]

This was very far from the end of the Liberal discomfiture. Gladstone's Liverpool speech proved to be his last great public utterance. On 19 May 1898 he died, and was buried amid scenes of public grief which never before or since have attended the funeral of a subject, and amid the most touching and impressive valedictions from almost everybody except the Queen whom he had served so loyally. Thus was removed the last great figure for whom all Liberals felt veneration.

On 14 December 1898, the Liberal Party suffered another major departure by its leadership not one whit less dramatic – or irresponsible – than that of Rosebery. An exchange of correspondence was published, in which Harcourt withdrew from chairmanship of the Liberal M.P.s, and John Morley, who had been Secretary for Ireland in the old Administration and stood next in seniority, expressed his approval of Harcourt's stand.[3] Harcourt's resignation was not officially based on any current issues of disagreement over policy, but on a refusal 'to be a candidate for any contested position'. This appears to refer to the current criticisms of his leadership; but these criticisms came mainly from supporters of the imperialist movement, which was becoming increasingly popular in the country, and was influencing a large section of the Liberal Party.

The Harcourt–Morley correspondence came as a complete thunderbolt. Two Liberal front-benchers had had a couple of days' notice, but only under seal of strict confidence.[4] There was naturally a great deal of resentment among the erstwhile colleagues of Harcourt and Morley. One of the leading figures, Sir Henry Fowler, threw their action in even worse light, referring to 'the reply to my letter in which I am informed that [Harcourt's] decision *was taken four months ago*. The only question was the time of announcement!!'[5]

The Harcourt–Morley incident removed the two leading Liberal

---

[1] Rosebery to W. E. Gladstone, 7 October 1896. Gladstone papers 44,290, fol. 267–8; W. E. Gladstone to Rosebery, 8 October, 1896. Rosebery papers 22.

[2] Rosebery to Asquith, 6 October 1896 (copy). Rosebery papers 1.

[3] Published in full in *Liberal Magazine*, vi (1898), pp. 554–7.

[4] Harcourt to Campbell-Bannerman, 12 December 1898. Campbell-Bannerman papers 41,219, fol. 191–2. Memorandum in Asquith papers 9, fol. 109–28.

[5] Sir Henry Fowler to Asquith, 17 December 1898. Asquith papers 9.

front-benchers in the Commons. This only left four members of the old Cabinet still available to take over the Parliamentary leadership of the Opposition: Sir Henry Campbell-Bannerman, Sir Henry Fowler, James Bryce, and H. H. Asquith. None of them stood markedly ahead of the others; but it appears that Bryce was never really considered, and Fowler little more. The real choice lay between Campbell-Bannerman and Asquith.

Sir Henry Campbell-Bannerman was a wealthy Scot, then aged sixty-two. In the Liberal interlude of 1892–5, he had been Secretary of State for War, where he had acquired some reputation among political sophisticates as an administrator, and had played a large part in dislodging the Queen's cousin, the Duke of Cambridge, from the post of Commander-in-Chief. Campbell-Bannerman was generally regarded as the occupant of a central position in the current dispute in the Liberal Party over imperialism, while the other Liberal front-benchers who remained after the departure of Harcourt and Morley were markedly on the imperialist side. To the public as a whole, he was almost unknown, even as a name, and there were some doubts whether his health was adequate.[1]

Asquith was a more or less self-made lawyer in his middle forties, with a thriving practice at the Bar. He had recently taken as his second wife a rather spectacular socialite, 'Margot' Tennant, a woman who was prone to make very shrewd, but often extremely indiscreet, comments on men and affairs. Asquith had been Home Secretary in the old Administration, and had been blamed – most unjustly – for his alleged part in the death of two miners in the riots at Featherstone in 1893. He was universally regarded as a rising force in politics, and Tom Ellis put some pressure on him to accept Liberal leadership in the Commons. Asquith refused, largely for financial reasons.[2]

Thus Campbell-Bannerman was left as the only available candidate for the post of Leader of the Liberals in the Commons. After a decent gesture of reluctance he accepted the post, and was unanimously elected on 6 February 1899. Like Harcourt before him, Campbell-Bannerman was not recognized as overall Leader of the Party, and it seems generally to have been assumed that the

[1] Lord Tweedmouth to Haldane, 22 December 1898. Asquith papers 9, fol. 143–4.
[2] Memorandum by Asquith, December 1898. Asquith papers 9, fol. 109–28.

likeliest man to head a Liberal administration was Lord Spencer, whom Gladstone had proposed to recommend to the Queen in 1894.[1]

At the very moment when the new Parliamentary leadership and the developing crisis in South Africa both demanded experience and co-ordinated action, the Liberal Party suffered a quite unexpected disaster by the death of the Chief Whip, Tom Ellis. As events would prove many years later, Campbell-Bannerman spoke even better than he knew when he described this loss as 'a complete calamity'.[2] With some imagination, Campbell-Bannerman did not follow the ordinary course of appointing Ellis's second-in-command, but prevailed upon Herbert Gladstone, fourth son of the Prime Minister, to accept the post. Technically, this was a step down, as Herbert Gladstone had been a junior Minister in the old Government.

His probity and personal character were of the highest order. As Chief Whip he worked tirelessly for Liberalism, and his personal fortune (which was not great) suffered considerably from his political devotion. When he became Chief Whip, the available funds were only £15–£16,000, which was less than the annual cost of running the Party machine. On two occasions Herbert Gladstone was even driven to borrowing £5,000 from his brother Henry, in order to make Party ends meet.[3] His skill in the day-to-day business of the Party was considerable, and his sometime Secretary, R. Humphrey Davies, has written to the present author of the 'splendid wisdom' by which Herbert Gladstone 'kept the Party differences and rivalries of Chiefs quite distinct from the work of organization'. Yet Herbert Gladstone's fatal weakness lay in his poor judgement on major questions. There had been signs of this as long ago as 1885, when he 'leaked' the news of his father's conversion to Home Rule in circumstances which greatly damaged the work of the older man. We shall later need to consider the disastrous effects which Herbert Gladstone's misjudgement would exercise on matters of even greater moment for the Liberal Party.

*   *   *

[1] E. Halévy, *The rule of democracy 1905–1914*, 1961 edn, p. 3. The possibility of a Spencer administration is also considered, e.g., in Grey to Asquith, 7 October 1903. Asquith papers 8, fol. 92–5.

[2] Campbell-Bannerman to Asquith, 7 April 1899. Asquith papers 9, fol. 177–8.

[3] Sir Charles Mallet, *Herbert Gladstone*, p. 195.

The outbreak of the Boer War – Britain's last great war of Imperial expansion – in October 1899 made the position of the Liberal Party even more difficult, for no secret was made of the fact that they were profoundly divided. When the war was already imminent, John Morley had given his solemn warning, which rings down the years to those who survey the tragic consequences which still persist, nearly three-quarters of a century on:

'You may carry fire and sword into the midst of peace and industry – such a war of the strongest Government in the world against this weak little Republic . . . will bring you no glory. It will bring you no profit, but mischief, and it will be wrong. You may make thousands of women widows and thousands of children fatherless. It will be wrong. You may add a new province to your Empire. It will still be wrong. You may give greater buoyancy to the South African Stock and Share market. You may create South African booms. You may send the price of Mr Rhodes's Chartereds up to a point beyond the dreams of avarice. Yes, even then it will be wrong.'[1]

Lord Rosebery, on the other hand, declared that, 'what we have to do is to join with all the energy and all the strength at our command in supporting those who have the direction of affairs'.[2]

At this time, three rising Liberal politicians were associated very closely with Lord Rosebery. One of them was Asquith, whom we have already had cause to consider. The other two were Sir Edward Grey and R. B. Haldane. Grey was a member of the famous Whig house which had produced the celebrated Earl Grey of the 1832 Reform Act. He was eventually to achieve great fame as the Foreign Secretary who was in office at the outbreak of the First World War. Haldane was a lawyer, like Asquith, and a man of phenomenal energy. He was noted as an authority on the German philosophers. This feature, as well as his own rather bleak character, earned him the sobriquet 'Schopenhauer' from Campbell-Bannerman. Haldane was strongly disposed towards caution, and avoiding a complete split among the Liberals, urging Campbell-Bannerman that 'the defective

[1] Speech at Manchester 15 September 1899. *Liberal Magazine*, vii (1899) pp. 488–9.
[2] At Edinburgh, 1 November 1899. *Liberal Magazine*, vii (1899), p. 566.

military preparations should give room for a nimble Liberal candidate to turn about in'.[1]

A substantial measure of agreement among the Liberal M.P.s was secured in support of a back-bench amendment to the Address, on 19 November 1899, condemning the Government's handling of the negotiations with the Boers but leaving aside the question of whether the war should be supported. Even on this line, Liberal cohesion was far from complete. Ninety-four Liberals supported the amendment, fifteen voted against it; forty-two were present but did not vote, and thirty-six were absent.[2] Nevertheless, such unheroic tactics might have served the Liberal Party well if the war had come to a speedy end; but the longer it lasted the worse the tensions became. With perhaps more logic than political wisdom, Grey remarked to Rosebery that 'either the war is a necessary war, or it is not; if the former it should be justified: if the latter it should be denounced'.[3] Other Liberals accepted Grey's argument from a very different side from Grey himself, and proceeded to denounce the war.

On 25 July 1900, Sir Wilfrid Lawson, one of the leading anti-war Liberals, submitted a motion of censure on Joseph Chamberlain, the Colonial Secretary. Campbell-Bannerman urged the Liberals to abstain; but in fact they split fairly evenly three ways, into those supporting Lawson, those supporting the Government, and those who followed the official advice.[4] Campbell-Bannerman threatened to resign if the Party split; but Grey, who seemed to take the threat seriously, nevertheless spoke against the censure motion.[5] The resignation did not occur, but evidently it was a near thing. Even so staunch a Liberal newspaper as the *Daily News* was driven to remark, with permissible understatement: 'We cannot honestly say that we think that the Opposition cut a very creditable figure in yesterday's debate'.[6]

* * *

[1] Haldane to Campbell-Bannerman, 9 November 1899. Campbell-Bannerman papers, 41,215, fol. 133–4.

[2] The behaviour of individual Liberal M.P.s is listed in the Viscount Gladstone papers 46,105, fol. 12 *seq*.

[3] Grey to Rosebery, 20 October 1899. Rosebery papers 23.

[4] The resolution was lost by 210 to 54. The 42 Liberals who were present during the sitting and abstained from voting are listed in Viscount Gladstone papers 46,105, fol. 101.

[5] Grey to Rosebery, 29 July 1900. Rosebery papers 23.

[6] *Daily News*, 26 July 1900.

By the late summer of 1900, it seemed that the Boers had been defeated, and only mopping-up operations remained. In what appeared to be the aftermath of a victorious war, the Unionists resolved to hold a General Election. Not surprisingly, the Liberals encountered considerable difficulties, both through refusals of subscriptions and the withdrawal of candidates from the field.[1] Instead of making play of the disunity among the Liberal ranks, the Unionists sought to brand all Liberals as 'pro-Boer' – which was palpably false.[2]

Again the Liberal machine served the Party well. In these desperate circumstances, the Liberals secured a handful more seats than they had held in 1895, although marginally less than they had had at the dissolution. Harcourt noted that, 'the result is better rather than worse than [one?] would have expected',[3] and the same point was made by a young Conservative who had just been returned for Oldham – Winston Churchill. Even where the Liberal vote fell, this was apparently not always attributable to the war or the internecine Liberal feuds; Campbell-Bannerman blamed the drop in his own majority at Stirling Burghs mainly on the Catholic Irish crossing over on educational questions.[4]

Perhaps it was just as well for the Liberals that the Government called the election when it did. The longer the war continued, the worse the Liberal divisions became.

From his precarious position on the fence, Campbell-Bannerman had striven to preserve unity, and had discouraged the Imperialists from setting up separate organizations.[5] He seems to have been concerned to keep Harcourt at arm's length.[6] But he was deeply outraged by the Army practice of herding Boers from 'cleared' areas into what were known as 'concentration camps'. This term had nothing of the frightful connotations which it later came to bear; but disease spread

---

[1] Herbert Gladstone to Campbell-Bannerman, 16 September 1900. Campbell-Bannerman papers 41,216, fol. 7–9.

[2] For some illuminating examples, see *Liberal Magazine* of November 1900, and the Supplement thereto.

[3] Sir William Harcourt to Campbell-Bannerman, 18 October 1900. Campbell-Bannerman papers 41,219, fol. 144–5.

[4] Campbell-Bannerman to Herbert Gladstone (copy), 12 October 1900. Campbell-Bannerman papers 41,216, fol. 22.

[5] Campbell-Bannerman to Grey, 29 November 1900 (copy). Campbell-Bannerman papers 41,218, fol. 17–19.

[6] Sir William Harcourt to Campbell-Bannerman, 5 December 1900. Campbell-Bannerman papers 41,219, fol. 157–8.

like wildfire, and mortality, especially among children, was fearful. Addressing the National Reform Union on 14 June 1900, Campbell-Bannerman attacked Arthur Balfour, the Unionist leader in the Commons, in the following words: 'A phrase often used was that "war is war", but when one came to ask about it one was told that no war was going on, that it was not war. When is a war not a war? When it was carried on by methods of barbarism in South Africa.'

This expression, 'methods of barbarism', made little impact for a day or two; but then it suddenly became one of the great slogans of politics. Campbell-Bannerman was belaboured with extreme savagery by the Imperialists, both inside and outside his own Party.

The Liberal cleavage was now complete. On one side, Campbell-Bannerman, Morley, Harcourt, Sir Robert Reid, Labouchère, and a rising young Welsh M.P., David Lloyd George. On the other, Asquith, Rosebery, Grey, Haldane, and Fowler.

The Liberals of the two groups maintained their dispute largely through a series of dinners – 'war to the knife and fork', in Sir Henry Lucy's expression. A great deal of concern and excitement seems to have been generated among people whom one might have expected to be busy with weightier matters, over the question of what dinners should be held, and who should attend them.[1]

But the Liberal battles were also fought on more serious issues. Before the end of 1900, there existed a Liberal Imperialist Council, under the chairmanship of Sir Edward Grey. The possibility that Grey and Fowler might secede from the Liberal Party altogether was considered with some complacency by Herbert Gladstone, although he felt more concern at the possibility that the secession might extend to Asquith and Lord Kimberley.[2] But the Chief Whip was extremely angry when the Imperialists contrived to secure the services of William Allard, Secretary of the Home Counties Liberal Federation, as Secretary of the new organization.[3]

Chafing under Campbell-Bannerman, the Imperialists had long hoped that Rosebery would return to the centre of politics. On 15

[1] As, for example, over the Asquith dinner arranged for 19 July 1901. Asquith papers 8, fol. 5–20.
[2] Herbert Gladstone to Campbell-Bannerman, 4 January 1900. Campbell-Bannerman papers 41,215, fol. 193–4.
[3] Herbert Gladstone to Campbell-Bannerman, 12–16 November 1901, Campbell-Bannerman papers 41,216, fol. 154–7; Herbert Gladstone/Haldane correspondence, 14–17 November 1901, Haldane papers 5905, fol. 122–7.

December 1901, the former Prime Minister delivered a major speech at Chesterfield. This was rather less divisive than some had expected on the question of the war itself; but Rosebery indicated a strong distaste for Irish Home Rule, and attacked the policies propounded by the N.L.F., in an astonishing metaphor, as 'fly-blown phylacteries'.

Herbert Gladstone seems, on the whole, to have been pleased with the Chesterfield speech. Campbell-Bannerman certainly was not[1] – regarding Rosebery's plea for a 'clean slate' on policy questions as 'an affront to Liberalism', castigating his plea for 'efficiency' as 'a mere *rechauffé* of Mr Sidney Webb, who is evidently the chief instigator of the whole faction', and writing with amusement of the 'fly-blown phylacteries'. Harcourt's views were similar, but perhaps less virulent.[2]

A great deal of uncertainty inevitably overhung Rosebery's speech. Was he returning to active membership of the Liberal Party, and, if so, in what capacity? In spite of his personal feelings, Campbell-Bannerman did what he could to bring Rosebery back into the camp, and met him late in December. Rosebery, however, refused cooperation, even on matters where there was no serious disagreement, declaring that 'he "was not of our communion" '.[3]

On 24 February 1902, Rosebery's political reappearance was celebrated by the establishment of a body known as the Liberal League, which was announced in the Press three days later.[4] Lord Rosebery was President, and the Vice-Presidents were Asquith, Fowler, and Grey. The Liberal Leaguers declared that, 'they had no intention of severing themselves from the Liberal Party but, on the contrary, intended to act with the rest of the Liberal opposition on the lines of that policy' – presumably meaning the Chesterfield policy. The League M.P.s continued to take the Liberal whip, and the Vice-Presidents performed the ordinary functions of Liberal front-benchers. Grey felt some concern about the relationship be-

[1] Herbert Gladstone/Campbell-Bannerman correspondence, 17–18 December 1901, Campbell-Bannerman papers 41,216, fol. 171–3.
[2] Sir William Harcourt to Campbell-Bannerman, 23 December 1901. Campbell-Bannerman papers 41,220, fol. 15–18.
[3] Campbell-Bannerman to Asquith, 7 January 1902. Asquith papers 8, fol. 52–3; Herbert Gladstone to Asquith 31 December 1901, *ibid.* fol. 41–2; R. W. Perks to Asquith, 2 January 1902, *ibid.* 34–8.
[4] Minutes of the inaugural meeting are given in Rosebery papers 106.

tween the new body and the old Liberal Imperial Council;[1] but the older body seems to have merged itself in the new, and Allard, about whose appointment there had been so much trouble, became its secretary.[2]

Large sums of money were raised by the League with very little effort; Harold Harmsworth (the future Lord Rothermere), for example, offered £1,000 a year for three years. At the beginning, 'the impression was fostered that there was almost fabulous wealth at the back of the League'.[3] According to the Minutes of the League's final meeting, 'In the earlier days of the League, from 1902 to 1907, we had an income within a few hundred pounds of £30,000. This amount was contributed mainly by seven very generous donors who gave us at least £3,000 each.'[4] In addition, a special campaign fund for the 1906 General Election raised £10,000, and evidently candidates with League sympathies received substantial sums.[5]

The officials of the Liberal Party did not penalize individuals whose sympathies lay with the League's policies, but discouraged candidates from actually joining it.[6] Nevertheless, at least twenty-eight M.P.s who sat in the 1900–5 House belonged.[7] Branches of the League were soon established in a considerable number of places. Large quantities of literature were produced, but this concentrated on attacking the Government, rather than on maintaining the internal dispute of the Liberal Party.

The Liberal League was one of the great 'might-have-beens' of modern history. Rosebery was a man of immense wealth, ability, and prestige. Some of the ablest men of the Party were willing to set their careers at risk in order to support him. Several others were well-disposed towards his policies. The movement seemed to wear the aspect of youth and vigour. But Rosebery's lack of consistent purpose, and his strange lack of responsibility towards his own followers, gradually dissipated all of these advantages. There was no climacteric dispute until the League was almost finished. Yet when the Liberals formed

[1] Rosebery to Grey (copy), 28 February 1902. Rosebery papers 106.
[2] Freeman-Thomas to Rosebery, 14 March 1902. Rosebery papers 106.
[3] Allard to Rosebery, 26 February 1906. Rosebery papers 107.
[4] Council of the Liberal League, 31 May 1910. Rosebery papers 107.
[5] Allard to Rosebery, 20 May 1907. Rosebery papers 107.
[6] Allard to Rosebery, 25 March 1902. Rosebery papers 106.
[7] Listed in an undated memorandum, probably written in 1904. Viscount Gladstone papers 46,107.

a Government at the end of 1905, not a single voice of importance was raised to insist that Rosebery should be included – much less that he should preside over it – and when the League expired in 1910, not a dog barked.

The wartime difficulties of the Liberal politicians spilled over into the Liberal Press, affecting the control and policy of two of the principal Liberal newspapers. At the outset of the Boer War, the *Daily News* was edited by E. T. Cook, a distinguished pro-war journalist, while the *Daily Chronicle* was edited by the no less distinguished opponent of the war, H. W. Massingham. In November 1899, Massingham was driven to resign,[1] and the *Daily Chronicle* swung to support of the war. In January 1901, the 'pro-Boers' counter-attacked[2] and an anti-war syndicate, said to have been organized by Lloyd George,[3] acquired control of the *Daily News*, forcing Cook in his turn from office, and replacing him by R. C. Lehmann, an opponent of the war. There was a good deal of bitterness about the way in which this was done; Cook knew nothing of the negotiations, and received two days' notice of dismissal.[4]

* * *

The South African war came to an end in May 1902, but even before this there were signs of impending trouble for the Government. A series of important Court decisions showed that the legal rights of Trade Unions were a good deal less than most people had imagined; and the Government's failure to introduce prompt remedial legislation caused great concern amongst workers, including those who had hitherto supported the Unionists. The Balfour Education Act of 1902 greatly disturbed the Nonconformists, and all Liberals of prominence – with the single exception of R. B. Haldane – condemned it.[5]

From that moment forth, everything went wrong for the Government. In the spring of 1903, Joseph Chamberlain began to express in public his wish to abandon Free Trade, and in the autumn he launched his famous 'Tariff Reform' campaign in favour of a revived

[1] D.N.B. 1922–40, p. 567.
[2] *The Times*, 10 January 1901.
[3] (Sir) Robert Ensor, *England 1870–1914*, p. 316.
[4] Campbell-Bannerman to Herbert Gladstone, 2 January 1901; Herbert Gladstone to Campbell-Bannerman, 15 January 1901. Campbell-Bannerman papers 61,216, fols. 65, 69–72.
[5] Dudley Sommer, *Haldane of Cloan*, pp. 129–30.

D

policy of Protection. In September 1903, Arthur Balfour, who had by then become Prime Minister, received the resignations both of Chamberlain on one flank and the leading Unionist Free Traders on the other. Even before these resignations, the Liberal leaders were expecting a General Election in the near future,[1] and friendly contact was established between Liberal headquarters and Unionist Free Traders – the possibility of giving such men unopposed runs being considered favourably.[2] The Free Trade Union, which was established in the middle of 1903, encompassed both Liberal and Unionist Free Traders. With some difficulty, even Rosebery was persuaded to join.[3] In those days, it was common enough for one or two M.P.s to cross the floor in the lifetime of a Parliament; but this time no fewer than eleven Unionists moved to the Opposition side, and only one Liberal and one Nationalist migrated the other way.

Among the men who joined the Opposition, by far the most famous was Winston Churchill; but there was also another future Cabinet Minister, J. E. B. Seely. When Seely withdrew support from the Government, he resigned his seat and stood as a candidate in the supervening by-election – but no one could be found to stand against him. Churchill defied the Oldham Unionists to demand his resignation, but they did not dare.[4]

The by-elections told the same story. In 1903, the Government lost five seats; in 1904 another seven, including the two which they had captured earlier in the lifetime of the same Parliament. In 1905 seven more were taken.

Towards the end of 1905, some irreconcilable statements were made by Unionists on the subject of Tariff Reform; while almost immediately afterwards there was an extraordinary Liberal fracas on the Irish question. Campbell-Bannerman had spoken on the subject in Stirling on 23 November; while on the two following nights, Rosebery addressed meetings in Truro and Bodmin. Apparently gauging the tone of Campbell-Bannerman's speech from an incom-

---

[1] Herbert Gladstone to Campbell-Bannerman, 24 June 1903. Campbell-Bannerman papers 41,216, fol. 281–2.

[2] Hugh Cecil to Gladstone, 6 July 1903. Campbell-Bannerman papers 41,216, fol. 286–93; Lord James of Hereford's memorandum, 21 December 1903, *ibid.* 41,217, fol. 59–66.

[3] Asquith/Rosebery correspondence, 9–27 July 1903, Rosebery papers 1. Freeman-Thomas to Rosebery, 4 July 1903, *ibid.* 106.

[4] Lady Violet Bonham-Carter, *Winston Churchill as I knew him*, p. 112.

plete Press account,[1] Rosebery took issue. The general reaction of
Liberals to Lord Rosebery – and not least that of his erstwhile partisans – was one of angry indignation.[2] By common consent, the
speeches of Asquith were among the most judicious and statesman-
like, and what could have become a savage and totally unnecessary
internecine battle was damped down.

Whether influenced by dissensions in the Liberal Party or in his
own Party, Balfour resigned on 4 December 1905. It followed that
the Liberals would be invited to form an administration. Lord
Spencer, who once seemed the likeliest candidate for the Liberal
Premiership, had been incapacitated by a stroke a few weeks earlier,
and although considerations both of politics and of health[3] cast
doubts on Campbell-Bannerman's suitability, he was invited to head
a new Government.

Tactics were of very great importance in this situation. The
Liberals do not seem to have had much doubt that the Unionist
Party would be defeated; but, even at the end of November,
J. A. Spender, one of the leading Liberal journalists and a man of
great political experience, wrote to Lord Rosebery that, 'the most
sanguine view in our camp is that, if the election took place now, the
thirty seats that make all the difference between a government dependent on and independent of the Irish would not be won'.[4] Both
past experience and current differences made that particular prospect
most unwelcome to the Liberals. However, Campbell-Bannerman
decided to accept office, and became Prime Minister on 5 December
1905.

The task of forming a Ministry presented great difficulties.
Harcourt had died in the previous year, and Rosebery had exasper-
ated everyone. But a great deal turned on three very able members
of the Liberal League: Asquith, Grey, and Haldane. A few months
earlier, the three men had concluded what became known as the
'Relugas compact' from the place on Grey's estate where it had been
agreed. They had agreed that none of them would serve under
Campbell-Bannerman, unless he took a peerage and gave Asquith

[1] Rosebery to Asquith, 28 December 1905 (copy?) Rosebery papers 106.
[2] Robert Hudson to Herbert Gladstone, 28 November 1905. Viscount Gladstone
papers 46,021.
[3] Herbert Gladstone to Asquith, 29 October 1903. Asquith papers 8, fol. 98–9.
[4] Spender to Rosebery, 29 November 1905. Rosebery papers 106.

the leadership of the Commons. Thus Campbell-Bannerman would find himself in a House where, as Rosebery had discovered, he could exert little control over events. The Lord Chancellorship, according to this plan, would go to Haldane, who would overshadow the Premier even in the Lords. Asquith would join the post of Chancellor of the Exchequer with Commons leadership, while Grey would receive the Foreign Office. Thus all the key posts would go to Imperialists, with reversion of the premiership as well.

Campbell-Bannerman was apparently prepared, if necessary, to constitute his Cabinet without any of them.[1] But it would make matters a good deal easier if they would join. Asquith was offered the Exchequer, Grey the Foreign Office and Haldane a choice of the Attorney-Generalship or the War Office. Asquith's position was crucial, and he explained his own dilemma in a letter to Haldane:[2]

'. . . After considerable hesitation and ostensible, probably actual, wavering, CB has, on the advice of his wife, declined to go at once to the House of Lords. . . .

'If I refuse to go in, one of two consequences follows: either (1) the attempt to form a government is given up (which I don't believe in the least would now happen) or (2) a weak government would be formed entirely or almost entirely of one colour.

'In either event in my opinion the issue of the election would be put in the utmost peril. It would be said that it was an issue about Home Rule, the Colonies, the Empire, etc., etc., and the defection of the whole of our group would be regarded as conclusive evidence. The *tertius gaudens* at Dalmeny [Lord Rosebery] would look on with complacency. I cannot imagine more disastrous conditions under which to fight a Free Trade election. . . .'

Some interesting light on the process by which Grey and Haldane were eventually brought into the Government is provided in an account written by F. D. Acland (later Sir Francis Acland) to his wife.[3]

[1] Grey to Asquith, 4 December 1905. Asquith papers 9, fol. 180–1.
[2] Asquith to Haldane, 7 December 1905. Haldane papers 5,906, fol. 243–6. See also Campbell-Bannerman to Haldane, *ibid.* fol. 247–8.
[3] F. D. Acland to Mrs Acland, 10 December 1905. Acland papers.

'. . . C.B. stiffened on getting Asquith with him and at 7.30 on Thursday Grey & Haldane came to see Father [that is, A. H. D. Acland] to tell him their definite conclusions, Grey having posted his refusal to serve at all, Haldane, having been offered high office, with his written refusal in his pocket.

'Father then bombarded them for an hour and got Haldane nearly turned and both promising to consider and see him again that night. After dinner Haldane returned converted, and Grey later still stubborn. Father had found out meanwhile that the offices were not being filled up, and would be kept open till next morning, and he had been offered the Leadership of the Lords if that would in any way help Grey & Haldane to come in. He kept this back, but hammered Grey until he promised to go to C.B. next morning and accept Foreign Office. They also settled whether Haldane should take Attorney General, Home or War and decided War – which is good . . .

'Father has I suppose done C.B. as great a service as one man can do another, but he hasn't had a word of thanks from him & now they have got Grey and Haldane there is no mention of anything for Father. . . .

'I am rather proud of my father – Grey and Haldane are two of the stubbornest men going. He saved the party by turning them. I think the Liberals would not have won if they had stayed out.'

By this remarkable process, Asquith, Grey, and Haldane were brought into the Government. Of the other men associated with the Imperialist wing, Bryce obtained the very hazardous post of Chief Secretary for Ireland, Birrell the Board of Education, and Fowler the Duchy of Lancaster. On the other side of the Party, Sir Robert Reid became Lord Chancellor as Lord Loreburn, Morley became Secretary for India, and Herbert Gladstone Home Secretary. Lloyd George received the Board of Trade. The 'Lib–Lab' John Burns became President of the Local Government Board. Outside the Cabinet, several men who would later play an important role made their first appearance in Ministerial office. Among them were Winston Churchill, Reginald McKenna, Herbert Samuel, Walter Runciman, and the Master of Elibank.

And thus, in a few days, Campbell-Bannerman had drawn together a group of men who could very easily have dissolved into a rabble, and formed them into one of the strongest and most talented governments which Britain has ever known. They could look forward to the impending General Election with at least the reasonable hope that it would provide them with a working overall majority in the House of Commons.

*   *   *

On 12 January 1906 the first constituency polled, Ipswich. 'Ip-ip-ip-Ipswich!' was the placard of the radical London *Star*, for this Suffolk town, which had been represented in the old Parliament by a Liberal and a Unionist, now sent back two Liberals with convincing majorities. On the next day ten Unionist constituencies in Lancashire voted, and every one went either Liberal or 'Labour'. To general amazement, Balfour was unseated in Manchester East, which he had represented for twenty years. And so the tale went on. London, which had been overwhelmingly Unionist, swung to overwhelming support for the new Government. In the whole Principality of Wales, not a single Unionist seat remained. Less than a fifth of the seats in Scotland were still Unionist. When the nation had polled, the only remaining Unionist strongholds were the Presbyterian areas of Ulster, the entirety of Birmingham, most of Liverpool, some rural areas, particularly in South-East England, a few wealthy districts near the large towns, most of the University seats, and isolated, scattered constituencies where local or personal factors had affected the result. Apart from the ex-Prime Minister, six members of the old Cabinet were unseated, although one of them, Walter Long, found a new constituency before the election was over. In so doing, he provided the Unionists with their only Irish gain, and their only seat South of the Boyne – County Dublin South.

The Liberals secured 400 seats, 60 of which were held by members of the Liberal League.[1] There were 129 Conservatives and 29 Liberal Unionists. The Irish Nationalists held 83, and a new organization, the Labour Representation Committee – soon to become the Labour Party – took 29. For most purposes the L.R.C. could be regarded as Government supporters, and form any purposes so could the Irish. A Conservative Free Trader, Austin Taylor of Liverpool, and a Liberal Unionist Free Trader, Robert Glendenning of Antrim, decided to take the Liberal whip. Thus, the effective Government

[1] Listed (27 January 1906) in Rosebery papers 107.

majority was brought to 358, while, even in the improbable event of the Irish and the L.R.C. voting with the Unionists, it was still in excess of 130.

Few indeed were the Liberal losses to counterbalance just over 200 gains. The Unionists took 13 Liberal seats and the L.R.C. took 2.[1] Most commentators regarded the 23 L.R.C. gains from the Unionists as part of the Liberal victory.

---

[1] Nine of the thirteen Unionist gains were reversals of losses either in by-elections or by accretion of M.P.s. Two more – Govan and N.W. Lanarkshire – were held by narrow majorities in 1900, and the Liberal loss seems to be explained by the intervention of a third 'Labour' candidate who polled substantially. The remaining two – Maidstone and Hastings – might repay detailed study. The L.R.C. gains from the Liberals were Gorton, and one Dundee seat.

3

The Top of the Hill

*And the land shall not be sold in perpetuity; for the land is
Mine: for ye are strangers and sojourners with Me.*

Leviticus xxv, 23

The achievements of the Liberal Government which took office in
1905 have been told many times.[1] We are here concerned primarily
with the effect of events upon the Liberals, rather than with the effect
of Liberals upon events, and hence much of that story is outside our
present concern. Nevertheless, some considerable part of it is relevant
here, for it is only in this perspective that the character and behaviour
of the Liberal Party may be understood.

In the first couple of years, two great Ministerial reputations were
made. Asquith, as Chancellor of the Exchequer, dispelled some of
the principal 'Tariff Reform' arguments by producing Budget surpluses
in a Free Trade economy.

The other great administrative reputation was won by the President
of the Board of Trade, David Lloyd George. His early reputation
had been that of the 'guerilla leader' of a form of Liberalism
which was particularly popular in the Principality – with a strong
admixture of Welsh separatism, radical pacifism, and dissenting
religion. In 1902 he first appeared as a serious national politician,
winning his spurs as the 'nonconformist genius' who contested the
Education Bill clause by clause. As President of the Board of Trade,
he received general acclaim for the Merchant Shipping Act of 1907,
and the Patents and Registered Designs Act of the same year. Both
of these measures delighted his political friends, and were welcomed
by his opponents as well.

But his role as an industrial negotiator represented a very much

[1] A useful contemporary account is *The Government's Record 1906–1913*. Liberal
Publications Department 1913.

broader view of the scope of his office than any predecessor had taken. He intervened personally in industrial disputes, with conspicuous success, and also established arbitration machinery which proved of great value later on.

Yet events which lay outside the Government's control did not assist its reputation. The year 1906 had been one of general prosperity, but in 1907 a world-wide trade recession began. This was mirrored in the by-election results. In 1906, the Government lost only one seat, and this could reasonably be attributed to the appearance of a third candidate. But in 1907 they lost Brigg to the Unionists, Jarrow to Labour, and Colne Valley to an Independent Socialist. In the first three months of 1908, the Unionists captured three more Liberal seats, one of them with a very great overturn of votes.

*   *   *

But the first two years or so of the new Government gave clear indication of an impending struggle on constitutional matters. This had really been brewing for many years. The National Liberal Federation had repeatedly declared its wish to 'mend or end' the House of Lords. But even if the Liberal M.P.s and their leaders had all shared the N.L.F.'s enthusiasm (which they did not), the Lords would undoubtedly have thrown out any Bill from the Commons which sought to curtail their powers. Nor was there any indication of that sort of extra-Parliamentary pressure from the electorate which might overcome the Lords' reluctance. In 1894, Campbell-Bannerman had reported to Rosebery his own experience among his Stirling constituents: 'As to the heroic line on the H. of Lords I am satisfied that it has small support: there are very few abolitionists, nor does one hear the march of the unicameral men. I was obliged to coo like a dove, and I believe a suspensory veto is all my people wd. stand.'[1]

This, it must be remembered, was the climate of opinion in a strongly Liberal area, and there is little to show that it had changed much a dozen years later.

The House of Lords had long settled into a routine when measures were set before them by the Commons. To a Unionist administration, they gave little trouble. To contentious Liberal measures, they adopted very skilful tactics. If the Bill was obviously popular, they would let it through without cavil. But if it was likely to be of restricted

[1] Campbell-Bannerman to Rosebery, 9 December 1894. Rosebery papers 2.

interest, they would have no compunction in either throwing it out or introducing wrecking amendments. Thus a Liberal Government, however large its majority, would be compelled either to acquiesce in defeat or else to appeal to the electorate in circumstances where the large and crucial mass of central opinion could be expected to resent an election which seemed to them pointless and to visit their resentment upon the Government.

This pattern of behaviour was well illustrated by the Lords' treatment of contentious Bills which the Liberals sent up to them in the first few years of their new administration.

While the Unionists were still in office, they had set up a Royal Commission on Trade Disputes and Trade Combinations. This Commission reported while the General Election was actually in progress, and in March 1906 the Liberal Attorney-General, Sir Lawson Walton, introduced a Bill which closely followed the Commission's recommendations.

Walton had indicated that the Government would be willing to accept modifications of the Bill in certain directions, including the liability of Trade Unions in tort. A Labour member, Walter Hudson, introduced an alternative measure, which sought to remove from the Trade Unions all liability in tort. The Prime Minister intervened in favour of Hudson's Bill, which duly passed the Commons.[1] In the final stages, the Unionists did not oppose the Bill, and by the end of the year the Lords had passed it as well. The Trade Unions were completely satisfied.[2]

At first sight, the Lords might quite reasonably have refused to pass the Bill. It had not been foreshadowed – not in the form which it took, in any event – at the General Election a few months earlier. It was not even the Government's own Bill. It introduced completely new principles which could reasonably alarm the lawyer. Yet it was apparently popular, and any resistance by the Lords would be likely to prove injurious to themselves, and injurious to the Unionist Party.

But the new Government was a good deal less successful in satisfying the aspirations of its sympathizers over the education question. In order to remove those features of the Balfour Act of 1902 which had enraged the Nonconformists, Augustine Birrell, President of the

---

[1] No Liberal, Labour, or Irish members opposed Hudson's Bill. Seven Unionists supported the Second Reading, although sixty-seven voted against.

[2] G. D. H. Cole, *British Working-Class Politics, 1832–1914*, p. 189.

AGRICULTURAL AND SITE VALUE.

[From the *Westminster Gazette*.

Mr. Lloyd-George: What are you using this acre field for?

Owner Agricultural purposes. I turn my pony in here!

Mr. Lloyd-George: It can't be worth more than £50 for that purpose—couldn't you do something better with it?

Owner: There's no need for me to do anything—the builders over there are doing it all for me. They'll be wanting to build here soon. Why, I could get £500 to-morrow for this acre!

Mr. Lloyd-George: Then, surely, it won't hurt you to pay a tax of a halfpenny in the £ on an increased value which you have had nothing to do with making!

[Mr. Lloyd-George's Budget proposes to levy a tax of a halfpenny in the pound on undeveloped land, excluding (*a*) all land worth less than £50 an acre and (*b*) all land solely valuable for agricultural purposes.]

Published by the LIBERAL PUBLICATION DEPARTMENT (in connection with the National Liberal Federation and the Liberal Central Association), 42, Parliament Street, Westminster, S.W., and Printed by the National Press Agency Limited, Whitefriars House, London, E.C.

Leaflet No. 2231.]   25/6/09.   [Price 5s. per 1000.

THE BIG DOG AND THE LITTLE ONE.

[From the *Westminster Gazette*.

LORD HALSBURY: I don't think much of that paltry little thing—it's a mockery of a dog.

AGED PENSIONER: Well, my lord, 'tis only a little 'un, but 'tis a wunnerful comfort to me. Us bain't all blessed wi' big 'uns!

[Lord Halsbury, in a speech at Budleigh Salterton on January 6th, spoke of the Pensions given by the Liberal Act of Parliament as "so paltry as to be all but a mockery." Lord Halsbury himself draws a State Pension of £5,000 a year, or nearly £100 a week.]

Published by the LIBERAL PUBLICATION DEPARTMENT (in connection with the National Liberal Federation and the Liberal Central Association), 42, Parliament Street, Westminster, S.W., and Printed by the National Press Agency Limited, Whitefriars House, London, E.C.

LEAFLET No. 2207.]   1/2/09.   [Price 4s. 6d. per 1000.

Board of Education, brought forward an Education Bill, which proposed to exclude denominational teaching completely from the
elementary schools. The Irish opposed it, but the Bill passed the
Commons. The Lords proposed some unacceptable amendments,
and the Government was forced to let the Bill drop. Another Bill was
submitted in 1908. Again the Bill passed the Commons; again there
were difficulties in the Lords; and again the Bill was eventually
withdrawn.

These Education Bills could fairly be criticized even by people who
agreed with what they were trying to accomplish. But this sort of
criticism could not be brought against the famous Scottish Land
Bills. The 1907 Bill was designed to obtain a general valuation of land
in Scotland, as a necessary preliminary to the application of Land
Value Taxation. The Bill was clearly popular in Scotland, but it was
defeated in the Lords. Rather ominously, Lord Rosebery ranged himself among the opponents of the Bill.[1] The Government introduced
another Bill to similar effect in 1908. This Bill again passed the
Commons with a massive majority. It was not formally rejected by
the Lords, but was amended in a way which defeated its purpose,
and the Government decided to withdraw it. No doubt this would
infuriate the people of Scotland, but Scotland only returned twelve
Unionists out of seventy-two constituencies, and the issue was not
one on which the Government could appeal with confidence to an
electorate which was predominantly English.

But resentment was building up, and some men were already
spoiling for battle, long before the Government decided that it was
propitious to attack the enemy. On 26 June 1907, two resolutions
were moved in the House of Commons. The first, originating from
the Labour benches, called for the outright abolition of the Upper
House. This was heavily defeated, but secured the support of 102
M.P.s: 40 Liberals, 26 Labour, and 36 Irish. Campbell-Bannerman
moved a more moderate resolution, which demanded that the power
of the Lords to reject or alter Bills from the Commons 'should be
so restricted by law as to secure that within the limits of a single
Parliament the final decision of the Commons shall prevail'.

*   *   *

Thus, coming events were already casting their shadows by 1908.

[1] Rosebery to Freeman-Thomas, 4 September 1907. Rosebery papers 107.

Enthusiasts for reforms of many different kinds had either seen their cherished proposals wrecked by the Lords, or had good reason for believing that they would be so treated if and when they were sent up from the Commons. From their very different viewpoints, they all saw the House of Lords as their enemy, although the public as a whole was still largely unmoved.

Early in 1908, Campbell-Bannerman's health collapsed completely. He resigned early in April, and died later in the month. There is no evidence that he ever formally recommended his successor to the King, but everyone assumed – correctly – that it would be Asquith. The most notable promotion in the new Ministry was David Lloyd George, who was advanced from the Board of Trade to the Exchequer; while Winston Churchill succeeded to the post which had thus been vacated.

The new Prime Minister himself introduced the 1908 Budget, which he had prepared while at the Exchequer. But the Chancellor contrived to stand at the storm-centre of a series of violent controversies almost immediately afterwards.

The issue of Old Age Pensions had been prominent in politics for over a decade. Chamberlain had more or less promised them in 1895, and again in 1900.[1] The general contention of the Unionists was not that Old Age Pensions were undesirable, but that increased revenue from tariffs was necessary before they could be granted. Free Traders pointed out, with much logic, that a tariff which is successful as a protective device will necessarily fail to produce revenue. The Government's Bill had been the subject of consideration by a Committee of the Cabinet for some months,[2] but Lloyd George was the moving spirit behind it in the Commons.

The Unionists, by reason of their past promises, could scarcely put up more than a half-hearted fight; but spirited opposition came from certain Liberals, or erstwhile Liberals. Lord Rosebery considered that his sometime followers were 'dealing a blow at the Empire which may be almost mortal',[3] while a Liberal M.P., Harold Cox,[4] headed the opposition to the Bill on *laissez-faire* grounds; but when his amendment to the Second Reading was moved, only one other

[1] Speech at Hanley, 12 July 1895; speech at Birmingham, 29 September 1900.
[2] Cabinet Letter 1 May 1908 (draft). Asquith papers 5, fol. 25.
[3] House of Lords, 20 July 1908.
[4] Cox sat for Preston. In January 1910 he defended the seat as an Independent Liberal, but finished bottom of the poll.

Liberal voted with him. The Unionists were split; twenty-nine supported Cox, forty-two voted with the Government and ninety-one abstained. On the Third Reading, Cox was the only Liberal to oppose the Bill. Twelve Unionists voted with him, and eleven with the Government, while the great majority abstained.

When the Bill went to the Lords, an attempt was made to amend it by restricting the operation to a trial period of seven years; but the Commons threw out the amendment, and the Lords did not care to press their point when the Bill was returned to them. So it received Royal Assent at the end of the Session, and came into operation at the beginning of 1909. With certain exceptions, necessitous people over seventy years of age received five shillings a week, which in the values of the times was something like the level of subsistence.

Lloyd George's first Budget produced a far greater measure of public controversy. The Chancellor introduced it on 29 April 1909, declaring it to be 'a war budget . . . for raising money to wage implacable war against poverty and squalidness'.

The Chancellor proposed to raise £13·6 million more in taxation.[1] The largest single item was £3·5 million from a new graduated system of income tax and surtax. A further £3·4 million was to be raised from tobacco and spirits, and £2·6 million from liquor licences. £2·85 million was to be obtained from increases in estate duties, and £0·75 million from stamp duties.

But the fundamental departure which Lloyd George made from traditional finance was in his Land Taxes. There were three main proposals. The first was a tax of 20 per cent on land value increments, payable on transfer of land. The second was a tax of one halfpenny in the pound on the value of undeveloped land. The third was a tax of 10 per cent on the value of leasehold reversions. All of these land taxes together were only designed to raise half a million pounds in the current financial year.

Many people supposed that Lloyd George's land taxes represented the application of Henry George's economic doctrines. This was not so,[2] and some later economists have criticized him for applying a complex system of measures, without producing the positive benefits

[1] Itemized in Cabinet Letter, 28 April 1909. Asquith papers 5, fol. 106–7.
[2] See unsigned article, 'Land Reform in Politics', *Land and Liberty*, February–March 1964, and Sir Edward Harper's address to the International Conference on Land Value Taxation, Edinburgh 1929.

of land value taxation. It may seem remarkable that such contro-
versial measures ever got through the Cabinet; indeed, there seems
little doubt that Lloyd George had a great struggle with many of his
colleagues, but was upheld mightily by Asquith.[1] Lewis ('Loulou')
Harcourt, usually a very shrewd observer, passed a card to Walter
Runciman at the Cabinet meeting of 24 March 1909: 'This Budget
will ensure the triumph of Tariff Reform'.[2]

Lloyd George encountered the inevitable opposition from people
who disliked his taxes on alcohol; but he was at no pains to rally the
temperance workers. He enraged the very rich; but he did not try to
turn the battle into one of rich *versus* poor. It was the land taxes on to
which he desired to focus attention.

The Chancellor rapidly took the struggle from the walls of Parliament to the public hustings. At Limehouse, in the East End of
London, he made one of the most celebrated speeches in political
history to a working-class audience of four thousand on a sweltering
night in July.

The bulk of the Limehouse speech was a closely reasoned examination of the manner in which the activities of all other sections of the
community, from the richest *entrepreneur* to the poorest labourer,
redounded to the profit of the landowner, without any corresponding
service on his part. The mordant and provocative sarcasm which
accompanied the logical arguments would have come well enough
from anyone who was not a Minister; but in the mouth of one of the
most senior members of the Government it horrified many people
beyond measure, and gave the word 'limehousing' to the English
language.

The Opposition exploded. Even King Edward VII, by no means
a diehard, remonstrated with Asquith. A little more oratory of this
kind drove the Unionists to fight the Budget tooth and nail on its
passage through the Commons. Outside the walls of Parliament, the
Duke of Beaufort declared that he would like 'to see Winston
Churchill and Lloyd George in the middle of twenty couple of dog
hounds'.[3]

But there could be little doubt that the general effect of the

---

[1] Lucy Masterman, *C. F. G. Masterman*, pp. 133–4.
[2] Runciman papers.
[3] At Cirencester, 7 August 1909. Just possibly, the Duke was jesting; but, if so,
the joke was a very bad and a very dangerous one.

Budget was very salutory from the Liberal point of view. The High Peak by-election of July 1909 was something of a test-case. Oswald Partington, the Liberal M.P. for the constituency, was appointed a Junior Lord of the Treasury, and under the law as it then stood he was required to defend his seat at a by-election. The seat was far from safe, and Partington's Unionist opponent was the same man who had stood there in 1906. On his own statement, Partington fought the contest entirely on the Budget.[1] The Liberals retained the seat; the poll of both Parties was increased, and the Liberal majority was only slightly reduced.

One of the side-effects of the Budget controversy was to clarify the position of Lord Rosebery. He had been showing unquiet at the radicalism of the administration for some time.[2] But at Glasgow on 10 September 1909 he announced that: 'I have long ceased to be in communion with the Liberal Party, and I have long since been an independent politician.' He went further, saying that: 'I think my friends are moving on the path that leads to Socialism. How far they are advanced on that path I will not say, but on that I, at any rate, cannot follow them an inch.'

This speech really finished the Liberal League. Asquith, as Vice-President, wrote to Rosebery, virtually calling for his resignation from the Presidency.[3] Rosebery, as usual, gave no very clear reply, although his complete disagreement with the Budget and the current behaviour of the Liberal Party was not in doubt. The League showed very little sign of grasping the nettle.[4] It tottered on ineffectually for several months more, but was finally wound up on 31 May 1910. Unlike most political bodies at the moment of their dissolution, the Liberal League still possessed very substantial financial assets.[5]

Rosebery did not pass into alliance with the Unionists; with one or two intermissions, he vanished from politics. His eldest son,

[1] *The Times*, 24 July 1909.
[2] Rosebery to Freeman-Thomas, 4 September 1907; Allard to Rosebery, 16 November 1907; Rosebery to Allard, 21 November 1907. Rosebery papers 107.
[3] Asquith/Rosebery correspondence, 11–20 September 1909. Rosebery papers 1.
[4] Rosebery to Allard, 19 June 1909; Allard to Rosebery, 28 June 1909; Minutes of Liberal League Executive, 28 June 1909. Rosebery papers 107.
[5] Council of Liberal League, 31 May 1910. Rosebery papers 107. The League had a balance of about £1,500, and unexhausted subscriptions of nearly £3,000 for three years.

Viscount Dalmeny, continued to sit as a Liberal M.P. for the remainder of that Parliament, and another son, Neil Primrose, was elected to Parliament in 1910 as a Liberal. The latter was, for a short time, Lloyd George's Chief Liberal Whip.

As the Budget controversy developed, Lloyd George began to use a new line of tactics. In form, he issued solemn warnings to the Lords; in fact, he was provoking them to do the very thing which was the subject of his admonitions. On 9 October, he made a speech at Newcastle which is not as famous as his earlier utterance, but which was really far more ominous, far more alarming, than anything he had said at Limehouse. The Lords, he declared, 'are forcing a revolution. The Peers may decree a revolution, but the people will direct it. If they begin, issues will be raised that they little dream of. Questions will be asked which are now whispered in humble voice, and answers will be demanded with authority. . . .'

This speech, and more besides, drove the Lords into the trap which Lloyd George had improvised for them. Early in September, the Cabinet had already considered the situation which would arise if the Budget were rejected.[1] By the beginning of November, Asquith was warning the King that rejection was 'probable', and the Cabinet was discussing the financial consequences if taxes which required annual ratification were not authorized.[2] On 30 November 1909, the House of Lords threw out the Finance Bill by 350 votes to 75.

Entering into the spirit of the new situation, Asquith moved and carried a resolution in the House of Commons two days later, describing the action of the Lords as 'a breach of the constitution and a usurpation of the rights of the Commons'.[3] So now at last an issue had been forced between the Liberals and the Lords where the people might reasonably be expected to side with the Liberals. To large sections of the public, the Lords' behaviour looked very much like extremely rich men violating the rules of the political game, for no better reason than that the Government was proposing some relatively small incursions on their personal wealth. As Lloyd George

[1] Cabinet Letter (draft), 8 September 1909. Asquith papers 5, fol. 150–1.
[2] Cabinet Letters (draft), 3 and 17 November 1909. Asquith papers 5, fols. 167–8; 169–70.
[3] Lord Knollys, the King's Secretary, validly observed to Asquith's Secretary, Vincent Nash, that the wording of the resolution was infelicitous; the Lords' action would have been better described as 'contrary to constitutional practice'. Knollys to Nash, 1 December 1909: Asquith papers 1, fol. 233.

jubilantly put it, 'Their greed has overcome their craft, and we have got them!'

On the day after Asquith's resolution was carried, Parliament was dissolved, and a General Election was fixed, to commence on 14 January 1910.

*   *   *

No Party could derive a full measure of satisfaction from the results of that election. The Liberals secured 275 seats, the Unionists 273, the Irish 82, and Labour 40. Thus the Liberals had lost their overall majority, but the Unionists had not won a majority. The increase in Labour representation was more apparent than real, and was due only to the accretion of some of the miners' M.P.s who had formerly sat as 'Liberal-Labour'.

Viewed in more detail, the election of January[1] 1910 presents a most interesting picture. The sensational Liberal gains in the South, which had given the victory of 1906 its landslide proportions, were swept away. The Unionists recaptured their old strongholds. But in the North, in Scotland, and in Wales, the position was very different. Taking these areas as a whole, the Liberals more or less broke even. A few losses were counterbalanced by a few gains. In the North-East of England, the Liberals and their allies actually made a marginal improvement on 1906.[2]

The Labour Party, as we shall see in a later chapter, was dependent on Liberal votes for practically every seat it held, and it was more or less bound to continue to do what it had done for some years – to make occasional protests when playing to its own gallery, but to give support to the Liberals on critical issues in the division lobbies.

The Irish, in theory, were masters of the whole situation, for at any moment they could put the Liberals out by voting with the Opposition. But the real position was far more complex, and presented some

----

[1] Strictly, polling lasted from 14 January to 10 February.

[2] If we do not distinguish between Liberals and Labour, we find that in Scotland the Government made five gains and five losses; in Wales, no gains and two losses; in Northumberland and Durham, four gains and two losses; in Yorkshire one gain and two losses; in Lancashire four gains and seven losses. But in the South-East corner of England (the area covered by the London and Home Counties Federations of the Liberal Party, there were only three gains to forty-eight losses. In the areas covered by the Western Counties and Devon & Cornwall Federations, there was only one gain – itself a reversal of a by-election loss – to nineteen losses.

exceedingly difficult problems both for the Liberals and for the Irish.

It was well known that Liberals varied considerably in their enthusiasm for Home Rule, and any situation which compelled them either to legislate or formally to abjure Home Rule would be likely to present them with serious difficulties both within Parliament and outside it. Many people who would vote Liberal for Free Trade, for social reform, or to tweak the tail of the House of Lords, would be hesitant or even downright opposed if politics came to centre again on Ireland.

The Irish Party faced problems of a different kind. It is widely considered that the best thing which can happen to a relatively small Party is to hold the balance of power. All modern British examples have shown that such a situation is an unmixed disaster for that Party. The Irish people could now reasonably expect their Parliamentary leader, John Redmond, to deliver them Home Rule. Already some had broken away from him, and a substantial contingent of 'Independent Nationalists', most of whom hailed from County Cork or nearby, looked to William O'Brien as their leader, and were a good deal less well disposed towards the Liberals than was Redmond.[1]

John Redmond and his friends were placed in a most uncomfortable position. The Budget was extremely unpopular in Ireland, largely because of the liquor taxes. The Irish Party would gladly have voted against the Budget – particularly now that the O'Brienites were offering a serious threat. Such a vote, however, would have defeated the Government, and would either have put the Unionists in office or precipitated another General Election. But Home Rule was even more important than the Budget in Irish eyes, and there was no question of getting Home Rule unless the Liberals remained in office, and the power of the House of Lords was curtailed.

T. P. O'Connor, Irish Nationalist M.P. for a Liverpool constituency, wrote to Lord Morley, threatening that his Party would vote against the Budget unless the Government promised a Bill dealing with the Lords' veto in the current year.[2] Obviously, no Government

[1] For discussion of the O'Brienites, see memorandum dated 1910, Elibank papers 8,802, fol. 39.
[2] Cabinet letter (copy), 10 February 1910. Asquith papers 5, fol. 180–1. O'Connor was, however, amenable to other suggestions. See T. P. O'Connor to Master of Elibank. Elibank papers 8,802, fol. 18.

KEY-PLAN TO "THE ATTACK ON THE LORDS."

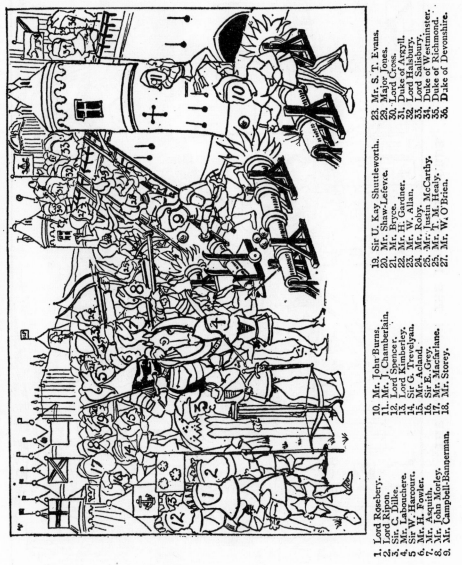

1. Lord Rosebery.
2. Lord Ripon.
3. Sir. C. Dilke.
4. Mr. Labouchere.
5. Sir W. Harcourt.
6. Mr. H. Fowler.
7. Mr. Asquith.
8. Mr. John Morley.
9. Mr. Campbell-Bannerman.

10. Mr. John Burns.
11. Mr. J. Chamberlain.
12. Lord Spencer.
13. Lord Kimberley.
14. Sir G. Trevelyan.
15. Mr. Acland.
16. Sir E. Grey.
17. Mr. Macfarlane.
18. Mr. Storey.

19. Sir U. Kay Shuttleworth.
20. Mr. Shaw-Lefevre.
21. Mr. Bryce.
22. Mr. H. Gardner.
23. Mr. W. Allan.
24. Mr. Roby.
25. Mr. Justin McCarthy.
26. Mr. T. M. Healy.
27. Mr. W. O'Brien.

28. Mr. S. T. Evans.
29. Major Jones.
30. Lord Cross.
31. Duke of Argyll.
32. Lord Halsbury.
33. Lord Salisbury.
34. Duke of Westminster.
35. Duke of Richmond.
36. Duke of Devonshire.

THE ATTACK ON THE HOUSE OF LORDS.

(*Picture Politics*)

could submit to such a threat, and a concession to the Irish on the
spirit duty was intolerable.[1] At one moment, some members of the
Cabinet seriously considered the resignation of the Government,
although this idea was quickly withdrawn.[2]

In the middle of April, the Government submitted three Resolutions, which in fact anticipated almost exactly the eventual Parliament Act of 1911. They proposed: (1) that the Lords should be
disabled from rejecting or amending a Money Bill, (2) that Bills
passed by the Commons in three successive sessions of Parliament
should become law in spite of the Lords' opposition, and (3) that the
maximum duration of Parliament should be reduced from seven
years to five years. A Parliament Bill embodying these proposals was
read for the first time on 14 April. Apparently reassured, the Irish
who followed Redmond supported the Government on the Budget,
while the O'Brienites voted with the Opposition. The Budget therefore passed the Commons on 27 April, and on the following day the
Lords let it through without a division.

The Government's Resolutions in the Commons were not the first
Parliamentary proposals for House of Lords Reform to be made in
the session. On 9 March Lord Rosebery had proposed in the Lords
that, 'the possession of a peerage should no longer give the right to sit
and vote in the House of Lords', and this was carried by the Lords
later in the month. By the standards of the time, it was a remarkably
radical proposal; not long beforehand, Lord Knollys indicated that
such a reform would seriously curtail the Prerogative.[3] But it would
not satisfy the Government: for, however the composition of the
Lords might be improved by removing the most stupid members, it
would still remain predominantly Unionist. The Government was
therefore concerned primarily to reduce the power of the Lords, and
only secondarily to reform its constitution.

This stage of what we might call preliminary sparring between the
Liberals and the Lords was marked by one feature of minor, but per-
sistent, interest, for it was at this time that Asquith used the three
words, 'Wait and see', which were to plague him for the rest of his
life. The context, however, is generally misunderstood; as his
daughter pointed out, they were actually used 'in one of his rare

[1] Cabinet letter, 13 April 1910 (draft). Asquith papers 5, fol. 208–11.
[2] Cabinet letter, 25–6 February 1910 (draft). Asquith papers 5, fol. 192–4.
[3] Knollys to Nash, 3 December 1908. Asquith papers 1, fol. 90.

moments of exasperation, not as an appeal to patience, but as a threat – that is – "You wait and see what's coming to you!"'.[1]

The Budget had just passed, and the two sides were beginning to take up their positions in preparation for the constitutional struggle, when King Edward VII suddenly died, on 6 May 1910. In order to reduce the burden on the new sovereign, George V, and to attempt a compromise settlement, a Conference was held at which four members each of the two main Parties sought to hammer out a solution. Lloyd George, who was one of the Liberal tetrad, came soon to contemplate something much more than a Constitutional Conference – rather, a full Coalition which would settle most of the major political problems of the day. This proposal was considered sympathetically by most of the leading Unionists, and by Sir Edward Grey and Lord Crewe at least among the Liberals.[2] It did not become public until years later, but it shows that the germ of an idea existed in the minds of Lloyd George and some of the leading Unionist statesmen. No doubt there would have been a political earthquake if the news had 'leaked' in 1910; but, as will be seen later, the eventual consummation of this idea would prove even more spectacular.

For reasons which may have been related to Unionist reactions in the constituencies, or perhaps to certain aspects of the Irish question,[3] the Unionists suddenly cooled to the idea of a coalition. And likewise the Conference itself collapsed in failure, after months of work, on 10 November 1910. On the same day, the Cabinet met, and asked the King for an immediate dissolution. Perhaps the Government was reassured by Jesse Herbert's calculation that the Liberal and Labour Parties would make a net gain of twenty-nine seats in England and Wales at an immediate General Election.[4]

The King refused a dissolution until the Parliament Bill had been submitted to the Lords. If the Lords failed to pass the Bill, then a dissolution would be granted. The Lords adopted the Rosebery proposals as their own in place of the Government's recommendations.

---

[1] Lady Violet Bonham-Carter (Baroness Asquith), *The Listener*, 18 March 1948, p. 454; Parl. Deb. (Commons) xiv 3 March 1910, 972; *Ibid.* xvi 4 April 1910, 25 and 26.

[2] Sir Austen Chamberlain, *Politics from Inside*, pp. 291–3; Roy Jenkins, *Asquith*, p. 217. Lloyd George had given much detailed attention to the idea; see Memoranda in Lloyd George papers C/16/9/1 and 3.

[3] Roy Jenkins, *Asquith*, p. 217; Sir Austen Chamberlain, *op. cit.*, p. 213.

[4] Herbert to Elibank, 9 November 1910. Elibank papers 8,802, fol. 129–30.

TARIFF REFORM

MEANS HAPPIER DUKES.

Published by the LIBERAL PUBLICATION DEPARTMENT (in connection with the National Liberal Federation and the Liberal Central Association), 42, Parliament Street, Westminster, and Printed by Field, Dowsett, Morland & Co. Ltd., 170, Edmund Street, Birmingham.

LEAFLET No. 2262.]   Price 5/- per 1,000.

HANDS OFF!

Why do the Lords refuse to pass the Budget?

They give plenty of excuses, but everybody knows that one of the real reasons is that the Budget taxes land values.

The Tory cry is—"HANDS OFF THE LAND!"

The Liberal policy is—TAXATION OF LAND VALUES AND THE BEST USE OF THE LAND IN THE INTERESTS OF THE COMMUNITY.

Published by the LIBERAL PUBLICATION DEPARTMENT (in connection with the National Liberal Federation and the Liberal Central Association), 42, Parliament Street, Westminster, S.W., and Printed by Waterlow & Sons Limited, London Wall, London; and 49, Parliament Street, Westminster.

LEAFLET No. 2263].   1/12/09.   [Price 5s. per 1,000.

The gauntlet was down. Parliament was dissolved on 28 November, and polling took place in the following month.

The result was almost exactly the same as in January. The Liberals had 272 seats, against 275 in January; they had gained twenty-three seats from the Unionists, while losing twenty-four to the Unionists and one (West Fife) to Labour. The Unionists also had 272 seats, as against 273 in January. They made two net gains from the Liberals, three gains and four losses to Labour, and two losses to the Irish Nationalists.

It is difficult to see much pattern in the changes which occurred. The Unionists made substantially more gains than losses in Devon and in the North-West of England; the Liberals made substantially more gains than losses in South-East England. But the transfers of votes were slight. Seventeen of the twenty-three Liberal gains from the Unionists and seventeen of the twenty-four Unionist gains from the Liberals represented swings of under 500 votes. Nearly all of the remainder are explicable by obvious changes like the intervention or withdrawal of third candidates.

* * *

The possibility still remained that at some point it would be necessary to create a large number of Government peers to swamp the Unionist majority in the Lords and force through the Parliament Bill. It was well known that William IV and his ministers had contemplated that step in 1832; it was less well known that it had actually been followed in 1713 to ensure acceptance of the Treaty of Utrecht. Neither Edward VII nor his son viewed the prospect with pleasure; but George V gave a reluctant and secret undertaking shortly before the December election to create the necessary peers if the Government were returned, and requested this exercise of the Prerogative.[1] According to Lord Derby's account, the King asked Asquith what would happen if he refused – to which the reply was, 'I should immediately resign and at the next election should make the cry, "The King and the Peers against the People".'[2] Lord Crewe, who was present with Asquith at the interview, endorsed the statement, and assured the King that the whole Cabinet agreed.

[1] Harold Nicolson, *King George V*, p. 138.
[2] Memorandum by Lord Derby, 20 August 1911 (Derby papers). Quoted by Randolph Churchill, *Winston Churchill*, ii, pp. 342–3.

The King was most anxious that information about the 'contingent guarantees' should not pass beyond the Cabinet.[1] It certainly did leak to a degree,[2] but did not become extensively known.

By 20 July 1911, it seemed likely that the Unionist peers would try to amend the Bill, and Asquith made the King's undertaking officially known to the Unionist leaders, although, unofficially, they had known it at least a day earlier.[3] They were given to understand that the amendments were unacceptable to the Government. The Unionist leaders capitulated, and Lord Lansdowne, leader of the Unionist peers, advised his followers to abstain.

This led to the incredible 'Die-hard Revolt', headed by the Earl of Halsbury – already near the end of his ninth decade. The possibility that such a situation would arise appears to have been recognized by Lord Knollys before most people; as early as Christmas Day 1910 he confidentially warned Asquith that one important Conservative M.P., Lord Hugh Cecil, was prepared to resist the Bill, even if this entailed a mass-creation of peers.[4] It soon became apparent that there were more 'Die-hard' peers than Liberal peers. Some, at any rate, of the Unionists must actually vote with the Government if the House of Lords was not to be swamped. The possibility that a mass-creation might become necessary was taken sufficiently seriously for the Ministers to draw up a very substantial list of potential peers,[5] and for 'Loulou' Harcourt, First Commissioner of Works, to make plans for seating the enlarged House of Lords in Westminster Hall.[6] Inevitably, the King's name was brought into the discussions, and although he agreed to this[7] he much resented the way in which it was done.[8]

Meanwhile, Lord Crewe was in contact with Lord Cromer, one of the more moderate of the Unionist peers, and was authorized by the Cabinet to tell Cromer how many Liberal peers could be counted upon to support the Government, in order that sufficient Unionists

[1] Knollys to Nash, 11 December 1910. Asquith papers 2, fol. 83.
[2] Knollys to Asquith, 3 July 1911. Asquith papers 2, fol. 233.
[3] Knollys to Asquith, 19 July 1911. Asquith papers 2, fol. 250.
[4] Knollys to Asquith, 25 December 1910. Asquith papers 2.
[5] Elibank papers 8,802, fol. 252–65.
[6] Colin Cross, *The Liberals in power*, p. 125.
[7] Asquith papers 2, fols. 233–68, etc.
[8] Knollys to Nash, 9 August 1911. Asquith papers 2, fol. 272. The letter is interesting; Asquith's pencilled comments are even more so.

should vote in the Government lobbies to defeat the Halsburyites.[1]

In the last speech of the debate, the Earl of Selborne rose to the drama of the occasion: '. . . The question is, shall we perish in the dark by our own hand, or in the light, killed by our enemies?'

The majority of Lord Selborne's colleagues chose the less heroic course, and on 10 August 1911 the Government scraped home with a composite majority of seventeen – including several bishops, cross-benchers like Lord Rosebery, and thirty-seven Unionist peers. Not a single Liberal voted in the minority. The King expressed immeasurable relief,[2] and eight days later the Bill received Royal assent.

---

[1] Cabinet letter, 3 August 1911 (draft). Asquith papers 6, fol. 64–5.
[2] Knollys to Asquith, 11 August 1911. Asquith papers 2, fol. 280.

4

The New Radicalism

Sound a blast for freedom, boys, and spread it far and wide,
  March along to victory, for God is on our side,
While the voice of Nature thunders o'er the rising tide,
  'God gave the land to the people!'
The land! The land! 'Twas God who gave the land!
  The land! The land! The ground on which we stand!
Why should we be beggars with the ballot in our hand?
  God gave the land to the people!

The Liberal Land Song (Tune: 'Marching through Georgia')

In the three years which lay between the passage of the Parliament Act and the outbreak of the First World War, there were more signs of a truly revolutionary situation developing in Britain than at any other time in the last hundred years. The Government came under intense pressure from a wide variety of people of very disparate persuasions. Some of them were Government supporters who sought to take advantage of the constitutional changes which the Act had brought about to compel the passage of reforms which the Lords would formerly have blocked. On the other hand, the Unionist Opposition was determined to take a stand against the Government whenever this could be done without political damage to themselves; and they were prepared to carry this opposition to the very verge of civil war. Mortified by the Budget and the Parliament Act, they turned to curse the apostate peers, and to blame defeat on to the pusillanimity of their leaders. Balfour was driven from office and replaced by Bonar Law. The nominal distinction between Conservatives and Liberal Unionists was wiped out, and the two Parties were amalgamated on 9 May 1912.

Some indication of the prevailing atmosphere is provided by C. F. G. Masterman, who narrowly held the Liberal seat of SW. Bethnal Green in a by-election just before the Parliament Bill passed the Lords. He told the Press:

'I feel as if I had just emerged from a mudbath. I found pleasant-spoken women had been informing the electors in the dark that we were shooting down working men in South Wales, that my chief delight was in flogging children who subsequently died, that I had written books insulting Bethnal Green, that Mr Pickersgill, who after twenty-five years had become more an institution than a member, was bitterly opposed to my candidature. The Kensitites stated that I wished to revive the fires of Smithfield; it was explained to the Jewish voters that the Government was deliberately trying to ruin them through the Shops Bill, by shutting their shops on Sundays. . . .'[1]

A more famous example of the same attitude is provided by the 'Marconi scandal', which began to erupt in the summer of 1912. The details of this long and involved story do not concern us here. The 'scandal' turned at first on the allegation that certain Ministers stood to derive personal profit from Government transactions with the British Marconi Company over wireless installations. On this score, the Ministers were exculpated completely. At a later stage, the point at issue was whether two of these Ministers – Lloyd George and Sir Rufus Isaacs – should have disclosed to Parliament some private transactions in an American Company which also carried the name Marconi. This Company's financial relationship with the British Company was such that no profit could be made from 'inside knowledge' of the Government's dealings, and therefore they had every right to invest in those securities.

About the same time, a statement appeared in the Press to the effect that the Master of Elibank, when he was Liberal Chief Whip, had invested £9,000 of Liberal Party funds in the American Marconi Company. No transactions in Marconi shares of any kind were recorded in the Party's books, but it is possible that shares may have been purchased through Elibank's private broker. It appears that Elibank later suffered through the defalcations of this broker,

[1] Lucy Masterman, C. F. G. Masterman, pp. 198–9.

and it is possible that the Liberal Party may have suffered as well.[1]

A Select Committee was established to inquire into the Marconi proceedings, under the chairmanship of a back-bench Liberal M.P., Sir Albert Spicer.[2] Unfortunately, the conclusions reached by the Committee were not unanimous, and a rather mild motion of censure against Lloyd George and Isaacs was met by a division of the House of Commons on Party lines,[3] and was therefore defeated.

*   *   *

Before the passage of the Parliament Bill was complete, the Government inaugurated the very important National Insurance Bill of 1911, which provided two separate systems of State insurance, one against sickness and one against unemployment. The 'backstage' work, particularly in the later stages, was largely the achievement of C. F. G. Masterman, while the Parliamentary conduct of the Bill was in the hands of Lloyd George. Difficulties were encountered from a number of quite separate quarters – ranging from doctors through insurance collectors to a fatuous body known as the Servants' Tax Resisters' League, where mass-meetings of domestic servants listened with dutiful respect to the invectives of titled personalities against the iniquity of the Government requiring them to lick insurance stamps. The Unionists did not contest the principle of the Bill, but opposed a number of its provisions. After it had passed the Commons, the Lords let the Bill through without debate.

The pressure of various groups avid for a wide range of different reforms was stepped up. The suffragettes are most famous for their extra-Parliamentary deeds, but a great deal of Parliamentary activity

[1] The information about Liberal Party funds was communicated to the present author by Mr R. Humphrey Davies, who was at the operative time Secretary to the Chief Whip, and a sort of unofficial registrar of Party funds. Apparently Elibank's predecessor had dealt through a bank and not a broker.

[2] *Albert Spicer 1847–1934* by One of his Family. Simpkin Marshall Ltd, 1938, pp. 39–41.

[3] The resolution submitted by Bonar Law, which represents the most hostile view of the Ministers, was in these terms:

'That this House, having heard the statements made by the Attorney-General and the Chancellor of the Exchequer, acquits them of acting otherwise than in good faith, and reprobates the charges of corruption which have proved to be wholly false, but regrets their transactions in the shares of the Marconi Company of America and the want of frankness displayed by them in their communications to the House.'

also took place. In 1911, a Memorial was signed by ninety M.P.s, calling for full adult suffrage. The Prime Minister indicated to the deputation which presented this Memorial that a Bill would be drafted in a form which would allow the House of Commons to extend the vote to women if it wished.[1] The Government's Franchise Bill was introduced in June 1912. In its original form, it proposed universal male franchise, the abolition of plural voting, and the abolition of the University constituencies.[2] Three different amendments were proposed at the Committee Stage, each seeking to extend the vote to women. The broadest of these would have given women equal franchise; the other two sought to enfranchise more limited classes of women. The Cabinet decided that members of the Government should be free to express diverse views on the subject of these amendments.[3] Suddenly, the Speaker (who happened, by an interesting coincidence, to be a Unionist), decided to rule the women's suffrage amendments out of order. As Asquith wrote to the King, this was 'a flat contradiction of the assumptions on which all Parties in the House have hitherto treated the Bill', and, in the Prime Minister's view, 'entirely wrong and impossible to reconcile with what took place in the case of the previous Franchise Bills of 1867 and 1884'. But he dolefully concluded that 'there is practically no right of appeal against the dictum of a Speaker in such matters'.[4]

By general agreement, the Bill was then withdrawn. Time was made for a private member to introduce a Bill soon afterwards, which would have enfranchised large numbers of women, but would not have given equal franchise. In the Second Reading debate, in May 1913, the whips were not put on. Sir Edward Grey spoke in favour of the Bill, and Asquith spoke against it. When the House divided, the Bill was lost.[5] In the following year, however, the National Liberal Federation declared clearly in favour of women's suffrage, and

[1] *Liberal Magazine*, 1911, pp. 712–14.

[2] *Liberal Magazine*, 1912, pp. 360–5.

[3] Cabinet letter (draft), 22 Jan. 1913. Asquith papers 7, fol. 5.

[4] Cabinet letter (draft), 25 January 1913. Asquith papers 7, fol. 7–8.

[5] *Liberal Magazine*, 1913, pp. 301–8. For the Bill: 146 Liberals (+ 9 paired); 28 (+ 12) Unionists; 34 (+ 3) Labour; 13 Nationalists. Against the Bill: 74 (+ 5) Liberals; 140 (+ 19) Unionists; 54 Nationalists. Members of the Cabinet who voted for the Bill were: Birrell, Buxton, Grey, Isaacs, Lloyd George, Runciman, and McKinnon Wood. Members of the Cabinet who voted against were: Asquith, Churchill, Harcourt, Hobhouse, Pease, Samuel, and Seely. The only Opposition Frontbencher who supported the Bill was Stuart-Wortley.

Asquith seems to have decided that the measure should receive Government support.

Another very live issue which concerned the franchise was plural voting – that is, the right of people with property in more than one constituency to use more than one vote. A Government Bill to abolish plural voting had been introduced in 1906. It had passed the Commons, but had been rejected by the Lords. On the failure of the Franchise Bill of 1912, a private Member brought a new Bill to abolish plural voting. In the following year, a Government Bill on the subject passed all its stages in the Commons, but was rejected by the Lords, like its predecessor. It was the Government's intention eventually to give the proposal effect through the Parliament Act, but the earliest possible date was June 1915.

The advocates of the taxation of land values also began to step up their campaign. The Budget of 1909 had touched the fringe of the land question. Liberals who had been advocating the doctrines of Henry George for over twenty years were now determined to set those doctrines into effect. On 18 May 1911, three months before the Lords at last accepted the Parliament Bill, a deputation waited on Asquith and Lloyd George, and presented them with a Memorial signed by no fewer than 173 Liberal and Labour M.P.s.[1]

This Memorial was strong in its defence of Free Trade and its advocacy of land value taxation. Both Asquith and Lloyd George evinced sympathy with the aims of the memorialists.[2] But land values could not be taxed until they had been assessed. Lloyd George told the delegates that it was expected that valuation would be complete within five years of the passage of the Budget – information which can scarcely have satisfied the more eager land taxers. But they had no immediate means of exerting effective pressure.

In the middle of 1912, however, a means was found, through the Hanley by-election, which we shall have cause to consider in more

---

[1] 166 of these are listed in *Land Values*, June 1911, pp. 17–18. 121 Liberals signed without reservation, five with reservations. Thirty-eight of the Labour M.P.s signed without reservation and two (Hardie and Jowett) with reservations. The only signature missing from the Labour list is that of Ramsay MacDonald. No Unionists signed, nor did any members of either wing of the Irish Party.

[2] *Liberal Magazine*, 1911, pp. 356–8. The full text is given in *Land Values*, June 1911. For further discussion of the Liberals and the Rand question, see H. V Emy, 'The Land Campaign' (pp. 35–68 of *Lloyd George: twelve essays*, ed. A. J. P. Taylor, 1971).

detail in a later chapter. An ardent land-taxing Liberal, R. L. Outhwaite, captured a Labour seat and pushed the defender to a derisory third place.

When the Government was prodded into vigorous action, the effect was enormous. In the autumn of 1913, a land campaign was commenced in earnest. Thus wrote Lloyd George:

'Swindon was electric. I have rarely addressed such an enthusiastic audience. . . . The land caught on. Winston found the same thing at Manchester. His allusion to our programme was received with wild cheering.

'But we must not let it flag. You cannot leave it even for a season. The Tory press have evidently received instructions to talk Ulster to the exclusion of land. If they succeed we are "beat" and beat by superior generalship.'[1]

Asquith had a similar experience when he came to consider the land problem at the N.L.F. meeting in Leeds. Percy Illingworth, Chief Liberal Whip, wrote ecstatically to Lloyd George, 'The Prime Minister's speech last night was I think the best I ever heard him make. "Land" went like hot cakes at the delegates' meeting.'[2]

The old problem of the Welsh Church also came into active consideration as soon as the Lords' veto was removed. In April 1912, a Welsh Disestablishment Bill was introduced in the House of Commons. The Bill came in for some criticism from a few Liberals who sought to allow the Welsh Church to retain certain endowments, and on the other side from some Liberal and Labour M.P.s who wished to nationalize its cathedrals.[3] The Bill passed the Commons but was rejected by the Lords. In the following Session, it met the same fate. In 1914, the Bill again passed the Commons, and was actually set on the Statute Book under provision of the Parliament Act in September. But by this time war had broken out, and the operation of the Act was suspended.

Irish Home Rule was a far thornier problem than the Welsh Church. For the Unionists, it took on a new aspect. Until 1910, they

[1] Lloyd George to Percy Illingworth, 24 October 1913 (copy). Lloyd George papers C/5/4/7.
[2] Percy Illingworth to Lloyd George, 28 November 1913. Lloyd George papers C/5/4/8.
[3] Parl. Deb. (Commons), xlv, cols. 1,045; 1,551.

could always persuade themselves that Home Rule could never take effect within the lifetime of the current Parliament, for the Lords would be certain to reject it, and at least one General Election would be necessary before any Government could set it into effect. But after the Parliament Act, the Opposition was forced to recognize the real possibility that Ireland might attain Home Rule in the lifetime of the Parliament then sitting, and their persistence took on a desperate character. It was perhaps no accident that Bonar Law, whom the Unionists had chosen for their new leader, was a man with strong Ulster connections.

In 1912, the House of Commons passed the Government of Ireland Bill. This provided for the establishment of a bicameral Irish Parliament. The Irish Parliament would be subject to the overriding authority of the United Kingdom Parliament; but, within those limits, it would have power to legislate on most, but not all, purely Irish affairs. Matters specifically excluded from its control included treaties with foreign countries; war and peace; defence; and most questions of external trade. Thus, the proposed powers of the Irish Parliament were to be very similar to those which the Northern Ireland Parliament possesses today.

Irish M.P.s would continue to sit at Westminster, but their number would be reduced to forty-two. This reduction was justified on two grounds: first, that Ireland had long been over-represented at Westminster on the basis of population; and second, that many of the legislative functions would now be discharged by the Irish Parliament. The reduction would, of course, prove electorally disadvantageous to the Government; but Birrell eventually produced a scheme, which lacked nothing in craft, to ensure that this reduction did not occur before the next General Election.[1]

The issue on which the Unionists would take their main stand was by no means predetermined, but their tactics turned on exploiting to the uttermost the situation in what they were pleased to call 'loyal Ulster'. In the Protestant areas of the North, men flooded to sign the 'Ulster Covenant', and it became increasingly clear that they were ready – or many of them were ready – to defend the exclusion of the

[1] Cabinet paper, 9 August 1913. This proposed a carefully designed timetable to ensure that the Home Rule Bill would receive Royal assent in December 1914. The Plural Voting Bill would pass, despite the Lords' veto, in June 1915, and be followed by a General Election. The reduction of Irish representation would take effect in December 1915.

Protestant parts of Ulster even to the limit of civil war. Eventually, a force of 100,000 'Ulster Volunteers' was raised.

Inevitably the Bill passed the Commons, and equally inevitably it was rejected by the Lords. In the next Session of Parliament it again passed the Commons, and was again rejected by the Lords.

When the Bill was again prepared for submission to Parliament, it was evident that the provisions of the Parliament Act would enable it to become law, whatever the Lords might do, and therefore both sides realized that the struggle this time was crucial. It was no longer simply a question of how the politicians would handle a political question, for the irresistible force of Southern nationalism was set on a collision course with the immovable object of Ulster truculence.

The Government made great efforts behind the scenes to secure some kind of compromise which would satisfy the aspirations of the South without violating too flagrantly the wishes of the Protestant parts of Ulster.[1] None of these placated the Unionists, but eventually Asquith proposed an amendment to the Second Reading of the Bill, on 9 March. This would authorize the Protestant counties of Ulster to vote themselves out of Home Rule for a period of six years. Such a plan would have allowed two General Elections to occur, and would have deferred the question of the Protestant counties until people could form an assessment of how Home Rule was working. But the Unionists vigorously attacked the proposal, arguing that it represented a mere 'delay in execution'. Later in the same month, doubts were cast on the loyalty of the army units stationed in Ireland, should they be called upon to suppress violence by Ulster Unionists. A considerable number of officers stationed at the Curragh, in central Ireland, indicated that they would prefer to accept dismissal if they were ordered north. Although the Cabinet had insisted that 'an officer or soldier is forbidden in future to ask for assurances as to the orders which he may be required to obey', J. E. B. Seely, the Secretary for War, made certain unauthorized concessions to the officers. He was forced to resign, and Asquith took the War Office himself.

Still Asquith sought a settlement which would be, if not acceptable, at least tolerable, to both sides. On 9 May, he met Bonar Law and also Sir Edward Carson, the leading figure among the Irish Unionists, to discuss the possibility of placating Ulster by some

---

[1] See Cabinet letters (drafts), 26 November 1913, 23 January 1914, 4 March 1914. Asquith papers 7, fols. 77, 90–1, 101–2.

Supplemental Bill which would receive Royal assent at the same time as the Home Rule Bill. But the Unionist leaders were intransigent, and there were strong hints that they were not in complete control of their own followers. As Asquith reported to the King:[1]

> 'Carson fears that the Third Reading would otherwise be followed by demonstrations in Ulster, with inevitable collisions and bloodshed, leading to a general outburst. Bonar Law fears that his Party, who are growing averse to any kind of settlement, would kick over the traces, and that subsequent negotiations would become impossible.'

One last, desperate attempt was made to secure a peaceful solution. On Asquith's advice,[2] the King summoned a Conference at Buckingham Palace, under the Chairmanship of the Speaker, to which were invited two representatives each of the Liberals, the Conservatives, the Nationalists, and the Ulster Unionists.

Many Liberals were furious about the Conference. Charles Trevelyan, a junior Minister, wrote to Walter Runciman in great alarm of his experiences at a gathering of Liberals from his own constituency of Elland, and nearby Halifax, and Sowerby Bridge:[3]

> '. . . They were entirely faithful men. They did not use violent language.
> 'But they say that the whole of the Liberal working-class is on the point of revolt; that the prestige of the government is gone, and that the great mass of working-men think that the government is funking. They have never approved of leaving Carson alone, they were more angry about the gun-running, and the[y] are quite furious about the Conference. There is *no one at all* in favour of it. I have never seen such unanimity. . . . The Government has got to show itself top dog *now*, or the Liberal Party will disintegrate, even in the West Riding. . . .'

[1] Asquith's report of meeting with Law and Carson, sent to the King, (draft) 6 May 1914. Asquith papers 7, fol. 123-4.

[2] Cabinet letter (draft), 17 July 1914. Asquith papers 7, fol. 143-4. The King to Asquith, 18 July 1914. Asquith papers 3, fol. 237.

[3] Charles Trevelyan to Runciman, 25 July 1914. Runciman papers. The date is just after the collapse of the Conference; presumably the letter is misdated, or else the news had not yet reached Trevelyan.

But Trevelyan need not have worried on that particular score; the Conference collapsed after four days, on 24 June 1914.

The situation had more or less passed out of the hands of the politicians. Neither the Liberals, the British Unionists, the Nationalists, nor the Ulster Unionists could be certain of controlling the anger of their followers in any compromise which they might seek to make. The existence of the Ulster Volunteers had led to the establishment of a compensating body, the National Volunteers, in the South. In April, large stores of ammunition from Germany had been landed for the use of 'loyal Ulster'. On 26 July, two days after the failure of the Home Rule Settlement Conference and a week before the British declaration of war, German rifles were landed at Howth for the use of the southerners. In the ensuing affray, three members of the Dublin crowd were killed and many wounded.[1]

Thus Lloyd George had shown a remarkable understanding of the depths of the situation when he spoke in Newcastle in October 1909 of the issues which would be raised which the peers little dreamt of. Ireland was on the point of civil war. A series of alarming strikes with syndicalist overtones had occurred in Britain. The famous 'Triple Alliance' between miners, railwaymen, and transport workers had been forged. The movement for women's rights had taken a course quite different from that which occurred anywhere else in the world. The suffragettes had embarked on a policy of violence, and the measures which the Government had applied to deal with that violence had cast discredit upon it in the eyes of some of its supporters.[2]

*　　*　　*

[1] The growth of both volunteer movements had been rapid. Printed papers for the Cabinet trace the origin of the Ulster Volunteers to the manifesto of the Grand Orange Lodge of Ireland on 7 December 1910, and the simultaneous appeal for Orange Lodges 'to take active steps to resist [the] enforcement' of Home Rule if it became law. In February 1912, about 12,000 Ulstermen had been drilled; by 30 September 1913 the Ulster Volunteers totalled 56,651 and had 4,986 rifles; by 31 March 1914 there were 84,000 Volunteers. The National Volunteers started later. On 28 March 1914, there were only 10,489; by 28 April there were 19,206; on 15 June Birrell wrote that about 80,000 had been enrolled. On 5 July, the total strength of the two opposing forces was about 200,000.

[2] Thus, seven Liberals and sixteen Labour M.P.s had voted for Lord Robert Cecil's motion of censure on McKenna for his treatment of imprisoned suffragettes. Parl. Deb. (Commons) xl, 28 June 1912, 717.

There was not much indication of substantial changes in public opinion, although the by-elections were telling against the Government. By the outbreak of war, the Government had lost sixteen seats to the Unionists for one gain from them; but a considerable number of these losses could reasonably be attributed to the intervention of third candidates where there had been straight fights in 1910. There was no sign of crumbling on the Liberal front, as the Unionists had crumbled in 1903–4, or the Liberals in 1895. Perhaps the Government would have been defeated at the General Election which was due about 1915, although this was far from certain. But they would not have become a rabble.

The Liberal Party's organizers were gradually improving the operation of what Mr Humphrey Davies has called the 'engine room'. In 1908–10, the system of Area Federations was reorganized, extended to cover the whole country, and brought under the aegis of the Whips' Office.[1] For many years – apparently until the middle or late 1920s – the Area Federation Secretaries met regularly in London to pool experience, and for mutual consultation. It is evident that considerable benefits sprang from this arrangement. In the next couple of years, the same Federation system was applied to the Liberal M.P.s, and a Junior Whip was appointed to each Federation area.

Nevertheless, the system of Headquarters organization had its imperfections. In 1910, when the Chief Whip found 'the double load of work in the House of Commons and formal organization . . . too much for any man', Sir Jesse Herbert was made chief of the staff at Headquarters and Chief Organiser in the country. An evidently informed commentator writing a number of years later expressed the opinion that 'grave decadence' came from the free hand given at the time to the Chief Organiser.[2] But the abilities of the Whips were not disputed. The Unionist *Pall Mall Gazette* described Elibank (1910–12) as the 'cleverest Whip of modern times'.[3] His successor, Percy

---

[1] W. Finnemore, 'The District Federations', *Liberal Agent*, September 1930, pp. 140–2.

[2] Document in the Runciman papers headed 'Headquarters & Party Organisation' – with pencilled comment 'Uncorrected'. This was included in the same envelope with a letter from Viscount (Herbert) Gladstone to Runciman, dated 31 July 1924, and a memorandum referred to in that letter. It may be the notes of a speech by Viscount Gladstone, or, conceivably, Runciman.

[3] *Pall Mall Gazette*, 17 May 1912; A. C. Murray, *Master and Brother*, p. 34.

WILLIAM EWART GLADSTONE (1809–98), and granddaughter.

Mr Gladstone doubtless believed that on the Day of Judgement he would be called to account for every thought and action of his life, and, unlike many people who shared that belief, acted accordingly. His influence on Liberal thought and action, not only in his own lifetime but for long after his death, was probably greater than that of any other man.

(photograph by courtesy of the National Liberal Club.)

SIR HENRY CAMPBELL-BANNERMAN (1836–1908)

In the middle 1890s he was an elderly statesman of the second rank, of whom the public as a whole knew nothing. Yet in 1905–6 he drew together a party which was in danger of falling to pieces, and led one of the most talented administrations of modern times to an overwhelming victory.

(photograph by courtesy of the National Liberal Club.)

HERBERT HENRY ASQUITH (1852–1928)

Asquith 'outstripped all others and dominated the scene' in a succession of Cabinets which included such men as Lloyd George, Churchill and Balfour.

(*photograph by courtesy of the Radio Times Hulton Picture Library.*)

'SAMS AND SIMS' Viscount (Sir Herbert) Samuel (1870–1963) and Viscount (Sir John) Simon (1873–1954) were both among the brilliant younger men who served in Asquith's Government, and who were defeated along with their leader in 1918. In the early 1930s, they headed the two main groups of the Liberal Party – Samuel insisting on the duty of Liberals to stand by their Free Trade principles, and Simon leading the group which eventually disappeared without trace among the Conservatives.

(photograph by courtesy of the Liberal Party Organization.)

Viscount (Sir Herbert) Samuel

Viscount (Sir John) Simon

(photograph by courtesy of the Popperfoto Library.)

Illingworth (1912–15), was apparently an even greater Chief Whip. When he stood as Liberal candidate in the hitherto Unionist seat of Shipley in 1906, the seat was not defended, and he registered a gain for his Party without a contest. When, tragically soon, his obituary came to be written, Sir Robert Hudson spoke of his 'simple honesty of purpose, coupled with plain, straightforward speaking', justly describing him as 'the friend of everyone on both sides of the House'.[1]

These organizers were upholding a most remarkable Government, which Asquith guided in such a manner that the tremendous and often disparate personalities employed their skills with constructive effect. Mrs Masterman, widow of C. F. G. Masterman, who served in that Cabinet, writes thus:[2]

> 'There has been a tendency lately among historians to try to "write off" Asquith, not, I think, endorsed by anyone who served with him. My husband always said that no one knew Asquith's stature who had not served in Cabinet with him, when he clearly outstripped all others and dominated the scene.'

Inevitably, there were some clashes of personality among the Ministers.[3] The really remarkable thing is that they were kept so effectively within bounds, and did not disrupt the business of government. Few men have towered so completely over opponents and friends alike as did Asquith at the outbreak of the First World War.

[1] 'Percy Illingworth: an appreciation', *Liberal Agent*, January 1915.
[2] Lucy Masterman, 'Recollections of David Lloyd George – 1', *History Today*, March 1959, p. 163.
[3] For examples, see Barry McGill, 'Asquith's predicament 1914–1918', *J. Mod. History* xxxix, No. 3 (September 1967), pp. 283–303.

5

Lib-Lab Politics

I have never advocated or asked for special rights or special sympathy for working men. What I stand for is equal rights for all men.

HENRY GEORGE, shortly before his death in 1897

ὅταν δὲ δαίμων ἀνδρὶ πορσύνῃ κακά
τον νοῦν ἔβλαψε πρῶτον.

Whenever a divinity brings evil on a man, he first makes him mad.

EURIPIDES, Fragments

We have seen abundant evidence of public preoccupation with political questions at the turn of the nineteenth and twentieth centuries, and of the deep and general conviction that politics really mattered, and had real bearing on people's lives. In this context, it is not surprising that working men who felt aggrieved at their condition in life should look to Parliamentary activity as a means of remedying their grievances.

It did not follow that working men were bound to seek independent Parliamentary representation. Other goups, who sought reforms on matters such as temperance, or ecclesiastical reform, or reform of the House of Lords, were content to exert their political influence mainly through established political parties, although they naturally formed *ad hoc* bodies to deal with matters of especial complaint. Furthermore, both Liberal and Conservative or Unionist Governments had secured the enactment of important measures which eased the lot of the workers.

There was no necessary conflict of interests between the Liberal Party as a whole and those whose primary concern lay in removing the many just grounds of grievance which troubled the working classes. Many Liberal Associations in the latter part of the nineteenth century must have consisted in the main of working men. In many – probably in most – Liberal constituencies, working men formed the preponderant section of the electorate.

It was natural enough that working men should wish to see some of their own number elected as Members of Parliament, because such men could speak with especial authority on matters which aggrieved their class. The Liberal Party was glad enough to accommodate and encourage them. In 1874, two mining Trade Union officials, Thomas Burt and Alexander Macdonald, were elected to Parliament as Liberals. Macdonald died a few years later, but Burt continued to sit in Parliament as a Liberal until his retirement in 1918. Henry Broadhurst, a former stonemason, was a Minister in Gladstone's short-lived Government of 1886. By the early 1890s, there was a small, but very influential, group of 'Liberal-Labour', or Lib-Lab, M.P.s who accepted the Liberal whip, but laid especial emphasis on matters which concerned the workers. At the Newcastle conference of the N.L.F. in 1891, Gladstone eulogized the Lib-Labs, expressing his wish to see more of them; and the Marquis of Ripon made a powerful plea for the downtrodden farm labourers.

Nor may this be interpreted as a mere 'playing to the gallery' for the votes of working men. The L.C.A., as we have already noted, was a body whose high subscription made it necessarily a preserve of the wealthier classes; but the minutes of its annual meeting[1] on 4 June 1891 record, with evident pleasure, that all current 'Labour' – that is, Lib-Lab – members would be offering themselves for re-election, and notes the adoption of seven other Trade Unionists as candidates – adding that 'several other arrangements are in progress which it is believed will give satisfaction to the advocates of Labour representation, and tend to promote the union of the Liberal Party'. A few years later, although the Liberal Party was torn by the Imperialist schism, the two wings of the Party were united in their enthusiasm for 'Labour' representation. There seems to be no evidence that any substantial section of the Liberal Party was in any way opposed to the idea, and most of the leading figures expressed themselves at some time or other in strong sympathy.

[1] The author is grateful to Mr R. Humphrey Davies for this information.

Yet in most of the constituencies where working-class voters formed the preponderant part of the electorate, the Liberal candidates were not 'working men'. The main consideration which limited the number of working-class M.P.s was money. No working man could hope to fight an election campaign out of his own resources. Still less could he hope to maintain himself financially if he were elected, at a time when M.P.s were unpaid. While a body with access to Trade Union funds might be persuaded to finance a working-class M.P., most working men seem to have been quite happy that a man of more comfortable circumstances should defray the necessary expenses from his own resources, or from those of his friends.

The idea that working men should sit in Parliament in complete independence from both of the older Parties took a long time to develop. There were a few 'independent Labour' candidatures, mostly with discouraging results, in the 1880s. The first victory of an 'independent Labour' candidate was recorded by Keir Hardie, who won West Ham South from the Unionists in a straight fight in the General Election of 1892.[1]

In the following year, the Independent Labour Party (I.L.P.) was established, and Hardie adhered from the start. But in its early days the I.L.P. seems to have been far from clear whether its object was to secure the election of working men (whether they were socialists or not), or the election of socialists (whether they were working men or not) – or whether it insisted on both requirements.

The Liberal reactions to the new movement were predictable, and many Radical working men no doubt endorsed the views of Lord Rosebery:[2] 'An independent Labour organization will not catch a single Tory vote. Such votes as it does carry away will be Liberal votes, and in that way in some districts . . . it may hamstring and even cut the throat of the Liberal Party in those localities.'

In 1899, the T.U.C. decided, by a rather small majority, to instruct its Parliamentary Committee to convene a 'special congress . . . to devise ways and means for securing the return of an increased number of Labour members to the next parliament'. This, of course, was in no sense a call for an independent political party – but in any

---

[1] Some books suggest that John Burns and Havelock Wilson, both first elected in 1892, were also at first independent. But see William Kent, *John Burns, Labour's Lost Leader* (London 1950), p. 55; and on the offer of financial help from the Liberals, p. 50. On Havelock Wilson, see D.N.B., 1922–30, p. 917.

[2] Speech at Manchester, 2 May 1894. *Liberal Magazine*, ii (1894), p. 186.

case the co-operative societies, most of the miners, and many other unions, declined to co-operate.[1]

In Scotland, where traditions of industrial militancy were stronger than in England, a body known as the Scottish Workers' Parliamentary Elections Committee (S.W.P.E.C.) was established in January 1900, with much wider working-class support; this body was later renamed the Scottish Workers' Representation Committee (S.W.R.C.). The conference promoted by the English T.U.C. was held in the following month, and established a body known as the Labour Representation Committee (L.R.C.). But while the Scottish body strongly affirmed its independence of the old Parties, the L.R.C. left this point, for the time being, unsettled. For some purposes (but not for Parliamentary elections) the L.R.C. described itself as the Labour Party. The use of this term, however, did not necessarily imply independence, for the Welsh Liberal M.P.s often called themselves the Welsh Party, while accepting the Liberal whip.[2] The L.R.C. chose as its Secretary J. Ramsay MacDonald, former secretary to a Liberal M.P.

In the 1900 General Election, the L.R.C. fielded fifteen candidates, and secured the election of two – both in highly exceptional conditions.

In Merthyr Tydfil, two Liberals were defending their seats in a two-member constituency. The mineowner D. A. Thomas (the future Viscount Rhondda) belonged to the pacifist wing of the Party, while W. Pritchard Morgan was an Imperialist. The Unionists had been so soundly trounced in the past that they did not fight at all. Keir Hardie, unlike some of his L.R.C. associates, was opposed to the Boer War, and Thomas implied to his supporters that they should give their second vote to Hardie and not Morgan. Thomas comfortably headed the poll, Hardie was elected with him, and Morgan was unseated.

The other successful candidate was Richard Bell, who ran in close co-operation with a Liberal against two Unionists in the two-mem-

---

[1] For general accounts of events up to 1906, see P. Poirier, *The advent of the Labour Party* (London 1958), and F. Bealey and H. Pelling, *Labour and Politics, 1900–1906* (London 1958). See also F. Bealey, 'Negotiations between the Liberal Party and the L.R.C. before the General Election of 1906', *Bull. Inst. Research 29* (1956), 261–74; F. Bealey, 'The electoral arrangements between the L.R.C. and the Liberal Party', *J. Mod. Hist. 28* (1956), 353–73.

[2] See *North Wales Observer*, 26 May 1899.

ber constituency of Derby. There was little or nothing to distinguish
Bell from a typical Lib-Lab. Indeed, he had wished to stand as a
Liberal; but he had been compelled by the headquarters of his
Union to stand in the L.R.C. interest.

In addition to these actual gains, the L.R.C. probably affected the
result in a few other constituencies, where enough votes were taken
from the Liberals to give the Unionists the seat. But the seven L.R.C.
candidates who had to face both Liberal and Unionist opposition
finished, without exception, bottom of the poll.

It would be wrong, however, to imagine that the finances of the
L.R.C. all came from working-class sources. One of its constituent
bodies, the I.L.P., certainly received a contribution of £500 from
George Cadbury, a well-known Liberal manufacturer. It is probable
that Cadbury played a very important part behind the scenes in the
relations between the Liberals and the L.R.C. in the years which
followed. He was also paying £300 a year towards the salary of Jesse
Herbert, political secretary to Herbert Gladstone, the Liberal Chief
Whip.[1] More important still, he had become proprietor of the *Daily
News* after the strange machinations at the beginning of 1901, and
from then onwards this paper became the advocate of a Liberal–
L.R.C. alliance.

*   *   *

When the L.R.C. was formed in 1900, the Liberal prospects looked
grim, and within a year they looked worse. The Liberal Party was
split from top to bottom on questions both of policies and personalities. At a time of bitter antagonisms between the leading personalities of the Party, both Campbell-Bannerman and his Chief Whip
Herbert Gladstone seem to have regarded the Liberal Imperialist
organizations and the L.R.C. as essentially similar bodies – with the
difference that they were a good deal more anxious to accommodate
the L.R.C. Towards the Liberal League, Herbert Gladstone took (at
least in theory) the very reasonable attitude that a Liberal might
hold the League's views, but should be discouraged from joining a
divisive organization; but towards the L.R.C. no such qualifications
were made. Right down to 1914, and even afterwards, the Party

---

[1] 'Cadbury . . . himself brought out J. H. & *pays half his salary.*' Herbert Gladstone to Campbell-Bannerman, 19 November 1899. Campbell-Bannerman
papers 61,215, fol. 144–50.

Whips fought off those people who contended that the existence of a separate Labour organization would at best split radical votes, and at worst threaten the existence of the Liberal Party. The genius of William Ewart Gladstone provided the main force of cohesion in the Liberal Party, while the misjudgement of his high-principled, but politically accident-prone,[1] son Herbert was to prove of crucial importance in bringing about its ruin, and indirectly doing great harm to the interests of the workers themselves.

The history of the early relations between the Liberals and the L.R.C. must be studied largely through the various by-elections of the period. Much of this story would have seemed unimportant to contemporaries, and it is only in the light of what happened later that its significance may be appreciated.

In the North-East Lanarkshire by-election of September 1901, a Liberal seat was being defended. The local Liberal Association put forward Cecil Harmsworth, a candidate of the Imperialist wing. The Liberal whips gave public support to the S.W.P.E.C. nominee, Robert Smillie.[2] A constituency which was usually Liberal in straight fights was captured by the Unionists. The S.W.P.E.C. vote was unimpressive, but it was enough to unseat the Liberal.

Then the Liberal seat of Dewsbury fell vacant. The L.R.C. did not fight, but the Social Democratic Federation (S.D.F.), an avowedly socialist organization, nominated Harry Quelch. The local Liberals were encouraged by headquarters to withdraw their candidate, Walter Runciman, whom Campbell-Bannerman obviously disliked.[3] The Dewsbury Liberals refused to accept this advice, and Runciman was victorious, with Quelch a poor third.

The next important by-election arose in Clitheroe, Lancashire, a Liberal constituency in a part of the country which was largely Unionist. The L.R.C. announced that their candidate would be David Shackleton, a Trade Union official with strong Liberal sympathies. The local Liberals were apparently willing to support him if he stood as a Lib-Lab, but the L.R.C. would not agree.

---

[1] The author is grateful to his colleague Dr Michael Burstall for this felicitous expression.

[2] The *Daily Chronicle*, 28 August 1906, inconveniently reminded the Master of Elibank, the future Liberal Chief Whip, that he had written to Smillie at the time, cordially wishing him success.

[3] Campbell-Bannerman to Herbert Gladstone, 30 October 1901. Viscount Gladstone papers 45,987, fol. 199–200.

On 10 July 1902, two leading Clitheroe Liberals, Alderman Catlow and a Mr Reed, met Herbert Gladstone and Campbell-Bannerman in London.[1] The national officials urged the local Liberals to unite on Shackleton. Catlow inclined to agree and Reed to disagree; but Herbert Gladstone himself recorded in his note of the interview that, 'both resent[ed] the way they had been treated'.

On 21 July, a large and representative body, the Clitheroe Liberal Council – known locally as the 'Six Hundred' – met, and was confronted by a recommendation from the local Executive, under strong pressure from London, that Shackleton should not be opposed. The Council overwhelmingly defeated its own Executive's proposal, and invited Catlow himself to be the candidate. He promised an answer within thirty-six hours; but it proved the inevitable negative.

Apparently with the intention of forestalling any further action by the local Liberals, one of the junior Liberal Whips moved the Clitheroe writ on 25 July. The Unionists, who evidently perceived their own chances to be hopeless, did not advance a candidate. When nomination day arrived, on 1 August, Shackleton was unopposed.

The aftermath of Clitheroe was predictable. Within a week of Shackleton's return, Herbert Gladstone was hearing about local Liberal 'heartburnings'. The Liberal Association was utterly dispirited. In the local elections of 1903, the L.R.C. made great advances in the constituency. By October 1903, we find Catlow telling the Liberal clubs of Lancashire that Labour – presumably meaning the L.R.C. – regarded what had happened as a sign of Liberal weakness.

During 1902, there was some argument for the view that support of the L.R.C. did not imply repudiation of the Liberals. But this ambiguity was soon removed. In February 1903, the L.R.C. held a most important conference at Newcastle. At this conference, L.R.C. candidates and M.P.s were required 'to abstain strictly from identifying themselves with or promoting the interests of any section of the Liberal or Conservative Parties'. The L.R.C. M.P.s were instructed to constitute themselves a separate group in the House of Commons, and an amendment to invite the 'Lib-Labs' to join was defeated.[2] Affiliated Trade Unions were required to contribute substantially to a Parliamentary fund, out of which the L.R.C. M.P.s were paid an annual salary of £200. Inevitably, this last decision was of immense

[1] Viscount Gladstone papers 46,484.
[2] G. D. H. Cole, *British Working Class Politics 1832–1914*, p. 171.

importance in persuading working-class candidates who were not supported by wealthy Trade Unions to stand under the auspices of the L.R.C. rather than the Liberal Party.

While the L.R.C. was engaged in its Newcastle conference, a by-election was being fought in the London suburb of Woolwich, whose main industry was the famous arsenal. It was a Unionist seat which the Liberals had not fought in 1900, and where the Liberal organization was more or less defunct. The L.R.C. put forward as candidate Will Crooks, a popular Trade Unionist. Like Shackleton, he would have excited no comment if he had called himself a Liberal – indeed, he had the active support of two London Liberal newspapers, and even received a telegram of support from the N.L.F. On 11 March 1903, he secured a sensational victory.

Soon, another Liberal seat fell vacant – Barnard Castle, in County Durham. It was a largely mining constituency with a long Liberal tradition. The late M.P. was Sir Joseph Pease, and his agent, for the past seven years, had been Arthur Henderson. This fact did not prevent Henderson from securing nomination as an L.R.C. candidate, but no particular constituency had been allocated to him. No one seems to have explained how the various individuals and organizations involved reacted to the dual loyalty thus involved. However, in February 1903, Pease indicated his intention not to fight the seat again because of his age. In the same month, the L.R.C. conference decided in favour of total independence, and therefore Henderson could not stand as a Liberal. A prospective Liberal candidate, Hubert Beaumont, was adopted. In June 1903, Sir Joseph Pease died. Henderson went forward as the L.R.C. candidate for the constituency. Attempts were made to secure Beaumont's withdrawal, but they failed.

There were cross-currents in the election. There was some rather unconvincing evidence that Beaumont was not a sound Free Trader, and it may well be that some Liberals decided that Henderson was for that reason the better Liberal of the two, whatever their labels.[1]

---

[1] William Emerson, Chairman of Beaumont's election committees, described him as a 'thorough Liberal' (letter to *Daily News*, 6 July 1903). Another letter appeared in the *Daily News* on the same day from Samuel Storey, in which he claimed that his own support for Beaumont was endorsed by all the Northern Counties Liberal Presidents. Although Storey himself eventually abandoned Free Trade, it is difficult to believe that his statement could be true if Beaumont's attitude on so fundamental a matter was in doubt.

The Liberal press was split, the *Daily News* and the locally influential *Northern Echo* supporting Henderson. Nearby Liberal M.P.s and candidates gave Beaumont little support – perhaps fearing L.R.C. intervention in their own constituencies if they did. On 24 July, the constituency polled. Henderson scraped home with the desperately narrow majority of forty-seven over the Conservative, with Beaumont third. For the first time ever,[1] a 'Labour' candidate standing outside the two main political parties had secured a majority in a three-cornered contest. What is even more important, the L.R.C. had gained the full and undivided services of a man who would serve them with high devotion for the rest of his life, and was destined to be the first member of the Labour Party to become a Cabinet Minister.

*   *   *

The Barnard Castle by-election began to cause real alarm among Liberals. By then, it was evident that the L.R.C. was not a body of working-class Liberals, but, in the words of a contemporary Liberal,[2] 'an outside body composed of Liberals, Tories and Socialists'.

Four of the L.R.C. M.P.s, it is true, held views indistinguishable from those of many Liberals, and the opinions even of the fifth would not have been impossible to match among Liberal M.P.s. Nevertheless, even Jesse Herbert – whose activities we shall shortly need to consider – perceived that it was 'a separate group unpledged to support of the Liberal Party, a group which will harass every Government, and whose representatives in Parliament will probably decline the Liberal whip'.[3]

Not for the first time, and certainly not for the last, the Liberal workers in the constituencies recognized dangers far more acutely than the leadership, for the very good reason that they were in much closer contact with the ordinary voters.

Samuel Storey, Chairman of the Northern Liberal Federation and

---

[1] When Havelock Wilson was elected for Middlesbrough in 1892, he had both Liberal and Conservative opponents, but in those days it was not unusual for two candidates supporting the same Party to oppose each other at elections – and, as we have seen, Wilson took the Liberal whip.

[2] Samuel Storey, *Daily News*, 6 July 1903.

[3] Memorandum to Herbert Gladstone, probably 6 March 1903. Viscount Gladstone papers 46,025, fol. 132.

one of Beaumont's staunchest partisans, wrote to the *Daily News* in the course of the Barnard Castle campaign. He noted the tendency of the L.R.C. to put forward candidates in Liberal constituencies in his area, and the situation created by the L.R.C. conference decisions which forbade Henderson not merely to support ordinary Liberals, but even to support 'Lib-Labs'. He concluded with a most disturbing prophecy:

'. . . And I venture to warn you and the Party Whips and those M.P.s who would apparently cheerfully cast Barnard Castle to the wolves in the hope, perhaps, of keeping them from their own doors, that the effect of surrendering to this new policy will be the destruction of organized Liberalism here in the North. Consider the present state of the Liberal organization in Clitheroe, and pray beware! . . . Depend upon it, there are thousands of middle-class Liberals, thousands of Radical workmen, who, if they are not encouraged to fight for their own (and Barnard Castle always has been their own), will perforce return to their tents and watch with dismay the process by which some of the Liberal leaders and Whips are nursing into life a serpent which will sting their Party to death.'[1]

The salient facts of Clitheroe, Woolwich, and Barnard Castle were for the most part known to the public, and the disquiet which many Liberals were feeling was all too evident. But before Barnard Castle or even Woolwich had polled, some vital decisions of an even more far-reaching nature had been taken.

Undeterred by the recent conference of the L.R.C., Jesse Herbert met Ramsay MacDonald, Secretary of the L.R.C., on 25 February 1903, and in a memorandum to his chief[2] noted, with apparent sympathy, that the L.R.C. was seeking 'no alliance, no treaty, but a free hand in certain constituencies in return for which friendliness they will demonstrate friendliness in every constituency where they have influence'. He argued that:

[1] *Daily News*, 6 July 1903. It is extraordinary that this apparently devoted Liberal and former Liberal M.P. was later to be elected to Parliament again (January 1910) – but as an 'Independent Tariff Reformer'.

[2] Jesse Herbert to Herbert Gladstone, 6 March 1903. Viscount Gladstone papers 46,025, fol. 126–36.

'... The L.R.C. can directly influence the votes of nearly a million men. They will have a fighting fund of £100,000. . . . Their members are mainly men who have hitherto voted with the Liberal Party. Should they be advised to vote against Liberal candidates and (as they probably would) should they act as advised, the Liberal Party would suffer defeat not only in those constituencies where L.R.C. candidates fought, but also in almost every borough, and in many of the Divisions of Lancashire and Yorkshire. This would be the inevitable result of unfriendly action towards the L.R.C. candidates. *They* would be defeated, but so also should we be defeated.

'If there be good-fellowship between us and the L.R.C. the aspect of the future for both will be very bright and encouraging. They will probably fight 35 constituencies, which should save the Liberal Party funds to the extent of £15,000 and win 10 seats from the Government. They will bring a not inconsiderable addition to the strength of the Liberal vote in many constituencies where that addition will mean the success of the Liberal candidate.'

Herbert Gladstone evidently approved of his political secretary's proposals. On 13 March 1903, a week after Jesse Herbert's memorandum, the Chief Whip sent to Campbell-Bannerman a schedule, not of thirty-five, but of fifty-five, seats where the L.R.C. might possibly be given a free run by the Liberals.[1] A revised list was drawn up on 7 August. There was no reciprocal obligation on the part of the L.R.C. to abstain from intervening in places where such intervention would be likely to damage Liberal M.P.s. Local L.R.C. enthusiasts were only with difficulty dissuaded from putting up a candidate in Herbert Gladstone's own constituency of West Leeds.

But the whole situation was suddenly and dramatically transformed by the inauguration of Chamberlain's Tariff Reform campaign. A great new enthusiasm swept the Liberal Party, as it rallied in defence of the Free Trade cause. Money began to flood in. It was

---

[1] The list, and the full text of Jesse Herbert's memorandum, are published in F. Bealey's paper in the *Bull. Inst. Hist. Res. 29* (1956). See also Herbert Gladstone to Campbell-Bannerman, 7 August 1903. Campbell-Bannerman papers 41,217, fol. 1–2.

no longer possible to hold back Liberal Associations from the attack – much less from the defence when their own constituencies fell vacant.

At Norwich, in January 1904, a Unionist seat was at stake. An I.L.P. member stood in the interest of the L.R.C. In spite of the effect of this candidate in splitting the anti-Government vote, the Liberal was comfortably victorious. This time, it was the L.R.C. men who were coy about supporting their own nominee. Bell went even further, and sent a telegram of congratulations to the victorious Liberal. As a result, he was removed from the L.R.C. lists, and contested the next election – successfully – as a 'Lib-Lab'.

From the beginning of 1904 until the General Election, the Liberals did extremely well in the by-elections. Whatever the L.R.C. Conference had said, it was impossible to discipline not merely Bell but also Shackleton, Crooks, and Henderson, all of whom were active in support of individual Liberal candidates. Perhaps some Liberals still looked over their shoulders in fear of L.R.C. opposition; but the L.R.C. must have known that they were doomed almost to a man should the pact break down, while they had the lively hope of substantial Parliamentary representation if it could hold until the General Election. Few people outside the central councils of the two organizations seemed to have any glimmering of the opportunities which the pact was to open for the L.R.C.

* * *

In the 1906 General Election, the L.R.C. fielded fifty candidates. Thirty-one of them stood without Liberal opposition.[1] Twenty-four of these thirty-one were elected, while only five L.R.C. candidates were victorious in the face of Liberal opposition. Only one Liberal seat (in Dundee) was lost to the L.R.C. The new M.P.s included two future senior Ministers of the Crown, Ramsay MacDonald and Philip Snowden, both of whom ran in double harness with Liberals in two-member constituencies.

The concordat between the Liberals and the L.R.C. did not extend to Scotland. Every one of the four Scottish L.R.C. candidates had to face both Liberal and Unionist opposition, and two of them were victorious. The S.W.R.C. contested five Scottish constituencies.

[1] Twenty-one had straight fights against Unionists in single-member constituencies; ten ran in double harness with Liberals in two-member constituencies.

All faced three-cornered fights, all secured a 'respectable' vote, but all ran third.

It is not entirely clear how many M.P.s should be designated Lib-Lab, but the highest estimate seems to be twenty-five. There were some very marked differences between the L.R.C. and the Lib-Labs. The great majority of the L.R.C. members had unseated Unionists, while most of the Lib-Labs represented traditionally Liberal areas, like the mining constituencies. The L.R.C. was strongest in Lancashire and Cheshire, where there were no fewer than thirteen L.R.C. seats, but not one Lib-Lab.[1] Superficially, the new body seemed to provide a much stronger threat to the working-class Unionist vote than to the Liberals.

It is rather difficult to analyse the effect of the Gladstone–MacDonald pact on the voting behaviour of the electors who were affected by it. Above all, we cannot test the accuracy of Jesse Herbert's view that it would direct working-class votes to the Liberals in constituencies where the L.R.C. did not stand. The impression which is left from a comparison of voting figures in various constituencies suggests that the L.R.C. alliance benefited the Liberals in the North-West, but that elsewhere it did little good, and possibly some immediate harm, to the Liberals.

But the officials of the Liberal Party were obviously delighted with the result of their negotiations with the L.R.C. After reviewing the results, Jesse Herbert commented thus to Herbert Gladstone:[2]

'. . . No avowed socialist won.[3] The sum of the matter is that in England and Wales Liberals and Labour-men hold 367 seats out of 495, i.e., a majority of 239, and there are only two cases in which we have any just ground for complaint against the Labour people and one case in which they have just ground of complaint against us.

'Was there ever such a justification of a policy by results?

'In Scotland Labour had in no case a free run. There were ten three-cornered fights. . . . We lost six seats thereby, and of these

[1] Unless we so classify W. P. Byles of Salford North.

[2] Jesse Herbert to Herbert Gladstone, 16 February 1906. Viscount Gladstone papers 46,026, fol. 190–1.

[3] Whether Keir Hardie was in truth a 'socialist' is open to doubt. But Herbert can hardly have failed to notice that he avowed himself a socialist.

Labour won two. That was their result in seventy-two seats, whilst our result was in 495 seats.

'Moreover the attitude of the Labour M.P.s has been greatly influenced by our past relations. They are strongly favourable to the Government. There are not more than seven irreconcilable. Even they are very friendly with me. There is no reason to anticipate any change in their attitude if the same policy be continued. But will it be?'

In Scotland, as Jesse Herbert had indicated, the situation was completely different from that in England and Wales. This difference seems attributable to the different attitude of the Scottish 'Labour' organizations, and not to any difference of approach by the Scottish Liberals. A Memorandum prepared for Campbell-Bannerman by the chief professional workers of the Scottish Liberal Federation a couple of years later outlines the difference.[1] It is noticeable that no distinction is made between the S.W.R.C., the L.R.C., and the other 'Labour' candidates.

'At the General Election of 1906 practically all the Labour candidates were Socialists . . . eleven Labour candidates went to the poll, nine might be described as Socialists, one with Socialist leanings, and one Independent Radical. None of these contests took place in the West of Scotland, and in every instance where a Labour candidate was in the field before a Liberal candidate was selected, negotiations were opened with the view of arriving at some arrangement, but in all cases the supporters of the Labour candidates refused to come to any understanding whatever, and the Liberals therefore decided to run their own candidates. In the other cases where Liberal candidates were on the field before the Labour candidates, no negotiations were carried on, so that in the eleven instances in Scotland where Labour candidates stood the Liberals also fought the seats. Only two Labour candidates succeeded in being elected, one capturing a seat from the Tories, and one from the Liberals, although in other instances two seats were

---

[1] Memorandum on the Socialist and Labour movements in Scotland, prepared by Mr A. D. Wood and Mr Wm Webster, Joint Secretaries of the Scottish Liberal Association, and Mr E. Wilson, Special Organiser (carbon copy) – with ms. inscription – 'Prepared by my instructions for the Prime Minister. A.O.M. Feb. 1908'. S.L.A. Memorandum Elibank papers 8,801, fol. 145–50.

lost to the Liberal Party which were previously held by them, and other seats that might have been won were retained by the Tory Party, representing a minority of the electors who voted.'

The compilers of the document contended that Labour drew a considerable number of Unionist votes as well as Liberal votes, and that in some areas they captured the entire Irish vote.

* * *

On 12 February 1906, a few days after Jesse Herbert's complacent letter to Herbert Gladstone, the twenty-nine L.R.C. M.P.s and one Lib-Lab (J. W. Taylor of Chester-le-Street) decided to constitute themselves the Labour Party, with its own organization and whips, and to sit on the Opposition side of the House. This latter decision was probably inevitable because the Government side was over-crowded, while there was plenty of room on the other. The Lib-Labs resented the choice of name, considering that it was they alone who were entitled to such a designation. They accordingly constituted themselves the 'Trade Union Labour Group' within the Liberal Party.

The separation of the Labour Party was not, at first, total. J. W. Taylor had not merely adhered to the Labour Party, but had also defeated an official Liberal candidate; yet he continued, for a time at least, to take the Liberal whip as well as the Labour whip.[1]

The Labour Party at this stage was a very loose body indeed. The M.P.s acted together in the House of Commons – but that was about all. One of these early Labour M.P.s, John Jenkins, stated the position baldly when he defined his own relationship to Keir Hardie: 'I am not a member of the Independent Labour Party. Mr Keir Hardie is not my leader; he is my chairman. . . . What he says on the public platform we, as members of the Labour Representation Group, have nothing to do with.'[2]

Outside Parliament, the Labour Party was no more cohesive. A

---

[1] Through the kindness of Mr R. Humphrey Davies, the present author has inspected a document, evidently a carbon copy of one prepared for the Chief Whip, and bearing the date '1906'. This lists the L.R.C. men and adds, 'The above 30 Members have accepted the Labour Whip, and, with the exception of Mr Taylor, do not receive the Government Whip. At present, Mr Taylor receives both.'

[2] *Liberal Magazine*, 1906, p. 620.

member of one of the affiliated Trade Unions, or of the I.L.P., or of the Fabian Society, was *ex officio* a member of the Labour Party,[1] whatever his political sympathies might be. Right down to the closing stages of the First World War, there were very few constituencies in which it was possible for a sympathizer to join the Labour Party directly. Elsewhere, he could only join *via* one of the affiliated bodies; and it was these bodies, at the local level, which decided on Parliamentary candidates. As we shall later see, these affiliated bodies sometimes contained a large number of members who had grave doubts about the utility of the Labour Party itself; and from these doubts some rather startling situations occasionally arose.

*   *   *

In the first year of the new Liberal Government, co-operation between the Liberal and Labour Parties was generally close, and the first fruit of that co-operation was to be seen in the Trade Disputes Act of 1906.

The trade recession of 1907–9 redounded to the benefit of both the Unionists and the Labour Party at the expense of the Liberals. The Unionist successes have already been considered in an earlier chapter; but this rather dismal period was also signalled by two by-election victories of the official Labour Party, and one of an independent Socialist.

The first of these by-elections was Jarrow. The octogenarian Liberal M.P., Sir Charles Palmer, was a very popular local employer, who had reluctantly forgone retirement at the General Election in order to retain for the Liberals a constituency whose allegiance was otherwise much in doubt. In the spring of 1907 he died, and there was a four-cornered contest for the vacancy – the fourth candidate being an Irish Nationalist. All four candidates secured a substantial vote, but the seat was won by Peter Curran for the Labour Party, and the Liberal came third. Labour was beginning to establish itself in the hitherto Liberal North-East. William Allard, Secretary of the Liberal League, took a jaundiced view of the contest, telling Lord Rosebery that, 'the three Democratic candidates . . . may be regarded as Socialists. Perhaps the most dangerous of the three is the official Liberal candidate, S. L. Hughes.'[2]

---

[1] See G. D. H. Cole, *History of the Labour Party since 1914*, p. 5.
[2] Allard to Rosebery, 11 June 1907. Rosebery papers 107.

A fortnight later, the result in Colne Valley was no less impressive. A Socialist, without the official backing of the Labour Party, won a Liberal seat in a very closely-run three-cornered contest; less than five hundred votes separated the three candidates. The new M.P., Victor Grayson, nevertheless accepted the Labour whip.

Nearly two years later, in May 1909, the official Labour Party recorded another gain from the Liberals, in the Attercliffe Division of Sheffield. As in Jarrow, there was a four-cornered contest – the fourth candidate this time being an independent Unionist. As in Colne Valley, the result was extremely close, for the four candidates were less than eight hundred votes apart.

These Labour victories were indicative of a strong general movement towards the Labour Party. In Scotland, for example, meetings were held and branches inaugurated on a very large scale throughout the country, and the Labour Party was very anxious to emphasize its distinctiveness from both of the older Parties.[1] But the most important development about this time concerned the English and Welsh miners.

In 1906, the Miners' Federation had conducted a ballot on the proposal that it should affiliate to the Labour Party. This was narrowly defeated; but a second ballot two years later gave a clear, though by no means overwhelming, majority in favour of affiliation.[2] There were enormous regional variations in the miners' views. At one extreme, Lancashire – traditionally Unionist – voted in favour of affiliation by a majority of more than two to one; while at the other extreme the Derbyshire and Leicestershire miners gave something like three-to-one majorities against. Not surprisingly, the miners in those areas gave a great deal of trouble to the Labour Party.

The decision to implement the majority opinion and apply for affiliation to the Labour Party was made '. . . on the understanding that the present members now representing the Federation in Parliament be not called upon to sign the Labour Party constitution, except in the case of a by-election or at the next General Election'.

The Labour Party set up a sub-committee to consult with the Miners' Executive, and a meeting was held on 11 December. On 2

---

[1] 'S.L.A. Memorandum'. Elibank papers 8,801, fol. 145–50.
[2] 213,137 votes to 168,446, on a 69 per cent poll. See Roy Gregory, *The Miners and British Politics 1906–1914* (Oxford 1968), p. 28 *seq.*

January 1909, the terms were agreed. Although many accounts suggest otherwise, it seems clear that the Lib-Lab miners did not cross the floor of the House in the course of 1909, but continued to receive the Liberal whip.[1] However, as we shall see, most of them defended their seats as Labour Party candidates in January 1910.

In June 1909, the Liberal M.P. for Mid-Derbyshire died. Many of his constituents were miners, but he was an 'ordinary' Liberal, not a Lib-Lab. On 26 June, a representative meeting of the local Liberals was held. The Chairman reported that the miners proposed to recommend a candidate to the Liberal Association, and the name of J. G. Hancock was mentioned as a possible contender. Hancock had signed the constitution of the Labour Party, but declared nevertheless he had been a Liberal all his life, and still was a Liberal. A few days later, the Mid-Derbyshire Liberals adopted him as their candidate; and on 7 July the National Executive Committee of the Labour Party also endorsed his candidature.

There was some apprehension – but, apparently, no consternation – in the local Liberal ranks; a Special Correspondent of *The Times* reported that a 'leading Liberal' in the constituency told him:[2]

> 'The miners . . . are not Socialists or I.L.P. men; many of them belong to the Liberal Association; Mr Hancock himself is a Liberal, and if we had not adopted him he would not have stood as a candidate at all. . . . So Liberal are the miners that we have had more difficulty with some of them than with any other class on account of our adoption of Mr Hancock. They have hesitated to endorse the candidature lest it should imply a slight upon Liberalism. . . .'

Thus, the Liberal Association had adopted a candidate who was pledged to sit with the Labour Party in the House of Commons. He was duly returned with a large majority over his Unionist opponent in a straight fight.

[1] This was implied in the 1908 resolution of the Miners' Federation. It is confirmed by the Parliamentary report presented to the 10th Annual Conference of the Labour Party in January 1910. This Report covers the whole of 1909, and states, 'During the year our numbers were increased by the election of Mr J. Pointer (Attercliffe) and Mr J. G. Hancock (Mid-Derbyshire).' No reference is made to the Lib-Lab miners.

[2] *The Times*, 12 July 1909.

The *Labour Leader*, organ of the I.L.P., drew its own conclusions from the events in Mid-Derbyshire:[1]

> '[The Labour Party] has gained a great victory both in form and in substance. Here was a constituency recognised as a stronghold of Liberalism, and here was a candidate whose sympathies were avowedly Radical, yet the candidate was forced by the irresistible pressure of events to sign the Labour Party's constitution and to stand as a Labour Party candidate, and the former Liberal stronghold is destined henceforth to be one of the recognised strongholds of Labour.'

As the General Election of January 1910 approached, the miners' M.P.s who had hitherto sat as Lib-Labs were forced to decide whether to follow the recommendation of the Miners' Federation and defend their seats as Labour candidates, or to continue as Lib-Labs accepting the Liberal whip. Strong pressures were put upon them to sign the Labour Party's constitution,[2] but there seems to be no evidence of any counter-pressure by the Liberals at the national level to persuade them to remain.

In the old House, there had been fifteen miners' M.P.s (not including J. W. Taylor) accepting the Liberal whip. Of these, twelve stood as Labour candidates and three as Lib-Labs. These three who persisted in their old allegiance included no less a figure than Thomas Burt, who had been sitting since 1874.[3] But the old 'Trade Union Labour Group' which had been formed after the 1906 General Election, and of which the miners had formed the backbone, soon disappeared.

*   *   *

Relations between the Liberal and Labour Parties in the General Election of January 1910 varied considerably. The Liberals counter-attacked in Jarrow and Colne Valley. There was no Liberal candidate at Attercliffe, which Labour had won in the 1909 by-election,

---

[1] *Labour Leader*, 23 July 1909.

[2] See criticism in *Labour Leader*, 5 November 1909, p. 43, of those miners' M.P.s who insisted on remaining Liberals.

[3] The other two were Charles Fenwick (Wansbeck), and John Wilson (Mid-Durham).

WANTED—A WARRANTY.

Chief Ministerial Whip. "I CAN RAISE THE CORONETS ALL RIGHT; BUT I CAN'T ANSWER FOR THE 'NORMAN BLOOD.'"

Prime Minister. "NEVER MIND THE 'NORMAN BLOOD'; IT'S THE 'KIND HEARTS' AND THE 'SIMPLE FAITH' THAT I'M WORRYING ABOUT."

(The Master of Elibank and Asquith)

MR. K— H—: "Can't get in myself, but I can keep a few others out anyway."

[WESTMINSTER GAZETTE, *July* 17.]

(Keir Hardie)

and the only place where a Lib-Lab miner who had gone Labour was faced with Liberal opposition was Gateshead.

The Liberals went to the extreme of self-abnegation in Manchester East, which they had captured in 1906 from Arthur Balfour himself. The Liberal M.P. – who had probably never dreamed that he would be returned at all – decided not to stand again. In his place, L. W. Zimmerman was adopted to defend the seat in the Liberal interest. The Miners' Federation nominated a Labour candidate, who refused to withdraw. So Zimmerman withdrew instead!

Just as the Liberals varied considerably in their tenderness towards the Labour Party, so did Labour show a wide range of different attitudes towards the Liberals. In most of the critical constituencies, the pacts which had been devised before 1906 continued, and the leaders of the Labour Party were evidently well content with this arrangement. With more zeal but less prudence, Ben Tillett, one of the leading activists of the Labour Party, wrote to the Press in angry condemnation of these pacts,[1] and the *Labour Leader* noted that, 'it is the Liberals . . . who will be from an election point of view the most dangerous foes of the Labour Party candidates'.[2]

The Labour candidates varied considerably in their eagerness to proclaim their Party. Some, like Keir Hardie in Merthyr Tydfil, or Robert Smillie in Mid-Lanarkshire, were quite unambiguous. Others, like Fred Hall (Normanton) and W. Abraham ('Mabon', of Rhondda), omitted the word 'Labour' entirely from their election addresses.

Superficially, the Labour Party, which had forty seats in the new Parliament, had improved its position substantially. In fact, this apparent improvement was due entirely to the accession of the reluctant and rather shamefaced miners. Labour made only one gain from the Unionists, against six losses. The only Labour gain from the Liberals, apart from the miners, was Manchester East, where the Liberal deliberately withdrew. Against this, the Liberals recaptured Jarrow, which they had lost in the by-election, and Gateshead where the formerly Lib-Lab miners' M.P. defended his seat in the Labour interest. On polling day, eight thousand miners marched through the streets of the town, demonstrating against him.[3] The Liberals also

---

[1] *The Times*, 28 December 1909.
[2] Quoted in *The Times*, 10 December 1909.
[3] Roy Gregory, *op. cit.*, p. 79.

retook Colne Valley, where Victor Grayson finished bottom of the poll.

The Labour Party put up a miserable performance in three-cornered contests. Although several L.R.C. men had defeated both Unionist and Liberal opponents in 1906, there was not a single Labour Party candidate with a three-cornered fight who was successful in January 1910, and only five who secured as good as second place.[1]

The General Election of December 1910 altered the position only very slightly. The representation of the four parties was scarcely altered. Labour made four gains from the Unionists, against three losses. There was this time one Labour gain from the Liberals in West Fife. In January there had been a three-cornered contest; the Liberal had a fair lead over Labour, with the Unionist a bad third. In December the Unionist did not fight. A comparison of figures suggests that most of the Unionist votes, and some of the Liberal votes, transferred to Labour. This tendency for Labour in some parts of Scotland to pull votes heavily from the Unionists had been noted by the Scottish Liberal organizers long before the election.[2]

Between 1910 and the outbreak of war, there were two important measures which bore on the relationship between the Liberal and Labour Parties. The first might well have led to the obliteration of the Parliamentary Labour Party within a few years. The second probably did more than any other measure ever passed by Parliament to assist the Labour Party and damage the Liberals.

On the same day as the House of Lords passed the Parliament Act, 10 August 1911, the House of Commons agreed to the payment of M.P.s at the rate of £400 a year. The Labour Party therefore decided to discontinue the separate payments to Labour M.P.s.[3] With this powerful inducement to support the Labour Party removed, a number of Labour M.P.s began to cast sympathetic eyes towards the Liberals.

But the Trade Union Act of 1913 operated in a very different way. The celebrated Osborne case of 1909 had arisen because a Liberal

[1] 'Double harness' constituencies are not, of course, considered as three-cornered fights. The five second places were Jarrow, West Fife, Huddersfield, Montrose Burghs, and Bow & Bromley.
[2] S.L.A. Memorandum. Elibank papers 8,810, fol. 145–50.
[3] 12th Annual Report of the Labour Party, 1912, pp. 14, 16.

railwayman of that name objected to the Trade Union of which he was a member paying money to the Labour Party. The judgement established that it was unlawful for a Trade Union to devote money which it had received from subscriptions to political objects. Thus the Labour Party was not lawfully entitled to receive those funds which (then as now) formed the major part of its revenue.

The judgement disturbed many M.P.s, both Liberal and Labour. Eventually a Trade Union Bill was introduced, and passed both Houses with comparatively little difficulty. The effect of the Bill was to legalize Trade Union contributions for political purposes, but at the same time to enable a member who objected to his money being used in this way to 'contract out' of the political levy. Bonar Law, for the Unionists, accepted the Bill in this form.[1]

The Trade Union Act required that the political funds of Trade Unions should be kept quite separate from their ordinary funds.

A number of M.P.s, Liberal as well as Labour, sought a simple reversal of the Osborne Judgement, and Asquith had considerable difficulty in preserving the principle of 'contracting out'.[2] In retrospect, although no one seems to have recognized this at the time, it was an unqualified disaster for the Liberals, and a tremendous boon for the Labour Party, that contracting-out and the separate political fund were introduced, instead of a simple return to the *status quo*. The effect has been summarized, perhaps with some exaggeration, by A. J. P. Taylor:[3]

'The political fund could not be used for anything else. In the old days a Union felt generous if it subscribed £100 to the Labour Party. Now it thought nothing of handing over £5,000, if the money was lying idle in the political fund. Not all the political fund was paid to the national Labour Party. Some went to Union M.P.s; some to assist local associations and to assist the local ex-

[1] *Annual Register*, 1913, pp. 32–3.

[2] See J. A. Spender and Cyril Asquith, *Life of Lord Oxford and Asquith*, I, pp. 355–6. A. J. P. Taylor states (*English History, 1914–1945*, p. 114) that the contracting-out provision 'was intended to hamper their political activity', and that the Act was 'designed to cripple the Labour Party'. The present author knows of no evidence for either of these contentions. The Labour Party was still – in general – an ally of the Liberal Party; and if, for some reason, the Liberals nevertheless desired to cripple it, the simplest thing for the Government to do was nothing at all. Yet the Bill was a Government Bill, sponsored by the Law Officers.

[3] A. J. P. Taylor, *English History, 1914–1945*, p. 114.

H

penses of elections. All the same, the income of the Labour Party multiplied by ten overnight, and it shot up further when Unions increased their membership during the war.'

*   *   *

The Trade Union Act so closely antedated the First World War that its effects were not fully felt before that war. But there were considerable signs of the effect of payment of M.P.s, and people who had been drifting towards the Labour Party were returning to the Liberals in some numbers. From 1911 to 1914, the Labour Party's by-election record was dismal indeed. Not only did they fail to take a single seat from either the Liberals or the Unionists, but four by-elections occurred in Labour-held seats, and Labour lost them all.

In the middle of 1912, Enoch Edwards, Labour M.P. for Hanley, died. He was one of the Lib-Lab miners who had adhered to the Labour Party in the 1910 elections, and he had had a straight fight against the Unionist on both occasions.

When the Liberals decided to intervene by setting R. L. Outhwaite against the Labour nominee, S. Finney, the initial reaction of the Labour Party was to threaten that the Labour M.P.s would withdraw for a fortnight from the House of Commons in protest! This ridiculous piece of petulance was soon recognized as futile, and abandoned.

The report of the Special Correspondent of *The Times* provides a revealing picture of the campaign at its height:[1]

'. . . There can be no doubt that the new land taxation campaign is at the bottom of the present business. Mr Outhwaite's attack in Hanley cannot be explained in any other way, for it must be remembered that the Liberals are raining their blows, not on the heads of the Socialist wing of the Labour Party, but on the miners' group, which has been on the whole more friendly to the Government than any other working class organization. There is a growing impression here that a small knot of advanced Liberals took the risk of alienating the Labour leaders in the hope that Hanley might do for land taxation what High Peak did for the Budget in 1909.

'. . . The Labour people expect many Hanley Liberals to vote for Mr Finney, and they could certainly do so with a clear conscience. Mr Finney holds sound Liberal views and is one of the type of old-

[1] *The Times*, 8 July 1912.

fashioned trade union officials. . . . But for his Labour Party label he should be *persona grata* with the Liberals. . . . His address is not nearly so sensational as that of Mr Outhwaite, who for all immediate and practical purposes has a much more revolutionary programme.'

The present author, who has had the opportunity of consulting the election addresses concerned, will freely confirm the view of *The Times* Special Correspondent about the two documents. The Liberal and Labour candidates do not seem actually to have disagreed on anything, but the Liberal laid major stress on the land question, in the spirit of the Memorial presented to the leaders of the Government a year or so earlier.

The result of the Hanley by-election was a convincing victory for Outhwaite and his land policy, and a crushing defeat for the Labour Party, which ran a very bad third.[1] It is rather notable that the *Liberal Magazine* does not exult over this massive triumph; which suggests that the principal officials of the Liberal Party may not wholly have approved.

The year 1913 saw another interesting Lib-Lab by-election, this time in Chesterfield. In several respects this was an almost exact reversal of the result in the similar and contiguous mining constituency of Mid-Derbyshire four years earlier.

James Haslam of Chesterfield was another miners' M.P. who had been elected as a Lib-Lab in 1906, and had defended his seat in 1910 in the Labour interest, but without Liberal opposition. In June 1912, he announced that he would not seek re-election. The closeness of his relationship with the local Liberals is indicated by the fact that he made his announcement to the annual meeting of the Chesterfield Division Liberals, and went on to tell them, 'If it should happen to be a Liberal candidate that is put into the field and he is a man I can respect, then, no matter what Labour may say, I personally shall support that man's candidature.'

The Liberals selected a candidate, one Alderman Eastwood, and the Labour Party announced that their man would be Barnet Kenyon, treasurer of the Derbyshire Miners' Association.

---

[1] Hanley, 13 July 1912   R. L. Outhwaite (Lib.)   6,647 (—)
(December 1910 in brackets) G. H. Rittner (U.)   5,993 (4,658)
                             S. Finney (Lab.)   1,694 (8,343)

On 31 July 1913, Haslam died, and a by-election resulted.[1]

Eastwood announced immediately that he would not be prepared to stand. Thereupon, the Liberals proceeded to support Kenyon, who was already the Labour Party's candidate. It appears that the Liberals did not formally adopt him, although they gave him full and active assistance throughout the campaign. It was soon made clear that Kenyon proposed, if elected, to accept the Liberal whip, but to claim full freedom in relation to labour and mining questions.

The Labour Party repudiated Kenyon, but did not advance another candidate; however, an Independent Socialist, John Scurr, was nominated.

Two of the Labour M.P.s for nearby Derbyshire seats campaigned actively on Kenyon's behalf. They were W.'E. Harvey of North-East Derbyshire, whom *The Times* described as 'the real leader of the revolt against the inquisition of the Labour Party',[2] and – such are the ironies of politics – J. G. Hancock, who had been the central figure of the Mid-Derbyshire by-election of 1909. The Unionists entered the field with a third candidate.

By the later stages of the campaign, the Liberals were treating Kenyon as fully one of their own. Both Asquith and Lloyd George sent him telegrams of good wishes; and the Prime Minister rather rubbed salt in Labour's wounds by addressing his missive to the 'Central Liberal Committee Rooms'. Alderman Eastwood, who had been Prospective Liberal Candidate, addressed the eve-of-poll meeting on Kenyon's behalf. Kenyon duly captured the seat.

After Chesterfield, there were further signs of disaffection among Labour M.P.s for the mining constituencies. In March 1914, J. G. Hancock, and also William Johnson of Nuneaton, were called upon by the Executive Committee of the Miners' Federation to explain why they had made no attempt to form Labour organizations in their constituencies.[3] There was a further complaint against Johnson that he was still addressing Liberal meetings. As a result, the Labour whip was withdrawn from both of them. Johnson then proceeded to take the Liberal whip. Hancock took no immediate action,

[1] For the antecedents of the Chesterfield by-election, see *The Times*, 1 August 1913. For the course of the campaign, see issues of 2, 7, 8, 11, 13, 14, 15, 16, 18, 19, 20, and 21 August 1913.

[2] *The Times*, 19 August 1913.

[3] Report of Executive Committee to the Labour Party, 1914–15. January 1916, p. 15.

but defended the new constituency of Belper in 1918 as a Liberal.

In the early months of 1914, at least three other former Lib-Lab miners' M.P.s who had transferred to the Labour Party were showing little enthusiasm for their new associates. One of them, William Harvey of NE. Derbyshire, was another West-Midlander; but the remaining two, John Wadsworth of Hallamshire and Fred Hall of Normanton, came from the West Riding coalfield.[1] Thus the Liberal 'contagion' was already spreading out of the Midlands into Yorkshire.

Harvey died soon afterwards, and at the ensuing by-election in NE. Derbyshire, a Liberal intervened. In both of the 1910 elections, Harvey had been comfortably victorious in straight fights; but this time the Labour candidate defending his Party's seat ran a poor third. The seat, however, was won by the Unionist, with the Liberal just behind him.

Even in those mining areas where Labour was relatively strong, it was not predominant. The Liberal held Houghton-le-Spring in the 1913 by-election, and NW. Durham in the following year – both in three-cornered contests, with Labour a bad third. Such results were almost impossible to explain, except on the assumption that most miners were voting Liberal in preference to Labour.

But the 'showdown' between the Liberal and Labour Parties was mutual, for Labour was able to prove its nuisance value. Several of the Liberal by-election losses were clearly due to the intervention of Labour or Socialist candidates, even though all of these intervening candidates came third, and usually a bad third at that.[2] No doubt the officials of the two parties were highly embarrassed at the activities of Liberal land-taxing enthusiasts like Outhwaite and of Socialist enthusiasts like Scurr, who were busily disrupting the alliance they had been building since 1902. In the middle of 1914, *Liberal Magazine* concluded from the Unionists' gains in three-cornered contests that, 'what is clearly wanted is a policy of accommodation between Liberal and Labour, which will reproduce in the constituencies the co-operation which obtains at Westminster'.[3]

The predictable result of three-cornered contests was that both

[1] *The Times*, 20 March 1914.

[2] Unionist victories explainable in this way were South Lanarkshire (1913), Leith (1914), and SW. Bethnal Green (1914); and probably Oldham (1911), Crewe (1912), and Poplar (1914).

[3] *Liberal Magazine*, 1914, pp. 323–4.

Parties would lose a lot of seats on the 'split' vote at the ensuing General Election. This might well drive the Liberals from Government to Opposition, while the Parliamentary Labour Party would virtually cease to exist. Even if the Party officials contrived to restore the electoral arrangements of the previous three General Elections, there were plenty of people in both Parties who would be delighted to sabotage their efforts.[1] There was nothing to suggest that the Liberal Party was soon to be obliterated, and that the Labour Party would become the principal Party of Change.

What divided the Labour Party from the Liberals at the outbreak of the First World War was not any difference of political outlook, but the mere accident of the social class from which the M.P.s derived. Even this social difference was becoming less. Not only did the patriarchal working-class figures of Thomas Burt and Charles Fenwick continue to sit on Liberal benches, but more and more Labour M.P.s were looking towards the Liberals. It would not be difficult to parallel the opinions held by almost anyone on the Labour benches with a similar set of opinions held by a man who sat on the Liberal benches. In the 1890s, there had been some argument for the view that the Liberal Party was no longer a satisfactory champion for the aspirations of working men, and that they could better fulfil those aspirations by establishing a new political organization of their own. The tremendous radical vigour of the Liberals from 1906 onwards destroyed that argument. It is difficult to see how any administration could have acted faster or gone further than the Liberals did in that great era of social reform.

Although the Labour Party may have helped the Liberals by attracting the votes of working-class Unionists in Lancashire in the early years of the century, yet by 1914 it could only serve to divide and weaken the forces of change, and its continued existence would help nobody but the Unionists. The price which was paid for the Liberal Whips' squeamish refusal to strangle the Labour Party in its cradle was the division and confusion of radicals throughout the inter-war years, and the eventual establishment of 'Labour' administrations which had remarkably little in common with the wishes and needs of the workers themselves.

[1] See G. D. H. Cole, *British Working Class Politics 1832–1914*, p. 224.

6

The Lamps Go Out

'After the declaration of war in 1914, I was called to the office of the Chief Liberal Whip, Percy Illingworth. I found him in tears. He was so shaken that for a minute he could not find speech. Then he muttered, "Liberalism is dead." '

FRANCIS NEILSON, *Modern Man and the Liberal Arts*, p. 171

The First World War presented the Liberal Party with a series of agonizing dilemmas. There was a Liberal case for entering the war, and there was a Liberal case for the view that Britain was under no obligation – whether moral, economic, or military – to do so. There was a Liberal case for accepting various unpalatable measures to prosecute that war, and there was a Liberal case for the view that these measures were not necessary, even if the war itself was necessary. There was a Liberal case for urging a negotiated peace, and a Liberal case for fighting the war to a finish. There was a Liberal case for upholding Asquith, and a Liberal case for bringing him down.

Yet many historians have made too much of these dilemmas, and have written as if the war made Liberal disruption somehow inevitable. Tensions not much less severe existed in the Unionist Party, which preserved itself intact, and tensions a great deal sharper existed in the Labour Party, which derived enormous political profit. What shattered the Liberal Party was not the vital issues of principle which divided Liberals, and on which Liberals – whatever their views – had both the right and the duty to speak out; but rather a series of largely accidental factors which arose both during and after the war.

*   *   *

Lord Rosebery had foreseen in 1904 that the *entente cordiale* which was concluded with France in that year predetermined the course of events, and had made war with Germany inevitable.[1] In 1911, he told an audience in his worshipping Edinburgh that the existing international arrangements 'might lead to an Armageddon such as was not dreamed of by Napoleon'.[2] On this view, it was Britain's decision to move from her nineteenth-century isolation, and to lean, however tentatively, towards the Franco-Russian alliance, which produced the reassemblage of the nations and the armed forces of Europe, and led inescapably to the holocaust. One may consider that Britain had opportunities long after 1904 to reverse the trend of events; but this would have required a degree of vision seldom vouchsafed to the wisest of men. Whatever we may think of Rosebery as a constructive statesman, it is difficult to deny that his genius as a prophet was sometimes almost uncanny.

Many Liberals were far from happy about Britain's role in the new pattern of events. Asquith later wrote of the profound unwillingness of Liberals at all levels, from the Cabinet downwards, to countenance increased armaments.[3] In 1909, the Cabinet was deeply divided over the proposal to build eight 'Dreadnought' battleships, and the eventual agreement was a compromise.[4] Even so, forty-one Liberals (including Lib-Labs) supported a motion of censure on the Government's naval shipbuilding programme a few months later.[5] In March 1911, thirty-seven Liberal M.P.s voted for the reduction of military and naval expenditure;[6] in July 1912 twenty-three voted against the Supplementary Estimate for extra men and boys for the Navy;[7] and in March 1913, fourteen voted against increased naval estimates.[8]

Although these were relatively small minorities, it is not difficult to believe that there were many other Liberal M.P.s who felt a greater or lesser measure of unquiet on such matters, but either deferred to the judgement of their leaders, or did not care to stand up and be counted.

Right at the head of the Government, the same controversy went

[1] Frank Owen, *Tempestuous Journey*, (1954), p. 260.
[2] *Ibid.*, p. 211.
[3] H. H. Asquith, *The genesis of war*, pp. 106–10, etc.
[4] Cabinet letter, 24 February 1909 (draft). Asquith papers 5, fol. 86–7.
[5] *Liberal Magazine*, 1909, p. 397.
[6] Parl. Deb. (Commons) xxii, 13 March 1911, col. 1,995.
[7] *Ibid.*, xli, 22 July 1912, col. 945.
[8] *Ibid.*, l, 28 March 1913, col. 2,055.

on. Unexpectedly, Lloyd George adhered to those who sought to 'warn off' Germany – and signalled that view in a famous speech at the Mansion House in 1911. Later in the same year, however, Morley objected in the Cabinet, 'to discussions which had taken place between the British and French General Staffs without Cabinet authority'.[1]

The possibility of close friendship – much less an alliance – with Czarist Russia was viewed by many Liberals with unmitigated alarm. Campbell-Bannerman publicly deplored the collapse of the Russian Parliament, the Duma, at the Inter-Parliamentary Conference of 1906 – adding the trenchant words, 'The Duma is dead; long live the Duma!'[2] On 4 June 1908, eighteen Liberals supported a motion of censure when Edward VII made a State visit to the Czar.[3] Sir Charles Dilke brought a similar motion of protest when the Czar returned the visit a year later, and attracted twenty-three Liberal votes.[4] This same loathing for Czardom and all it meant brought Morley to write, just after war was declared: 'I don't like a policy which leaves us to face any mess into which bankrupt France may be dragged by barbarian Russia.'[5]

When the European war began in 1914, Britain was not committed by treaty to either France or Russia, and it was by no means certain that she would be involved. The Foreign Secretary, Sir Edward Grey,[6] and Asquith as well, probably believed that Britain would be destroyed unless she rallied to the aid of France, but many Liberals were unconvinced. Lord Beaverbrook[7] lists seven doubtful members of the Cabinet, and there may be others who would have been likely to resign, and a sufficiently large section of the country as a whole would probably have supported them to make conduct of the war impossible.

It is widely believed that Britain was under a treaty obligation to Belgium. The letter which Asquith drafted for the King on 30 July

---

[1] Cabinet letter, 1 November 1911 (draft), Asquith papers 6, fol. 75–6.
[2] *Liberal Magazine*, 1906, pp. 435–6.
[3] *Liberal Magazine*, 1908, pp. 356–7. They are described as 'Liberal and Labour Members', but the eighteen listed were all either ordinary Liberals or Lib-Labs at the time.
[4] *Liberal Magazine*, 1909, p. 397.
[5] Morley to Rosebery, 7 August 1914. Rosebery papers 37.
[6] G. M. Trevelyan, *Grey of Falloden*, p. 250.
[7] Lord Beaverbrook, *Politicians and the War*, i, pp. 25–6.

1914, before Belgium was invaded – indeed, before France and Germany were at war – deserves to be quoted. Asquith wrote:[1]

> '. . . The Cabinet carefully reviewed the obligations of this country in regard to the neutrality of Belgium arising out of the two treaties of April 1839, and the action which was taken by Mr Gladstone's Government in August 1870.
>
> 'It is a doubtful point how far a single guaranteeing State is bound under the Treaty of 1839 to maintain Belgian neutrality if the remainder abstain or refuse. The Cabinet consider that the matter if it arises will be rather one of policy than of legal obligation. After much discussion it was agreed that Sir E. Grey be authorised to inform the German and French ambassadors that at this stage we were unable to pledge ourselves in advance, either under all conditions to stand aside, or in any conditions to join in. . . .'

But at a later Cabinet meeting, on 2 August, 'it was agreed, without any attempt to state a formula, that it would be made evident that a substantial violation of the neutrality of [Belgium] would place us in the situation contemplated by Mr Gladstone in 1870, when interference with Belgian neutrality was held to compel us to take action'.[2]

Belgium had not yet been invaded; but Runciman pencilled on his convening notice for that Cabinet meeting the observation, 'The Cabinet which decided that war with Germany was inevitable.'[3]

While all was yet in doubt, John Burns declared, on the night of 1 August, that he intended to resign from the Cabinet. Asquith persuaded him not to announce his resignation until the next day. On 2 August, Germany issued her ultimatum to Belgium, demanding passage for troops into France. At lunchtime that day, several Ministers who had grave doubts about intervention met: Morley states that Beauchamp, Simon, Lloyd George, Harcourt, Samuel, Pease, and McKinnon Wood were present, adding, 'not sure about Runciman'. Morley commented, however, that, 'It wore all the look

---

[1] Cabinet letter, 30 July 1914 (draft). Asquith papers 7, fol. 151–2. Contrast article by Sir Herbert Samuel, *Manchester Guardian*, 25 October 1928.

[2] Cabinet Letter, 2 August 1914 (draft). Asquith papers 7, fol. 153–4.

[3] Convening notice (1 August 1941) for Cabinet Meeting of 2 August 1914. Runciman papers.

of an important gathering, but was in truth a very shallow affair.'[1]

By the same evening, the only undoubted recalcitrants were Morley, Burns, Simon, and Beauchamp. All four were reported at the Cabinet meeting of 3 August to have tendered their resignations.[2] Later that day, however, Asquith won over Simon and Beauchamp,[3] leaving only Morley and Burns. These two, however, were implacable, and with them resigned a third, much more junior, member of the Government, C. P. (later Sir Charles) Trevelyan.

The three men resigned for very different reasons. Trevelyan seems to have taken a pacifist position. Burns most certainly did not behave like a pacifist. He used to march with the troops, and 'spoke with great satisfaction of his experiences with the territorials'.[4] There is a strange inconsistency in Burns's position. While his letter of resignation declared that, 'The decision of the Cabinet to intervene in an European war is an act with which I profoundly disagree'[5] – and he was one of the very few people who foretold the cost of the war in life and money[6] – yet we find him writing to Asquith and others, soon after the outbreak, urging that police recruiting be stopped, 'to divert Police Recruits into the Army'.[7] Morley would probably find most echoes among contemporary Liberals, as he wrote:[8] 'In a Council of War I can find no place – not from a squeamishy conscience but because I should neither find much interest nor be of the slightest use to other people. . . .'

Several years later, Morley wrote to Haldane, perhaps not with complete seriousness, 'I count "the guilt of Wilhelm Hohenzollern" as far less than the guilt of three English Ministers'.[9]

When war was almost certain, the Unionists and the Irish immediately and authoritatively pledged support. Ramsay MacDonald, Chairman of the Parliamentary Labour Party, was apparently

---

[1] Viscount Morley, *Memorandum on Resignation August 1914*. Macmillan 1928, p. 15 (published posthumously). It seems that Runciman was not present. Runciman to Samuel, 14 January 1943. Samuel papers A/45, fol. 43.

[2] Cabinet Letter, 3 August 1914 (draft). Asquith papers 7, fol. 155–6.

[3] Morley, *op. cit.*, pp. 27–8; Cabinet Letter, 4 August 1914 (draft), Asquith papers 7, fol. 157–8.

[4] Percy Preece to Runciman, 25 September 1908. Runciman papers.

[5] Draft of 2 August 1914. Burns papers 46,282, fol. 158.

[6] Newspaper cutting (not identified) of 14 April 1928. *Ibid.*, 46,304, fol. 147.

[7] *Ibid.*, 46, 282, fol. 175–₁.

[8] Morley to Rosebery, 7 August 1914. Rosebery papers 37.

[9] Morley to Haldane, 16 August 1920. Haldane papers 5,914, fol. 224.

opposed; but the Labour M.P.s rapidly replaced him by the pro-war Arthur Henderson. A small band of Liberal and I.L.P. pacifists provided the only opposition to a war which nearly everyone believed would be brief, glorious, and victorious.

Within the Government, there was some reorganization as a result of the three resignations, and also Asquith's determination to be rid of the Secretaryship for War, which he had accepted at the time of the Curragh 'mutiny' earlier in the year. Earl Kitchener received that post, as a 'non-political' appointment. In general, the administration continued to be a Party government of the old kind; but the Party battle was to a degree muted. The silencing, however, was far from complete. The Government of Ireland Bill and the Welsh Disestablishment Bill had both passed the Commons three times when war broke out. They awaited Royal assent in despite of the Lords. The Government intended to enact the Bills, but also to enact a Suspensory Bill which would prevent them taking effect for the duration of the war. The proposal to enact the Irish Bill was bitterly attacked by Bonar Law,[1] and the King tried very anxiously to avoid serious damage to national unity.[2] On 28 August 1914, an electoral truce was arranged between the three British Parties – but not the Irish. This gave each Party the right to fill its own by-election vacancies without opposition from the others. It was concluded for four months in the first instance, and was then from time to time renewed for varying periods.[3]

* * *

As soon as the war began, the wonderful machine of the Liberal Party almost fell to pieces. Sir Robert Hudson went to the Headquarters of the British Red Cross Society, and was soon appointed Chairman of the Joint War Finance Committee. For the rest of the war, his main attention was devoted to that cause rather than politics. Sir Jesse Herbert's remaining energies were mostly applied to the work of the Parliamentary Recruiting Committee.

Not only did innumerable M.P.s, candidates, agents, and constituency workers for the Liberal cause become drawn into the vortex

[1] See Barry McGill, 'Asquith's Predicament 1914–1918'. *J. Mod. Hist.* xxxix, No. 3, September 1967, p. 284.

[2] The King to Asquith, 25 August 1914. Asquith papers 4, fol. 4; Lord Stanfordham to Asquith, 11 September 1914, *ibid.*, fol. 12.

[3] Asquith papers 26, fols. 13 to 23.

of war, but the Party officials did not even press upon the constituencies the need to preserve some skeleton organization. There was
almost a deliberate and conscious disbandment of the Liberal Party.
It is true that something comparable happened with the Unionists;
but organization was never as important for them as it was for the
Liberals. Personal influence and contacts played a much greater
part in their electoral campaign.

Towards the end of 1914, Percy Illingworth, Chief Liberal Whip,
ate an oyster. As a result, he contracted typhoid, and died early in
January 1915.

We have already seen that Illingworth was a man of quite extraordinary ability and character. But the real significance of Percy
Illingworth lies in the fact that the two most important men in the
Liberal Party and the Government both held him in immense
regard. Asquith described him as 'one of the straightest men I have
ever known and one of the most loveable'.[1] Lloyd George went much
further, and stood on record with the opinion that Illingworth would
have prevented the rift which eventually developed between himself
and his chief.[2] This may well be an exaggeration, for some men who
were in a good position to judge events have been strongly persuaded
that the split would have come in any case. But the oyster certainly
did tremendous damage, for there were few people indeed whom
both men admired as they admired Illingworth.

On Illingworth's death, the Prime Minister first offered the vacant
post to J. H. Whitley, the Deputy Speaker.[3] But Whitley would not
leave his official position. The second plan was to establish a sort of
condominium between John Gulland and Wedgwood Benn, two of
the Whips who had worked under Illingworth. This also failed.[4] So
the post was eventually given to Gulland. John Gulland – known
from his swarthy appearance as 'black John Willie' – was a man of
commendable character. He was noted for his work in Parliament on
behalf of crippled children. He was honest and straightforward, a
competent Parliamentarian, and a man with a methodical mind.
His loyalty to Asquith was absolute, although there are indications

[1] H. H. Asquith, *Memories and Reflections*, i, p. 192.
[2] D. Lloyd George, *War Memoirs*, New edn, i, p. 448.
[3] Asquith to Lord Murray (Master of Elibank), 18 March 1918. Elibank papers
8,804, fol. 156.
[4] Runciman to Sir Robert Chalmers, 7 February 1915. Runciman papers.
Quoted in Barry McGill, *op. cit.*, 1967, p. 289.

that Asquith and Elibank both felt some reservations about his capacity as Chief Whip.[1] In different circumstances, his public career would have been regarded as useful and successful. It was his own tragedy as well as that of his party that events followed the course which they did.

Thus the men who were best fitted to hold the Liberal Party together through the stresses of war had vanished from the centre of politics within six months of the outbreak, while entirely new issues arose to cut right across the lines of political allegiance. Although fewer Liberal M.P.s than Unionists were on active service[2] – perhaps through age, perhaps through different family traditions – this was not necessarily a source of strength to the Liberals, either in Parliament or in the country.

*   *   *

At the beginning of the war, there was no movement to alter the Party character of the administration. But on 17 May 1915, Bonar Law wrote to Asquith, threatening questions in the House and a demand for a debate, unless there were 'some change in the constitution of the Government'.[3] On the same day, Asquith wrote to the King's Secretary, indicating that he had come to the conclusion that the Government must be reconstituted, 'on a broad non-party basis.'[4] Although Asquith had said five days earlier that no Coalition was being planned,[5] this did not mean that he would not favour one if circumstances changed enough to make it politically practicable. Several reasons have been suggested for Asquith's sudden decision[6] – but there seems no need to doubt that the primary reasons were those which he circulated to the Cabinet: that a 'broad-based' Government was necessary to prevent public controversies in Parliament which would damage the war effort.[7]

[1] Asquith to Elibank, 18 March 1918. Elibank papers 8,804, fol. 156. Elibank to (?) Lord Cowdray, 15 June 1915. Elibank papers.

[2] Barry McGill, op. cit., p. 285, quoted the Curzon papers as showing that in January 1915 there were 139 Unionists in the forces, against 41 Liberals, 1 Labour, and 3 Nationalists. By January 1916, the numbers were 125, 32, 1, and 5 respectively (p. 291).

[3] Quoted in R. Blake, The unknown Prime Minister (London 1955), pp. 246–7.

[4] Asquith to Lord Stamfordham, 17 May 1915. Asquith papers 27, fol. 162.

[5] Parl. Deb. lxxi (12 May 1915), 1642.

[6] Barry McGill, op. cit., pp. 286–8, and citations.

[7] Asquith's notes for Cabinet, 17 May 1915.

Whatever the arguments, there can be no doubt that there was tremendous Liberal resistance to the proposal of a Coalition, and that it was only overborne by the strongest pressure from Asquith himself.[1] The Unionists and the Labour Party both entered the Government – with Henderson and eight Unionists in the Cabinet – but the Irish Party was unrepresented.[2]

Lloyd George consented to move to a completely new office, the Ministry of Munitions. Whatever criticisms may be levelled at him for his later conduct, there can be no doubt that this was an act of profound self-abnegation. As Chancellor, he held that office which most commonly leads to the Premiership, and none could have doubted that he was Asquith's heir-apparent. In the new post, he was far down in the Cabinet hierarchy, and stood to catch the blame for almost everything that went wrong at the front. The Liberals insisted that the new Chancellor should be a Liberal, and Reginald McKenna was given the office – but on the understanding that he was no more than *locum tenens* for Lloyd George.

To his great personal regret, Asquith was forced to drop Lord Haldane and Winston Churchill from the Cabinet, because of invincible Unionist opposition. Asquith has been much criticized for acceding to the demands for Haldane's removal, but it is difficult to see what else could be done, once the fatal decision for a Coalition had been taken.

During the period of Asquith's Coalition, many Liberals became increasingly tried by issues which confronted them with terrible dilemmas between their Liberalism and their determination to fight the war. It was all too apparent that measures which the Government was proposing in order to confront wartime emergencies were likely to persist when the war was over. Nor was it by any means certain that they were really necessary for the conduct of the war itself; and to some Liberals they looked like concessions to the Unionists which were being made for political rather than military reasons.

First came McKenna's Budget of September 1915, which proposed a 33⅓ per cent *ad valorem* tariff on what are usually described as 'luxury' imports, in order to save shipping space. But when it is

[1] Lady Violet Bonham-Carter (Lady Asquith), *Winston Churchill as I knew him*, pp. 403–4.
[2] See Redmond to Asquith (a) undated, (b) 25 May 1915. Asquith papers 27, fols. 184, 192.

noted that these imports included such items as tea and cocoa, it seems that the concept of 'luxury' was a broad one. A Unionist Chancellor would have had far more difficulty than McKenna in piloting those duties through the Cabinet and Parliament. Perhaps he would not have tried. Even McKenna faced some quite substantial Liberal opposition, although he beat it down.[1] On a number of divisions, about thirty Liberals and some Labour M.P.s voted against the Government. No doubt many others felt grave disquiet.

The issue of conscription was even more agonizing. Late in 1915, the Government applied a scheme promoted by Lord Derby, which, viewed from different eyes, was either the last, desperate attempt to avoid conscription, or was an essential preliminary in order to make conscription politically acceptable.[2] When the Government eventually decided, at the turn of the year, that not enough men had enlisted under the scheme, and resolved to conscript them, the Liberal Ministers were set in a fearful position. The Home Secretary, Sir John Simon, resigned – and himself joined the Air Force, being later mentioned in dispatches. Four other Liberal Ministers contemplated resigning with him: the Chancellor of the Exchequer, Reginald McKenna; the President of the Board of Trade, Walter Runciman; the Chief Secretary for Ireland, Augustine Birrell; and even the Foreign Secretary, Sir Edward Grey. Eventually they were persuaded to remain, but there were marks of strong reluctance, which only the authority of Asquith could overbear.[3] When the Prime Minister sought leave to introduce the Conscription Bill to the House of Commons, there was a substantial body of M.P.s who opposed him: thirty-five Liberals, thirteen Labour and fifty-nine Nationalists.[4] Nearly all the Nationalists abstained in the later stages, when it was made clear that the Bill would not extend to Ireland, but substantial bodies of Liberal and Labour M.P.s continued to dispute its passage.

Similar lines of cleavage were seen again when the Government proposed to extend conscription to married men, in May 1916.

[1] Parl. Deb. (Commons), lxxiv, 30 September–20 October 1915, cols. 1,033, 1,659, 1,683, 1,759, 1,851, 1,857, 1,939.

[2] This and cognate problems are discussed by the present author in 'Voluntary enlistment in the First World War and the work of the Parliamentary Recruiting Committee', *J. Mod. Hist.* 42 (1970) pp. 564–85.

[3] See Trevor Wilson, *The downfall of the Liberal Party*, pp. 70–83.

[3] Parl. Deb. (Commons) lxxvii, 6 January 1961, col. 1,255.

Twenty-eight Liberals voted against the Second Reading, twenty-seven against the Third.[1] Again one may be sure that many others deliberately abstained from voting, or voted with profound doubts in their minds.

The 1916 Easter Week rising in Dublin again recalled all the old political struggles. Most of the principal figures responsible for Irish administration, including Augustine Birrell, the Chief Secretary, were driven to resign. Executions were ordered in Ireland, which may or may not have been morally justified but were certainly politically disastrous. Asquith visited Ireland to investigate the situation on the spot, and then gave Lloyd George the task of negotiating a solution. His proposals won the initial support of both the Redmondite Irish and the Ulster Unionists. But there was soon a powerful revolt by British Unionists.[2] Within the Cabinet, the Unionists were completely split; Bonar Law and Balfour favoured acceptance; Lansdowne and Walter Long demurred.

From a political point of view, there was everything to be said for Asquith forcing Lloyd George's Irish proposals through the Cabinet, accepting the resignations of any recalcitrant Unionist Ministers, and facing with equanimity the prospect of a General Election if he was challenged. But for reasons of a purely patriotic kind, Asquith was concerned at all costs to avert a General Election.[3]

Stalemate on the Western Front continued, and Asquith suffered the usual fate of a wartime Minister who fails to deliver the anticipated victories: his political position at home became steadily weaker, and men began casting round for a charismatic leader who symbolized success rather than failure.

After Kitchener's death on 5 June 1916, Lloyd George was offered the War Office, but was reluctant to accept the office under the conditions which had circumscribed his predecessor.[4] An attempt was made to give the post to Bonar Law, but he would not accept – and finally, on 6 July, it was given to Lloyd George, with more or less the powers he was demanding. The long delay in making so vital an appointment was clear evidence of a power-struggle, and the

[1] Parl. Deb. (Commons) lxxxii, 4 and 16 May 1916, 263 and 1,487; *Liberal Magazine*, 1916, p. 228 lists them.

[2] Cabinet Letter, 27 June 1916. Asquith papers 8, fol. 171–8.

[3] McGill, *op. cit.*, pp. 291–2.

[4] McKenna's letter to Runciman (19 June 1916; Runciman papers) throws some interesting light on the early stages of the negotiations.

I

terms on which Lloyd George received the post made it equally clear who had won. Thus wrote the Premier's irrepressible wife, 'Margot', that night in her diary: 'We are out, it is only a matter of time when we shall have to leave Downing Street'.[1] Such judgements tend to be self-serving.

*   *   *

On 8 November 1916, it was the turn of the Unionists to be severely split. The division occurred in a debate arising out of the disposal of enemy property in Nigeria. Sixty-four Unionists voted one way, and seventy-three the other. The Liberals were a good deal less badly split on that occasion; but, as one recent historian has pointed out, Bonar Law 'began to see that while Asquith could not save him from his own rebels, he might save himself by joining them and destroying Asquith's government'.[2]

For the second time Asquith's position was undermined, not because the Unionists were united against him, but for the very reason that they were divided.

On 13 November 1916, Lord Lansdowne, Unionist leader in the Lords and Minister without Portfolio, presented a most important memorandum to the Cabinet, which implied the desirability of negotiated peace with Germany.[3] At the time, of course, it was a highly confidential document, but it may have played a vital and catalytic part in changing the whole character of the Government.[4] In both the Liberal and Unionist Parties there were Ministers completely committed to the vigorous prosecution of the war at all costs, and there were also 'War Committees' of back-benchers with similar views, who may have exerted considerable influence.[5] All of these people may have been spurred into prompt action by the knowledge or suspicion of the Lansdowne memorandum. There is nothing to suggest that Asquith ever inclined to Lansdowne's view; but in politics what people are thought to have done is often more important than what they have in fact done.

By the end of November 1916, a lot of people were determined to

[1] See Frank Owen, *Tempestuous Journey*, pp. 315–20.
[2] Barry McGill, 'Asquith's Predicament 1914–1918'. *J. Mod. Hist.* No. 3 (1967), at p. 294.
[3] Lord Oxford, *Memories and Reflections*, pp. 138–47.
[4] Lord Beaverbrook, *Politicians and the War*, ii, pp. 19–20.
[5] McGill, *op. cit.*, pp. 290, 292–3.

establish a small committee with overriding powers to conduct the
war. On 1 December, Lloyd George submitted proposals of this kind
to Asquith. The Prime Minister did not dissent from the proposals,
but insisted that he should be Chairman. His letter to that effect was
promptly communicated by Lloyd George to Bonar Law.[1] On 3
December the leading Unionists met, and urged Asquith to tender
his resignation – in default of which they would resign themselves.
There seems to be some doubt whether the purpose of this was to
break Asquith or to prove him indispensable – either because of their
admiration for his intellectual powers, or because the likely alternative was Lloyd George, whom they found more distasteful. Just possibly, some had one aim and some the other. Asquith asked them to
defer their decision until he had met Lloyd George, which he did
later in the day. The Prime Minister was prepared to concede the
Chairmanship of the War Committee, and the two men reached a
large measure of agreement – notably:

'The Prime Minister to have supreme and effective control of War
policy.
   'The Agenda of the War Committee will be submitted to him;
its Chairman will report to him daily; he can direct it to consider
particular topics or proposals; and all its conclusions will be subject to his approval or veto. He can, of course, at his own discretion,
attend meetings of the Committee.'[2]

A little before midnight, it was officially announced that Asquith
had advised the King to consent to a reconstruction of the Government. On the following morning, 4 December, a leading article
appeared in *The Times*. This was derogatory to the Prime Minister,
and had clearly been written by someone who knew of the discussions
of the previous day. There is continuing argument as to how *The
Times* got hold of the information; but some people believed that
Lloyd George was directly or indirectly the informant. The article
further implied that Lloyd George had won a victory over the Prime
Minister. There followed a quick exchange of letters between the two

[1] The correspondence between the main figures was published in part in the
Atlantic Monthly, February 1919 – to the great annoyance of both Asquith and
Lloyd George.
[2] J. A. Spender and Cyril Asquith, *Life of Lord Oxford*, ii, p. 264.

men, in the course of which Asquith expressed concern over the political implications, but not the source, of *The Times* article, and stated the terms of the agreement.

Later in the same day, Asquith submitted to the King the resignations of his colleagues, but not of himself, and received authority to form a new Government. Soon afterwards, he wrote again to Lloyd George, indicating that he had 'come decidedly to the conclusion that it is not possible that [the War] . . . Committee could be made workable and effective without the Prime Minister as its Chairman'.[1] Lloyd George did not see the letter until the following day, 5 December, but he then replied, tendering his resignation. In the early afternoon, the Liberal members of the Cabinet, with the exception of Lloyd George, conferred with Asquith. All but Edwin Montagu (who had succeeded Lloyd George as Minister of Munitions) agreed in advising Asquith to meet Lloyd George's challenge by resigning.

Earlier in the same day, Bonar Law had informed Asquith that he was unwilling to continue in the Government unless the War Committee proposal was proceeded with in the form initially agreed between Asquith and Lloyd George. As Lloyd George had adopted the same position, Asquith consulted some of the leading Unionists, and they indicated their unwillingness to continue in the Government without Law and Lloyd George. The same evening Asquith resigned. The King thereupon invited Bonar Law to form an administration.

On the following day, 6 December, there were numerous discussions between the leading political figures. One of the most important of these was another conference between the Liberal members of the old Cabinet – not including Lloyd George, but including Arthur Henderson from the Labour Party. It was agreed, but not quite unanimously, that Asquith should not accept a subordinate post in a Bonar Law Government, and Asquith, who concurred, conveyed the information to Law in the early evening. Law then went to the King and resigned his commission. Lloyd George was called to the Palace and invited to form a Government.

While all of this was taking place, one of the junior Liberal Ministers, Dr Christopher Addison (Parliamentary Secretary to the Ministry of Munitions), was taking active steps to assist the replacement of Asquith by Lloyd George. He discovered that, of the 260 or

[1] *Ibid.*, p. 266.

so Liberal M.P.s, 49 were 'out and out' supporters of Lloyd George, and 126 more would support him if he could form a Government.[1]

Just why Asquith resigned in the middle of the crisis has been, and will probably remain, a subject of speculation. The extreme hostile view is stated by A. J. P. Taylor:[2] 'He defied Law or Lloyd George to form a Government: "then they will have to come in on *my* terms". Asquith was not manœuvred out of office. He deliberately resigned office as a manœuvre to rout his critics.'

Asquith's most recent biographer, Roy Jenkins, has argued that the resignation was, 'not . . . a tactical manœuvre, but because he did not have sufficient support to carry on'.[3]

The extreme Asquithian view was put by Asquith's daughter, Lady Violet Bonham-Carter:

' "I shall never cease to wonder", wrote Mr Churchill, "why Mr Asquith, with a large Liberal majority at his back, did not invoke the expedient of a Secret Session." Mr Churchill believed, as I do, that Parliament would have undoubtedly confirmed my father in power. Why, then, did he not seek a vote of confidence? Mr Churchill answered his own question when he wrote later that "disinterested patriotism and inflexible integrity were his only guides". My father was convinced that a campaign would have been conducted outside Parliament, in the Press and on the platform, which would have done grave injury to the war effort and to the national cause. He could fight for a principle, for his party, above all for his country. What he could not fight for was himself.'[4]

Perhaps we may resolve these views by suggesting that Asquith would have preferred to remain in office if he could have done so without constant intrigue and crisis; but that he was far from dismayed at the prospect of resignation, and had not the least intention of fighting the Germans and his own colleagues at the same time. In the period which immediately followed his resignation, he showed

[1] Christopher Addison (Viscount Addison), *Politics from within, 1911–1918* (London 1924), i, pp. 270–1.

[2] A. J. P. Taylor, *English History 1914–1945*, p. 69.

[3] Roy Jenkins, *Asquith*, p. 454.

[4] Lady Violet Bonham-Carter (Lady Asquith), *The Listener*, 18 March 1948, p. 454.

what certainly looks like genuine relief. This would be understandable in a man of sixty-four with many interests, whose son had recently been killed in the war, who had held senior public office for eleven consecutive years and the Premiership for nearly nine.

* * *

Just as we have no reason for doubting Asquith's willingness to leave office, so also have we no reason for doubting his successor's categorical assertion that he 'neither sought nor desired the Premiership'.[1] Lloyd George was adept at the *suppressio veri*, and highly tendentious comments, but – in the teeth of his reputation to the contrary – he was not particularly addicted to lying. It is difficult to believe that either he or anyone else had foreseen the outline of events, a few days before he became Premier. Lord Beaverbrook suggests that Lloyd George told Law, in effect, 'I have not been fighting for the premiership, but simply to get rid of the Asquith incubus. Give me the Chairmanship of the War Council and I am perfectly content. I would prefer to serve under you.'[2]

This remark is in character to the extent that Lloyd George cared little for the trappings of office, but much for the realities of power. He was probably more or less indifferent whether Asquith, Law, or himself were Prime Minister, provided that he had effective control of the war effort. He was quite willing to play Mayor of the Palace to someone else's King. When at last it became plain to him that he could only secure effective control at the price of a break with Asquith and most of his Liberal colleagues, then he took office without hesitation.

In all three Parties, Lloyd George encountered great difficulty. He knew that Asquith would not accept office under him. It was widely believed that an understanding existed between Asquith and his Liberal Ministers that none of them would join. Runciman, however, assured Cecil Harmsworth that there was no foundation for this belief.[3] Apparently Runciman was never invited to join the new Government. Herbert Samuel was invited to continue, and refused; but he made it clear that he was speaking for himself alone and not his colleagues. It appears that Samuel had no confidence in the

[1] Lloyd George, *War Memoirs* (new edn, 1938), i, p. 596.
[2] Lord Beaverbrook, *op. cit.*, p. 283.
[3] Cecil Harmsworth to Runciman, 10 December 1916. Runciman papers.

viability of the administration.[1] Churchill, who had been excluded
from Asquith's Coalition, was apparently willing enough to accept
office under Lloyd George, but the Unionists would not tolerate
him. It was only with considerable difficulty, and several months
later, that Lloyd George managed to smuggle him back into the
Government. The most impressive Liberal name the Prime Minister
could secure was Christopher Addison, whom he made Minister of
Munitions. A number of more junior Liberals joined as well, but
they were mostly lightweights, with no potential of becoming much
more.

After a series of complicated intrigues, the Unionists decided to
join – Lloyd George agreeing not to remove Haig from the post of
Commander-in-Chief; not to bring Churchill or Lord Northcliffe
into the Government, and not to commit the Government to Home
Rule. The support of the Labour Party was only given by an extremely narrow margin, largely because Lloyd George indicated his
willingness to enforce State control of mines, and possibly shipping.
By such means, and at such a price, was Lloyd George able to form
his Government.

The Liberal Chief Whip, John Gulland, played no active part in
the affair. Lloyd George's second wife, then his secretary, has noted
that Gulland approached neither Asquith nor Lloyd George.[2] This
statement has been denied elsewhere.[3] But even if it were true, it
would not necessarily imply a failure of duty by Gulland. The officials of the Liberal Party no doubt saw that a crash was coming, and
perceived that there was nothing they could do to avert catastrophe.

---

[1] Samuel papers A/56, fol. 13 (Memorandum of 7 December 1916); McGill,
op. cit., p. 295.
[2] Countess Lloyd George's introduction to Malcolm Thomson, *David Lloyd
George* (London 1948), p. 24.
[3] Discussion of Sir Eric Drummond's statement in McGill, *op. cit.*, p. 300 n.

7

The Coupon Election

οὐκ ἔστιν οὐδὲν δεινὸν ὧδ' εἰπεῖν ἔπος,
οὐδὲ πάθος οὐδὲ συμφορὰ θεήλατος,
ἧς οὐκ ἂν ἄραιτ' ἄχθος ἀνθρώπου φύσις.

*There is nothing terrible which may be told – neither suffering
nor divine visitation – which may not be the lot of man.*

EURIPIDES, *Orestes*, 1–3

'We have been swept away as no Party ever was, or ever will be
again.'

Those were the words of the Liberal Party's chief professional
worker, Sir Robert Hudson,[1] a few days after the results of the 1918
General Election had been declared. Hudson was an organizer of
vast experience, and not a man given to extravagant hyperbole. It
therefore falls upon us to examine the origins, the course, and the
conclusion of this catastrophic election.

On 8 December 1916, the day after Lloyd George assumed office
as Prime Minister, Asquith addressed a meeting of Liberal members
of both Houses at the Reform Club in London.[2] In the course of a
factual description of events, he clarified several matters which were
in doubt.

He explained that he had acted upon the advice of friends and
colleagues in refusing himself to accept office under Lloyd George,
and that he had advised his Ministerial colleagues, both individually
and collectively, on what action they should take if they were approached to join the new Government: 'Exercise your own judgement; consider how you can best serve them. If you think you can

---

[1] J. A. Spender, *Sir Robert Hudson*, p. 162. Letter from Hudson to Frank Wright,
2 January 1919.
[2] *Liberal Magazine*, 1916, pp. 621–6.

serve them by going in, for God's sake go in; if you can best serve them by remaining with me outside, stay outside. I do not quarrel with your judgement or attempt to exercise any pressure upon you one way or the other.'

Asquith also made clear his own position in relation to the Liberal leadership: 'We are here today because I felt it my duty to resign, not the leadership of our party, though I am quite prepared to do that if I am asked, but I have been compelled to resign the headship of the Government.'

The same meeting, at which prominent partisans of Lloyd George were present, affirmed its 'unabated confidence' in Asquith as Leader of the Liberal Party.

Asquith took his new seat in the House of Commons in the place recognized for the Leader of the Opposition, and he performed the procedural and ceremonial functions usually associated with that office.[1]

* * *

Once the new Government had been formed, there were two quite separate Liberal bodies in Parliament. Asquith was unquestionably Leader of the Liberal Party, and John Gulland remained the Chief Liberal Whip. But one of the offices which any Prime Minister must fill is that of Parliamentary Secretary to the Treasury, which is the official designation of the Chief Government Whip in the Commons. When Asquith formed his Coalition in May 1915, he appointed two men to hold the post jointly: John Gulland, for the Liberals, and Lord Edmund Talbot for the Unionists. When Lloyd George took office in December 1916, Gulland, like the other close associates of Asquith, either was not invited to continue in office or refused. Lloyd George first tried to persuade Cecil Harmsworth – brother of the 'Press Lords' Northcliffe and Rothermere – to become Chief Government Liberal Whip,[2] but on Harmsworth's refusal, contrived with some difficulty to secure Neil Primrose, son of Lord Rosebery.[3] In 1917, Primrose was replaced by Capt. F. E. ('Freddie') Guest, and a few months later was killed in the war.

[1] *Ibid.*, p. 629, both text and footnote.
[2] Harmsworth to Lloyd George, 1 May 1917. Lloyd George papers F/87/1/1.
[3] Lloyd George/Primrose correspondence, 12–13 December 1916. Lloyd George papers F/42/11/1–3.

'Freddie' Guest demands a great deal of attention in our studies. He was a son of Viscount Wimborne, and connected by marriage to Winston Churchill. Like his more famous relative, he had originally been a Conservative. His father's peerage had been conferred by Beaconsfield, but the family had moved to the Liberals at the time of the Tariff Reform controversy. Guest had been one of the junior Liberal Whips under Asquith from 1911 to 1915.

While Asquith, in his capacity as Leader of the Liberal Party, presided over the 'official' organization of the Party, operated by John Gulland as Chief Whip from the Liberal offices in Abingdon Street, Lloyd George presided over a completely separate organization operated first by Primrose and later by Guest from the Treasury offices in Downing Street. It appears that the Lloyd George whip was sent to all Liberal M.P.s, whatever their sympathies,[1] and it may be reasonably assumed that the Asquithians did the same.

The two Liberal organizations faced difficulties in Parliamentary by-elections. The 'Party Truce' arrangements expired at the end of 1916, and were not officially renewed at the time, although the good sense of all concerned ensured their continuance in practice until the Armistice. Several attempts were made to secure a renewed arrangement with four signatures instead of three – the two Liberal Whips acting separately. But it remained uncertain which Liberal organization should fill the vacancy when a Liberal seat fell vacant. Arrangements were made *ad hoc* between Gulland and the Government Liberal Whip. In July 1918, Guest complained to Lloyd George[2] that:

'In practice the only seats which the official Liberal Party are prepared to concede to us are:
 1. Those held by Liberal Ministers.
 2. Those where the official party machine has no hopes of getting a candidate of their own complexion returned.'

Thus, after the death of Neil Primrose in 1917, the selection of a candidate for his seat of Wisbech was left to Guest; but at Banbury in 1918, even though the retiring M.P. had been a Lloyd Georgeite,

[1] T. Lough's letter to Guest, *Manchester Guardian*, 23 November 1918.
[2] Guest to Lloyd George, 6 July 1918. Lloyd George papers F/21/1/25.

an Asquithian was at first proposed.[1] When a Liberal Association sought a candidate, the application was normally made to Liberal Headquarters, and Gulland naturally recommended people who were acceptable to his own organization.

Before the end of the war, the Lloyd Georgeites had considerably extended their political machine. In order to secure the nomination of Lloyd George candidates, they divided the country into areas considerably smaller than the Federations of the 'official' Liberals, and established such local contacts as they could.

In spite of the existence of these separate organizations, Asquith for a long time exerted all his authority to prevent any action being taken which might embarrass the Government, seeking by example to preserve national unity.[2] But he would not serve under Lloyd George, and refused the office of Lord Chancellor when it was offered to him in May 1917.

Social contacts between the two men did not entirely break down,[3] but the division between them gradually grew deeper. Thus, when E. S. Montagu, hitherto reckoned an Asquithian, joined the Cabinet in June 1917, Asquith wrote to him in terms very different from those which he had used to the Liberals six months earlier – indicating that he found it 'difficult to understand, and still more difficult to appreciate, your reasons for the course which you propose to take. But, in these matters, every man must be guided by his own judgement and conscience.'[4]

Asquith's stoical refusal to rally his colleagues for a Party attack on the Government was maintained even when that Government was violating Liberal precepts in a manner not necessitated by the exigencies of war. In March 1917, he would not act as the centre of disaffection when the Government sought to introduce protection for the Indian cotton industry. Nor would he make the Irish question a matter for Party dispute. In April 1918, the Government sought power to apply conscription to Ireland by Order in Council. The Liberals were severely split – sixty-six supporting the Government

[1] Guest to Lloyd George, 24 November 1917 and 6 July 1918. Lloyd George papers F/21/2/8 and 25.

[2] See Roy Jenkins, *Asquith*, p. 465.

[3] Dame Margaret Lloyd George to Lloyd George, 7 June (? or January) 1918. Lloyd George papers I/1/2/33; Grey to Runciman, 5 June 1918. Runciman papers.

[4] Asquith to Montagu, 19 June 1917. Asquith papers 18, fol. 11–14.

and thirty-nine voting against it – yet Asquith and his chief associates abstained from voting.[1] Nevertheless, some of Lloyd George's
more sensitive adherents, such as that remarkable political chame-
leon, Christopher Addison, were already beginning to resent
Asquith's very gentle criticisms of the Government right at the
beginning of 1918.

At the turn of 1917–18, the apparent stalemate in Europe led to a
very substantial movement in favour of a negotiated peace. A further
statement was issued by Lord Lansdowne – this time a letter published in the *Daily Telegraph* on 29 November 1917, which raised in
public the matters which had been the subject of his Cabinet memorandum a year earlier. Philip Kerr (later Marquis of Lothian) considered that Lansdowne had been inspired by Lord Loreburn, the
former Liberal Lord Chancellor, and suggested that, 'M'Kenna and
presumably the other Liberal leaders strongly approve of it.'[2]

It has been established that Lord Buckmaster, who was Lord
Chancellor during the first Coalition, took the same line as Lansdowne.[3] Thus Lloyd George had reason to believe that not only his
own Premiership and his particular methods, but also the whole
issue of fighting the war to a conclusion, might need to be tested.
Documents which were confidential at the time reinforce this view.
In late August 1917, McKenna wrote to Runciman, with astonishing
good sense:[4]

> 'Meanwhile I reflect on the war. Don't you think the time has
> come for us to make up our profit and loss account? A year of war
> costs us in round figures 250,000 dead, 250,000 permanently
> maimed, 500,000 other casualties, and £2,000,000,000 addition to
> the debt. What can we hope to get in return over and above what
> we could get now? Belgium and France we must have uncondi-
> tionally free. But beyond this we can look for nothing but giving
> Alsace and Lorraine, in whole or part, to France. No doubt a
> good thing, but is the chance of it worth the price? If the chances
> were a certainty I should be inclined to think the price too high,
> but it is far, far from a certainty. . . .'

[1] *The Times*, 15 April 1918, analyses the voting.
[2] Kerr to Lloyd George, 4 December 1917. Lloyd George papers F/89/1/9.
[3] Letter to A. G. Gardiner, 2 December 1917, cited by Trevor Wilson, *The
downfall of the Liberal Party*, p. 105.
[4] McKenna to Runciman, 27 August 1917. Runciman papers.

Some months later, Lewis Harcourt, another Liberal ex-Minister, wrote:[1] 'I fear this means that Ll.G. will carry on till someone – or *everyone* – is at the last gasp: then there will be a belated demand for a *man to make peace* and most people will turn to Ed. Grey.'

But there is not the slightest reason for thinking that Asquith himself ever inclined towards these views. The Lloyd Georgeites recognized this point; in August 1918 Guest wrote that the people who were prepared to enter into negotiations with the German Government included 'the Asquithians (except Mr Asquith)'.[2]

There was no clear picture of what the political line-up would be in a wartime election; but before the end of January 1918, Lloyd George's associates – including Addison, Guest, and Sir Gordon Hewart (the future Lord Chief Justice) – were actively discussing a possible programme for submission to the electorate.[3] The Unionists were prepared to contemplate an alliance for a wartime election, but they were anxious to ensure that the Coalition should not remain in office after the war – at least without a fresh appeal to the electorate.[4] For a long time the Lloyd George Liberals kept their minds open to examine a wide range of political possibilities.[5]

*   *   *

The matter which was to prove of greatest importance in deciding the orientation of parties arose unexpectedly. Early in May 1918, Maj.-Gen. Sir Frederick Maurice, who had recently been deposed from the post of Director of Military Operations, sent a letter to the Press, in which he contended that certain public statements of Lloyd George and Bonar Law on the subject of British military strength in France were false. Asquith demanded a Select Committee to inquire into the allegations. Bonar Law, for the Government, recommended a tribunal of two judges instead. The Opposition rejected this offer, and Asquith formally moved for a Select Committee.

Asquith did not discuss the merit or otherwise of Maurice's attack, but argued that the existence of the charges called for investigation.

---

[1] Lewis Harcourt to Runciman, 21 May 1918. Runciman papers.

[2] Guest to Lloyd George, 3 August 1918. Lloyd George papers F/21/2/30.

[3] Christopher (Viscount) Addison, *Politics from Within 1914–1918*, ii, p. 242.

[4] Sir George Younger to Bonar Law, 16 March 1918. Bonar Law papers 83/1/9.

[5] This and other aspects of the period are discussed by the present author in 'The background to the "Coupon" election arrangements', *Eng. Hist. Review*, (awaiting publication).

Lloyd George treated the issue as one of confidence, and defended the Government against the substance of Maurice's charges – thus destroying not only the idea of a Select Committee but also the Government's own proposal for a judicial inquiry. On the Division[1] the Government won by 295 votes to 108, including tellers. The minority consisted of ninety-eight Liberals, nine Labour members, and one Unionist. Seventy-one Liberals supported the Government. For the first time, and for the only time in that Parliament, the official Liberal Whips told one way and the Government Whips told the other.

It is likely that Asquith went to his grave believing that Lloyd George had lied, while Lloyd George went to his believing that Asquith had clutched at the straw of some unsubstantiated assertions by an unbalanced soldier, in his desperate desire to wreak revenge on the Government. There is now evidence[2] that Lloyd George was relying on information supplied by Maurice's own department, which was later corrected – but that, through failure by Lloyd George's secretariat, the Prime Minister did not see the correction. But some doubt has been cast even on this apparently plausible explanation.[3]

The figures of the division suggest such a massive Government victory that the issue was never in doubt. This was far from being the case, for several accidents were of crucial importance. The Irish M.P.s, who might have been expected to support Asquith, were so profoundly disaffected that they were out of the country. The Unionist leaders apparently believed before the debate that the Government figures were wrong and Maurice was right, but decided for political reasons to support the Government.[4] At least one prominent Unionist M.P. has gone on record with the admission that he was swayed by the Prime Minister's arguments.[5] Indeed, the natural reaction of Conservatives confronted with a dispute between politici-

---

[1] Parl. Deb. (Commons) cv, 9 May 1918, col. 2,401.

[2] Lord Beaverbrook, *Men and Power 1917–1918*, pp. 262–3.

[3] See Lord Templewood (Sir Samuel Hoare), *The Spectator*, 2 November 1956, p. 676, and the correspondence which it provoked – especially the letters of Nancy Maurice (16 November and 7 December) and of the Dowager Countess Lloyd George (23 November).

[4] Letter of Lady Violet Bonham-Carter (Lady Asquith) to Viscount Templewood, 24 October 1956. Templewood papers, xvii, 9.

[5] Lord Templewood, *op. cit.*

ans and soldiers would be to support the soldiers. The Maurice debate seriously threatened the Government's existence from an extraordinary coalition of very disparate people: the Irish who could not forgive the wrongs of their own country; the pacifists who opposed the Government on principle; the Asquithian leaders who had not forgotten December 1916 – and some of whom were contemplating a negotiated peace; the Liberal rank and file who would normally look to their official leaders; and the mass of Unionist M.P.s who resented Lloyd George's continual 'interference with the soldiers'. More by luck than judgement the Government had won a resounding victory; but no one could be sure that another challenge would not succeed at a later date.

On the day after the Maurice debate, Cecil Harmsworth, one of the Liberal M.P.s who had voted with the Government, wrote to Walter Runciman, who had supported Asquith:[1]

'There seems to be a dangerous likelihood of this division becoming permanent.

'If, as I think I said on a former occasion, such a division took place on a point of vital principle, I should have nothing more to say. But what is Genl. Maurice to us, or are we to Genl. Maurice? & why should it be assumed that on a point of principle the Liberals in the Govt. must necessarily take a different, and antagonistic, stand from that of Liberals outside the Govt.? I am equally familiar with both sides & observe no such rigid divergence. Is it yet too late to stop the rot?'

But whether men like Harmsworth liked it or not, the gage was down after the Maurice debate, and the partisans of Asquith and Lloyd George began to take up their respective positions.

As in the Boer War, the Liberal Press was a field of conflict. There were four Liberal newspapers of national importance: the *Daily News*, the *Daily Chronicle*, the *Manchester Guardian*, and the *Westminster Gazette*. The *Daily News* was controlled by its staunchly Asquithian editor A. G. Gardiner, and the *Westminster Gazette* by the no less staunch Asquithian J. A. Spender. The redoubtable C. P. Scott of the *Manchester Guardian* was not the sort of man whom any politician could ever have in his pocket, but for the time being his sympathies

[1] Cecil Harmsworth to Runciman, 10 May 1918. Runciman papers.

lay strongly with Lloyd George. The *Daily Chronicle* was edited by Robert Donald. In earlier times he had been a Lloyd Georgeite, but by 1918 he was becoming increasingly hostile to the Government, and virtually declared war on the Prime Minister in May 1918 by appointing Major-General Maurice as his newspaper's military correspondent.[1]

Lloyd George now determined to secure control of the *Daily Chronicle*. Early in October,[2] it was announced that Sir Henry Dalziel, a Lloyd George Liberal M.P., acting for himself and associates, had bought outright the business of the *Daily Chronicle* and *Lloyd's Weekly News*. It subsequently transpired that a company had been formed to purchase these two papers, and also a controlling interest in the *Edinburgh Evening News* and the *Yorkshire Evening News*; and that the trustees of the 'Lloyd George Fund' – an entity which we shall later need to consider at some length – had taken 525,251 out of 616,498 ordinary shares in that company.[3] From then until the *Daily Chronicle* was eventually sold, that newspaper was the mouthpiece of Lloyd George.

* * *

Before the Maurice debate, there had apparently been a lull in the discussions between Lloyd Georgeites and Unionists on the question of a wartime General Election – perhaps as a result of division among the Unionists. But the debate, and the adverse fortunes of war about the same time, increased the likelihood of such an election, and on 12 July 1918 a meeting of Lloyd Georgeites was held, under Addison's chairmanship, to consider a programme.[4] On the following day, Guest wrote to the Prime Minister,[5] urging the immediate conclusion of an agreement with the Unionists over candidates, and also that steps should be taken to draw up an agreed programme.

For a long time yet, it was by no means clear whether an election appeal would be made by Lloyd George personally, or whether he would be in alliance with the Unionists, and this uncertainty considerably handicapped the Lloyd Georgeites in their organization

---

[1] For Maurice's reply to the Prime Minister, see *Daily Chronicle*, 17 May 1918.
[2] *The Times*, 5 October 1918.
[3] Sir Ivor Jennings, *Party Politics*, ii, p. 264.
[4] Addison, *op. cit.*, ii, p. 246.
[5] Guest to Lloyd George, 13 July 1918. Lloyd George papers F/21/2/27.

work.[1] But discussion with the Unionists about a possible wartime
election persisted, and Guest was still apparently assuming that the
contest would be held in these circumstances when he wrote to Lloyd
George on 3 August.[2] By 25 September, the idea of an alliance seems
to have been approved by the Prime Minister, for his associates compiled a memorandum, entitled 'Suggestions for terms of a definite
alliance with the Unionist Party'.[3] This document examines two
possible bases of agreement, one of which bears a striking resemblance to the terms which were eventually concluded after the
Armistice. Nevertheless, it was very far from certain that the Unionists would reciprocate, and on 5 October Bonar Law wrote to
Balfour, in evident apprehension that such an arrangement might
produce a split in the Unionist ranks.[4]

In spite of these negotiations with the Unionists, the Prime
Minister by no means abandoned the idea of a *rapprochement* with
Asquith. Late in September 1918, Lloyd George met Lord Murray –
the former Master of Elibank – who was virtually the only acceptable
intermediary between himself and Asquith. The Prime Minister and
Murray parted 'with the understanding that off [his] own bat
[Murray] would propose to Mr A. a reconstructed Government in
which he should hold the post of *Lord Chancellor, and nominate two of
the Principal Secretaries of State, and six Under Secretaries*'.[5] The proposed
'deal' included the passage of Home Rule with the exclusion of
Ulster, and the application of conscription to Ireland. There should
also be an immediate General Election. Lord Murray considered
that Lloyd George, 'wishes to be in a position of issuing orders; at
present he can do nothing without negotiations. Therefore, he wants
a General Election because he thinks now is the moment to "market
his popularity".'

When Murray met Asquith, however, he discovered, 'that the one
fact that Lloyd George wants a General Election to him made such
a proposition unworkable. . . . "Moreover I am by no means prepared to accept L.G.'s Irish policy . . ." Mr Asquith added that he

[1] Guest to Lloyd George, enclosing notes of Sir Henry Norman, 19 September
1918. Lloyd George papers F/21/2/29.
[2] Guest to Lloyd George, 3 August 1918. Lloyd George papers F/21/2/30.
[3] Guest to Lloyd George, 25 September 1918. Lloyd George papers F/21/2/40.
[4] R. Blake, *The unknown Prime Minister*, p. 384.
[5] Memorandum of meeting with Lloyd George, 24 September 1918. Elibank
papers 8,804, fol. 193–6.

K

had no wish to become Lord Chancellor, and never had any, and that my information that Lloyd George would sweep the country by no means tallied with his own.'[1]

From this encounter, Murray drew the baleful conclusion: 'Unless I am very much mistaken, in these two conversations I have been present at the obsequies of the Liberal Party as I knew it.'[2]

For some time yet, the Lloyd Georgeites remained in doubt about the position of the Asquithians, and in his negotiations with the Unionists, Guest left the door carefully open for the possible admission of Asquith and some of his associates into the Government.[3] Guest gave his very shrewd estimate of the attitude of Liberal supporters in the country:

'The bulk of the officers of the Associations, and practically all the Agents, are firmly Asquithian, but in many parts of the country the hold of the Association machinery over the rank and file would depend, at the Election, upon
(1) the personality and qualifications of the candidate, and
(2) the programme you put forward.'

Even this letter, written three weeks before the Armistice, implies that at least part of the duty of the next Parliament would be the prosecution of the war.

By 29 October, however, the die was cast. Guest wrote to Lloyd George that he had concluded an agreement with Law to the effect that the Unionists would support 150 Lloyd George candidates – while, in addition, 'all Labour candidates who support you will be to the good'.[4] On 2 November, Lloyd George wrote to Bonar Law with formal proposals for the continuance of the Coalition into peacetime, and for an early General Election. The Unionists took some time in replying, and it was not until 12 November, the day after the Armistice, that they accepted the proposals.

On the same day, a meeting of Liberal supporters of the Coalition was held, and Lloyd George indicated that he and Bonar Law would

[1] Runciman's judgement was better. See Runciman to Samuel, 5 January 1919. Samuel papers A/46, fol. 9.

[2] *Idem.*

[3] Guest to Lloyd George, 21 October 1918. Lloyd George papers F/21/2/43. Compare also Addison, *op. cit.*, ii, p. 249.

[4] Guest to Lloyd George, 29 October 1918.

fight the forthcoming General Election with the Coalition intact, under a joint manifesto. Declaring that he had done nothing in the past two years to make him ashamed to meet his fellow-Liberals, he added, 'Please God, I am determined that I never shall'.[1] On the following day Asquith said that this speech was a perfectly clear and satisfactory statement of Liberal policy, and did not impede the unity of the Liberal Party.[2]

Asquith continued to oppose the idea of an early General Election – indeed, the King held the same view.[3] But the decision had been taken, and a formal announcement of the impending dissolution was made by Bonar Law on 14 November.

Just after the Armistice, Lloyd George again offered the Lord Chancellorship to Asquith, although perhaps in a rather perfunctory manner.[4] Again it was refused. How the Prime Minister's relations with the Unionists would have been sorted out if the answer had been different is an interesting subject of speculation.

The Coalition's Manifesto was issued over the signatures of Lloyd George and Bonar Law on 22 November. On the whole it was a document very acceptable to Liberals, but it foreshadowed some illiberal fiscal policies. For some time, Lloyd George continued to talk language which, while not of the highest Cobdenite orthodoxy, was at least consistent with Liberal ideas on other subjects. On 24 November, he asked rhetorically, 'What is our task?', and replied, 'To make Britain a country fit for heroes to live in!' That answer was destined to plague him for many a long day.

But the attitude of the public as a whole was completely different. In working-class districts in particular, the main interest seemed to be revenge.[5] Lloyd George, ever sensitive to popular feeling, began to talk the same language. By 11 December, he was urging that Britain should 'exact the last penny we can get out of Germany to the limit of her capacity' – and his supporters were speaking much stronger language than that.

Although Guest had apparently expected a good deal of Labour support for the Coalition, the Labour Party decided by a convincing majority to withdraw. The most profound change had in fact come

[1] *Daily Chronicle*, 13 November 1918.
[2] *Manchester Guardian*, 14 November 1918.
[3] Harold Nicolson, *King George V*, pp. 328–30.
[4] Roy Jenkins, *Asquith*, pp. 476–7.
[5] Wilson, *op. cit.*, p. 40.

over the Labour Party in the previous fifteen months. In August 1917, Arthur Henderson left the Government in circumstances of bitter and mutual recrimination, and devoted his energies to the task of remodelling the Labour organization, and – even more important – eliciting large sums of money from Trade Unions, whose political funds were lying idle, and could not lawfully be used for any other kind of activity. In June 1918, a policy drafted by Sidney and Beatrice Webb was accepted by the Party Conference. Men who had known the Labour Party before 1914 took years to take the measure of the new entity with which they were dealing.

A small number of former Labour men – of whom the chief examples are G. N. Barnes and G. H. Roberts – continued to support the Government, and stood without Labour backing. There was also a comparatively new and quite separate organization, the National Democratic Party (N.D.P.), whose supporters are sometimes confused with these 'Coalition Labour' men. Some, but not all, of the N.D.P. candidates were former Labour Party men, or were of working-class origin, or both. A number of them had evidently been put forward with the primary object of unseating Liberal or Labour M.P.s whose attitude to the war had been unacceptable to the Government. Among these was Clem Edwards, who had sat as a Liberal M.P. for a Welsh seat in the old House, and who stood against Arthur Henderson in East Ham South.

*   *   *

Although the Lloyd George Liberals and the Unionist leaders had established their own *concordat*, both Liberal and Unionist Parties had local organizations in almost every British constituency – even though they had been partly dismantled during the war – and these organizations were anxious to derive what benefit they could from the election. A glance through the election literature of the period shows how very difficult it was to determine which candidates were Government supporters and which were not. It would require a very astute voter indeed to pick through their varying reservations. The greater the detail with which the election addresses are examined, the more confused the whole situation is seen to be. The test which the voters were eventually offered was not what the candidates said, but what the Coalition leaders said.

The official approval of the leaders was conveyed in the form of a

letter signed jointly by Lloyd George and Bonar Law. A number of
these approval letters were quoted in candidates' election addresses.
Those letters which the author has seen were all dated 20 November
1918, and all had the same form:

'Dear . . .
'We have much pleasure in recognizing you as the Coalition
Candidate for . . .
'We have every hope that the Electors will return you as their
Representative in Parliament to support the Government in the
great task which lies before it.

'Yours truly,
'D. Lloyd George.
'A. Bonar Law.'

These letters of support were dubbed 'Coupons' by Asquith, by
analogy with the tickets employed in wartime rationing.

In a considerable number of cases, there is still doubt whether a
candidate received the Coupon or not. This particularly applies to
some of the Liberal candidates who were returned unopposed. There
were a few other cases of Liberal candidates who apparently did not
receive the Coupon, but who had no Unionist opponent, and where
the circumstances strongly suggest that some collusive arrangement
had been reached.[1] With reservations of this kind, the approximate
number of recipients of the Coupon were 364 Unionists, 159 Liberals,
and 20 N.D.P. candidates. Thus, for about sixty British seats there
were no Coupons issued. In Ireland, the only recipients of the
Coupon seem to have been the two Unionists in Cork City – both of
whom fared disastrously. When the allocation of the Coupons is examined in detail, it illustrates the immense confusion which sur-
rounded the whole election.[2]

In some cases, it was obvious enough to whom the Coupon would

---

[1] A classification of the Liberals who were elected is given in Guest's letter to
Lloyd George, 30 December 1918 (Lloyd George papers F/21/2/56). Unfortunately
there are a number of omissions and several demonstrable inaccuracies – and it
gives no help with the candidates who were not successful.

[2] The matter is discussed at length by Wilson in the book cited, in his paper
'The Coupon and the British General Election of 1918' (*J. Mod. Hist.* xxxvi (1964),
pp. 28–42), and in his Oxford D. Phil. thesis (1959), 'The Parliamentary Liberal
Party in Britain 1918–1924'.

go. Where a British M.P. was a Government supporter and sought
re-election he usually received the Coupon as a matter of course.
This rule could be applied easily enough to the Unionists. Outside
Ireland, all but four of the Unionists who sought re-election received
the Coupon. These four did not include Lt-Col. Herbert, who voted
against the Government in the Maurice debate. But it was excessively difficult to decide on a satisfactory test for Liberals. As a
general rule, Liberal M.P.s who supported the Government in the
Maurice debate received the Coupon, and Liberal M.P.s who voted
against the Government on that issue were denied the Coupon, but
this rule was not followed invariably. About eleven M.P.s who voted
against the Government received the Coupon, and about four who
supported the Government found that it was used for an opponent.

During the Maurice Debate, two Liberal M.P.s, W. M. R. Pringle
and J. M. Hogge, had indicated that Liberal supporters of the
Government had been promised immunity from Unionist attack
at the next General Election. Cecil Harmsworth, who was one of the
Liberals who supported the Government on that occasion, categori-
cally denied that any such suggestion had been made to him, or that
he had heard of its being made to anyone else.[1] Nevertheless, this
happened in most cases when the election came.

Vital as the Maurice Debate was for the election, it is possible to
overstate its importance. There was a substantial band of Liberals
who, not once but repeatedly, had voted against the Government
during the war, and who needed no prompting from the Liberal
Whips to continue doing so. Such people would obviously have been
refused Coalition support, whatever happened in that particular
division.

There were some other constituencies which could be disposed of
fairly simply – for example, places where one candidate was obviously a Government supporter and the other candidates were
opponents. Men with distinguished Service records also received
favourable treatment. In other places, the decision about Coupon
allocation was taken jointly by Sir George Younger, the Unionist
Chairman, and Capt. Guest, Chief Coalition Liberal Whip, and
their respective subordinates.

In some places, the situation was bedevilled by the uttermost
confusion. A few of the many examples must suffice. F. C. Thorn-

[1] Harmsworth to Runciman, 10 May 1918. Runciman papers.

borough,[1] of Morpeth, was a very staunch Asquithian, who had not sat in the old House. He was, therefore, amazed to receive a Coupon in the post one morning. It transpired that his Chairman at Blyth had a relative on Lloyd George's staff, who had procured the Coupon as a friendly act. Thornborough refused to use it, and an attempt to produce a rival candidate for whom it could be used failed; but if it had lain in his conscience to display it, there can be no doubt that he would have been returned, and duly recorded as a 'Coalition Liberal'.

Thornborough's case may be contrasted with that of H. J. Craig, who was defending his seat of Tynemouth. Craig had not voted in the Maurice debate. He issued to the local Unionists a statement of his attitude, which they considered to be satisfactory. Within hours of Lloyd George's announcement of 12 November, he saw Guest, informed him of his entire approval of the Premier's view, and indicated his intention to stand as a Coalition candidate. Guest told Craig to get into the field quickly, and hold a public meeting at once – which Craig did. Nevertheless, he learnt soon after that the Unionist would receive the Coupon. Craig tried in vain to persuade Guest, 'publicly and explicitly to explain in what respect my pledge of support to the Government . . . falls short of that which you have received from other candidates, both Liberal and Conservative, to whose candidature you have given your official approval'.

At Paisley, Liberal and Unionist disagreement resulted in a *tertius gaudens*. The outgoing Liberal M.P., Sir John McCallum, was on the Coalition black list over the Maurice debate, even though he had agreed to support the Coalition Government. Therefore the Liberals and Unionists compromised, and awarded the Coupon to the N.D.P. candidate.[2] However, McCallum contrived to hold the seat.

In most of the constituencies where no Coupon was issued, there seems to be a fairly simple explanation.[3] A special example was East Fife, where Asquith was being opposed by a Unionist. The Coupon could not be given to Asquith, while Lloyd George could hardly pose as a Liberal if he sanctioned its use against his nominal leader. Lloyd George afterwards claimed – and there seems no reason to dis-

---

[1] Personal communication to the author from the late F. C. Thornborough, J.P.
[2] W. Dudley Ward to J. T. Davies, 14 January 1920. Lloyd George papers F/22/1/1.
[3] Discussed in Wilson's D.Phil. thesis, pp. 59 *seq.*

believe him – that he and Bonar Law 'both deprecated the setting up
of a candidate against him and did our best to persuade him [the
candidate] to stand down, and when he finally refused to do so we
withheld the co-called "coupon" from him'.[1]

In four places[2] Coalition Liberals were actually set up against
nominees of the local Liberal Association. But there were many cases
where Coalition Liberals gave support to Coalition Unionists who
were opposing Liberals, and these doubtless caused great distress and
dissension. The effect of the Coupon was immediate and dramatic.
It is well described by (Sir) Percy Harris, who had sat as Liberal
M.P. for Harborough in the old House, and found the Coupon
issued to his Unionist opponent.[3]

'It took the electors completely by surprise. . . . It was interpreted
as a personal reflection on me in particular, and it was assumed
that I must have done something wrong for a member of my own
Party, Lloyd George, to sign a letter supporting my opponent.

'Until then all had been going well, but now my friends melted
away like snow in the night. I could get few speakers to come out
on my behalf. . . .'

This must have been a typical experience for a Liberal candidate
who had the Coupon used against him. Whatever the political
sophisticates might have known or understood, the great mass of the
voters had never thought of themselves as supporters or opponents
of the Coalition. If they had applied any label to themselves at all,
it was merely that of 'Liberal' or 'Unionist'. Many of them had had
no previous occasion to do even that.

The behaviour of some of the candidates scarcely helped to clarify
matters. We have already seen something of the antics of Barnet
Kenyon, of Chesterfield, in the 1913 by-election. In 1918 he stood as
a Liberal and was unopposed, although there seems some conflict of
authority as to whether he received the Coupon or not. Probably he
did. Certainly his nomination papers included the signatures of local
Unionist officials. Yet he gave his public support to the uncouponed

[1] Lloyd George to Haydn Jones, 18 November 1924. Lloyd George papers
G/30/3/41.
[2] Huddersfield, Caernarvon, Oldham, Berwick & Haddington.
[3] Sir Percy Harris, *Forty years in and out of Parliament*, p. 76.

Labour and Independent Unionist candidates who were contesting the two-member seat of Derby, even though there were a Liberal and an N.D.P. candidate also in the field; while in West Derbyshire, where the Coupon was given to the Unionist, Kenyon gave his equally public support to the Liberal.[1]

The Liberal Press was completely split.[2] Of the great Liberal newspapers, the *Daily News* and the *Westminster Gazette* were hostile to the Coalition, and the *Manchester Guardian* was now largely hostile; while the *Daily Chronicle* was – inevitably – favourable. The *Star*, the *Northern Echo*, and the *Liverpool Post* were hostile, while the *Glasgow Herald* was favourable.

The Representation of the People Act 1918 had altered the franchise profoundly. Almost every man over twenty-one, and almost every woman over thirty, received the vote. So, for the duration of the war only, did men over nineteen who were serving in the forces. The electorate was nearly three times as large as it had been before the war under the old 'household franchise'. When allowance is made for deaths and for people who had not reached voting age in 1910, it appears that at least three-quarters of the people who were qualified to vote in the 1918 General Election had never had a vote before at all, and many had had no 'political education' whatever in the ordinary sense of the term.

It is difficult to see how the Coalition could have failed to triumph. A pure Unionist Government was impossible because the Unionist leaders were pledged to continue the Coalition. A pure Liberal Government was impossible because there were only about 250 Liberal candidates in the field who were not committed to the Coalition. A pure Labour Government was theoretically possible, for there were a little under 400 Labour candidates – but no one can seriously have believed that it would happen. Perhaps some sort of Liberal–Labour alliance would have been credible, but again no one seems to have believed in it. A cursory glance at the disposition of candidates and the allocation of Coupons made it virtually certain that the Unionists would be the preponderant Party both in the Coalition and in the House.

These were the facts as they stood before the country went to the polls. Lloyd George has been accused of many things, but no one has

---

[1] *Derbyshire Courier*, 21 December 1918.
[2] Press attitudes are listed in detail in Lloyd George papers F/21/2/49.

suggested that he was other than astute, or that he was blind to political portents. Why, then, did he consent to this arrangement?

One of the strangest features of the whole business is the fact that Lloyd George not only failed to obtain more Coupons for his Liberal associates, but apparently did not attempt to secure agreement for more than 150 Liberal Coupons in total. Early in the campaign, Guest even wrote that, 'I do not think the Conservative Whips expect us to *realise* more than about 125.'[1]

The answer seems to be connected partly with arrangements which were being prepared as far back as July, when Lloyd George was contemplating a wartime election, whose underlying issue – whether stated in public or not – would be prosecution of the war *versus* peace negotiations. On 20 July, Guest sent Lloyd George detailed lists of Liberals who should not be opposed by the Unionists in a wartime election.[2] Ninety-eight names are listed, and another forty-four are suggested to be left over for further consideration. Guest also mentions sixteen candidates, who are not individually listed – making a grand total of 158. Eighty of the M.P.s listed for definite protection went to the polls in December, and of them seventy-seven either received the Coupon or had no Unionist opponent, or both. Twenty-seven of the 'possibles' went to the polls; eleven of them received Coupons, and a further five stood in places where no Coupon was issued. Furthermore, even where the Liberals for whom protection was sought or contemplated did not stand themselves, it was frequently granted to their Liberal successor. It very much looks as if the number 150 was conditioned more by the number of places where the local Liberals could be expected to nominate a Lloyd Georgeite than by the number of places where Lloyd George might – if he had wished – have granted Government support to a Liberal.

There has been much argument as to whether the Coupon was designed by Lloyd George to destroy the Liberals, or to save as many as he could from Unionist attack. He certainly had good reason to protect as many as he could of those Liberals whom he could trust to follow him wherever he led. On the other hand, if he had desired to protect the Liberal Party as a whole, he could have promulgated a programme so patently Liberal that the majority at least of the

[1] Guest to Lloyd George, 15 November 1918. Lloyd George papers F/21/2/47.
[2] Guest to Lloyd George, 20 July 1918. Lloyd George papers F/21/2/28.

Unionists would have been compelled to disavow him. He would be appealing to the country as Prime Minister, and his own *imprimatur* would be enough certification to help a goodly proportion of Liberal candidates to victory. The truth seems to be that Lloyd George was not much interested in whether he saved the Liberal Party or whether he destroyed it. Provided that he could command events, he cared little either for parties or for men.

*   *   *

The National Liberal Federation was an organization which encompassed all sorts and conditions of Liberals, and it was particularly anxious to prevent a rupture between Liberal supporters of the Coalition and Liberals who opposed it. On 22 November, the Executive issued a statement that:

> '. . . Liberal candidates should be free to promise support for the Coalition Government so long as it exists for the purpose of:
> (a) securing a clean and durable peace;
> (b) of promoting such consequential measures of social and political reconstruction as do not contravene in any vital particulars the declared policy of the Liberal Party.'

This statement begged some very important questions; but the Whips and the Liberal Central Association were no less concerned to avoid disruption. The policy and practice of Liberal Headquarters were set out soon after the election.[1]

> 'The Liberal Party fund [was] administered in the interests of the Party as a whole. Every legitimate effort [was] made to secure the adoption by Liberal Associations of Liberal candidates sound on the question of leadership, but where a Liberal Association adopted a candidate who [was] known to be an adherent of Mr Lloyd George the decision was loyally accepted by Headquarters. Before and during the election, general communications from Headquarters, from the National Liberal Federation and from the

[1] Statement prepared when seeking legal opinion to controvert any possible Coalition Liberal claim on Party funds. Undated, but from internal evidence written at the end of December 1918 or the beginning of January 1919. Asquith papers 148, fol. 71–92.

Liberal Publication Department were sent to every Association without any attempt at discrimination. Some of the candidates calling themselves Coalition Liberals either received from Liberal Headquarters or were promised, but did not claim, contributions towards their election expenses.'

Asquith was evidently concerned to preserve what unity he could, and would not pronounce emphatically against the Coalition. Like the N.L.F., he used formulae of uncertain import. But his Chief Whip, John Gulland, engaged in a lively and public controversy with Winston Churchill while the election was in progress.[1] Runciman went further. He examined the Liberal programme, and concluded that there was little hope of the Coalition putting it into effect.[2]

*   *   *

For the first time, all elections were held on the same day,[3] which on this occasion was Saturday 14 December 1918. An uneasy fortnight elapsed, during which the Forces' votes were collected, before the results were finally declared on 28 December.

The Coalition secured a massive landslide, with well over 470 seats. If the uncouponed Unionists are included (which, for all practical purposes, they may be), the number exceeds 520. The Coalition itself consisted overwhelmingly of Unionists, who outnumbered their Liberal partners by five to two. Outside the Coalition, the largest Party was Sinn Fein with seventy-three; but Sinn Fein could not constitute the Parliamentary opposition because its members refused to sit at Westminster. The next largest Party was Labour, with about sixty members, while the Asquithian Liberals were reduced to a figure which has been variously given within the range twenty-six to thirty-four.[4] The Irish Nationalists were down to seven, and there were a number of assorted 'oddments'.

[1] *Liberal Magazine*, 1918, pp. 651–4.
[2] *Ibid.*, pp. 669–70.
[3] Except for Kennington, where polling was delayed by the death of a candidate.
[4] In the author's view, the following twenty-nine Liberal M.P.s did not receive the 'Coupon': F. D. Acland, S. Arnold, W. Wedgwood Benn, Sir F. D. Blake, Sir T. A. Bramsdon, F. Briant, G. P. Collins, W. H. Cozens-Hardy, C. F. Entwistle, J. Gardiner, H. J. Glanville, J. M. Hogge, J. S. Holmes, S. G. Howard, H. H. Jones, J. D. Kiley, G. Lambert, Sir J. McCallum, J. A. M. Macdonald, Sir D.

Examined in further detail, the position thus baldly stated comes out in even sharper relief. In more then eight cases out of nine, the Coalition had piloted its candidate to Westminster.

The Labour Party made substantial overall advances, although less than some commentators had expected. But its candidates fared variously. The known or believed pacifists, like MacDonald and Snowden, were heavily defeated. Arthur Henderson also suffered defeat. Thus the Labour Party was practically leaderless in the House of Commons. But in industrial constituencies, Labour did not usually come worse than second in triangular contests – while before 1914 they had mostly run third.

The fate of the Asquithian Liberals was absolutely appalling. Asquith himself was two thousand votes behind a Unionist in East Fife, which the Liberal leader had represented for thirty-two years. *The Times* graphically describes the fate of his colleagues:[1]

'If Mr Asquith felt the whip, his principal associates were chastised with scorpions. All the Liberal ex-Ministers who followed him into opposition at the fall of the first Coalition Government were defeated. Other ex-Ministers who have thrown in their lot with him since suffered the same fate. His Chancellor of the Exchequer, Mr McKenna, two of his Home Secretaries, Mr Herbert Samuel and Sir John Simon, his President of the Board of Trade, Mr Runciman, two of his Secretaries for Scotland, Mr McKinnon Wood and Mr Tennant, his Postmaster General, Sir Charles Hobhouse,[2] and his Chief Whip, Mr Gulland, were all casualties. Their case differed from that of Mr Asquith in that they were not

Maclean, Dr D. Murray, J. T. Rees, T. Thomson, G. R. Thorne, C. F. White, A. Williams, P. Williams, J. W. Wilson, E. Hilton Young. Some M.P.s who received the 'Coupon' were never Government supporters, and some who did not receive it were supporters from the beginning. J. Havelock Wilson, whom the author regards as a Coalition Liberal, was certainly not a member of the N.D.P. Two M.P.s whose classification presented contemporaries with difficulties are still alive, and the author has consulted them. A. H. Moreing was a Coalition Liberal; F. V. Willey (Lord Barnby) was a Coalition Unionist.

[1] *The Times*, 30 December 1918.

[2] Hobhouse seems to have offered to surrender his constituency of Bristol East if Lloyd George would grant him a directorate of the Suez Canal Company. (Guest to Lloyd George, 15 November 1918; Lloyd George papers F/21/2/47.) Lloyd George followed Guest's advice – 'to leave him to flounder harmlessly in disgruntled and leaderless opposition'.

merely defeated but hopelessly outclassed.[1] Mr McKenna, Mr Runciman, Mr Herbert Samuel, Sir Charles Hobhouse, Mr McKinnon Wood, and Mr Tennant were engaged in three-cornered contests. All six were at the bottom of the poll with Coalition and Labour candidates above them. Two or three obtained only an insignificant fraction of the total number of votes polled; Mr McKinnon Wood and Sir Charles Hobhouse made such a poor showing, with little more than 1,000 votes in each case, that they actually forfeited their deposit of £150 by polling less than one-eighth of the total number of votes recorded. . . . The fate which befell Mr Gulland overtook all his Assistant Whips, Mr Geoffrey Howard, Mr Walter Rea, and Sir Arthur Marshall. Only three non-Coalition Liberals who have ever sat on a Front Bench survived the catastrophe – Mr George Lambert, Mr F. D. Acland, and Captain Wedgwood Benn. . . . None of the three has held office of Cabinet rank. . . .'

Even among the tattered band who did scramble home, good luck played a large part. Less than twenty had defeated a Coalition opponent. Fewer still had withstood a three-cornered contest.

The Liberal pacifists were blotted out to a man. C. P. Trevelyan in Elland, R. L. Outhwaite in Hanley, and D. M. Mason in Coventry were not even supported by their Liberal Associations, and stood as Independents with Asquithian Liberals among their opponents. E. T. John had already defected to the Labour Party. Noel Buxton in North Norfolk was nominated as a Liberal, but was narrowly defeated by an independent supporter of the Coalition.

The naïve, or optimistic, Liberal could set a cheerful face on these results. He could argue that there were over 160 Liberals in the House of Commons to about 380 or so Unionists and about 60 Labour representatives. No doubt many of the Unionists owed their election to the fact that they had fought in the shadow of Lloyd George, and would soon be out of the House. The slaughter of Liberal leaders was fearful – but, then, there had been a massive slaughter of prominent Unionists twelve years earlier. Was 1918 any more than 1906 in

[1] This is a considerable exaggeration. Asquith was 2,002 votes behind the victor in what was virtually a straight fight (there was a third candidate, an Independent, but he only polled 591 votes). McKenna, Runciman, and Samuel were all within 2,800 votes of the victor in contests against Unionist and Labour opponents. Samuel actually approached the victor more closely than did Asquith.

reverse? The Liberals were still undeniably the second Party of the
State. They had an immensely impressive band of leaders, still available to assume public office. There were innumerable people
throughout the land who thought of themselves as Liberals, and who
had not even begun to think of transferring their allegiance elsewhere. Would not the Government eventually lose popularity, fall
from office, and thus make way for the Liberals to return to their
inheritance?

But to those who dared read the signs of the times, the situation
was far graver than this facile view suggested. Confidence had been
utterly shattered. Many Liberals accepted, in part at least, the
calumnies of Northcliffe and the other Press lords, who considered
Asquith a drifter who had only been removed in the nick of time to
save the country from defeat. Others would never be brought to
trust Lloyd George again. Here was the genesis of the splits and
schisms which would tear the Liberal Party to pieces in the ensuing
fifteen years.

PUNCH, OR THE LONDON CHARIVARI.   [JUNE 2, 1915.

THE COMING OF THE COALITION.

[With acknowledgments to GUIDO RENI's fresco of Phœbus, Aurora and the Hours in the Palazzo Rospigliosi at Rome.]

from left to right: Viscount Grey, Sir Edward Carson, Sir Austen Chamberlain, Asquith, Winston Churchill, [?] Walter
Long, A. J. Balfour, Marquis of Lansdowne, Lloyd George, Bonar Law.)

8

The Hard-Faced Men

*'. . . filled with hard-faced men who looked as though they had
done very well out of the war'.*
Description of the 1919–22 House of Commons, attributed
uncertainly to STANLEY BALDWIN

One hill cannot shelter two tigers. – Chinese proverb.

When the results of the 1918 General Election were declared, there
was a superficial similarity between the positions of the Liberal and
Unionist Parties in the House of Commons. In both Parties, the
majority of M.P.s had pledged support for the Government and had
received the Coupon. In both Parties there was a not inconsiderable
minority who had been elected without the Coupon, or even in
defiance of the Coupon. Few M.P.s in either Party had fought their
campaign in open and general opposition to the Government, and
therefore there was no necessary implication that any substantial
group either of Liberals or of Unionists would regard themselves as
members of a true Opposition.

But there was a great practical difference between the two Parties.
The leading Unionists were all either members of the Government
or pledged to support it. Many of the leading figures of the Liberal
Party had deliberately excluded themselves from the Government,
and were acquiring an increasing reputation as critics of the administration.

At the end of 1918, the Liberal Party was, ostensibly, a single and
united body. No Liberal had formally challenged Asquith's position
as Leader of the Party – although whether Liberals were prepared
to follow his lead was a very different matter. Nor was it by any
means clear which Liberals would support whom if it did come to a
showdown, and both Asquithian and Lloyd Georgeite officials took

a pretty sanguine view of the extent of their own support. The *Liberal Year Books* seem to imply that all Liberals who had not received the Coupon could be considered Asquithians. Capt. Guest's analysis of the Liberal M.P.s, compiled for Lloyd George's benefit immediately after the election, was even more unrealistic, for he lists only five M.P.s as 'hostile' to the Government and five more as 'doubtful'.[1] As the Liberals whom Guest 'understood to be friendly' included such intransigents as Frank Briant, J. D. Kiley, and F. D. Acland, it is certain that Guest had been grossly misinformed. Some uncouponed Liberals, like Sir Francis Blake, had evidently been omitted from the Government list by accident, just as Liberals like P. W. Raffan, who were never Lloyd Georgeites, had received the Coupon by accident.

Nor were those Liberals who managed to scramble home without the Coupon a uniform group in any way. They were not noticeably concentrated in particular regions of the country. They did not represent any particular brand of Liberalism to a preponderant extent – but were, in fact, a more or less random sample of all the various attitudes which Liberals held on policy questions.

We often call them 'Asquithians', as if they were distinguished by some strong personal allegiance to their Leader – but nothing of the kind was true. Some were very soon reconciled to Lloyd George and estranged from Asquith. Men like J. M. Hogge and H. J. Glanville, who had sat in the old House, had voted again and again in the division lobbies not merely against Lloyd George's Coalition, but also against Asquith's – and, for that matter, against Asquith's Government before the war. It is probably true to say that every one of the uncouponed Liberals who was returned in 1918 could be matched with another Liberal who held very similar opinions who had received the Coupon, while there were other Asquithians – or Independent Liberals, as they were often called – from whom he differed sharply. If we may be permitted to glance ten or fifteen years ahead, each group included men who would remain Liberals for the rest of their days, men who were destined to join the Labour Party, and men who would finish up, actually or for all practical purposes, members of the Conservative Party.

The Asquithians had suffered disaster at the polls, but they still

[1] Guest to Lloyd George, 30 December 1918, where the M.P.s are listed. Lloyd George papers F/21/2/56. See also F/21/3/5.

L

retained great assets. The central 'machine' of the Liberal Party was theirs. The loyalty of the permanent officials and of all the Area organizations outside Wales was not in doubt. Quite apart from any ideological considerations, many of these organizations received large subventions from Asquithian headquarters. As recently as 22 March 1918, the General Committee of the N.L.F. had formally re-affirmed its confidence in Asquith's leadership.[1] The Asquithians retained the prestige and goodwill associated with the name 'Liberal' among those innumerable people who regarded the Liberal Party as their friend, and who could be expected to go on voting Liberal for the rest of their lives, whoever happened to be the leader and where-ever he happened to lead.

The central funds of the Party, at that particular moment, were in a very healthy state, even though there had been no contributions since 1916,[2] and a sum of a little under £100,000 had been disbursed on candidates' expenses during the 1918 election.[3] Five years, and two General Elections, later, the annual disbursements were still estimated at £50,000 (not counting special General Election ex-penses) – of which £30,000 went to the upkeep of Headquarters and the Federations, and £20,000 in grants to the constituencies.[4]

Just after the election, the *Manchester Guardian* explained the power of the Chief Whip over Party finance:[5]

'The central party fund is in his hands entirely. Morally it is a trust for the Party, legally it is his personal property, and if he chose to go away to South America with it he would commit no offence against the law. The Chief Whip is appointed by the Liberal Leader of the day, but he does not need to recognize any change in Liberal leadership. He has, in fact, the practical power to say which Liberal leader he recognizes.'

*   *   *

[1] Typed memorandum, 'The Liberal Leadership', December 1918/January 1919. Asquith papers 148, fol. 79.
[2] Viscount Gladstone to Asquith, 1 August 1924. Asquith papers 34, fol. 133.
[3] Asquith papers 141, fol. 1.
[4] Notes of meeting between Guest and Geoffrey Howard, 19 December 1923. Lloyd George papers G/8/13/1.
[5] *Manchester Guardian*, 31 December 1918.

Asquith and Gulland had both lost their seats at the General Election. There were precedents for a Liberal Leader without a seat in the House of Commons, but a Chief Whip could not possibly discharge his duties unless he was an M.P. Asquith, while he remained Leader, was presumably entitled to appoint a new Chief Whip – although this right was soon to be challenged – but anyone whom he appointed might decide to recognize a different Leader. Furthermore, if Asquith relinquished the leadership, or if he could be deposed from the leadership, then in whose hands did the choice of a new Leader lie?

The majority of organized Liberals in the country were probably not followers of Lloyd George at the end of 1918, and were most certainly not followers of Lloyd George a year later. Yet Gulland at first anticipated that the Liberal M.P.s would meet and elect Lloyd George leader. He did not consider it likely that Lloyd George would claim the funds, but indicated that he was 'preparing to defend them'.[1]

Certain parliamentary arrangements needed to be made at once. John Gulland wrote to Walter Runciman[2] that:

'The situation in the House is not an easy one. It is very difficult to draw accurately a list of the free men, and to differentiate between the Coalition Liberals and the others. We [that is, Asquith, Gulland, and a few others] rather came to the conclusion that it was not wise in the meantime to attempt to distinguish between them, but to hope for an early issue that would bring men definitely to our side. Nothing definite has been settled, but it looks as if Donald Maclean would lead our men in the House and Wedgwood Benn be Whip.'

But the decision to appoint a Parliamentary Leader and a Chief Whip inevitably implied separation sooner or later. Indeed, if for any reason Asquith had not been prepared to make such a separation, there is no doubt that many Liberals both in Parliament and in the country would very soon have sought affiliation elsewhere.

*   *   *

[1] Gulland to Runciman, 4 January 1919. Runciman papers.
[2] *Idem.*

At the beginning of the new Parliamentary session, on 3 February 1919, a meeting of Liberal M.P.s who were regarded as opponents of the Government was held. This meeting was convened by Capt. Wedgwood Benn,[1] who at one time had been a junior Whip, but it does not seem clear on what basis the invitations were issued. Twenty-three M.P.s attended.[2] Even in this tiny nest there were several cuckoos. Lt-Com. Hilton Young was later to become Chief Whip of the Lloyd George group. George Lambert and Godfrey Collins were also to become prominent on the Government side. Josiah Wedgwood's candidature has been given various appellations, but 'Independent Radical' seems to fit him best. However, he joined the I.L.P. and took the Labour whip soon after the meeting.

There was much confusion and argument to cross purposes.[3] Not without opposition, this group of M.P.s agreed to the motion that they should constitute themselves the Liberal Parliamentary Party and proceed to elect officers. Sir Donald Maclean, a man much admired by those who knew him well, but not a particularly colourful character, was unanimously elected sessional Chairman. Asquith had in fact approached him on the subject four weeks earlier[4] – while George Lambert was reported to be 'a little sore' at the proposal.[5] Lambert's attitude was not wholly unreasonable, for he was a good deal senior to Maclean both as an M.P. and in the public offices he had held; nor had Maclean a record of such outstanding brilliance that these considerations could be ignored.

Then the second dispute arose. It was announced to the meeting that Asquith had appointed G. R. Thorne as Chief Whip in place of John Gulland, who had been defeated at the election. Thorne had not been Asquith's first choice; his earliest approach had been to Wedgwood Benn.[6] The appointment of Thorne was promptly challenged by Members who denied that even Asquith could impose an officer upon them, and who asserted that the Liberal M.P.s should

[1] *Manchester Guardian*, 4 February 1919.

[2] Listed in *Liberal Magazine*, 1919, p. 89.

[3] Trevor Wilson, *The downfall of the Liberal Party*, pp. 189–90; *The Times*, 4 February 1919, etc.

[4] Maclean to Asquith, 8 January 1919 (dated 1918). Asquith papers 18, fol. 39–40.

[5] Gulland to Runciman, 11 January 1919. Runciman papers.

[6] Benn to Asquith, 11 January 1919. Asquith papers 18, fol. 41; Sir Robert Hudson to Viscount Gladstone, 28 June 1921. Viscount Gladstone papers 46,476.

choose their own Whips. Eventually, Thorne was appointed Joint Whip with J. M. Hogge – a pugnacious radical who had held East Edinburgh rather narrowly in a by-election in 1912, and had contrived to increase that majority substantially in 1918, in face of a couponed opponent. Hogge was not *persona grata* to the Asquithian leadership. Before and during the war, he and W. M. R. Pringle had been a noted pair of rebels – although Pringle was later accepted into the Asquithian 'establishment'. There were also objections to Hogge of a more personal character. Maclean particularly detested him, observing that he was 'born crooked and a natural wrecker',[1] and later noting that ' "fairies" and bookmakers run away with a lot of money'.[2] These attributes were unusual for a man who was a licensed preacher of the United Free Church of Scotland and Honorary Secretary of the National Anti-Gambling League.

Rounding off the meeting, the little band engaged in some trenchant criticism of the leadership and the whole organization of the Liberal Party. The Asquithian Liberals who had thus set up their own Parliamentary organization were known as the 'Wee Frees', by analogy with a small and strict Scottish Presbyterian sect.

Two days after the 'Wee Free' meeting, another important Liberal gathering was held. All Liberal M.P.s who did not hold office in the Government were invited, whether they were reckoned Coalition supporters or opponents. The meeting was convened by six M.P.s, of whom one – Godfrey Collins – was considered an Asquithian, while the others were Coalitionists.[3] The meeting was fairly representative, the most notable absentee being Sir Donald Maclean.

The meeting decided to establish a committee to promote unity, which committee should consist of four members from each group. The joint committee met several times, but negotiations finally broke down on 6 March. The Asquithians failed to secure acceptance for a verbal formula which would have made it impossible for the Lloyd Georgeites to support Coalition Unionists when they were opposed by Liberals, while the Lloyd Georgeites sought unsuccessfully to obtain a declaration that the Parliamentary Liberal Party

[1] Maclean to Runciman, 8 January 1920. Runciman papers.
[2] Maclean to Viscount Gladstone, 28 February 1923. Viscount Gladstone papers 46,474. The colloquial meaning of the word 'fairy' appears to have altered substantially.
[3] *Westminster Gazette*, 3 February 1919.

comprised 'all Members who were selected as candidates by their local Liberal Association' – which would have given control to the Coalitionist majority. A memorandum by Sir Henry Norman, sent with apparent approval by Guest to Lloyd George,[1] complained about 'the evident fact that the Independent Liberals (inspired by Hogge and Benn) would not accept *any* terms of reunion'. Meetings of the two groups may have enabled them to define their differences, but were of no value in healing the breach.

Another meeting of all Liberals without Government office was summoned for 27 March, to elect a sessional Chairman. Most of the 'Wee Frees' decided not to attend, but three of them turned up. George Lambert was elected Chairman without opposition.

At the beginning of the Parliament, the Government Liberal whip had apparently been sent to all Liberal M.P.s – even those who had beaten couponed candidates.[2] Hogge reacted violently to this, publicly asking Guest, 'why do you now send me a whip to attend the House of Commons, seeing you did everything in your power to prevent my getting there'.[3] On 4 April, the 'Wee Frees' as a body formally requested Guest to cease sending them the Government whip; and on 10 April they showed their displeasure with Lambert by withdrawing their whip from him.

Thus by the early spring of 1919 a formal decision had been taken on the whipping of Liberal M.P.s, and this probably forced most of them to make a personal decision one way or the other. Nevertheless, there was a good deal of coming and going across the floor of the House. No doubt there were some M.P.s who simply regarded themselves as 'Liberals', who were prepared to examine the Government's legislative proposals individually on their merits, and who were only with reluctance brought to tie the appellation 'Asquithian' or 'Lloyd Georgeite' around their necks. At least one M.P., Sir John McCallum of Paisley, contrived to receive both whips,[4] although he seems better classified as a 'Wee Free'. Godfrey – soon Sir Godfrey – Collins of Greenock was apparently[5] reckoned an Asquithian at the

[1] Guest to Lloyd George, 13 March 1919. Lloyd George papers F/21/3/9.

[2] *Daily News*, 31 January 1918.

[3] *Daily News*, 4 February 1919.

[4] W. Dudley Ward to J. T. Davies, 14 January 1920. Lloyd George papers F/22/1/1.

[5] But see *Lloyd George Liberal Magazine*, vol. 2, p. 848 (June 1922) for a different view.

election and for a short time afterwards. Later he took junior office in the Government, but by 1922 he was again an Asquithian.

In spite of these turbulent events in the Commons, there seems to have been little trouble in the House of Lords. The Marquis of Crewe had been Liberal Leader in the Lords since 1908, and simply continued in office with equanimity – appointing Whips and convening the Liberal peers as if nothing had happened.[1] The Government also had its Liberal Whips in the Lords, but there does not seem to have been anything of the enforced polarization of rank-and-file members which prevailed in the Commons.

*   *   *

The Asquithian Liberals were compelled to consider not only their relationships with the Lloyd Georgeites, but also problems of internal organization. Sir Jesse Herbert had died a few weeks after the establishment of Lloyd George's Coalition. Charles Geake died in April 1919 at the early age of fifty-one – and for him there could be no replacement. Sir Robert Hudson returned from the Red Cross, but those who only came to know him after the war do not seem to have held him in the same regard as those who had known him in earlier days. John Gulland and Lord Murray, whose advice would have been invaluable, were not long available for consultation, as both died in 1920. As for Asquith himself, McKenna wrote to Runciman, soon after the election, complaining that 'The old man is stoical to the point of indifference, but he hasn't the slightest intention to resign'.[2] With Asquith as with Hudson, the strain of war or the onset of old age seems to have made him a different man after 1918 from what he had been in earlier days, and men who remembered him in his days of glory sometimes did not fully realize this fact.

In other places, too, there was evidence of decline. Neither Thorne nor Hogge was comparable in stature with the great Chief Whips of the past, and the estate to which they succeeded was not the full inheritance of Gulland and his predecessors. Thorne and Hogge concentrated on Parliamentary work, while questions relating to the control and finance of the Party, and the selection of candidates, were handled by others. Until 1921, Sir Donald Maclean seems to

[1] Gulland to Runciman, 4 January 1919. Runciman papers. See also Viscount Gladstone to Samuel, 23 March 1919. Samuel papers A/29, fol. 55.

[2] McKenna to Runciman, 4 January 1919. Runciman papers.

have done this work,[1] while afterwards it was performed by Viscount Gladstone, Geoffrey Howard, and Sir Robert Hudson, in close co-operation with Asquith and Maclean.[2] These extraordinary arrangements must have presented considerable difficulties to the professional staff. Not only were the Lloyd Georgeites naturally anxious to secure control of the Party organization, but it seems that the men who operated it also feared aggression from Hogge[3] – who probably felt that he had been unreasonably excluded from participation in view of his position in the Parliamentary Party.

In the first year or two after the war, the Coalition Liberals had no proper political organization comparable with that of the Asquithians. They had to rely on the Government Liberal Whips and their staffs, and the personal associates of the Prime Minister. Lloyd George also established a very substantial staff of high ability at 10 Downing Street, which extended to the basement and the garden – whence the nickname, the 'Garden suburb'.[4] At this stage – and, indeed, for much of Lloyd George's life – there were numerous people, often of quite exceptional calibre, who were employed by Lloyd George as consultants, advisers, members of research committees, and so on. The lines between the staffs which he employed in various capacities seem to have been pretty blurred.

*   *   *

Although the 'Wee Frees' were a heterogeneous group in a condition of internal chaos, they immediately showed themselves extremely effective both inside and outside Parliament. The technical question whether the Leader of the Opposition was Maclean or William Adamson, Chairman of the Parliamentary Labour Party, was never finally resolved,[5] but there could be no doubt that Maclean far out-shone Adamson, and the 'Wee Free' Liberals were a far more power-

---

[1] Viscount Gladstone to Maclean, 13 January 1922 (copy). Viscount Gladstone papers 46,025, fol. 2–5.

[2] J. A. Spender, *Sir Robert Hudson*, pp. 165–6. Maclean and Hudson acted as trustees for Party funds – see Maclean to Asquith, 8 January 1919 (misdated 1918) – Asquith papers 18, fol. 39–40, while Howard was responsible for some aspects at least of outside organisation – see note by Viscount Gladstone, 6 December 1921 – Viscount Gladstone papers 46,820, fol. 2–4.

[3] Note by Viscount Gladstone, 6 December 1921. Viscount Gladstone papers 46,480, fol. 2–4.

[4] See T. Jones, *Lloyd George*, p. 94.

[5] See *Liberal Magazine*, 1919, pp. 90, 284.

ful Parliamentary opposition than the Labour Party. The fact that Adamson did not press his claim for Opposition leadership is of more than technical interest, for it shows that the Labour Party was still not taking itself seriously as a likely alternative Government. But the strength of the Independent Liberal opposition was itself a mixed blessing, for the dominant figures on the two sides of the House were both in name Liberals. Inevitably this led to more and more polarization of Liberal opinion in the country, and made the prospect of true reunion increasingly remote.

The Asquithians began winning by-elections almost at once. The first victory was Leyton West on 1 March 1919, where a two-to-one Coalition majority was wiped out. At Central Hull on 29 March the overturn of votes was even more impressive. At the General Election, the Liberal, with under 3,500 votes, had been 10,000 behind the Coalition Unionist; less than four months later another Liberal candidate, Commander Kenworthy, won the seat. In Central Aberdeenshire there was some confusion because the prospective Liberal candidate wished to run as a Coalitionist, while the local Liberal Association demanded that he should be an Independent. He eventually withdrew[1] and another man was chosen. The Unionist had been returned in a straight fight in 1918; this time the Liberal won the seat in spite of a substantial Labour vote. Yet after Central Aberdeenshire the by-elections quite suddenly but consistently showed that the initiative of opposition in the constituencies had largely passed from Liberals to Labour. In the remainder of 1919 there were three by-elections which were contested by Liberal, Unionist, and Labour Parties, and in every one the Liberal came a poor third. The Liberals' position was not helped by the considerable favour which the *Daily News* was showing to Labour about this time.

*   *   *

For the first few months of 1919, we might say that the issues between the 'Wee Frees' and the Coalitionists had been academic questions of who were the true Liberals and who were the false prophets – although questions of finance and power obviously lay behind them. But soon mighty issues of immediate political importance arose.

The Chancellor of the Exchequer was Austen Chamberlain. In his

[1] Guest to Lloyd George, 11, 19, and 29 March 1919. Lloyd George papers F/21/3/6, 11 and 13.

first Budget, on 30 April 1919, he inaugurated what he admitted to be a policy of Imperial Preference, by differential reductions in the wartime McKenna Duties. The nature of the Asquithians' attack on the Budget proposals was predictable; but it is striking to observe that many Coalition Liberals went so far as to abstain from voting or even to vote against the Government in the ensuing debates. Thus, when Wedgwood Benn's amendment to remove Imperial Preference from certain items was considered, not only did twenty-three Asquithian Liberals vote against the Government, but so also did seventeen Coalition Liberals; while no fewer than sixty-two Liberals who were in the House abstained from voting. This list includes such prominent Coalitionists as the Chief Whip, Capt. F. E. Guest; his destined successor, C. A. McCurdy; and Hamar Greenwood. Both from the by-elections and from the behaviour of the Liberals in the Budget debates, one is left strongly with the impression that electors and M.P.s alike were still thinking of themselves as either Liberals or Unionists in the spring of 1919, and had not really understood or accepted the logical implications of coalition.

The next great topic was the nature of the German treaty which was being concluded at Versailles. The line which Lloyd George was taking came to be attacked from two sides. A substantial body of Government M.P.s pressed for a particularly stern peace; while the 'Wee Free' Liberals were divided into those – headed by Maclean and Thorne – who welcomed the arrangements, and those – including Hogge and Acland – who opposed them.[1]

Much public interest was focussed on the first post-war meeting of the N.L.F. Council, which was held in Birmingham at the end of November 1919. This proved something of an Asquithian demonstration, and afforded the opportunity for recriminations between the majority of the delegates and those Lloyd Georgeites who ventured to attend. When the 'Coalie' M.P., Sir William Barton, said, 'I will tell you when reunion will take place . . .', a delegate expressed the general view by shouting, 'When you leave the Tories!' (In fact Sir William joined the Asquithians before the Coalition came to an end.)

Expressly or by necessary implication, the thesis of the meeting was a thoroughgoing condemnation of the acts and omissions of the

[1] See T. Wilson's D.Phil. thesis (Oxford 1959), pp. 146–7; *The Times*, 1 July 1919, etc.

Coalition. It was therefore startling to find the Prime Minister declaring at Manchester on 6 December[1] that, 'There is not one of those resolutions, to the best of my recollection, that the Coalition Government would not be prepared to pass – I won't say to accept or endorse, but to put into legislation.'

This caused visible embarrassment on the Government side. Bonar Law was driven to explain, in answer to a Parliamentary question, 'that the Prime Minister had read an account of the first day's proceedings of the Conference, and did not remember that this body was not likely to be satisfied with one day's discussion'.[2] This was hardly an adequate disclaimer, and the Executive Committee of the National Unionist Association went so far as publicly to express its regret that Bonar Law, the Party Leader, had not dissociated himself from the Prime Minister's remarks.[3] It is sometimes useful to observe that the public disagreements among Liberals were not without parallels elsewhere; and that while to Liberal eyes the Coalition looked Tory, to Unionist eyes it frequently seemed dangerously Radical.

*　　*　　*

While these developments were taking place, other events no less strange were occurring in connection with the extraordinary by-election in Spen Valley.[4] At the General Election of 1918, Sir Thomas Whittaker, who had already sat there for a quarter of a century, was returned as a Coalition Liberal, with the support of the local Liberal Association. When he died, the Liberal Association decided, by a majority, to nominate an Independent Liberal and not a Coalitionist. When the name of Sir John Simon, the former Home Secretary, was submitted to them, it was accepted – this time unanimously – at an exceptionally large meeting. The Coalition Liberals now sought a candidate to oppose Simon, and eventually secured one Colonel Bryan Fairfax for the purpose. They also obtained the backing of local Unionists.

On 8 December 1919, a large meeting of Liberal M.P.s, both 'Coalies' and Independents, was held. A Coalitionist, Gerald France,

[1] *Liberal Magazine*, 1919, p. 728.
[2] *Ibid.*, pp. 730–1.
[3] *The Times*, 19 December 1919.
[4] *Liberal Magazine*, 1919, pp. 712–16.

submitted a resolution protesting against the decision to oppose Simon. He was supported by another 'Coalie', Colonel A. C. Murray, brother of Lord Murray. Eventually the motion was withdrawn in view of an understanding that the whole question of the Government's attitude towards Liberal candidates would be considered early in the following session.

Help came to Simon from many quarters. One Coalitionist, Major Barnes, joined the 'Wee Frees'. Another, A. R. Barrand, spoke in support of Simon. Dr Macnamara, Coalition Liberal M.P. for NW. Camberwell, dared to accept a speaking engagement in Spen Valley in favour of Fairfax; he was repudiated in the most emphatic terms by his own Liberal Association. But the result of the election was that Labour captured the seat, with Simon a fairly close second, and Fairfax third.

We have already noted the rather dubious position of Sir John McCallum, Liberal M.P. for Paisley. In 1918, the constituency had been a 'triple marginal', in which fewer than 350 votes separated McCallum from the Co-operative and the Coalition N.D.P. candidates. When McCallum died, early in January 1920, the general view seems to have been that Labour would win the seat if there was a three-cornered contest.

The dilemma of the local Liberal Association was most remarkable, for the choice lay between a local Coalitionist and no less a person than Asquith himself.[1] The near-parity of the two factions was hardly complimentary or encouraging to the Party Leader: the Executive split 20:17 in his favour, and a full meeting of the Association divided 93:75. The minority agreed to fall in with the majority, and a unanimous invitation was issued to Asquith.[2] Some remarkable moves had been made at a higher level; Sir Donald Maclean was apparently in contact with the Unionist Party Chairman, Sir George Younger;[3] while Guest urged Lloyd George that, 'it is essential that you impress upon Bonar the vital necessity of putting forward a Unionist candidate should the local Liberal Association by any chance unanimously decide to invite Mr Asquith'.[4] Guest also

[1] W. Dudley Ward to J. T. Davies, 14 January 1920. Lloyd George papers F/22/1/1.

[2] *Manchester Guardian*, 22 January 1920.

[3] Guest to Lloyd George, 15–17 January 1920. Lloyd George papers F/22/1/3 and 5.

[4] Guest to Lloyd George, 16 January 1920. Lloyd George papers F/22/1/4.

made the interesting suggestion, 'that Messrs Hogge and Company have issued their ultimatum to Mr Asquith; in effect, that if he will not risk election at a by-election he will be repudiated as nominal head of the Independent Liberal Party.'[1]

But when Asquith took the field, a constituency which would have been interesting at any time became the focus of national excitement. On 12 February 1920, the Liberals secured a great victory, and the Coalition a most crushing defeat. Asquith was nearly 3,000 votes ahead of the Labour candidate – the same man who had stood as a Co-operative in 1918. Not only was the Coalition Unionist a bad third, but he actually forfeited his deposit.[2] Sir Donald Maclean gladly ceded precedence to his old chief.

Yet there was one feature of the Paisley by-election more ominous for the Liberal Party. Nine men who had sat in the past as Liberal M.P.s sent a message of support to the Labour candidate. Most of them had been noted in the past either as pacifists, as land taxers, or as both.[3] It would be interesting to know how those who lived into old age came to view the actions of their new Party on the very issues which drew them towards it, when the Labour Party received the plenitude of power.

* * *

There was a rash of important by-elections about this time. At North Edinburgh in April, Walter Runciman was rather narrowly defeated in his attempt to capture another place of traditional Liberal strength. While that campaign was being fought, a further by-election brought the whole question of the future relationship between Coalition Liberals and their Unionist allies under scrutiny. Both of the two Stockport seats became vacant, and two Coalition candidates – one a Liberal and the other a Unionist – were advanced. They were both quite comfortably returned – indeed, this by-elec-

---

[1] *Idem.*

[2] Paisley, 12 February 1920   H. H. Asquith (Lib.) 14,736 (7,542)
    (1918 in brackets)   J. M. Biggar (Lab.) 11,902 (Co-op. 7,436)
        J. A. D. MacKean (Co.U.) 3,795 (Co.N.D.P. 7,201)

[3] *Liberal Magazine*, 1920, p. 70, lists: C. R. Buxton; J. King; R. C. Lambert; H. C. Lees-Smith; R. L. Outhwaite; A. Ponsonby; C. P. Trevelyan; A. V. Rutherford, and Colonel J. Wedgwood.

tion was probably the most satisfying for the Government in its whole life.

The main interest of Stockport, however, does not lie in the result, but in the developments which were brought to a head while it was being fought. These had a rather long history.

In May 1919, a 'Coalition Committee' of both Liberal and Unionist supporters of the Government was set up, with the avowed object of establishing a durable political movement. Only new M.P.s were invited to serve, since it was considered that they would not be hampered by past associations.[1]

It seems certain that this 'Centre Party' movement was a spontaneous development, not owing its existence to the inspiration of any Party headquarters – in spite of the suspicious circumstance that 'Freddie' Guest's brother Oscar was the Chairman.[2] By the end of May there were 130 members – the great majority of them Unionists. In the middle of 1919, this idea of a 'Centre Party' based on the Coalition was widely canvassed, and received the public approval of such influential men as Captain Guest and Winston Churchill for the Liberals, and Lord Birkenhead for the Unionists; but by November the Secretary, Oswald Mosley, resigned, as he considered that the group was 'drifting'.

Unionist reactions to the 'Centre Party' idea were at least as mixed as Liberal reactions, and during the Stockport by-election Lord Salisbury, son of the former Prime Minister, wrote to local Unionists, urging them not to support the Coalition Liberal.[3] This seems so to have embarrassed Lloyd George and Bonar Law that they felt that the 'Centre Party' proposal had acquired a degree of urgency. They were further impelled in the same direction by a memorandum from ninety-three M.P.s which indicated, 'that this group, believing in the national necessity for the Coalition, express the hope that it might develop into a Single United Party'.

A few days later, Balfour submitted to Bonar Law a letter in which he argued for the amalgamation of the Coalition Unionist and Coalition Liberal organizations. Law showed the document to Lloyd George, who agreed to sound the Coalition Liberal Ministers.

[1] *The Times*, 14 May 1919.
[2] Guest to Lloyd George, 10 May 1919. Lloyd George papers F/21/3/21.
[3] For an account of Unionist reactions during the campaign, see R. Blake, *The Unknown Prime Minister*, pp. 415–17.

Lloyd George met the Liberal Ministers on 16 March 1920, and the meeting was reported in detail in the Press on the following day – to the fury of the Prime Minister. It became apparent that while some Ministers, like Churchill and Addison, were strongly in favour of fusion, others were not; and some expressed doubt whether their local Associations would accept it.[1]

A couple of days later, Lloyd George addressed a meeting to which all Liberal M.P.s, whether Coalitionists or not, had been invited.[2] He argued the inevitability of a Coalition of some kind – whether his own or some other. On the following day, Bonar Law spoke in a similar vein in favour of close co-operation. But by then it was quite obvious that a considerable number of men, both Liberals and Unionists, who were prepared to support the Coalition for the time being, would absolutely refuse to contemplate any permanent alliance, much less 'fusion'.

The idea of 'fusion' recurred in the correspondence of men like Lord Derby,[3] but those who had to face constituents seem rather quickly to have realized that it was politically 'not on'.[4] At least one of the Liberal Ministers, H. A. L. Fisher, urged Lloyd George to take a very different course: to break the Coalition and allow the Unionists to form a Government – which, in his view, would not have lasted long.[5]

*   *   *

Trouble continued between the two Liberal groups. Dr Macnamara, who had caused such anger in his constituency at the time of Spen Valley, was compelled to fight a by-election on his appointment as Minister of Labour. The Liberals of his constituency, NW. Camberwell, set up a candidate against him. The contest was a bitter one; Macnamara was returned, and Labour ran second. Thus, for the second time, the rival Liberal candidates were opposing each other in a hotly-fought and much-publicized by-election.

By the spring of 1920, relations between the two wings of the

---

[1] *The Times*, 17 March 1920.

[2] *Liberal Magazine*, 1920, pp. 139–49.

[3] Derby to Lloyd George, 21 March 1921; 18 November 1921. Lloyd George papers F/14/5/21 and 33.

[4] W. Ryland Atkins to Lloyd George, 25 March 1920. Lloyd George papers F/95/2/16.

[5] Fisher to Lloyd George, 20 March 1920. Lloyd George papers F/16/7/84.

Liberal Party were incomparably worse than they had been at the time of the Coupon Election. Until Spen Valley, the Asquithians had tacitly accepted that a Liberal Association could contain both Coalitionists and opponents of the Coalition; that it might support any brand of Liberal candidate, whether a Coalitionist or not; and that, while Headquarters might advise, they would not proscribe those who rejected that advice. But on 26 March 1920, Sir Donald Maclean made a forthright declaration of war on the Coalitionists.[1]

'Independent Liberals throughout the country should be at full and complete liberty in every constituency where the Liberal Association, however constituted, or the candidate, has entered into a compact or arrangement with the Conservative Party. In so far as headquarters in London can assist that, I can say on their behalf that it shall be done.'

From that moment, a Coalition Liberal seat was regarded by the Asquithians as a target quite as legitimate as any Unionist seat (and perhaps more delectable), whether the local Liberals were supporting the Coalitionist or not.

In May, the Leamington meeting of the N.L.F. General Committee provided the most flagrant exhibition of internecine fury in the Liberal Party thus far. A resolution was being considered which condemned the continuance of the Coalition, defended the independence of the Liberal Party, and warned Liberals not to ally with Unionists at the constituency level, but to preserve their organizations intact. The delegates cheered Maclean, but greeted Addison and the other Coalition Ministers as 'Rats'.

The real rumpus came when F. G. Kellaway, one of the 'Coalie' Ministers, asserted, 'I was fighting the Liberal cause when some of those who are making these interruptions were taking refuge in a tabernacle to assassinate Sir Henry Campbell-Bannerman'[2] – a statement no less enraging to the 'Wee Frees' for the element of truth which it contained. Chaos reigned until the Attorney-General Sir Gordon Hewart, fifty-seven M.P.s, and about twenty delegates left the hall in a body amid derisive cheers. Not a very good augury for Liberal reunion. Needless to say, the Asquithian resolution was

[1] Speech at Manchester. *Liberal Magazine*, 1920, pp. 166–7.
[2] Politically, that is – through the 'Relugas compact'.

carried.[1] The Coalitionists, however, did not abandon their interest in the N.L.F.; a representative body of Coalition Liberal Whips and private M.P.s decided that the Coalitionists should exert themselves to be present at the N.L.F. meetings in Bradford in November.[2]

The struggle for mastery went on. By February 1921, all of the English Area Federations, and the Scottish Liberals as well, had declared against the Coalition.[3] Only in the Welsh National Liberal Council was the influence of Lloyd George paramount – and in that body the Coalitionists signalled their victory by excluding all Opposition Liberals from the Executive Committee.[4] The Asquithians replied by establishing a rival body, the Welsh Liberal Federation, which was set firmly in Asquithian hands.

This cleavage went right down to the constituency level. In Wales, the constituency Liberal Associations seem to have declared for Lloyd George; in Scotland, twenty did so; in England, forty-five;[5] while in the great majority of places the local Associations remained in Asquithian hands. It is not difficult to visualize the acrimony which went on in nearly every Liberal organization in the land.

Even before it had become apparent to Lloyd George that he would neither capture the Liberal Party machine nor persuade his followers to accept 'fusion' with the Unionists, the Coalition Liberals began to set up their own organizations. On 16 April 1920, a Conference of English Coalition Liberal representatives was held. The delegates agreed to set up 'Area Advisory Committees' of Coalition Liberals, and also committees at constituency level. They decided that new bodies should be established in places where the seat was held by 'Wee Frees', Labour, or Unionists; while in Coalition Liberal constituencies the aim was to capture the local Liberal machine in the 'Coalie' interest.[6] In the course of 1920, the Coalition Liberals had some success in setting up Area Committees, but encountered much more difficulty at the constituency level. Even Liberal Associations supporting 'Coalie' M.P.s frequently adopted 'Wee Free' candidates when vacancies occurred.[7] Nor did the Coali-

---

[1] For account of meeting, see *Liberal Magazine*, 1920, pp. 275–9.
[2] Guest to Lloyd George, 1 November 1920. Lloyd George papers F/22/2/18.
[3] *Liberal Magazine*, 1921, p. 91.
[4] *Ibid.*, pp. 19–20. *Lloyd George Liberal Magazine*, vol. 1, pp. 125–6.
[5] Constituencies listed in Michael Kinnear, *The British Voter*, pp. 88–90.
[6] Guest to Lloyd George, 16 April 1920. Lloyd George papers F/22/1/30.
[7] Guest to Lloyd George, 23 December 1920. Lloyd George papers F/22/2/24.

M

tion Liberals find organization easier as time went on; in March 1922, one of the M.P.s was complaining to Lloyd George that constituency Coalition Liberal Associations were 'either non-existent or ineffective' outside Wales.[1]

The Lloyd Georgeites seem to have had rather more success with propaganda than with organization. The long-established *Liberal Magazine* was firmly Asquithian, but before the end of 1920, a rival periodical, called the *Lloyd George Liberal Magazine*, had appeared. Its quality was certainly inferior to the older publication, but in the spring of 1921 Sir William Sutherland was telling Lloyd George that, 'some 20,000 copies circulate monthly and at present it is the most successful political magazine'.[2]

Almost every major event served to exacerbate the Liberal schism. In 1920, the Government decided to remove the Land Taxes which Lloyd George had imposed ten years earlier. Although many had regarded these taxes as the precursors of land value taxation, they were only applied in such a limited manner that the revenue which they raised was negligible. Predictably, Lloyd George came under bitter Liberal attack.[3] Asquith himself was caught in some quite uncomfortable cross-fire from that land-taxing enthusiast Josiah Wedgwood, now set firmly in the Labour Party. Asquith gave the interesting answer that the Liberal Government was on the point of introducing land value taxation proposals in 1914. On this issue, as on others which harked back to the battles of old, the independent Liberals were unanimous for the traditional Liberal view, while the Coalition Liberals were severely split – eighteen supporting the Government and thirteen voting with the Asquithians against it.[4]

The matter which enraged the Opposition Liberals more than any other was the Government's Irish policy. The situation drifted from disaffection to open revolt. The Government enrolled that notorious irregular force, the 'Black-and-Tans', who only added fuel to the flames. 'Reprisals' were visited not only on the rebels, but on innumerable Irishmen who were quite uninvolved in the struggle. The

[1] Ernest Evans to Lloyd George, 21 March 1922. Lloyd George papers F/16/2/1.

[2] Sir William Sutherland to Lloyd George (undated). Lloyd George papers F/22/3/14.

[3] Lloyd George was not at a loss for answers. See *Lloyd George Liberal Magazine* No. 1 (October 1920), especially p. 6.

[4] *Liberal Magazine*, 1920, p. 394.

reactions of Asquith were not those of a politician trying to trip up an opponent, but of a man whose moral sense had been stirred to its depths against a policy which he regarded as one of wanton and brutal outrage.[1] The *Manchester Guardian*, under the editorship of C. P. Scott, swung violently against the Government, and so did innumerable Liberals who had been bred in the traditions of radical nonconformity. It is arguable that these Irish atrocities, more than anything else, made Lloyd George unacceptable ever afterwards to a large section of rank-and-file Liberal opinion. Lloyd George emerges very badly from these events – not least for the way in which he sought to evade responsibility.[2] Asquith not only described these Irish horrors as 'a policy of despair', 'a naked confession of political bankruptcy', and 'acts of blind and indiscriminate vengeance', but he also made a strong appeal for what he called 'Dominion Home Rule'. For this he encountered ridicule from Lloyd George[3] and also trouble from a most unexpected quarter – his loyal friend and colleague, Sir Donald Maclean, who dissociated himself from his Leader's views at a meeting which they both addressed in Ayr in October 1920.[4]

*   *   *

By the end of 1920, the Liberal Party seemed to be dissolving in utter chaos. Not only were the Asquithians and Lloyd Georgeites almost constantly at each other's throats, but each of the two groups included a very wide range of opinions on matters both of policy and administration. No war is as debilitating as civil war, and it was becoming increasingly evident that the common enemies of Liberalism – but particularly the Labour Party – were deriving more and more advantage from the contest. Viscount Haldane was moving perceptibly towards the Labour Party. Many lesser personalities had already crossed into that camp. But far more important than the loss of celebrities was the fact that Liberals, whether Coalitionists or Asquithians, were failing almost completely to win the support of the younger voters.

[1] See, for example, *Liberal Magazine*, 1920, pp. 652–6.
[2] Sir C. E. Callwell, *Field Marshal Sir Henry Wilson*, ii, p. 263; Donald McCormick, *The mask of Merlin*, pp. 186–7.
[3] *Liberal Magazine*, 1920, pp. 589–90.
[4] Discussed at length in Vivian Phillipps, *My days and ways*, p. 67. See also *Lloyd George Liberal Magazine* No. 1, p. 95.

The kind of consideration which was driving actual or potential Liberals into the Labour Party is well illustrated by a letter which C. P. Trevelyan wrote in May 1919. Trevelyan, it will be recalled, had been a junior Minister in 1914, but had resigned on the outbreak of war. In 1918 he had defended his old seat of Elland as an Independent, against candidates from all three Parties. Early in 1919 he joined the Labour Party. Yet he admitted that, 'It is not that I think the leadership of the Labour Party good. It is not so from any point of view.' There was nothing in this letter to suggest the enthusiasm of a convert; he evidently viewed Adamson with something approaching contempt, and decided that the Labour Party 'will pretty soon get hold of the government, probably to make a horrid mess of it'. The real reason for his move was despair of the Liberal hierarchy: 'Now both the intellectual leadership is lacking and what is far worse the moral. And the working class began to cease to vote Liberal at the last election and I am certain will never do so *en masse* again. That will again react and make the party more middle class, bourgeois, and eventually Whiggish than ever.'[1]

Trevelyan's prophecies were by no means all fulfilled, but it is not difficult to see his reactions as very characteristic of men who were of middle age or younger. Yet while Liberal confusions were resulting in many Liberals being drawn off into the Labour Party, those who seceded were not necessarily those who were most sympathetic with Labour views. In a letter written several years afterwards, Beatrice Webb recalled to Sir Herbert Samuel the 'long discussions' which he and Trevelyan had had in her presence – remarking that, 'In those days I should have prophesied that you would be more on the side of Labour than Trevelyan. But where exactly any Progressive finds himself in the present aftermath of war seems more chance than intention.'[2]

*   *   *

The by-elections were confirming the steady advance of the Labour Party. Liberals could still make headway in those rural constituencies where Labour had not yet entered the field – such as Louth (Lincs.) which they won in June 1920. But the urban industrial con-

[1] C. P. Trevelyan to Eleanor Acland, 24 May 1919. Acland papers.
[2] Beatrice Webb to Samuel, 23 January 1928. Samuel papers A/155(VII), fol. 6–8.

stituencies were being captured by Labour. This was certainly not a matter for which the very pedestrian Parliamentary Labour Party could claim credit. It is often said that the Labour Party 'displaced' the Liberals during the period immediately after the First World War. Rather should we say that the Liberals tore themselves to pieces, and the Labour Party, with considerable hesitation and very little leadership or sense of direction, moved cautiously yet clumsily into the space which the Liberals had vacated.

9

Nemesis

'England does not love coalitions.'

BENJAMIN DISRAELI, House of Commons
16 December 1852

For the first two years after 1918, the issues of political controversy, while vitally important, did not hit home at once to the ordinary voter in Britain. His satisfaction at the victorious conclusion of the war was reinforced by booming prosperity at home. No doubt, many voters who had been induced to vote for the Coalition candidates at the General Election withdrew their temporary support, but there was nothing afoot which threatened to bring the whole administration crashing in ruins.

At the end of 1920, the unemployment figures took a sudden upward swing, and by the middle of 1921 no fewer than 17·8 per cent of the insured workers were unemployed. From then until the Second World War, the national figures were seldom less than 10 per cent and sometimes more than 20 per cent. In areas of the old heavy industries, like coal and shipbuilding, they were much higher than the national average.

It is irrelevant to our story whether the Government was to blame or not. Insecurity and bitterness pervaded all classes, and the Government inevitably received a large measure of the blame.

The Liberal civil war continued. A further move was taken in the protectionist direction by the Safeguarding of Industries Act of 1921, which empowered the Board of Trade to impose a 33⅓ per cent *ad valorem* duty on imports of goods produced by 'Key Industries'. Sir William Barton, a former Coalition Liberal who had transferred to the Asquithians, moved an amendment to cut the period of operation of the Act from five years to one. Although the Government inevitably won in the division lobbies, the obvious restiveness of the

Coalition Liberals made it necessary for Charles McCurdy (who had succeeded Guest as chief Coalition Liberal Whip) to present a full report to his chief. This revealed that fifty-two voted with the Government, thirteen voted against, eighteen were marked in but did not vote, thirty-eight were absent, two were paired for the Government, and one was paired against.[1] There are plenty of other examples of parliamentary divisions on which Coalition Liberals were deeply split.

We have seen in the previous chapter how bad the relations between Coalition and Independent Liberals had become. The Coalition Liberals did not find their relations with the Unionists much easier. A theme which recurred repeatedly in the internal correspondence of the 'Coalies' was that the Coupon arrangements of 1918 had given the Unionists a large number of traditionally Liberal seats. Guest at one time listed forty-one seats which had been mostly or even invariably Liberal, right back to 1885, which had been captured in this way.[2] As early as the immediate aftermath of West Leyton, in March 1919, Alfred Mond wrote to Lloyd George, arguing that by-election candidates should be selected by both Coalition Whips in agreement.[3] Guest made a similar point after a Coalitionist had failed to hold Louth against an Asquithian in 1920: 'the only way to retain the *traditional* Liberal seats which [the Coalition Unionists] won with your Coupon at the General Election is peacefully to hand them back to Coalition Liberalism.'[4]

No doubt this was correct; but it is difficult to understand how experienced politicians like Mond and Guest can seriously have believed that the Unionists would abandon seats which they had captured, however exceptional the circumstances; or that local Unionist Associations would have countenanced such a practice even if their headquarters had desired to do so. Guest very properly recognized that Liberals blamed the Coalitionists bitterly for abandoning Liberal seats to the Unionists in 1918.[5] It is remarkable that he did not anticipate this very natural reaction when the Coupon arrangements were being made.

[1] McCurdy to Lloyd George, May 1921. Lloyd George papers F/34/4/8.
[2] F. E. Guest to Sir Robert Sanders, 23 December 1920. Lloyd George papers F/22/2/24.
[3] Mond to Lloyd George, 15 March 1919. Lloyd George papers F/36/6/46.
[4] Guest to Lloyd George, 18 June 1920. Lloyd George papers F/22/1/45.
[5] Guest to Lloyd George, 23 December 1920. Lloyd George papers F/22/2/24.

Although the Unionist leaders continued to praise the Coalition,[1] by the end of 1921 there were many signs of Unionist discontent in the constituencies, and men like Sir George Younger who were in close contact with constituency feeling were coming to the conclusion that the Coalition should be broken. The main hope of those who desired the Coalition arrangements to be continued indefinitely was to contrive an early General Election, with the Coalition intact, before either the Opposition outside, or the dissidents within, could organize themselves effectively.

In the course of 1921, Bonar Law retired from the Unionist leadership through ill health, and was succeeded by Austen Chamberlain. Lloyd George and Chamberlain were in close collusion about the possibility of an early election. A treaty was concluded with Ireland at the end of the year, and immediately afterwards the election proposal was put forward at a dinner party attended by Ministers and others. But Austen Chamberlain soon discovered that leading Unionists outside the Government were overwhelmingly hostile to an early election,[2] and Sir Malcolm Fraser, Chief Unionist Agent, reported that the Coalition would lose at least a hundred seats, and the Unionist Party would be thoroughly split. The proposal was therefore dropped.

Whether the Coalition was to persist or not, the Lloyd George Liberals now became conscious of the need to establish not merely local and *ad hoc* committees, but a full-scale and permanent national organization of their own. A conference was held in London on 19–20 January 1922. On the motion of Sir Gordon Hewart, a body called the National Liberal Council was established, and invited affiliation from Liberal organizations. (This, of course, bore no relation to the 'Liberal Nationals' established by Sir John Simon in 1931.) Hewart declared[3] that the body which was being set up was not a new Party – 'our Party is the Liberal Party – and nobody with our consent is going to expel or excommunicate us from it' – but the difference between the National Liberal Council and a new political party was rather difficult to discover.

*   *   *

[1] For examples see *Liberal Magazine*, 1921, pp. 251, 311–12.

[2] Chamberlain to Lloyd George, 4 January 1922. Lloyd George papers F/7/5/1. Sir George Younger to Chamberlain, 28 December 1921 (copy). Lloyd George papers F/48/5/4.

[3] *Lloyd George Liberal Magazine*, vol. 2, p. 395.

Some
Leading
LIBERALS

Mr LLOYD GEORGE

VISCOUNT GREY

THE MARQUESS OF READING

Mrs WINTRINGHAM

Mrs ... MAN

SIR JOHN SIMON

Mr WALTER RUNCIMAN

LADY VIOLET BENHAM-CARTER

Mrs CORB... ASHBY

EARL BEAUCHAMP

SIR HERBERT SAMUEL

THE MARQUESS OF CREWE

THE LAST GREAT BID FOR POWER

The front cover of a Liberal Party pamphlet, prepared for the 1929 Election.
In sheer calibre and capacity of their leadership, the Liberals of the interwar years far
overshadowed the other parties; and their failure to make greater advances in 1929 was
a major disaster for Britain and the world.

DAVID LLOYD GEORGE
1ST EARL LLOYD-GEORGE
(1863–1945)

As a young statesman (*left*); as a
enthusiast of water-divining (*below*
and (*right*) with his protégé the Prin
of Wales (now Duke of Windsor
Lloyd George has been called ':
inspired peasant'; and yet Winst
Churchill's judgement on his frie
and mentor was 'the greatest Wels
man since the Tudors'.

*(photograph by courtesy of the Ra
Times Hulton Picture Librar*

(photograph by courtesy of the Popperfoto Libra

(*photograph by courtesy of Syndication International.*)

SIR ARCHIBALD SINCLAIR, VISCOUNT THURSO
(1890–1970)

At a time when the National Government would countenance rearmament but failed to stand up to the dictators,
while the Labour opposition urged resistance to the dictators
yet voted against the Defence Estimates, Sinclair led the
Liberals to accept both the need to resist aggression and the
need to have the material with which to do so.

(photograph by courtesy of the Liberal Party Organization.)

While these strange events were taking place among the Coalition supporters, some manœuvres not one whit less extraordinary were occurring on the Opposition side of the House.

In the immediate aftermath of the General Election, the political orientation of the 'Wee Frees' was far from clear. An Asquithian as devoted as John Gulland complained that Asquith 'takes things very philosophically – rather too philosophically I think'.[1]

We have seen in the previous chapter the much more acid comments of Reginald McKenna. He was not one of those Liberals best disposed towards the Labour Party, but at the very beginning he seemed to assume that an alliance with Labour was desirable: 'Co-operation between the Liberal and Labour Parties won't come of itself; it will require months, perhaps a year or more, of patient negotiation. But I am sure it could be accomplished. Wedgwood Benn would be invaluable for the task.'[2]

Yet Gulland had even then decided that such an alliance was impossible: 'Labour will not go into the Government, but unfortunately they say also that they will make no sort of arrangement with us. This I regard as the saddest feature for the future.'[3]

A year later, some very tentative contacts began to be made in a different direction, with those Unionists who found the Coalition intolerable. Lord Robert Cecil, Unionist M.P., and son of the former Marquis of Salisbury, was frequently in correspondence with the Asquithians. In January 1920, he gave Runciman the advice that Asquith should retire from the Liberal leadership in favour of Grey,[4] adding: 'If that can be arranged the Liberal Party has a great future before it.'

Cecil returned repeatedly to the theme of a Government presided over by Grey as an alternative to the Coalition,[5] and some even of Asquith's strongest admirers like Professor Gilbert Murray reached a similar conclusion.[6]

---

[1] Gulland to Runciman, 4 January 1919. Runciman papers.

[2] McKenna to Runciman, 4 January 1919. Runciman papers.

[3] *Ibid.*

[4] Lord Robert Cecil to Runciman, 24 January 1920. Runciman papers.

[5] Cecil to Runciman, 13 January 1921 (Runciman papers); to Viscount Gladstone, 3 December 1921 (Viscount Gladstone papers 46, 476); to Asquith, 9 October 1922 (Asquith papers 18, fol. 78–82).

[6] Gilbert Murray to Viscount Gladstone, 21 April 1921. Viscount Gladstone papers 46,476.

Oswald Mosley, Unionist M.P. for Harrow, who had originally been associated with the abortive attempt to weld the Coalitionists into a 'Centre Party', now played a part in attempting to establish a rival alliance on the other side of the House. He has written[1] of 'a meeting at my house in the early 1920s between the Secretary of the Labour Party, Mr Arthur Henderson, and the Conservative, Lord Robert Cecil, to discuss the possibility of a government under the Liberal Lord Grey'.

Negotiations on these lines proceeded for some considerable while. On 29 June 1921, Asquith and Grey met, and discussed *open and avowed co-operation*, both in the declaration of general policy, and in the ultimate responsibilities of government, if and when the country should decide on the change'.[2] Grey protested that his eyesight was too poor to allow him to read papers, and so Asquith suggested for him some office like Lord President of the Council, with leadership in the Lords. A week later they met Crewe, Runciman, and Maclean, and also Lord Robert Cecil, to discuss the possibility of a broader appeal.[3] On 19 July the same men, and also Simon and Lord Cowdray, met again. Asquith was so satisfied that he wrote, 'I think that real progress was made, and that in another ten days we may see the thing on its legs'.[4] Sir Arthur Steel-Maitland, a past Chairman of the Unionist Party Organization and a member of Lloyd George's Government until the spring of 1919, also evinced interest.[5] Several further meetings were held,[6] and the matter continued under active discussion into the following year.

There were also some indications of friendship with the Labour Party. In the South-East Southwark by-election of December 1921, a Coalition Liberal seat was at stake; *Liberal Magazine* makes no secret that 'Liberals in the constituency gave general support to Mr Naylor, the Labour candidate', or that they were 'strongly and influentially urged' to do so.[7] Labour reciprocity was not strong, but 'Willie' Graham urged support for the Liberal in Oxford, and

[1] *New Outlook*, May 1966, p. 14.

[2] Notes of meeting 29 June 1921. Asquith papers 34, fol. 3–6.

[3] Notes of meeting 5 July 1921. Asquith papers 34, fol. 15–18.

[4] Notes of meeting 19 July 1921. Asquith papers 34, fol. 24–5.

[5] Steel-Maitland to Asquith, 29 July 1921. Asquith papers 34, fol. 26–7.

[6] Asquith papers 34, fol. 28–36. Cecil to Asquith, 9 October 1922, Asquith papers 18, fol. 78–82.

[7] *Liberal Magazine*, 1921, pp. 702, 720.

declared that, 'in the next House of Commons I am convinced that the problems that confront Liberal and Labour will largely settle themselves'.[1]

*   *   *

The main Unionist revolt did not centre on men like Cecil who were establishing contact with the Asquithians, but rather on men in the constituencies, in the Central Office, and on the Parliamentary back benches, who wished to make an independent appeal to the electorate. Such incidents as the 'Sale of Honours' scandal may have played a large part in fostering this attitude of mind.[2] It appears that knighthoods were offered at £10,000–£12,000 apiece, and baronetcies at £40,000. The scandal was thrown up at Lloyd George repeatedly in later years. He argued that:

'. . . Honours Lists during my Premiership . . . were prepared by the Chief Whips in the usual way. They were then submitted to the joint leaders of the Coalition, myself and Mr Bonar Law, and afterwards Mr Austen Chamberlain who succeeded him. . . . For my part I had no information as to who amongst the persons put forward had or had not subscribed towards the party funds. . . .'[3]

There seems little reason to disbelieve this disclaimer, so far as it goes. Lloyd George doubtless neither knew nor cared about the details of the transactions, but he must have known well enough the main story.[4] Perhaps the final judgement on the Coalition will be that they did not depart from common practice in the fact that honours were effectively sold; but they differed sharply from all modern governments in the scale on which it was done, the shamelessness of

[1] *Westminster Gazette*, 8 August 1922.
[2] For examples, see *Liberal Magazine*, 1922, pp. 431–4; Harold Nicolson, *King George V*, pp. 511–15, etc.
[3] *The Times*, 3 December 1927.
[4] The Unionists were in no position to cast the first stone. Mr R. Humphrey Davies, who was Secretary to the Liberal Chief Whip at the operative time, has written to the present author that, 'George Whiteley [Lord Marchamley, the Parliamentary Secretary to the Treasury] took stern and effective measures to suppress the touts who had evidently been active in the past' – that is, under the Conservative Government down to December 1905.

the touting system, and their total and cynical disregard for the worthiness and suitability of the recipient.

* * *

A couple of months after this scandal broke, the Coalition leaders made a further attempt to preserve their alliance by calling an election, and on 16 September obtained a Cabinet decision in favour of an immediate appeal to the country. But again the Unionist 'backroom boys' deflected them from this course, and this time drove their point home by informing Chamberlain that 184 constituencies had declared their intention of running Unionist candidates independent of the Coalition. By this stage it looked as if Lloyd George would succeed not only in smashing his own Party but in smashing the Unionist Party as well.

The fundamental weakness of the 'Diehard Unionists'' position was the absence of any credible body of alternative leaders within the Unionist Party – for all of their principal men were members of the Government. To this there was one exception – Andrew Bonar Law.

By the end of 1921, his health seemed largely restored. Bonar Law alone represented a possible nucleus of opposition opinion within the Unionist ranks.

In the early autumn of 1922, it seemed likely that Britain would become involved in a war between Greece and Turkey. This increased the murmurings among Unionist opponents of the Government, and gave some urgency to their arguments. The leaders of their Party who were ministers in the Government sought a showdown, and summoned a meeting of Unionist notables at the Carlton Club for 19 October 1922. The date was an unfortunate choice, for the result of a by-election in Newport became known just before the meeting assembled. In very unlikely territory, a Unionist who was not attached to the Coalition had captured a Coalition Liberal seat, with Labour second and the Liberal – also unattached – running third. With the news of this victory to sustain them, the rebels were victorious in the more crucial contest at the Carlton Club. Within a few hours, Lloyd George had resigned, and Bonar Law had been offered the King's commission to form a Government.

But with whom? Thirteen Unionist Ministers, headed by Austen Chamberlain, Lord Balfour, and Lord Birkenhead, issued a public statement that they refused to send Lloyd George 'a message of dismissal', and that they considered the Carlton Club decisions as 'unwise as they are ungrateful'. Evidently they were not convinced that Bonar Law could form a Government which would withstand a General Election, and they anticipated a renewal of the Coalition in the near future. Necessarily this outburst excluded from Bonar Law's administration most of the ablest and most experienced men in the Unionist Party. Although Law was unanimously elected Leader of his Party a few days later, the Government over which he presided was – in Churchill's famous phrase – the 'second eleven'. A measure of the Prime Minister's difficulty is given by his offer of the Chancellorship of the Exchequer to Reginald McKenna. Technically, McKenna was still a Liberal, although his Liberalism was evidently wearing thin, and he caused some consternation by addressing a Unionist meeting. But he refused Bonar Law's offer – although apparently for commercial rather than political reasons.

*   *   *

Some, at any rate, of the Asquithian Liberals seem to have been overjoyed at the defeat of Lloyd George, even though he was replaced by an overt Unionist. Asquith himself had declared that 'a government of reactionaries' was preferable to the Coalition,[1] and his wife wrote one of her effusive and tactless letters to Bonar Law, promising him (apparently without the slightest authority) 'no lack of generosity in my husband if and when he has to criticise'.[2]

Whether through the 'sale of honours' or by other means, the Coalition had amassed a very large fund, which has been estimated by a future Liberal Chief Whip, Vivian Phillipps, at something like £3,000,000.[3] The Unionists' share of the money (minus the considerable private deductions of their Treasurer, Lord Farquhar) seems to have gone straight into the central funds of their Party. The other section was to form the basis of what became known as the 'Lloyd George Fund' – of which the Liberal Party never had free disposal.

*   *   *

[1] Trevor Wilson, The downfall of the Liberal Party, p. 202.
[2] Margot Asquith to Bonar Law, 24 October 1922. Bonar Law papers 108/1/3.
[3] Vivian Phillipps, My days and ways, p. 110.

The 1922 General Election was fought in circumstances almost as extraordinary, and almost as damaging to the Liberals, as the previous one.

Lloyd George's National Liberals absorbed most of the Liberal Coalitionists, and also the nine National Democratic Party M.P.s who sought re-election. It is often exceedingly difficult, or even arbitrary, to decide to which group a Liberal candidate should be allocated, and a substantial number of Liberal M.P.s who had supported the Coalition defended their seats with the blessing of the Asquithians. Some candidates are often described as 'Liberals unattached', as they had not made it clear whom they proposed to follow. With rather splendid understatement, *The Times* attributes its own taxonomic difficulties to 'the confused state of Party politics resulting from the break-up of the Coalition'.[1] The number of National Liberal candidates may be set somewhere in the region of 150–160, but it is very difficult to be more precise. Most of these seats had been held in the old Parliament.

The relationship between the National Liberal candidates and the Unionists was, to say the least, highly ambiguous. Some of them were relying on local Unionist support, while others more or less made their peace with the Asquithians. A rather delightful example of the problems thus presented is given by the correspondence between Lloyd George and Sir Edward Rhodes, one of the principal Lloyd George Liberals in Manchester.[2] The arrangements of 1918 had resulted in no single Liberal, with or without the Coupon, being returned for Manchester or Salford, and repeated attempts by the Coalition Liberals to secure some accommodation with the Conservatives had failed. Hence neither group of Liberals had anything to gain from the *status quo*, and in 1922 the Liberals in both cities went to the poll without distinction of past associations. Rhodes attempted to secure official approval for this arrangement, but Lloyd George plaintively replied, '. . . As some of our candidates in other parts of Lancashire and elsewhere are working with the Conservatives, I could hardly give your pact a public blessing, otherwise I should certainly have done so.'

The Asquithians, with about 320 or so candidates, looked more

---

[1] *The Times*, 15 November 1922.
[2] Lloyd George/Sir Edward Rhodes correspondence, 6–8 November 1922. Lloyd George papers G/30/2/24 and 25.

like serious aspirants for office, and their relationships with the other Parties at the local level varied. In about twenty-four constituencies, Asquithians attacked seats held by National Liberals, and in five the National Liberals attacked an Asquithian seat. In Berwick & Haddington, and in East Ham South, no fewer than three *soi-disant* Liberals were contending for the seat.

Labour this time fielded 407 candidates. Their programme still bore marks of Liberal antecedents – notably in the fact that they (like the Asquithians, but unlike the Lloyd Georgeites) gave prominence to the taxation of land values. The Unionists, with 441 candidates, were fighting on the broadest front; but even they, it will be observed, left 174 seats uncontested. No doubt the long-standing uncertainty about their relationship with the Lloyd George Liberals explains many of these cases.

*   *   *

Contrary to most political calculations – including those of Sir George Younger[1] – the Unionists secured a comfortable working majority of about seventy seats over all other Parties and groups combined. Yet in spite of their overall victory they had lost about fifteen seats more than they had gained.

The National Liberals made their inevitable losses. The Asquithians made a considerable number of aggregate gains, with the result that the 117 Liberal M.P.s were approximately evenly divided between the two groups.

Labour had the most cause to rejoice, with sixty-five overall gains. For the first time there were more Labour M.P.s – about twenty-five more – than Liberals, even taking the two Liberal groups together. The status of the Labour Party as official opposition was undeniable. Nevertheless, the popular vote cast for the two Liberal wings together was almost exactly the same as the popular vote for the Labour Party.

The constituency results did not follow a national pattern with any exactitude. Asquithians, Unionists, and Labour made gains from, and losses to, each other in every possible direction. Only one thing was perfectly clear from the election – the inviability of the National Liberals as an independent Party. Not only could their eight gains

[1] Herbert Lewis to Lloyd George, 6 November 1922. Lloyd George papers, G/12/1/1.

be set against seventy-eight losses, but only four candidates – all of them in Wales – had contrived to hold their seats against Unionist opposition.[1] No doubt the great majority of the National Liberals who were returned owed their seats either to local agreements or else to the fact that the Coalition had collapsed so suddenly that the Unionists had not had time to select a candidate against them.

It was an election of freaks and surprises. The National Liberals lost Winston Churchill. At the head of the poll in his constituency of Dundee was the Prohibitionist E. A. Scrymgeour, victorious on his sixth attempt in this highly improbable place. Captain Guest finished third in East Dorset. One of the very few National Liberal gains was Caithness and Sutherland. The M.P. had sat in the old Parliament as a Coalition Liberal, but defended his seat as an Asquithian. He was defeated by a young baronet, destined to play a very important role in the Liberal Party – Sir Archibald Sinclair.

The Asquithians did a good deal better, yet they lost Sir Donald Maclean, who had held the fort so bravely in Asquith's absence, but was forced into third place in Peebles and South Midlothian. Sir John Simon avenged his by-election defeat by capturing Spen Valley from Labour in a three-cornered fight. Among the names as yet unknown, but of future importance, was Percy Harris, who took SW. Bethnal Green from the Conservatives in another three-cornered contest. There were other surprise victories, too: Oxford, which had been invincibly Unionist for many years, suddenly fell to the Liberals; and Penistone, which had been lost to Labour in the by-election, was recaptured. Dr Christopher Addison, who had said some peculiarly nasty things about the Asquithians in 1918[2] resigned from the Government in 1921 in circumstances which reflected little credit on either him or them; in 1922 he defended Shoreditch as an Asquithian, but ran third – a National Liberal recapturing the seat.

The Unionists' results were much less surprising; but Labour's great advance was marred by the very serious loss of Arthur Henderson, who was defeated at Widnes. Apart from this, they fared well. Ramsay MacDonald returned to the House as M.P. for Aberavon; and by a narrow majority the Parliamentary Labour Party elected him leader. Philip Snowden also returned to the House, as M.P. for Colne Valley, and George Lansbury regained Bow & Bromley.

[1] Carmarthen, Denbigh, Flint, Swansea West.
[2] *Manchester Guardian*, 3 December 1918.

INTO THE LIMELIGHT.

Ramsay MacDonald, Asquith, Lloyd George)

Sidney Webb took Seaham from the Liberals, and Clement Attlee took Limehouse from the Coalition Liberals.

In some areas, Labour made massive advances. Ten of the eleven county seats in Durham fell to them. Ten of the fifteen Glasgow seats returned Labour M.P.s – and seven of these seats represented gains from the Coalition.

More significant still was the nature of some of the new Labour M.P.s, who included a high proportion of able converts from the Liberals, such as C. P. Trevelyan and Arthur Ponsonby. Noel Buxton, who held North Norfolk as a Liberal in 1910, but lost the seat to the Coalition in 1918, now regained it in the Labour interest. The Unionist *Constitutional Year Book* for 1923 listed eleven former Liberal M.P.s who fought under the banner of the Labour Party in 1922.

For all Liberals, the writing stood plain on the wall. They were not the Government, and they were not even the Opposition. No longer could they assume that the 'swing of the pendulum' would return them to office sooner or later. The question now was not how to win the battle for power against the Unionist Party, but how to survive at all in face of the challenge from Labour.

10

Switchback

ἐκ Χάεως δ᾽Ἔρεβός τε μέλαινά τε Νὺξ ἐγένοντο.

Out of Chaos, Hell and black Night were born.

HESIOD, *Theogony* 123.

'. . . *I hate you being so far away. H.H.A. is not Ll.G. proof by any means. . . . We must not let L.G.* [sic.] *alone with H.H.A. more than we can help.*'

Letter from Sir Donald Maclean to
Viscount Gladstone, 29 December
1923. (*Viscount Gladstone papers
46,474, fol. 52.*)

Just after the 1922 General Election, the new National Liberal Chief Whip, Hilton Young, was asked by the Speaker whether his group regarded themselves as a section of the Opposition. He replied that he did not feel able to give a definite answer.[1] But Lloyd George had made up his own mind on the subject. A few days after the election, he published a manifesto calling for Liberal reunion. The body of the National Liberals – at least in Wales – seems to have taken the same view; Lord St Davids told Lloyd George that, 'the tone was very strong indeed in favour of Liberal reunion, much stronger than it has ever been before.[2]

But a number of Lloyd George's colleagues still hankered after a 'Centre Party', or some other kind of union with the Conservatives. On 4 May 1923, Winston Churchill said that he was, 'at a loss to see what the older parties were quarrelling about'; while, from the other wing of the old Coalition, Lord Birkenhead spoke in a similar vein a little over a month later.

[1] Vivian Phillipps, *My days and ways*, p. 91.
[2] St Davids to Lloyd George, 29 January 1923. Lloyd George papers G/17/6/1.

Captain 'Freddie' Guest also gave no signs of having abandoned the idea of a Centre Party. On 19 June 1923, he described 'the ideal of a coalition of all moderate-minded men' against Socialism as, 'not in the least distasteful', and declared that 'the role of Liberalism, therefore, has changed, and will be henceforth in my opinion no more than a political expression, and an attitude of mind, becoming as time goes on the left wing of a great national party, which intends to keep the Socialist out.'[1]

What was surprising was not so much the fact that Guest expressed these views – they had, after all, been the received opinion of the National Liberals a year or so earlier – but the vigour and authority with which they were repudiated. The *Daily Chronicle*, which was controlled, as we have seen, by Lloyd George, wrote of the 'total divergence between National Liberal policy and the policy which [Guest] put forward', and said that 'the National Liberals as a body cannot accept this non-Liberal view',[2] while Lloyd George himself repudiated his former Chief Whip in no uncertain terms.[3]

The official view of the Asquithians was strongly in favour of reunion. As *Liberal Magazine* put it:

'Whether [the National Liberals] were right or wrong in their theory that national safety required union between themselves and the Conservatives, they cannot now put it in practice because the Conservative Party has cut the knot. Thus the purpose for which the Coalition Liberals separated themselves has either been accomplished or has become impracticable. Why, then, should separation continue?'[4]

But within both groups there remained doubts and suspicions. The Asquithians seem at first to have set the blame on Guest rather than on Lloyd George. Viscount Gladstone wrote in January 1923 that:[5] 'L.G. clearly is bound to F[rederick] G[uest] & probably because F.G. knows too much. So I think F.G. is pulling the strings.'

But in Viscount Gladstone's view, Lloyd George was 'more or less

[1] *Daily Chronicle*, 20 June 1923.
[2] *Idem.*
[3] *Liberal Magazine*, 1923, p. 423.
[4] *Liberal Magazine*, 1922, p. 789.
[5] Viscount Gladstone to Maclean (copy?), 23 January 1923. Viscount Gladstone papers 46,474, fol. 29–30.

ready himself to come to fair terms'. It seems possible that Lloyd George was hampered, then and thereafter, by the fact that his political fund was not liquid, but was largely sunk in the *Daily Chronicle*.

Lloyd George for his part was not wholly convinced of the good-will of the Asquithians, writing to C. P. Scott that, 'the leaders of the Independent Liberals are determined that [Liberal reunion] should not occur. Simon is working against it; the Whips are whip-ping against it; Lord Gladstone and Geoffrey Howard are using every endeavour to persuade members of the party not to encourage it.'[1]

*   *   *

The Asquithians had difficulties of their own which were only obliquely related to the reunion question. It will be recalled that there had been much trouble over the appointment of Whips in 1919, but that this had eventually been resolved by G. R. Thorne and J. M. Hogge acting jointly as Whips in Parliament. After the 1922 Election, a third colleague, Sir Arthur Marshall, was added to these two.[2] In February 1923, Thorne resigned for reasons of health, and Asquith sought to take this as an opportunity to remodel the Whips' Office on the old plan, with a single Whip.

The appointment of a Chief Whip presented difficult problems. On paper, Hogge had by far the best claim, but the Asquithians not only found his personal character unacceptable, but had some doubts about his political reliability.[3] After Hogge, Sir Arthur Marshall seemed best qualified, but Maclean at any rate considered Asquith's former Secretary, Vivian Phillipps, to be a 'stronger' candidate,[4] and Phillipps was duly appointed. Although familiar with Parliamentary business, he was only a new M.P. A man of the highest probity, he was also one of the most virulent of all the opponents of Lloyd George, and his appointment could hardly be

---

[1] Lloyd George to Scott, 15 March 1923. Lloyd George papers G/17/11/6.

[2] The official position of Marshall is rather obscure. Compare Phillipps, *op. cit.*, pp. 80, 82; *Liberal Year Book*, 1923, p. 1.

[3] Thus, Maclean wrote to Viscount Gladstone, 28 February 1923, that Hogge 'has been in Sutherland's pocket for a couple of years'. (Viscount Gladstone papers 46,474.) Sir William Sutherland was a Lloyd Georgeite M.P. who was closely associated with Lloyd George's journalistic ventures.

[4] Maclean to Viscount Gladstone, 31 December 1922. Viscount Gladstone papers 46,474.

expected to help the cause of reunion. Phillipps appreciated the invidiousness of the situation, and told Asquith so[1] – but Asquith persisted, and Phillipps accepted the post.

Sir Arthur Marshall took, apparently without cavil, the position of English Whip, but Hogge refused to accept the corresponding Scottish post. There was a petulant and public exchange of correspondence – some of which appears to have been confidential[2] – but it seems that Asquith did not clearly inform Hogge what the position would be.[3] Although Phillipps was brought into the 'charmed circle' which controlled the L.C.A., he did not receive the overall control which Gulland and his predecessors had had. Thus the confusion of authority remained.

The ordinary M.P.s were a good deal more keen on reunion than some of the leaders. C. R. Dudgeon of Galloway[4] was elected as a Liberal *sans phrase*, and at first received neither whip. Finding it necessary to take some whip in order to keep informed of Parliamentary business, he asked for, and received, the Asquithian whip. Soon afterwards he asked for, and received, the Lloyd George whip as well. Neither group raised any objection to this arrangement. But there was a certain amount of altercation in the National Liberal ranks when Colonel Stephenson, who had been elected National Liberal M.P. for one of the Sheffield constituencies, decided to take the Asquithian whip as well.[5] Nevertheless, the practice of 'double whipping' seems to have become fairly common.

In March 1923, a group of seventy-three rank-and-file M.P.s from both sections signed a memorandum for speedy reunion. The numbers are even more impressive when it is noted that about twenty 'leaders' from the two sections were not invited to sign. Both Asquith and Lloyd George evinced sympathy with their aims; but Asquith argued that regular and continuous co-operation in the division lobbies was an essential condition precedent to the establishment of any formal machinery.

In the House of Lords, active steps were taken in the direction of

---

[1] Vivian Phillipps, *My days and ways*, p. 83.

[2] Viscount Gladstone to Sir Donald Maclean (copy ?), 14 February 1923. Viscount Gladstone papers 46,474.

[3] *Idem*.

[4] Information to the author from the late Major C. R. Dudgeon.

[5] Hilton Young to Lloyd George, 8 June 1923, etc. Lloyd George papers G/10/14/10 and 11. See *Liberal Magazine*, 1923, pp. 421–2.

reunion. In January 1923, Viscount Grey was elected Leader of all the Liberal Peers, whatever their past affiliations had been; although it seems that goodwill was not universal.[1]

There were plenty of signs of reunion in the constituencies. In 1922, an Independent had held Anglesey with a small majority over a National Liberal. When the M.P. died, a Liberal receiving support from both sections of the Party was able to take the seat with a majority over Labour and Conservative votes combined. Soon afterwards, another Liberal received the support of both groups in Ludlow; he did not win, but he much improved the Liberal position in the constituency. By-elections went rather well for the Liberals in 1923, except when they faced three-cornered contests in urban constituencies. East Willesden was captured by Harcourt Johnstone with a convincing overturn of votes in a straight fight on 3 March, and Tiverton was taken by Francis Acland on 21 June.

*   *   *

Changes in other quarters greatly hastened Liberal reunion, and provided a mighty boost for the Liberal Party. In May 1923, Bonar Law resigned, and was succeeded by Stanley Baldwin. Like his predecessor, Baldwin attempted to secure the services of McKenna at the Exchequer. This time McKenna accepted conditionally, but for technical reasons was unable to assume office.[2]

On 25 October 1923, Baldwin suddenly declared in favour of a policy of Protection as a means of dealing with unemployment. Various interpretations have been set on the reasons for Baldwin's pronouncement; but he explained it by saying that he regarded Bonar Law's pledge not to tamper with fiscal policies as binding on himself, and that he was prepared to submit to a General Election if he was challenged. The challenge, of course, was made.

This rendered Liberal reunion a matter of high urgency. On 13 November 1923[3] a consultation between the independent Liberals represented by Asquith and Simon, and the National Liberals represented by Lloyd George and Sir Alfred Mond, resulted in an announcement that, 'all candidates will be adopted and described as Liberals,

---

[1] St Davids to Lloyd George, 31 January 1923. Lloyd George papers G/17/6/2. *The Times*, 1 February 1923.

[2] See D.N.B. 1941–50, p. 554. But see also *Liberal Magazine*, 1923, p. 321.

[3] *Liberal Magazine*, 1923, p. 710.

and will be supported by the whole strength of the Party without regard to any past differences', and that, 'Liberal candidates will go to the poll in such numbers as to make united Liberalism a practical alternative to the present Government.'

This lead was followed in the constituencies, and at that election it was very rare for two nominal Liberals to oppose each other. The visible signs of past disunity were speedily suppressed. In most places, National Liberal organizations were dismantled as quickly as possible. The *Lloyd George Liberal Magazine*, which had existed since 1920, did not appear after the issue of November 1923.

Even men like Guest and Churchill, who were still Liberals on the Free Trade issue – if on little else – rallied unequivocally to join battle with the Conservatives. There was a widespread feeling of relief that the internecine battles were over. Thus Runciman wrote to Lloyd George of his 'great joy . . . to become united with you and those Liberals who have stood loyally by you'.[1]

It was agreed that £100,000 should be made available from the Lloyd George Fund. Headquarters certainly received £90,000 from that source,[2] but Lloyd George later stated that the actual sum given from the Fund was £160,000,[3] so much must have been given directly to candidates. The Liberals were able to field 454 candidates, against 536 Conservatives and 434 Labour. These numbers, it will be observed, indicate that all Parties were leaving many constituencies uncontested. This was partly due to various local arrangements between the three Parties.[4]

The key issue of the election was Free Trade, and this doubtless caused many Conservative Free Traders to support Liberal candidates in their constituencies.[5] But the Liberal campaign was not confined to the tariff issue. The election manifesto[6] was already demanding public works schemes as a relief for unemployment.

---

[1] Runciman to Lloyd George, 8 December 1923. Lloyd George papers G/17/4/1.

[2] Asquith papers 141, fol. 2.

[3] Malcolm Thompson, *David Lloyd George*, p. 369. For an intermediate stage in the negotiations, see Viscount Gladstone to Maclean, 30 November 1923. Viscount Gladstone papers 46,474, fol. 48–50.

[4] For some details, see R. W. Lynam, *The first Labour Government*, pp. 63–4.

[5] Phillipps, *op. cit.*, p. 96.

[6] *Liberal Magazine*, 1923, pp. 711–15.

While urging retrenchment, it opposed 'the starvation of, or false economies in, education'; demanded site value rating, and took a radical line on a wide variety of problems, including old age pensions, sex equality, and 'co-operation between employers and employed.'

*   *   *

Polling day was 6 December 1923. When the results were complete, an extraordinary picture emerged. The Conservatives were still the largest Party, with 258 seats, but they had lost their overall majority. Labour was next with 191, while the Liberals had 158. For once, the seats secured by the Parties bore a close relation to the number of votes polled. Although none of the three Parties gained or lost as many as 200,000 votes, this does not mean that the swing of opinion was small. The Conservatives had fifty-seven more candidates than in 1922, and their average vote per opposed candidate dropped from 48·6 per cent to 42·6 per cent.[1] The Liberal achievement is more impressive when it is recalled that there was some reduction in the number of candidates, and many National Liberals who were confronted with Conservative opposition in 1923 had had straight fights against Labour, and presumably received the Conservative vote almost entire, in 1922.

It is often observed that the Liberals 'swept the West Country'. Of the thirty-six seats in Cornwall, Devon, Gloucestershire, Somerset, and Wiltshire, the Liberals secured twenty-three. Asquith noted that it was possible to travel from Land's End to Oxfordshire without setting foot in a single constituency which was not Liberal. But it is not correct to consider that Liberals had been driven from the industrial heartland to the extremities of the British Isles. In some of the large towns, they did badly. The last Liberal seat fell in Glasgow, in Leeds, and in Sheffield. Like Labour, they failed to record a single victory in Birmingham. Yet in other places they did far better. Half or more of the seats were Liberal in such towns as Edinburgh, Manchester, Newcastle-upon-Tyne, Bradford, Hull, and Nottingham. The Liberals even took two seats in Liverpool. Numerous medium-sized industrial towns were Liberal. In many of the poorer areas of London, Liberals were meeting all comers on equal or more

[1] D. Butler and J. Freeman, *British political facts 1900–1960* (London 1963), p. 123.

than equal terms. A wide band of rural constituencies in the Midlands was Liberal. There were even Liberal victories in places like Aylesbury and Blackpool which had not been taken in 1906. In the exultation of their triumph, the Liberals could hardly be expected to notice that more than a quarter of their seats were held with majorities of less than a thousand, and that more than half had been won in straight fights with one or other of their opponents.[1]

Personal gains and losses were interesting and important. Winston Churchill, fighting his last battle as a Liberal, failed to capture West Leicester. Sir Donald Maclean moved to defend Kilmarnock, but lost the seat to Labour. Sir Alfred Mond was narrowly defeated in Swansea West. Those former National Liberals who had been most closely associated with the deeds of the Coalition often fared badly. Charles McCurdy and Hilton Young, who had followed Guest as National Liberal Chief Whips, were defeated. Few Liberal tears, perhaps, were shed over Sir Hamar Greenwood, who had been the instrument of the Coalition policy in Ireland at its most vicious phase; but he was still, technically, a Liberal. Among the Liberal gains, Charles Masterman, 'the unluckiest man in politics', at last returned to the House, representing the Rusholme division of Manchester; Ramsay Muir, that brilliant writer in the Liberal cause, took Rochdale, and 'Freddie' Guest captured Stroud. One of the very few contests where Liberal met Liberal was Cardiganshire. This was even more remarkable because the redoubtable Independent Liberal, Rhys Hopkin Morris, took the seat from the 'official' Liberal defender who was a Lloyd Georgeite. Hopkin Morris made rather a habit of winning when all the odds were stacked against him. Another 'habit' was signalled in the Labour Party, for Arthur Henderson was defeated (this time by a Liberal) in Newcastle-upon-Tyne East. Henderson was conspicuously successful in his by-elections and conspicuously unsuccessful in his General Elections.

*   *   *

Apparently on the King's suggestion, Baldwin did not resign at once, but remained in office to meet the new House. Everything

[1] For aspects of the campaign, and relationships between the Parties, see Chris Cook, 'A stranger death of Liberal England' (pp. 287–313 of *Lloyd George: twelve essays*, ed. A. J. P. Taylor, 1971).

turned on the Liberals. Would they sustain the Conservatives in
power, put Labour in, or make a serious bid for office them-selves?

The third of these possibilities is generally neglected by historians,
but it was by no means ridiculous. The Liberals, it is true, had only
a quarter of the seats in the House, but it was at least as reasonable
to invite a Party with 158 M.P.s and a Front bench full of experienced ex-Ministers to constitute the King's Government as to invite
the Labour Party, albeit with 33 more M.P.s, but with hardly anyone
who had had senior Ministerial experience, and not many who
were capable of it. The Liberal leaders themselves discussed the
allocation of offices in a Liberal Government in some detail, and
Asquith expressed the view that Labour was not ready to assume
office.[1] When Mond left the country at the beginning of January
1924, he wrote to Asquith offering his services, 'if by any chance
in my absence you may be called on and decide to form a Government'.[2]

The City of London Conservatives urged Baldwin to support a
Liberal Government if the Liberals could not be brought to support
a Conservative one, and other Conservatives seemed to favour the
same view. Winston Churchill put forward the suggestion that two
motions should be carried when the King's Speech was submitted
to the new Parliament – one censuring the Conservative Government
and the other repudiating socialism.[3] If Asquith had followed this
advice, it is difficult to see how any result could have emerged
except a Liberal administration. Many Conservatives, particularly
Free Traders in the Lancashire area,[4] were very unhappy about the
circumstances of the election, and would not have been likely to
object. Such an administration might well have proved viable, for
on most issues Asquith could expect the support of one or other of
the opposing Parties, and it was not necessary that it should always
be the same one.

But if the Liberals were forced to choose between Conservatives
and Labour, the outlook for Liberalism was grim. Some Liberals
palpably preferred Labour to Conservatives, and would be likely
to go Labour if the Party leaders decided to uphold a Conservative

[1] Phillipps, *op. cit.*, pp. 97–8.
[2] Mond to Asquith, 2 January 1934. Asquith papers 18, fol. 94–7.
[3] *The Times*, 18 January 1924.
[4] *The Times*, 18 January 1924, concerning Lord Derby and Sir Archibald
Salvidge.

Government. Others preferred the Conservatives, and would not be likely to remain long in the Party if it supported a Labour Government. There was a further peril in the situation. Voters who approved of the behaviour of the Government, be it Conservative or Labour, would tend to give credit to the Government, while voters who disapproved would be certain to blame the Liberals. Whatever happened, the Liberals could not fail to suffer.

Asquith rejected the idea of playing for a Liberal administration. Why he did so must remain a mystery; and it is arguable that this decision was the most disastrous single action ever performed by a Liberal towards his Party.

On 18 December 1923, Asquith spoke at the National Liberal Club. He had had previous consultation with Lloyd George,[1] and both Lloyd George and Simon 'expressed their hearty concurrence'[2] in the contents of his speech. It could admit of more than one construction; but it was universally taken to mean that Asquith was prepared to put Labour in office. It has been said that Lloyd George played a large part in causing this decision to be taken.

Although Lloyd George was fully implicated in Asquith's decision, he appreciated the political dangers, and told C. P. Scott that:[3] 'the Liberal Party is very divided on the question of supporting Labour. Quite a number of the "important and influential" emphatically dislike it, but if Ramsay were tactful and conciliatory I feel certain that the Party as a whole would support him in an advanced Radical programme.'

We shall later have cause to observe that Ramsay MacDonald was neither tactful nor conciliatory, and that no one could possibly call his programme either advanced or Radical. From these facts derived a great deal of trouble.

The speech which the Conservative Government set in the mouth of the King on 15 January 1924 was, as one historian says,[4] 'generous with promises it ran little risk of being asked to honour'. Rather strangely, this Speech made no mention of the Protection issue on which the election had been fought. J. R. Clynes, for the Labour Party, then submitted a simple motion of No Confidence. Asquith

---

[1] Asquith to Lloyd George, 14 December 1923. Lloyd George papers G/16/1/1.
[2] Lord Oxford, *Memories and Reflections*, vol. 2, p. 209.
[3] Lloyd George to Scott, 27 December 1923. Lloyd George papers G/17/11/8.
[4] C. Loch Mowat, *Britain between the wars*, p. 170.

made the Liberal position clear almost at the outset: 'I propose to vote, and advise all my friends to vote, in favour of that amendment.'

In the later stages of the debate, Baldwin made a very prescient statement. Turning to the Labour benches, he declared, 'The future lies between the honourable members opposite and ourselves.'

Not all Liberals were satisfied by Asquith's attitude. Winston Churchill (still out of the House) wrote a strong letter, which was communicated to the Press, indicating that, 'the enthronement in office of a Socialist government will be a serious national misfortune such as has usually befallen great States only on the morrow of defeat in war'. In the division which followed the Debate, the official support of the Liberal Party was, of course, given to Clynes's motion; but ten Liberal M.P.s went so far as to vote with the Government, and five more were 'absent unaccounted for'.[1] The Government was defeated, and the King invited Ramsay MacDonald to form an administration.

There were stories – perhaps apocryphal – of the Premier needing to consult an almanack to decide what offices needed to be filled, and his handling of Henderson was crude in the extreme. MacDonald had to draw from outside his Party – notably, Lord Parmoor from the Conservatives and Lord Haldane from the Liberals. It is striking that the sometime Liberal Imperialist Haldane should have ended his career as Labour's first Lord Chancellor, but he had been moving in that direction for some time,[2] and had been in contact with MacDonald since the election. It seems that Haldane made the first approach.[3] Asquith, while considering the decision ill-advised, bore his old friend no malice.[4] One of the Labour Law Officers gives an explanation[5] which is probably close to the truth: 'He was a Hegelian and looked upon the nation as a corporate entity –

[1] *The Times*, 23 January 1924. The Liberals who voted with the Government were: J. Duckworth; J. H. Edwards; Lieutenant-Colonel A. England; Sir E. J. Griffith; H. C. Hogbin; W. A. Jenkins; Sir Beddoe Rees; Sir T. Robinson; W. E. Robinson; J. B. Shirrock. The absentees were: General Spears; R. N. Kay; Sir R. Thomas; Sir Clifford Cory; Sir Murdoch Macdonald.

[2] Haldane/Asquith correspondence. Haldane papers 5,915, fol. 128, 131, 136–7, 143, 161, 164; *Liberal Magazine*, 1920, p. 86–7.

[3] Haldane/MacDonald correspondence, 19–22 December 1923. Haldane papers 5,916, fol. 75–7.

[4] Haldane/Asquith correspondence, 22–3 January 1924. Haldane papers 5,916, fol. 75–7.

[5] Sir Henry Slessor, *A history of the Liberal Party*, p. 159.

why he ever joined the old individualistic Liberal Party is more difficult to explain than his association with Labour.'

*   *   *

As some wise commentators had predicted at the time, the new Government was far more moderate than had been generally expected. MacDonald, who is now regarded as an indifferent Premier, acquired a high reputation in the office of Foreign Secretary, which he also held. The Housing Act, introduced by John Wheatley (one of the few so-called 'left-wingers' in the Government), was an important measure for municipal housing. The one Budget, introduced by Philip Snowden, was characterized by Liberal orthodoxy, if not Liberal imagination; the most notable feature was the repeal of the McKenna Duties – in the teeth of Protectionist wails of impending disaster – and a substantial reduction of import duties on foodstuffs.

A clear sign of the strain which this very qualified support for the Labour Government was putting on the Liberals is given by the rapid passage of Churchill towards the Conservative ranks. On 19 March 1924, he contested the Abbey division of Westminster as an Independent Anti-Socialist, against official candidates of all three Parties. He received strong support from individual Conservatives and from the Press, and was eventually defeated by the official Conservative by a hair's breadth – the Liberal securing a derisory vote. Later in the year, Churchill appeared in Epping as a 'Constitutionalist', where he received official Conservative support, and was elected.

The strain on the Liberal M.P.s was tremendous. The Labour Party had seventy seats fewer than the Conservatives. Therefore, Liberal abstention was not enough; in order to prevent the Government being defeated, the Liberals must actually vote with them in the division lobbies. Labour did nothing to help. As Vivian Phillipps writes:[1]

'The Government Whips were the last word in incompetence. They would put down motions for the suspension of the eleven o'clock rule without consulting me as to whether a sufficient number of our people would be able to stay after eleven o'clock

[1] Phillipps, *op. cit.*, p. 104.

to see them safe in Divisions. They would make arrangements with the Tories about the business to be taken on this or that day and would leave me in complete ignorance of the arrangements until the House met.

'Our people became increasingly restive and this was intensified by the Government attitude to them in the constituencies. On the platform in the country not only was there no acknowledgement of the fact that it was largely through our support that they were able to maintain themselves as a Government, but there was a constant stream of ill-natured criticism and frequently abuse of the Liberal Party.'

In the same way the Labour Party showed no sign of discriminating between those Liberal M.P.s who were close to the Conservatives and those who were well disposed to the Government. Although Labour obviously had neither the power nor the intention to contest every constituency in the land, yet they took an evident delight in advancing candidates in places where nobody but the Conservatives could possibly benefit – notably constituencies which had been narrowly captured or held by radical Liberals in 1923 in straight fights.[1] The Oxford by-election of 5 June showed the effect of this policy; the Labour candidate came a bad third, but polled enough votes to give a Liberal seat to the Conservative.

*   *   *

In spite of this sort of behaviour, the Government often survived through Liberal votes. On one notable occasion, however, it was the Conservatives who saved the Government. This was on the 'five cruisers' division of 18 March, when the Liberals divided the House against a Government proposal to speed up naval replacements. But the tenuous and qualified support which the Liberals generally gave to the Labour Government at last came to an end as a result of the 'Campbell case'. The official Communist organ, *Workers' Weekly*, had published two articles – one of which concluded by inviting members of the Armed Forces to, 'Refuse to shoot down your fellow workers. Refuse to fight for profits. Turn your weapons on your oppressors.'

On 5 August, J. R. Campbell, editor of *Workers' Weekly*, was

[1] See Trevor Wilson, *The downfall of the Liberal Party*, pp. 267–70.

arrested on a charge of incitement to mutiny. On the following day, the Attorney-General indicated that the arrest and prosecution had the support of the Government.[1] But when Campbell was brought before the Magistrates a few days later, the Crown asked for a discharge. Thereupon, the Communist Party revealed that the Defence had sought to subpoena MacDonald, Henderson, Clynes, and others as witnesses.

The Liberals opposed the prosecution from the start. As *Liberal Magazine* put it – long before the *dénouement*:[2]

'Mr Campbell's two articles contain hardly anything with which we agree, and a good deal that we should describe as against the public interest; but cases in which it is worth while to prosecute people for the public expression of their opinions on public questions are very few and far between, and this, in our view, is not one of them. What chiefly interests us is the fact that a Labour Minister's first impulse was for prosecution and suppression.'

When Parliament met after the summer recess, the Conservatives submitted a motion of censure on the Government for their handling of the case. If such a motion had been carried, there was no doubt that the Government would have been compelled, by ordinary constitutional practice, either to resign or to advise a dissolution of Parliament. The Liberals were placed in an agonizing position. They disagreed with the Government, yet for both political and financial reasons they did not wish to bring the Government down. They therefore moved the appointment of a Select Committee to examine the matter.

The Conservatives decided to support the Liberal amendment; and it was on this amendment that the crucial decision was taken. The Government resolved to make it an issue of confidence – although, of course, the Liberal intention in moving it had been the very reverse. Obviously the Liberals could not vote against their own amendment, and equally obviously they had no way either of persuading the Government to become less intransigent or of persuading the Conservatives to withdraw their embarrassing support. The Liberal amendment was therefore carried by 364: 198

[1] Parl. Deb. (Commons) clxxvi, 6 August 1924, 2,928–9.
[2] *Liberal Magazine*, 1924, p. 520.

o

on 8 October 1924. It is startling to note that the Government's support included not only twelve rebel Liberals and two Nationalists, but also two Conservatives.[1]

It is very difficult to escape the conclusion that the Labour Government actually sought the defeat which it received, for there was no need whatever to turn a motion for an inquiry into a vote of confidence. Perhaps the Government was moved by a different consideration, also related to the growing restiveness of the Liberals. A trade treaty which had recently been negotiated with Russia was receiving a very hostile reception among Press and public, and the Liberals had already indicated their intention to move a highly critical resolution.[2] This resolution would presumably have passed, and, if so, resignation or dissolution would have been inevitable. It may well be that the Government preferred defeat on the Campbell issue to defeat on the Russian treaty question, where public passions were a good deal stronger. But, whatever the Government's motives, MacDonald chose dissolution. Polling was to take place on 29 October.

* * *

The last thing on earth that the Liberals wanted was a General Election. The ordinary electoral difficulties which they faced were evident enough. But there was another difficulty of which the public did not know: the difficulty of finance.

The 'reunion' of 1923 did not entail union of the finances of the two wings of the Liberal Party. The Lloyd George fund was not amalgamated with the general funds of the Party. An adequate grant had been made in 1923, but dependence on grants of this kind was obviously not satisfactory. The 'official' headquarters of the Party, as we saw in an earlier chapter, were well equipped financially in 1916, but had received nothing since – unless we include money raised in *ad hoc* election appeals. Meanwhile the Party had been spending at the rate of about £50,000 a year, apart from elections. The 1918 General Election had cost about £100,000. Candidates'

[1] The twelve Liberals (of whom ten had had no Labour opponent in 1923) were: R. Alstead, J. M. Hogge, Commander Kenworthy, A. Rendall, Captain Berkeley, Colonel Hodge, Percy Harris, J. J. O'Neill, W. A. Jowitt, A. E. Hillary, Dr Spero, and Mrs Wintringham. The Nationalists were T. J. S. Harbison and T. P. O'Connor; the Conservatives Mitchell Banks and Collingwood Hughes.

[2] *Liberal Magazine*, 1924, p. 640; *Ibid.*, 'A sham treaty', pp. 523–31.

expenses alone in 1922 had totalled nearly £120,000, while gifts (including those received from Scotland) had amounted to rather less than £50,000, and the precarious nature of Liberal finance is indicated by the fact that four donors alone accounted for well over half of this money.[1] The Asquithians' share of the 1923 election expenses may perhaps not have exceeded receipts. Nevertheless, the Liberal Party seems to have disbursed over half a million pounds more than it received between 1916 and the 1924 General Election. With the threat of that election firmly in his mind, Viscount Gladstone decided that, 'we ought to run about 500 candidates, and even if we can do this on our scale it will mean £200,000.'[2]

In the view – probably correct – of the Lloyd Georgeites, the 'official' funds were 'very nearly exhausted' at the end of 1923.[3] Maclean first met Lloyd George early in 1924, and told him that £50,000 a year would continue to be necessary for ordinary organization expenses – 'to do it well but not extravagantly'.[4]

Considerations of finance and organization were very closely interwoven. Lloyd George was profoundly dissatisfied with the workings of Liberal organization. At a meeting between Guest and the Asquithian, Geoffrey Howard, in December 1923, drastic reorganization proposals had been advanced, including the establishment of an 'Organization and Election Committee', consisting of a rough parity of Asquithians and Lloyd Georgeites. It was also proposed that at least two prominent Lloyd Georgeites should be appointed to the Whips' Office.[5]

By the spring of 1924, the Asquithians were getting desperate at the uncertainty of the financial position. Towards the end of April Viscount Gladstone wrote to Asquith, 'The absolutely essential thing

[1] Information based on accounts in Asquith papers, box 141. Some of these accounts are a little difficult to follow, and slightly different figures are occasionally given for the same item. This suggests that some were only interim figures. The principal donors in 1922 were Lord Cowdray (£12,000); Sir Walter Runciman (father of the ex-Minister), £10,000; T. R. Ferens (£5,000); and Lord Forteviot (£3,000 on English and £2,000 on Scottish list). Fol. 43–4.

[2] Viscount Gladstone to Maclean, 30 December 1923. Viscount Gladstone papers 46,474, fol. 54.

[3] Notes of meeting between Geoffrey Howard and Guest, 19 December 1923. Lloyd George papers G/8/13/1.

[4] Memorandum by Maclean, 17 January 1924. Viscount Gladstone papers 46,474, fol. 68–71.

[5] Notes of meeting between Geoffrey Howard and Guest, 19 December 1923. Lloyd George papers G/8/13/1.

is the fixing of candidates. This cannot be done without some financial guarantee.' But he admitted that, to Lloyd George, 'I am just a red rag', and suggested that Asquith himself could make an approach more profitably.[1]

Early in July, Viscount Gladstone went further, and told Asquith that he could not accept responsibility for the next election as matters stood. 270 candidates could be financed from Headquarters resources, but at least 180 more were needed.[2] Meanwhile, Lloyd George contended that he was not sufficiently consulted in and out of the House of Commons on matters of policy and procedure – and refused to make a contribution until this was remedied.[3] Viscount Gladstone freely admitted 'that the arrangement here is a make-shift, born out of past events, and urgently requiring great alteration and development. For this we have had no opportunity with things between us and No. 18 unsettled, with no money and the continuous shadow of General Elections.'[4] In the same document, he accepted the 'need of an active live man as Secretary of the National Liberal Federation'.

Viscount Gladstone urged Asquith that, 'if the next General Election is to be fought by us as it should be fought we require now a definite guarantee of £130,000. . . . Lloyd George does not see his way to anything sufficiently definite for bank credit.'[5]

This terrible uncertainty over finance vitiated the Parliamentary strategy of the Liberal Party. Early in August, Lloyd George was in discussion with Asquith, 'as to the proper moment for "bringing this thing to an end" – in other words – for throwing the Government out'. But, as Vivian Phillipps observed, 'that golden moment is governed by certain sordid considerations upon which Lloyd George must be heard'.[6]

In the course of a rather lengthy memorandum to Asquith later in August, Lloyd George noted:

[1] Viscount Gladstone to Asquith, 28 April 1924, Asquith papers 34, fol. 132.

[2] Sir Charles Mallet, *Herbert Gladstone*, p. 286.

[3] Memorandum by Maclean, July 1924, Viscount Gladstone papers 46,474, fol. 89–94.

[4] Memorandum by Viscount Gladstone, enclosed in letter from him to Runciman, 31 July 1924. Runciman papers. No. 18 (Abingdon St) was the Lloyd George headquarters. No. 21 was the Asquithian headquarters.

[5] Viscount Gladstone to Asquith, 1 August 1924. Asquith papers 34, fol. 133.

[6] Phillipps to Maclean, 5 August 1924. Asquith papers 34, fol. 134–5.

'In the negotiations which took place between Donald Maclean and myself immediately after the election, I promised to find half the expenses of the Central Organisation at 21, Abingdon Street, provided that there was a reorganisation which would satisfy me that the money would be efficiently spent. That offer has not yet been accepted . . . Quite frankly, what I have seen and heard during the last few months convinces me that the most urgent need for the moment is not funds but a thorough overhauling of the whole organisation . . . I urge that you and I with, say, the assistance of Donald Maclean and Mond, should have a confidential talk . . .'[1]

Viscount Gladstone raised no objection to this enquiry into organization, adding that, 'L.G. wishes to get most of us out of this office and there will be no difficulty so far as I am concerned!'[2]

When the inquiry was eventually held, with Mond as Chairman, it was reported that the paramount need was for sufficient candidates.[3] But the situation was still unresolved a few days before the Campbell debate. Vivian Phillipps says that:

'On October 4th, Donald Maclean went down to Churt to put to [Lloyd George] the urgency of the position. To his amazement Ll.G. merely remarked, "Why should we have more than 300 candidates?"

'This was the death-blow. We had assumed that reunion meant reunion of resources. . . . We had striven at every stage to meet Ll.G.'s views in the long-drawn-out negotiations and we now found ourselves left without the means to put more than 300 candidates in the field.

' . . . Then, at the last moment, an ultimatum from Mond to Ll.G. resulted in a message to Gladstone that Ll.G. would contribute £50,000 but no more. As the election was likely to cost not less than £200,000, this was not exactly a "fifty-fifty" offer, but in any case it was too late. By a superhuman effort Gladstone managed within the next few days to bring our numbers to close upon 350, and with these attenuated forces we were left to face the electors.'

[1] Lloyd George to Asquith, 20 August 1924. Asquith papers 34, fol. 136–43.
[2] Viscount Gladstone to Asquith, 27 August 1924. Asquith papers 18, fol. 100.
[3] Phillipps, op. cit., p. 113. For some indication of the state of the Liberal organization at the time, see Chris Cook, op. cit., p. 173.

In fact the Liberals contrived to meet the 1924 election expenses with a little over £40,000 in donations, £50,000 from Lloyd George, and about £30,000 from their own depleted funds.[1]

It is not difficult to discern the thoughts which lay behind the various excuses and explanations which the apologists for the two sides have given.[2] The Asquithian hierarchy, 'more royal than the King, more Catholic than the Pope', loathed and distrusted Lloyd George both as a politician and as a man. Lloyd George for his part did not consider that he was receiving the control to which he was entitled in the councils of the Party, and also believed that any money which he gave would be handled incompetently by the Asquithians. 'Pooling the resources' sounded reasonable enough; but what would happen to those resources – or to Lloyd George – if they were pooled? Lloyd George became evasive, slippery. This confirmed the Asquithians in their judgement. The Asquithians, not knowing what money was likely to be available, could make no long-term plans. This confirmed Lloyd George in his judgement. When he wrote, just after the 1924 election,[3] that the Liberals 'went into action a disorganized rabble', he was not far wrong; but while much responsibility for this state of affairs lay elsewhere, a good deal lay with him. The efficient organization of any institution must presuppose at least a degree of mutual trust between the principal participants, and years of savage political battle had destroyed this trust at all levels of the Party. The Asquithians looked very much like a clique of high-minded, but ageing, men, and may fairly be blamed for failing either to adjust themselves to the new realities of post-war politics, or to make way for others who would, while Lloyd George may be blamed for acting in a manner which made confidence impossible.

*　　*　　*

Although the story of Liberal finances and organization was not generally known, it was plain to see that the Liberal Party had over a hundred fewer candidates than it had had a year before, and that

[1] Asquith papers 141, fol. 202.
[2] See also Trevor Wilson, *op. cit.*, pp. 291–8.
[3] Lloyd George to Viscount Inchcape (copy), 5 November 1924. Lloyd George papers G/30/3/35.

it could not be considered a serious aspirant for power. Not only was the Liberal Party short of money and candidates, but – for reasons already discussed – it was bound to suffer defections to both other Parties. The Conservatives could imply that the sinister figure of Russian Bolshevism stood behind the Labour Government; while Labour could proclaim with pride that it had proved itself able to govern. Each of these arguments was likely to influence substantial bodies of Liberals. Whatever happened in the election campaign itself, it is hard to see how the result could have been anything but a Conservative victory, with the Liberals a poor third. But it seems that these conclusions were exaggerated by the celebrated 'Zinoviev letter' – a document purporting to emanate from Gregor Zinoviev, President of the Communist International, and encouraging subversive activities in Britain. It is now known that the letter was forged, although it seems to have been used in good faith. Strangely, this forged letter attracted a great deal of public attention, while the genuine, and equally subversive, speech which he delivered at Riga a few days earlier[1] attracted relatively little.

The Conservatives secured a great landslide: about 415 seats, against 152 for Labour, and a figure which has been set between forty and forty-four for the Liberals. For the Conservatives, the triumph was unalloyed. For Labour, the setback was not particularly serious. They had lost fewer than forty seats, and their popular vote had increased by nearly a million – partly because they had put forward about ninety more candidates than in 1923.

The Liberals could hardly draw a crumb of comfort from the disaster. Nearly three-quarters of the Parliamentary Party had been wiped out. Asquith himself was beaten at Paisley, even though the Conservatives did not oppose him. This must be the only case in British political history when a man who had just defeated a major statesman of another Party was discovered shedding tears of grief in the hour of victory. Not long afterwards, the Labour M.P. thus elected, Rosslyn Mitchell, spoke to a great Labour rally: 'I only hope that when my turn comes to be cast aside, I shall be able to accept my rejection with the courage and dignity which was shown by that great gentleman.'[2]

[1] *The Times*, 20 October 1924.
[2] Letter of John Tristram, *The Guardian*, 6 November 1965.

By comparison, the fate of the other Liberal leaders was barely noticed, but it was no less grim. Every one of the Liberal Whips, headed by the Chief Whip, Vivian Phillipps, fell. So did figures like Macnamara, Seely, Hogge, Masterman, Muir, and Isaac Foot; even George Lambert, who had held South Molton since 1891, through all the disasters. Not one single constituency was captured from the Conservatives to compensate for well over a hundred losses. Even against Labour, only eight gains were registered, against sixteen losses. Seven of these eight gains had occurred in constituencies where the Conservatives did not fight. There were only seven seats in the whole country where a Liberal had been returned in a contest against both Labour and Conservative opponents. These seven were scattered almost at random, and were apparently personal rather than Party victories.[1]

The Conservatives deliberately stood aside in a few places where the Liberal candidate had some chance in a straight fight with Labour, while the Conservative had no hope whatever. Thus, they did not oppose Asquith in Paisley (yet this did not save him from defeat). Not did they oppose Simon in Spen Valley. In a few places, such as West Walthamstow, this practice resulted in Liberal gains from Labour.

In some areas, the Liberals fared particularly badly. In the South-West, where they had held twenty-three seats, they now held only two, and both of these were Bristol divisions where the Conservatives had stood down in favour of 'Liberals' who were very nearly Conservatives themselves. The story of the South-West was told again in other rural areas with a traditional Radical allegiance and a strong Nonconformist element – such as rural Lincolnshire and parts of rural Yorkshire. It is not difficult to believe that these were places where consternation over the 'Zinoviev letter' drove innumerable Liberals to 'play safe' and vote Conservative. Yet the fearful holocaust of Liberal seats was not paralleled by an equally severe decline in Liberal votes. The votes did drop, of course – from 4·3 million to 2·9 million – but this decline was partly due to the diminished number of Liberal candidates.

All of this was scant consolation for the Liberals. To the old stress of Asquithians *versus* Lloyd Georgeites was now added the new stress

[1] SW. Bethnal Green; Lambeth North; Western Isles; Merioneth; Devonport; Wolverhampton East; Swansea West.

of Liberals preferring Tories *versus* Liberals preferring Labour. To most impartial observers at the end of 1924, it must have seemed that the prophecy which Baldwin had made a few months earlier would be fulfilled sooner than even he had anticipated.

11

St Martin's Summer

Now Roman is to Roman
More hateful than a foe
And the Tribunes beard the high
And the Fathers grind the low.
As we wax hot in faction,
In battle we wax cold;
Wherefore, men fight not as they fought
In the brave days of old.

MACAULAY, *Horatius*, xxxiii

The internal relationships of the Liberal Party during the lifetime
of Baldwin's 1924 Government are of great importance. The period
divides sharply into three phases: eighteen months of rather uneasy
truce between the Asquithians and the Lloyd Georgeites; six months
of violent conflict, terminating in the complete victory of Lloyd
George; and then two and a half years of serious preparation for
the ensuing General Election.

The 1924 election had wrought damage on all sections of the Liberal Party, but the Asquithians had suffered worse than the Lloyd
Georgeites. Not only was Asquith out of the House and Lloyd
George still in it, but a simple counting of noses showed that most of
the M.P.s would be more likely to favour Lloyd George, should
trouble arise. The possibility that Asquith might return to the House
of Commons after a by-election was removed when it was announced
early in 1925 that he had accepted the Earldom of Oxford and
Asquith. Although this peerage made it virtually certain that he
could never again head an administration, yet he remained Leader
of the Liberal Party.

Neither Lloyd George nor any of his adherents made any move

to shift Asquith from his position of Leadership. Indeed, when he appointed Sir Godfrey Collins as Chief Whip in succession to the defeated Vivian Phillipps, no one called in question his right to make the appointment, as the 'Wee Frees' had done when Thorne was appointed. But Lloyd George was determined to hold the substance of power, if not the shadow. The office which he sought was the Chairmanship of the Liberal M.P.s.

When the Leader of the Liberal Party was a member of the House of Commons, the office of Chairman of the M.P.s was one of importance, always held by a senior man; yet it was not one which automatically conferred great power. But when the Leadership was vacant (as between 1896 and 1905), or when the Leader was out of the House of Commons (as in 1919–20), it was of crucial significance. In the old House it had been held by Sir John Simon. This time, it was sought by Lloyd George.

A gathering of the principal men in the Party was held just after the election. Lloyd George told them bluntly that the M.P.s were 'not going to tolerate any outside interference whether from defeated candidates or from anyone else'.[1] Asquith commented afterwards that he 'was certainly not going to put his head into that hornets' nest'.[2] Lloyd George was elected by twenty-six votes to seven.[3]

On the following day, the seven M.P.s who had voted against Lloyd George, plus three[4] who had not, constituted themselves the Radical Group. Runciman, who was the Chairman, held the office effectively, and not (as has been suggested) purely nominally. The Group declared its support for traditional radical policies in a wide range of matters, including land, education, Free Trade, pensions, and defence.[5] But although the Radical Group was characterized by its views on policy and not its views on leadership, several members were more conspicuous for their continued opposition to

[1] Vivian Phillipps, *My days and ways*, p. 121.
[2] *Ibid.*, p. 122.
[3] The seven were: Wedgwood Benn; Frank Briant; Mackenzie Livingstone; R. Hopkin Morris; G. R. Thorne; J. M. Kenworthy; W. T. Thompson. Three Liberal M.P.s were absent – David Davies, John Ward, D. M. Cowan, plus J. H. Whitley, the Speaker, who did not take part in Party affairs. There were six abstentions.
[4] Walter Runciman, H. E. Crawfurd, Percy Harris.
[5] *The Times*, 25 November 1924.

Lloyd George than for staunch devotion to the principles of radical Liberalism.

* * *

A political party which has suffered disaster at the polls frequently sets up an enquiry into its organization. As we have already seen, the Liberal Party had been conscious of the need for such an enquiry since long before the election. In the immediate aftermath, Asquith established a Liberal Enquiry Committee, consisting of three Asquithians and two Lloyd Georgeites.[1] Its labours were swiftly completed, and a Convention was held on 29–30 January 1925, with Asquith and Lloyd George both gracing the platform.

The most important event of the Convention was the inauguration of the 'Liberal Million Fund', which was launched amid tremendous enthusiasm by Vivian Phillipps. The Fund was established with the aim of raising a million pounds before the next election, by appealing to individuals and organizations within the Liberal Party. The idea of raising large sums of money by an appeal of this kind was completely new, not only to the Liberal Party but to all Parties. The 'Million Fund' organizers evidently hoped for a very large contribution from the Lloyd George Fund, and discussions about possible subventions continued. Lloyd George had some legitimate ground of complaint that the leading officials responsible for raising the Fund in the various areas of England and Scotland were almost all Asquithians.[2] He also expressed concern whether legal objection could be taken by Guest and others who had kept the Western National Liberal Organization alive in spite of the 1923 reunion.[3] Legal opinion was taken, and the conclusion was that Lloyd George had free disposal of the Fund.

The Liberal Million Fund was not a great success, and it soon became evident that it would not reach or even approach its target.[4]

[1] Sir Donald Maclean, Sir Godfrey Collins, Mrs Wintringham; C. A. McCurdy, Sir Robert Hutchison.

[2] Sir William Edge to Frances Stevenson, 9 March 1925. Lloyd George papers G/6/10/8.

[3] Meeting of Lord Oxford's colleagues concerning funds, 26 May 1925. Asquith papers 34, fol. 144–6.

[4] Towards the end of 1926, Liberal Headquarters had received 'over £80,000'. *Liberal Magazine*, 1926, p. 673.

Vivian Phillipps, who was Chairman of the Million Fund Raising Committee, believed that the main reason for this was that Liberals knew of the existence of the Lloyd George Fund, and assumed that it was available to the Party – and therefore refused to contribute. In November 1925, he told a meeting in Hull that there had been no pooling of money, and the Liberal Party did not have access to the Lloyd George Fund, adding that Lloyd George would not contribute until he knew the result of the forthcoming conference on the proposals of the Land Enquiry Committee which he had set up.[1] This revelation, however, was not followed by a large increase in contributions.

*   *   *

But although Lloyd George was reticent about subsidizing the Liberal Party – let alone merging funds – he was very willing to spend the money for other public purposes, and there is no reason to doubt his categorical assertion that 'not one penny of this fund have I ever touched for my private use'.[2]

In particular, Lloyd George was very glad to disburse money on a wide range of Inquiries, which were at least as well staffed and financed as Royal Commissions, and exhibited a much greater imagination and sense of urgency than is usual on those august bodies. The people who worked on these Inquiries were often men who had been 'discovered' through that remarkable Liberal institution, the Liberal Summer Schools, which were held annually from the early 1920s onwards. Many of the personalities had had Asquithian antecedents – but this did not trouble Lloyd George.

The first of these Reports, entitled *Coal and Power*, was actually published before the 1924 General Election. In October 1925, another Lloyd George enquiry, by a body known as the Liberal Land Committee, produced a report on rural land, under the title *The Land and the Nation*. This soon became generally known as the 'Green Book'. Among a large number of other proposals, it urged land nationalization. Soon afterwards, the Land Committee's urban report, *Towns and the Land*, appeared. This was usually known as the 'Brown Book'.

Whatever might be said for the intrinsic merits of the proposals

---

[1] Phillipps, *op. cit.*, p. 133; *Manchester Guardian*, 21 November 1925.
[2] *The Times*, 3 December 1927.

contained in these two[1] Land Reports, a great deal of resentment was caused by the manner in which they were introduced. In July 1925, Lloyd George offered a contribution of £20,000 a year for three years to the Liberal Party – but almost immediately made it clear that the offer was contingent on a favourable decision about the Land Reports, which were still unpublished. The offer and the conditions were not known beyond the inner ranks of the Liberal Party; but feelings were stirred again soon afterwards when Lloyd George launched a body called the 'Land and Nation League', under his own Presidency. This League operated on a considerable scale; its activities included the use of thirteen publicity vans.[2] When the subject-matter of the Land Reports became known, there was a great deal of opposition to the substantive proposals, which added to the general anger and confusion engendered by the manner of presentation.

In the winter of 1925–6, a number of Liberals seceded from the Party on the ostensible grounds that they disagreed with the proposals of the two Reports. The most important of these withdrawals was that of Sir Alfred Mond, M.P. On 26 January 1926, he announced his intention to join the Conservatives; about a week later, C. F. Entwistle, who had been one of the 'Wee Free' M.P.s of 1918, went with him. These two withdrawals at least were premature, for the Liberal Party had not even debated, much less adopted, the Land proposals.

The Liberal Land Conference was held in February 1926, and considered these Reports. The delegates were by no means prepared to give *carte blanche* to Lloyd George. The land nationalization proposals, which had caused such widespread criticism, were deleted, and the references to the taxation of land values were much strengthened. Those who were present at the Conference seem to remember it most keenly as the occasion on which Leslie Hore-Belisha, one of the younger M.P.s, slapped the face of the noted Asquithian, W. M. R. Pringle, in front of a thousand delegates for an offensive (and inaccurate) reference to Hore-Belisha's journalistic activities.

---

[1] A third Land Report, the 'Tartan Book', referred to land in Scotland, and was considered by the Scottish Liberal Federation in April 1928. *Liberal Magazine*, 1928, pp. 348–51.

[2] Lloyd George papers G/85/2, undated.

In the immediate aftermath of the Conference, a few more secessions to the Conservatives occurred: Hilton Young, the former Lloyd George Whip; H. C. Hogbin, who had been defeated at North Battersea in a straight fight with a Communist; and a group of prominent Liverpool Liberals. But so far as the Liberal leadership was concerned, from Lord Oxford downwards, there was no doubt that the proposals as modified by the Land Conference were now acceptable. Lloyd George also received – for a time – the support of Lord Rothermere's *Daily Mail*; but when he showed himself unwilling to accept some of Rothermere's 'advice,' this support became increasingly uncertain.[1]

*   *   *

The General Strike of May 1926 profoundly altered the whole position in the Liberal Party. The strike itself necessarily produced mixed feelings among Liberals. On the one hand, they had strong sympathy with the miners whose plight had led to the strike. But on the other hand they recognized that the General Strike necessarily sought to coerce, not the miners' employers, but the Government; and that if such a strike were successful it would create a precedent fraught with the most appalling dangers for the future.

At the beginning of the strike, the Liberal Shadow Cabinet – a body to which both Lord Oxford and Lloyd George belonged – declared unanimously that 'society was bound with all the resources at its command to make certain of victory' over the General Strike.

Three days after the Shadow Cabinet meeting, one of the most important statements on the strike was made in the House of Commons by Simon, who argued that 'every Trade Union leader who had advised and promoted that course of action [was] liable in damages to the uttermost farthing of his personal possessions'. Although Simon was a lawyer of very high standing indeed, it is by no means certain that his opinion was a correct statement of the law as it then stood. But there could be no doubt that he was telling the Conservatives exactly what they wanted to hear; and whether they knew anything of the law or not, they heartily endorsed Simon's very obvious sentiments.

[1] Rothermere to Lloyd George, 11 August 1925; 1 June 1927 to 18 October 1928. Lloyd George papers G/17/1/9 and 17–32.

While the strike was still in progress, another meeting of the Liberal Shadow Cabinet was summoned, for 10 May. Lloyd George wrote to the Chief Whip, Sir Godfrey Collins, indicating that he would not attend the meeting, as he was unwilling to join in declarations against the strike which did not also condemn the Government's handling of the situation; and, furthermore, that he could not endorse the Government's refusal to negotiate until the strike was over.

Lord Oxford's immediate reactions were unfavourable, but not violently so.[1] Nor did the behaviour of his colleagues give any indication of the storm which was brewing. On the day of the meeting Collins wrote to Lloyd George:[2] 'I read [the letter] to Lord Oxford and our colleagues.

'The general feeling was that you had probably overlooked, or had not an opportunity of reading, Lord Oxford's speech in the House of Lords, of which I enclose an extract. . . .'

There is nothing in this letter which suggests in any way that Lloyd George had cut himself off from his colleagues. But Lord Oxford's associates evidently put pressure on him to make this the occasion for a complete break with Lloyd George. On 20 May, ten days after the Shadow Cabinet meeting, Lord Oxford wrote sternly to Lloyd George, indicating that the latter's refusal to attend the meeting was 'impossible to reconcile with [Lord Oxford's] conception of the obligation of political comradeship'. With rather evident glee, Sir Donald Maclean wrote on the same day to Viscount Gladstone that, 'I never thought [Lord Oxford] would come right up to it but he has.'[3]

The whole atmosphere of the Liberal quarrel after the General Strike was a great deal more bitter than that of the first stages of earlier disputes, when the leading protagonists had apparently tried to avoid a permanent rupture, and had taken, so far as they could, positions which would not make future reconciliation impossible. This time it was different. It seems evident that both sides were determined to bring about a final showdown. The leaders of the Party and the various official bodies issued their long and angry

[1] Roy Jenkins, *Asquith*, p. 514.
[2] Collins to Lloyd George, 10 May 1926. Lloyd George papers G/5/1/10.
[3] Maclean to Viscount Gladstone, 20 May 1926. Viscount Gladstone papers 46,474, fol. 189.

statements to the Press, hot from the pen.[1] To Lord Oxford's letter, Lloyd George, inevitably, sent a reply – running to more than four pages of print. The Shadow Cabinet sat yet again, and the state of mind is indicated by the comment of the Lloyd Georgeite Earl Beauchamp: 'There never was any hope of any meeting, nor any wish for compromise. I was alone.'[2]

On this occasion Lord Oxford did not answer Lloyd George direct, but wrote instead a letter to the Chief Whip, Sir Godfrey Collins, in the course of which he said that, 'I have sat in many Cabinets under various Prime Ministers and I have not known one of them who would not have treated such a communication from a colleague, sent at such a time, as equivalent to a resignation.'

The parallel between the actions of a Prime Minister and the actions of the Leader of a Party with two score M.P.s may seem a little far-fetched; yet this is strangely characteristic of the Liberals in the 1920s. They did not seem to take any account of the immense weakening of their electoral position, but continued to act and think as if they were the only possible alternative Government.

On the same day as Lord Oxford wrote to Collins (1 June), twelve[3] members of the Shadow Cabinet wrote to Lord Oxford, in the most savage episode of the whole correspondence. Their letter was a general attack on Lloyd George's behaviour over a long period, and concluded: 'We have done our best in the interests of Liberalism to work with Mr Lloyd George in the councils of the Party, but we cannot feel surprised at your feeling that confidential

---

[1] For some of the views expressed, see *Recent Documents relating to the internal affairs of the Party*, published by L.P.D., 1926. The main documents were also published in the national Press, often in full.

[2] Earl Beauchamp to Lloyd George, 31 May 1926. Lloyd George papers G/3/5/18.

[3] Viscount Grey, Sir John Simon, Walter Runciman, Lord Lincolnshire, Lord Buckmaster, Lord Buxton, Sir Donald Maclean, Lord Cowdray, Vivian Phillipps, Geoffrey Howard, W. M. R. Pringle, Sir Godfrey Collins. *The Times* says (2 June 1926) that Lord Lincolnshire was not a member, but the document cited above, and also *Liberal Magazine*, 1926, p. 365, imply that he was. Six members of the Shadow Cabinet did not sign the letter. Ian Macpherson was away from London ill. Wedgwood Benn, although perhaps more violently opposed to Lloyd George than any of the others, was already showing increasing tenderness towards the Labour Party. The other four were regarded as Lloyd Georgeites: Earl Beauchamp, C. A. McCurdy, Dr Macnamara, and – in spite of his Asquithian antecedents – Charles Masterman.

P

relations are impossible with one whose instability destroys confidence.'

* * *

A more or less naked struggle for mastery was thus commenced, and it was waged in all the principal organs of the Liberal Party.

For a moment, the position was not clear even among the M.P.s. When Lloyd George had been elected Chairman by twenty-six votes to seven, his supporters had included H. A. L. Fisher who was now out of the House, and Hilton Young and Sir Alfred Mond who had joined the Conservatives. Six M.P.s had abstained, and three of these (Simon, Collins, and Runciman) were signatories of the letter from the 'Twelve Apostles' to Lord Oxford. Furthermore, some of Lloyd George's supporters at the beginning of the Parliament were numbered among those Liberals most sympathetic to the Conservative Government. Certain of these M.P.s were associated with a special appeal to Lloyd George, sent over the signature of Captain Guest.[1] They offered him support if he would assure them that he had no intention of allying with Labour or supporting the nationalization of industry. Apparently the required assurances were obtained, and the M.P.s supported Lloyd George by twenty votes to ten, with three deliberate abstentions.[2] A resolution was passed, deploring 'the publicity given to the differences between the Liberal leaders', and expressing 'the earnest hope that our leaders will use their best endeavours to restore unity in the ranks of the Party'.

One of the side-effects of the dispute was the extinction of the Radical Group. Runciman, the Chairman, wrote an article for the Group's weekly publication, in which he took a line broadly similar

[1] Guest's letter to Lloyd George (1 June 1926; Lloyd George papers G/8/13/4) lists the following M.P.s: Sir T. Robinson; Colonel England; Sir Murdoch Macdonald; Sir Beddoe Rees; Captain Guest; John Duckworth; J. H. Edwards; Walter Forrest; and C. P. Williams. Other lists given about this time show variations. Guest also listed ten M.P.s as 'likely supporters'.

[2] The ten were Wedgwood Benn, Frank Briant, Sir Godfrey Collins, H. E. Crawfurd, T. D. Fenby, Sir Robert Hamilton, Percy Harris, Mackenzie Livingstone, R. Hopkin Morris, and Walter Runciman. The three who abstained were David Davies, Sir John Simon, and D. M. Cowan.

THE SLEEPING BEAUTY SITS UP.

Liberal Party (*to the Fairy Prince Samuel*). "O LOVE, THY KISS WOULD WAKE THE DEAD!"

Tennyson: "*The Day-Dream.*"

[The success of the Liberal Party at two recent by-elections has been attributed to the return of Sir Herbert Samuel to its councils.]

THE RETURN OF THE PRODIGAL.

FARMER GEORGE. "HULLO, SAMUEL! SO YOU'VE COME BACK, HAVE YOU? WELL, I HOPE YOU'VE BROUGHT YOUR OWN VEAL SANDWICHES WITH YOU."

to that of Asquith, but more pungent.[1] Kenworthy and his associates violently disagreed with the article.

* * *

Immense excitement was building up in anticipation of the Annual Meeting of the National Liberal Federation, which was due to be held in Weston-super-Mare on 17 June 1926. Suddenly, dramatically, the whole situation was transformed. On 12 June, Lord Oxford had a stroke, which incapacitated him for three months. After that, no one sought to keep up the recriminations. The N.L.F. carried with only one dissentient a resolution of 'unabated confidence' in Lord Oxford as Leader of the Liberal Party. However, the Chairman assured a delegate in the course of the discussion that the resolution did not imply a censure on Lloyd George. In October, Lord Oxford resigned the Leadership. He played little further part in politics, and died on 15 February 1928.

* * *

The Liberal Party was now forced either to face a future without hope, or to capitulate to Lloyd George. In November 1926, the Million Fund Administrative Committee was invited to decide whether it would accept Lloyd George's terms for a massive grant from his Fund.[2] These terms included – in practice if not in theory – the removal of Vivian Phillipps from Headquarters. (Viscount Gladstone, Lloyd George's other particular hate, had departed after the election.) Those who desired to see the offer rejected received assistance from Sir Robert Hudson, but they were narrowly defeated, and the terms were accepted.

After the victory of Lloyd George, a major reorganization at the headquarters of the Liberal Party was inevitable. Not only did Phillipps go, but so also did Collins, who was replaced by the former

[1] In personal information to the author, Miss Barbara Bliss relates that she was working for the Radical Group at the time. She visited Lloyd George's headquarters in Old Queen Street to obtain news when the strike was on. There she met Colonel Tweed, one of Lloyd George's principal workers, who discussed an article which Lloyd George had written for an American magazine, and which had just appeared. In explanation, Tweed said that Lloyd George considered a revolutionary situation to be possible, and was determined to be on the right side of the barricades! When this incident was related to Runciman, he dictated the article which so angered some of his colleagues.

[2] J. A. Spender, *Sir Robert Hudson*, pp. 175–6.

Deputy Chief Whip, Sir Robert Hutchison – a strong supporter of Lloyd George, although personally acceptable to most of the Asquithians. Hudson, who had played so large a part before the war in the control of both the L.C.A. and the N.L.F., inevitably resigned – and his disappearance was almost unnoticed by the Party as a whole.[1] More attention was paid to the departure of R. Humphrey Davies, who resigned at the same time, although he was urged by Hutchison to remain. Of him, *Liberal Magazine* wrote an impressive and well-deserved tribute.[2]

Some of the Asquithians were far from pleased with the new arrangements, and determined to continue resistance to Lloyd George. Almost as soon as Lloyd George seized control, a body called the Liberal Council[3] was established by the intransigents. Lord Oxford himself was not included, but his daughter Lady Violet Bonham-Carter was one of the Vice-Presidents, while the President and moving spirit was his friend and political comrade Viscount Grey. The Vice-Presidents and members of the Committee included most of the leading Asquithians, but there was one very interesting absentee – Sir John Simon.

The Liberal Council produced a substantial quantity of literature. It also provided (although on a very much smaller scale) an alternative source of finance to the Lloyd George Fund, and assisted a number of candidates. It did not carry on a vendetta, but co-operated with the official organs of the Liberal Party. It probably kept within the Liberal Party many disaffected Asquithians who otherwise would have drifted out. The Liberal Council continued to operate, although on a diminished scale, until the middle 1930s; but after the death of Lord Grey in 1933, it gradually became inactive. The office was closed in 1939, and the Council was finally wound up in December 1946, when the scant remaining funds were transferred to the Free Trade Union.

*   *   *

Once he had secured control, Lloyd George sought to remodel the whole organization and approach of the Liberal Party. It is character-

---

[1] J. A. Spender, *op. cit.*, p. 177.
[2] *Liberal Magazine*, 1927, p. 13.
[3] See article, 'The Lloyd George Fund', by Barbara Bliss, *New Outlook*, November 1966, pp. 34–7. The Minutes of the Liberal Council are preserved at the National Liberal Club.

istic of the man that he never bothered to get himself elected Leader
of the Party,[1] and also that he was perfectly willing to advance
men who, in the past, had been his opponents. Thus, the key man
who was appointed on the organization side was Sir Herbert
Samuel, who had been Home Secretary in the closing period of
Asquith's Coalition, and had suffered the general fate of the Asquithians in 1918. He had then acquired a great and deserved reputation
as High Commissioner for Palestine, and later as Chairman of the
Royal Commission on the Coal Industry. The initiative for Samuel's
appointment seems to have come from the N.L.F., and Samuel
accepted with reluctance.[2] His presence undoubtedly made the new
régime more acceptable to the Asquithians than would otherwise
have been the case, although Runciman told Samuel ruefully that,
'the question of Mr Lloyd George's position in the Liberal Party'
was 'a subject on which we disagree . . . profoundly.'[3]

Colonel T. F. Tweed, who worked in close association with Samuel,
had been the leading organizer in Manchester in 1923, when the
Liberals made such spectacular gains in the city, but for some time
he had been on Lloyd George's staff. He was able and ruthless, but
made many enemies, partly through his want of tact. Margot
Asquith spoke of Tweed's 'untruthfulness and his treachery', warning
Samuel that 'he will do you infinite harm.'[4]

It was not difficult for percipient people to guess that the changes
announced at Liberal Headquarters bore some relation to the financial transactions of the Lloyd George Fund. A voice from the remote
past spoke to the public for the last time. Lord Rosebery wrote to
The Times early in 1927, asking, 'what is the sum, how was it obtained,
and what is its source?'[5]

No full reply was delivered at the time to Lord Rosebery,
although what we might call the 'Lloyd George organization' did

[1] Frank Owen states (*Tempestuous Journey*, p. 707) that, after Lord Oxford's
resignation, 'Lloyd George succeeded him', and Sir Ivor Jennings (*Party Politics*,
ii, p. 267) repeats the statement, citing Owen as his authority. Evidently Owen
was considering the predominant influence which Lloyd George exercised after
1926 as tantamount to 'leadership'.

[2] Samuel to Lloyd George, 26 October 1926; 9 February 1927. Lloyd George
papers G/17/9/2 and 4.

[3] Runciman to Samuel, 26 September 1928. Samuel papers A/46, fol. 7.

[4] Countess of Oxford to Samuel, 5 March 1927. Samuel papers A/155 (VIII),
fol. 76.

[5] *The Times*, 16 February 1927.

return a dusty answer in the Press a few days later. But towards the end of the year. Lloyd George was drawn to issue a comprehensive public statement about the Lloyd George Fund.[1]

Lloyd George declared that the Fund had never been handled by him personally. Until the 1923 reunion, it had been handled by the National Liberal Whips; afterwards, by a special committee. The money had been applied to various Inquiries, and publicity for their conclusions; and also to a 'Bureau for inquiring into the grievances of ex-Servicemen and others'.

So far as it goes, this statement may be presumed to be correct. But there exists among the Lloyd George papers a copy of an instrument dated 5 May 1925, dealing with the control of the Fund.[2] Sir John Davies is appointed Chief Trustee, the other Trustees being Charles McCurdy, Gwilym Lloyd George, Sir William Edge, and Henry Fildes. The Trustees declare the Fund to be 'held by us to be used under [Lloyd George's] direction for the furtherance by political action of the following causes . . .' – where follows a list of political objects. Power is given to the Chief Trustee and one other acting with him to disburse assets.

Some more facts are now known about this Fund.[3] Much of the money was invested in the *Daily Chronicle*, which proved a very profitable venture. A subvention of £300,000 was made towards the expenses in preparation for the next General Election, and a further £20,000 at the time of the election itself. It has been said – although this does not seem certain – that £105,000 more was contributed to the Million Fund. Between 1925 and 1930, £60,000 was disbursed for expenses at Liberal Headquarters. The Land and Nation League received about £240,000, and the various inquiries organized by Lloyd George are said[4] to have cost a further £650,000. Lloyd George is also known to have spent very large sums of money on other public purposes, both before and after the 1920s. On 9 July 1929 – that is, after the General Election – Lord St Davids told Samuel that the capital amount of the Fund then stood at £765,000 – although certain charges on the Fund had not yet been met. There were also 279,000 *Daily Chronicle* Ordinary Shares,

[1] *The Times*, 3 December 1927.
[2] Lloyd George papers G/86/3.
[3] See Frank Owen, *Tempestuous Journey*, pp. 685–94.
[4] Sir Ivor Jennings, *Party Politics*, vol. 2, p. 265.

but these had paid no dividend, and did not seem likely to do so.[1]

* * *

Many of the people whom Lloyd George employed were Liberals with Asquithian antecedents, and most of them had been 'discovered' through that remarkable Liberal institution, the 'Summer School'. Liberal Summer Schools commenced in 1922, with a session in Oxford, and from that date forward they were held annually. They provided an excellent opportunity for the more active Liberal minds to benefit from lectures by acknowledged authorities, to join in informal discussions, and to generate new ideas. Among the people who achieved prominence in this manner, and were assiduously cultivated by Lloyd George, were Maynard Keynes himself – whose influence on the economies not only of Britain but of all Western countries since 1945 is probably greater than that of any other man. Other notable men whom Lloyd George brought forward included figures like Walter Layton, Ramsay Muir, and H. D. Henderson. Such people had very little interest in old quarrels, but much interest in the future.

The most famous and important product of Lloyd George's research teams was the Liberal Industrial Inquiry report – officially entitled *Britain's Industrial Future,* but always known as the 'Liberal Yellow Book', which was published at the beginning of 1928. It was a comprehensive and diffuse document, whose conclusions cannot be summarized adequately in brief compass. By common consent, it represented the most thoroughgoing set of proposals on the general field of industry and employment which was advanced by any organization whatever in the whole inter-war period. On 28–9 March 1928, the Industrial Conference of the N.L.F. declared in favour of the great majority of the 'Yellow Book' proposals.

Not long afterwards, the Liberals amplified their proposals with specific reference to the besetting issue of the time, and produced a book entitled *We can conquer unemployment.* This title formed the great campaign slogan of the Liberal Party, and the authors were so bold as to declare 'that within twelve months [of a Liberal Government taking office] unemployment would be brought down to normal proportions'.

* * *

[1] Lord St Davids to Samuel, 9 July 1929. Samuel papers A/71, fol. 26.

Whether by coincidence or not, the Liberal by-election results turned from bad to excellent almost immediately Lloyd George and Samuel took control. In the early period of the Conservative Government, the Liberals lost two seats which they had held – the English Universities, which fell to the Conservatives on 12 March 1926; and Central Hull, which was won by Labour on 29 November of the same year. Commander Kenworthy had switched to Labour almost immediately after Lord Oxford's retirement[1] and defended his seat in the new interest. He was comfortably returned, and the Liberal suffered the ignominy of a lost deposit.

The first sign of a substantial improvement came, paradoxically, when another popular Liberal M.P. decided that his constituents should not be burdened with a Member who could no longer uphold the opinions of his supporters. Captain Wedgwood Benn, of Leith, seceded to Labour; but, unlike Kenworthy, did not himself contest the seat in his new interest. Benn had had a straight fight against Labour in 1924; the new Liberal candidate, Ernest Brown, had to face a three-cornered contest in an unfamiliar place. Liberals therefore took much encouragement from the fact that he scraped home, though with the barest of majorities, in this industrial constituency. Four days later, another Liberal victory was signalled in Southwark North. This was even more encouraging, as it represented a gain – and a gain from Labour at that – in a working-class district of London.

In general, the urban victories went to Labour, while the Liberals did extremely well in the rural areas. In June 1927, they captured Bosworth, and just missed taking Westbury. In February 1928 they won Lancaster; in March Mrs Runciman took St Ives, and Kingsley Griffiths held Middlesbrough West in a triangular fight. In April Linlithgowshire was captured, although in July Halifax was lost to Labour. But the St Ives by-election, although a Liberal victory, provided indications that the truce between Asquithians and Lloyd Georgeites was much less than peace. Sir Herbert Samuel, who spoke for Hilda Runciman, incurred a lambasting from Lloyd George for his pains.[2]

[1] Kenworthy to Collins, 23 October 1926, enclosed in letter of Collins to Lloyd George, 25 October 1926. Lloyd George papers G/5/1/12.

[2] Samuel–Lloyd George correspondence, 26–8 February 1928. Samuel papers A/71, fol. 16–18.

The Liberal tide still flowed. When Sir Alfred Mond transferred from the Liberals to the Conservatives, he did not permit his Carmarthen voters at once to review the question of their representation; but when he was eventually elevated to the peerage, the Liberal held the seat, with a very narrow majority over Labour. On 20 March 1929, the Liberals won Eddisbury. Two days later, James Blindell captured Holland-with-Boston. This was to be the last by-election gain which the Liberals would make for nearly thirty years.

As the General Election of 1929 approached, the Liberals poured out an enormous amount of literature and propaganda of every kind. The 'Yellow Book', the new volume, *We can conquer unemployment*, and, to a lesser extent, the 'Green Book' and the 'Brown Book', sold in enormous numbers, and exerted a great effect on public opinion. Organizations, sometimes of an ostensibly non-Party character, were set up to promote one or other item of the Liberal programme.

The leading personalities of the Liberal Party – including the members of the Liberal Council – were supporting the new programme almost to a man. Vivian Phillipps expressed his doubts about Lloyd George's claim to reduce unemployment to 'normal' dimensions within twelve months without cost to the taxpayer or ratepayer; but even he did not dissent from the substantive merits of the proposals.[1]

Meanwhile, the 'Lloyd George Fund' was poured into the pre-election and election campaigns. The Liberals were offering a wholly credible alternative Government, much higher in calibre than either of the other front benches.

Yet there were strange signs of doubting, even in the moment of battle. The Liberal literature sometimes suggests that the propagandists themselves no longer really believed that a Liberal Government was possible, and Liberal spokesmen were repeatedly asked how they would act if they held the balance of power between the other two Parties.

Polling day was 30 May 1929. No fewer than 1,729 candidates disputed 615 seats. The Conservatives advanced 590, Labour 570, and the Liberals 512. Only half a dozen constituencies – all Conser-

---

[1] *The Times*, 3 April and 13 April 1929. But compare the Samuel–Lloyd George correspondence, above.

vative – were uncontested. In more than three-quarters of the constituencies, Liberal, Labour, and Conservative candidates all stood. This made the election particularly open. Even in a more normal election, the result turns on electoral swings in a relatively small number of marginal constituencies; in 1929, the effect of Liberals and Labour both fighting a large number of constituencies which they had not contested for several elections – if at all – made the result even more in doubt. The electorate had changed greatly, both through the passage of nearly five years, and through the recent enfranchisement of the 'flappers' – women aged between twenty-one and thirty, who had not received the vote in 1918.

The election itself was comparatively uneventful. The Conservatives campaigned under the slogan 'Safety First'. Labour argued that the Liberal plan to conquer unemployment was the right policy in the hands of the wrong Party.

Some rather heavy pressure was put by Lloyd George on the few candidates who would not accept the 'Lloyd George programme'.[1] He sought to deny them funds, and even recognition as official Liberal candidates. As usual, Liberals resented pressures of this kind, and an alternative source of finance and general assistance was provided by the Liberal Council, which had raised a substantial sum with the assistance of Viscount Gladstone.[2] However, one Liberal M.P. who sought re-election was proscribed with general approval. This was 'Freddie' Guest, whose support for the Conservative Government had involved him in a good deal of trouble with the Liberals in his own constituency and elsewhere for a couple of years.[3] Another Liberal candidate was set up against him, but both were defeated.

In one important constituency a rather surprising accommodation was made. This was Sir John Simon's seat of Spen Valley. A Conservative candidate – David Maxwell-Fyfe, the future Lord Chancellor[4] – had been adopted, but Baldwin intervened to persuade him to

---

[1] See article by Barbara Bliss, *New Outlook*, November 1966, p. 35.

[2] Miss Barbara Bliss, who was Assistant Secretary of the Liberal Council, considers that a hundred would be a fair guess for the number of Liberal contests which were supported to a greater or lesser extent by the Council.

[3] *Liberal Magazine*, 1927, pp. 466–7; 1929, pp. 1–2, 76, 264, 341.

[4] Lord Kilmuir (David Maxwell-Fyfe), *Political Adventure*, p. 34.

withdraw. No Liberal could have had much hope of holding Spen Valley in a three-cornered contest; but Baldwin's political instinct was acute, and this apparent act of self-abnegation was to prove highly beneficial to the Conservatives and disastrous to the Liberals a couple of years later.

*   *   *

No Party secured an overall majority, either of votes or of seats. The Labour Party obtained most seats, the Conservatives most votes. For more than five and a quarter million votes, the Liberals returned only fifty-nine M.P.s.

Nearly half of the M.P.s in the country had secured a minority of the votes cast in their constituencies. In two-thirds of the constituencies, all three Parties stood, and all three candidates were taken sufficiently seriously to save their deposits. In all, Labour forfeited thirty-five deposits, the Liberals twenty-five, and the Conservatives seventeen.

The Liberals made overall gains from the Conservatives – twenty-nine gains to one loss – and losses to Labour – seventeen losses to two gains. There were a further twenty seats where the Liberal came within a thousand votes of victory. Although in 1924 they had done so very badly in three-cornered contests, yet in 1929 no fewer than forty-four Liberal seats were held or captured against opposition from both other Parties.

There was a marked tendency for the Liberals to do best in remote and rural constituencies, especially in the 'Celtic fringe' – but this was not the universal experience. About a quarter of the Liberal seats were in industrial areas, and these were widely scattered. Only two were in London – the two Bethnal Green constituencies – but two other working-class London constituencies were narrowly lost. Most of the leading Liberal personalities who had sat in the old Parliament were returned; apart from Guest, perhaps the most notable exception was Mrs Runciman. She transferred from St Ives to Tavistock, which she missed by only sixty-two votes; while her husband, moving from Swansea West (which the new candidate narrowly lost), clung on to her Cornish constituency. Another rather serious loss was Frank Briant, who was defeated by Labour in Lambeth North. There were two interesting returns to the new House

– Sir Donald Maclean, who captured North Cornwall, and Sir
Herbert Samuel, who took Darwen.

*   *   *

Why did the Liberals not fare better in 1929? All of the features
which a political party needs for victory seemed to be present:
unity; a sense of purpose; enthusiasm; personalities; money;
organization.

A party often reaps the benefit, or suffers the damage, not from
its actions in the immediate past, but from what happened years
earlier. The actual rights and wrongs of Asquithians or Lloyd
Georgeites simply passed the electors by. The long-winded letters
with which the disputants belaboured each other in the Press were
not studied or analysed in detail. Still less was the whole business
remembered in detail. The one impression which was left on the
minds of the ordinary voters was that the Liberals were having a
long and savage running fight, which seemed to have no meaning,
no beginning, and no end. And when at last the din within the
Liberal ranks was silenced – about a year or eighteen months before
the election – the time was much too short even for a man with
the genius of Lloyd George to pull them together. People had
developed their voting habits. Then, as now, most people voted for a
particular political party primarily because they were accustomed
to do so. People did not look at the election of 1929 in the light of the
problems of 1929 or the solutions advanced. To agree with what a
man says is a very, very different matter from voting for him – a
fact which many a candidate has learnt to his cost. The recent
General Elections, and particularly the election of 1924, had
encouraged those voters who 'vote for a Government' to turn away
from the Liberals.

The personal record of Lloyd George was a very dubious asset.
Liberals could, and did, argue that in the war he 'got things done'.
But could men who had written in 1926 of Lloyd George that,
'confidential relations are impossible with one whose instability
destroys confidence' expect to carry much conviction three years
later when they declared that he was the best possible leader for the
nation? And when Lloyd George made sweeping promises about
conquering unemployment, even though those promises were upheld
by serious professional economists and others, men were all too

inclined to recall the disappointments and the real – or alleged – broken promises of the Coalition.[1] For all his genius, and for all his quite genuine concern for the poor and downtrodden, a vast number of people both inside and outside the Liberal Party utterly mistrusted him as a man.[2]

But the Parliamentary weakness of the Liberals in 1929 was not merely the loss sustained by a political party; for the dynamic which the leading Liberals possessed was not to be found anywhere else. Britain and the whole world were to be losers when nonentities without vision came to control our country at one of the great turning-points of the human race.

---

[1] Lloyd George met, and seemingly abolished, the Labour accusation of broken promises of 1918 at Bangor in May 1929. See *Liberal Magazine*, 1929, pp. 354–5, with especial reference to 'Hang the Kaiser' and 'Land fit for Heroes'.

[2] See Vivian Phillipps's letter to *The Times*, dated 12 June 1929, quoted in *My days and ways*, pp. 199–200.

12

Disruption

'A Rolls-Royce mind without a driver.'
STANLEY BALDWIN, *on Sir John Simon*

In other circumstances, the Liberal result of 1929 might have looked like a victory on a modest scale. Yet in truth it was an utter disaster, and the Liberals themselves seemed to recognize this fact.[1] Not only had they failed to make the anticipated advances, but the 'balance of power' position in which they found themselves was bound to produce the same result as it had produced in 1924: they would be blamed for all the shortcomings of the Party which they sustained in office, and would receive credit for none of its achievements.

The Liberals were spared the immediate decision of whom to set in office. Instead of waiting to be defeated in the new House, Baldwin resigned at once, and MacDonald was invited to form a Ministry. Neither MacDonald nor Baldwin had any contact with Lloyd George to ascertain what support, if any, he was prepared to offer. As the Labour Party was rather larger than the Conservative Party in the House of Commons, the Liberals were not bound actually to vote with the Government to avoid precipitating another General Election. At least they could permit themselves the luxury of abstention.

Defections from the Liberal Party began almost at once. William Jowett, one of the Liberal M.P.s, underwent a rapid conversion to the Labour Party which has had few parallels since the celebrated experience of the Apostle Paul. Unlike St Paul, whose rewards were spiritual and posthumous, Jowett received a temporal and immediate reward in the office of Attorney-General. Liberals like Mackenzie Livingstone soon followed in the Labour direction. Others, like 'Freddie' Guest, joined the Conservative Party.

[1] See N.L.F. statement, *Liberal Magazine*, 1929, p. 662.

No less baleful for the Liberal Party was the abrupt termination of most of the Lloyd George subventions. As early as February 1927, Sir Archibald Sinclair had urged Lloyd George to continue his contributions for a substantial period after the election, suggesting a sum like £20,000 to enable the Party to grade down its expenditure.[1] The Fund trustees continued to pay £2,000 a year to the Parliamentary Party until 1931,[2] but the main contributions soon ceased.

Very soon, the Liberals began to feel the inevitable tensions of the Parliamentary situation. The first major contentious measure was the Coal Bill, which was published in December 1929. The Liberals accepted some of the proposals, but objected sharply to the quota system, which meant bolstering up inefficient pits. In the Second Reading division of 19 December, the Liberals officially opposed the Bill; but two Liberals voted with the Government and six purposely abstained.[3] The Government scraped home by eight votes. If all the Liberal votes had been cast against the Government, it would have been defeated. It is, however, equally evident that the Conservatives did not put their full force into defeating the Government – otherwise, in spite of the Liberal 'splinter', it would have fallen.

At this stage of the Bill, the Liberals in the country seem to have been pleased with the relative cohesion exhibited by their M.P.s.[4] But neither the satisfaction nor the cause of it lasted much longer. In the Committee stage of the Bill, a Liberal amendment against the quota system was moved by Clement Davies. This again was narrowly defeated – by 282 votes to 273. Four Liberals voted with the Government and eight purposely abstained. The Chief Whip, Sir Robert Hutchison, offered his resignation, but was persuaded to remain.[5]

Soon afterwards, the Liberal attitude underwent a most remarkable

[1] Sinclair to Lloyd George, 2 February 1927; (Sir) Ronald Walker to Lloyd George, 30 January 1927. Lloyd George papers G/18/4/4.

[2] Sinclair to Samuel, 3 November 1931. Samuel papers A/84, fol. 10.

[3] With the Government: Sir William Edge, Geoffrey Mander. Abstentions: Walter Runciman, Sir Donald Maclean, E. D. Simon, Leif Jones, Duncan Millar, Percy Harris. *Liberal Magazine*, 1930, pp. 45–6.

[4] Ramsay Muir to Lloyd George, 18 February 1930. Lloyd George papers G/15/6/22.

[5] Hutchison to Lloyd George, 28 February 1930. Lloyd George papers G/10/9/8.

change. On 10 March, Lloyd George was expected to launch a swingeing attack on the Government's record over unemployment. The attack did not materialize; instead, Lloyd George expressed unwonted sympathy with J. H. Thomas, the Minister responsible. Still more startling was the Liberal behaviour on 20 March, when district minimum prices were being considered in connection with the Coal Bill. Several Liberal M.P.s had put their names to an Opposition amendment. On Lloyd George's recommendation, the Liberals abstained and the amendment was thus defeated. Lloyd George gave the totally incredible 'explanation' that the Liberals were taking this action to avoid embarrassing the Government during a critical stage of the current Naval Conference! In spite of considerable temptation, the Liberals preserved this attitude throughout the rest of the history of the Bill, which was duly carried.

*   *   *

But issues of greater moment than the Coal Bill were casting their shadows across the political scene. Much the gravest of these was unemployment. Although this problem had been chronic since 1920, it took a serious turn for the worse during 1930. On 18 June, Mac-Donald said that the unemployment question called for the co-operation of all Parties. Lloyd George pledged assistance from the Liberals, but the Conservatives would not co-operate. Discussions therefore began between the Liberals, represented by Lloyd George, Lord Lothian, and Seebohm Rowntree, and the Government, represented by MacDonald, Snowden, and Vernon Hartshorn. These discussions were friendly, but unproductive.

Nevertheless, close contact was now established between the Government and the Liberals. But when the wider question of future relations between them was raised, on 18 September,[1] Lloyd George indicated that Liberals could only support the Government if electoral reform were introduced as a *quid pro quo*. He reinforced this point by mentioning that the Conservatives were prepared to promise not to oppose at the next election any Liberal M.P.s who would help them turn out the Labour Government; but that he personally would prefer co-operation with Labour. It requires no 'wisdom after the event' to recognize that this veering towards the

[1] Viscount Snowden, *Autobiography*, vol. 2, p. 884 *seq.*

Government would prove disastrous. In February 1929, Lloyd George, in a conversation with Samuel, had 'said that if any attempt were made in the next Parliament to induce the Liberal Party to support a Socialist Government the Party would be split from top to bottom'.[1]

*   *   *

The storm-clouds were gathering over the Liberal Party. Late in October, just before the new session began, Sir John Simon wrote to Lloyd George, informing him that if 'the question arises as to confidence in the Government, I shall feel obliged to vote in such a way as to show that I, at any rate, have no confidence in it'.

On 3–4 November 1930, a Conservative motion on the King's Speech was considered. The official Liberal line was to abstain; but five Liberals voted in favour of the motion and four against it.[2] As the anti-Government rebels included the Chief Whip, Sir Robert Hutchison, he now insisted on the resignation which he had tendered earlier in the year, and was replaced by Sir Archibald Sinclair.

On the same day as Hutchison resigned, Simon's letter to Lloyd George was published in the Press. It was no longer a question of isolated rebels opposing Lloyd George on isolated measures; rather, Simon had publicly declared war on Lloyd George's whole policy towards the Labour Government. The course which Simon was proposing to take was not to judge issues on their merits and to vote against the Government if necessary, but to ally himself with the Conservatives in order to bring down the Government at the earliest possible moment.

The Liberal Party was now entering one of the most acute crises of its whole existence, and the key figure of one side of the struggle was to be Sir John Simon. As an impecunious young barrister, he had so impressed the Walthamstow Liberals with his sincerity that they chose him unanimously for their candidate before the 1906 Election, in preference to a man who could have made substantial

---

[1] Samuel's note of 13 February 1929. Samuel papers A/72, fol. 1.

[2] Against the Government: Sir R. Hutchison, R. M. Kedward, George Lambert, Sir M. MacDonald, Sir J. Simon. With the Government: Sir G. Collins, Sir W. Edge, Sir D. Maclean, Walter Runciman. All of the anti-Government rebels eventually became Liberal Nationals; so, more surprisingly, did three of the four who rebelled in the opposite direction.

contributions to their funds. He was later to become one of the brightest luminaries of the Bar. We have seen him as the Home Secretary whom Asquith called 'the Impeccable', who resigned as a matter of principle over the question of conscription, but who volunteered himself for the services, and served with bravery and distinction. We have seen him as the hero of the Spen Valley by-election of 1919, whom all of the Asquithians and many of the Coalitionists regarded as a grievously wronged man when he lost the seat through the intervention of a Coalition Liberal; and we have seen him triumphantly regain that seat in 1922. All of these events were still very recent; and Simon seemed the very antithesis of Lloyd George, whom so many Liberals regarded as uncertain in his beliefs and tricky and devious in his actions. 'He wouldn't know a principle if he met it in the street', was Morley's judgement of Lloyd George. It seemed unthinkable that a situation could arise in which the course of Simon would be sly and opportunist, and Lloyd George would be loyal to fundamental Liberal principles.

The man who would eventually become the second figure of the revolt was Walter Runciman. He seemed to be even more of a Liberal purist than Simon. He was the Free Trader of all Free Traders; the man who thoroughly understood the theory of Free Trade, and also, as the son of a great shipowner and a practical man of business himself, was convinced of its application to the current problems of the commercial world. But in 1930 there was still no hint that Runciman might join Simon's revolt. As we have seen, he sometimes took an independent line in Parliament; but he was as likely to support the Labour Government when the official Liberal view was to abstain or oppose it, as to do the reverse. In any event, he was becoming increasingly interested in business rather than politics.

*   *   *

Lloyd George was not the man to endanger his own political position without reciprocal concessions from the Government, and it soon became obvious what those concessions were. The Liberals had a very just grievance against an electoral system which had given them such a poor Parliamentary return for such a massive popular vote. The King's Speech at the beginning of the new Parliamentary session promised an Electoral Reform Bill; but when the text of the Bill became known, it was clear that the clauses which interested the Liberals most were proposing 'second preference' voting and not the Liberals' own idea of Proportional Representation. Not surprisingly, Lloyd George had calculations made of the effect which second preference voting would have on the Liberal representation in the House of Commons. On some rather doubtful assumptions, it was shown that in 1929 the Liberals would have gained about fifty-three seats in England by this system, and Labour would have gained about twelve.[1] Simon promptly and publicly opposed the Government's recommendation.[2]

Simon showed early signs of deviation from the 'official' Liberal position on a matter far more fundamental than these tactical considerations. On 3 March 1931, he made an important speech in Manchester, in the course of which he invited those who had 'inherited Free Trade traditions . . . to ponder on the fiscal methods we may be bound to adopt'.

At the time, this speech caused much joy to the Protectionists, and alarm to the Free Traders; but this hint was certainly not definite enough to justify the view that Simon had abandoned the faith of a lifetime.[3]

Few Liberals were prepared to follow Simon's real or imagined deviations on Free Trade; but there was much unquiet about Lloyd George's tactics in the House of Commons. The depth of the Liberal split was shown at the unhappy N.L.F. Conference of May 1931, where the relationship between the Liberal M.P.s and the Government was debated. The Lloyd George line was championed by G. R. Thorne, who had been Asquith's Whip in 1919; the opposite view by Leslie Hore-Belisha, an M.P. generally regarded as a Lloyd Georgeite. A number of those Liberals who were destined within six months to be linked indissolubly with the Conservatives were heard loudly beating the drum of 'independence'.

The next indication of the crumbling of the Liberal Party arose rather unexpectedly. One of the few ways in which the Government showed signs of applying positive Liberal measures was in Snowden's Budget, introduced on 27 April 1931. This included proposals for

---

[1] Ramsey Muir to Lloyd George, 12 February 1930 (? misdated for 1931). Lloyd George papers G/15/6/21.

[2] *The Times*, 12 and 15 December 1930.

[3] *Liberal Magazine*, 1931, pp. 150–2.

the valuation of all land, and then – commencing two years later – the imposition of a land tax of a penny in the pound on capital values. The introduction of a tax which could not possibly apply in the current financial year is very unusual, and it was only brought into the 1931 Budget for reasons of Parliamentary procedure, to ensure that the valuation proposals would not be subjected to the Lords' veto.[1] No Liberal M.P.s opposed the suggested new tax,[2] but there was much confusion as to how it would integrate with existing taxation, and the upshot was a far from satisfactory compromise between the Government and the Liberals.[3] But this baleful and muddled episode does not end with that compromise. On 26 June 1931, three prominent Liberal M.P.s, Sir John Simon, Sir Robert Hutchison, and Ernest Brown, took it as the occasion to resign the Liberal whip.[4]

*   *   *

Simon's defection took place at a time of economic gloom and disaster. Unemployment, for which MacDonald had promised a 'complete cure', was twice as great as when he assumed office. Abroad, great banks were defaulting. No one could see the faintest sign of any alleviation of the situation, and everyone with anything to lose – whether his property or his job – was becoming desperately worried. Those with neither property nor job must have begun to feel that any change would be for the better.

The Conservatives were raising the cry of Protection with growing insistence. Desperate men did not weigh arguments; they panicked. The propensity to panic was not one whit less marked among the educated and intelligent than it was among the ignorant and stupid. Many politicians tried later to fish in some very muddy waters; but this is not the same thing as saying that they had deliberately stirred up the mud. Most of them were in too extreme a state of panic to do anything so lucid.

The Liberals' objection to the Second Labour Government was not that it was imposing socialist policies – no one could accuse it of that – but that it was incompetent in dealing with the problems of

---

[1] Snowden, *op. cit.*, Vol. 2, p. 905.

[2] *Liberal Magazine*, 1931, pp. 289–90.

[3] See Milner Gray's article, *Liberal Magazine*, 1931, pp. 307–9.

[4] For Lloyd George's view of Simon, see Parl. Deb. (Commons) ccliv, 3 July 1931, 1,667.

the day, especially unemployment. The Conservatives might or
might not prove more competent, but it was certain that they would
strike at Free Trade if they had the opportunity, while Labour would
not. Some members of the Government, Snowden in particular, were
staunch Free Traders. Others had no strong beliefs one way or the
other – or else believed (like MacDonald) that an undefined entity
called 'socialism' would somehow resolve the whole problem.

Lloyd George decided that the Labour Government might be
coerced into applying the unemployment policies which the Liberals
had proposed, and Labour had apparently endorsed, in 1929. He
was in discussion with MacDonald, and both men seem to have
agreed that Lloyd George should receive senior office in the Cabinet
under MacDonald.[1] No doubt this would drive Simon, and perhaps
some other Liberals, into even closer contact with the Conservatives;
but this would be a small price to pay if the final result were to coerce
the Labour Government to do Liberal things, and avert the threat
of Protection. But a series of events in the late summer of 1931
destroyed that hope for ever.

On 27 July 1931, Lloyd George became suddenly and dangerously
ill, and for a number of weeks was out of action, while diverse
events of climacteric importance were taking place. The management
of the Liberal Party devolved upon the Deputy Chairman of the
Liberal M.P.s, Sir Herbert Samuel. Lloyd George could, and did,
see other Liberals, and express strong opinions; but he was not in
close and intimate touch with events. On 31 July, Parliament rose
for the summer recess. On the same day a report was published from
a committee of inquiry which the Government had set up earlier in
the year, under the Chairmanship of Sir George May. This reported
that a Budget deficit of £120 million could be anticipated by the end
of the financial year unless drastic action was taken.

For three weeks and more, the Government talked round and
round possible economies. Driven to the last ditch, the Cabinet at
last authorized MacDonald and Snowden to approach the Opposition leaders to enquire whether they would give support if the
Government effected economies to the extent of about £78 million,
including a 10 per cent cut in unemployment benefit. The Opposition leaders seemed prepared to accept this, provided that a bank
loan could be raised sufficient to bridge the gap.

[1] Frank Owen, *Tempestuous Journey*, p. 717.

On Sunday 23 August 1931, the King saw the Prime Minister. On MacDonald's advice he met Baldwin and Samuel. For quite accidental reasons, he saw Samuel first; and the Deputy Chairman of the Liberals indicated that he favoured a National Government under MacDonald. When the King met Baldwin during the afternoon, the Conservative Leader concurred with this view.

When it became clear that some of the Labour Ministers would not accept the proposed economies, MacDonald left the Cabinet to tender the Ministers' resignations to the King. On the morning of Monday 24 August, he returned to the last meeting of the Cabinet of the Second Labour Government to tell them that he had agreed to head a new Government, which would include Conservative and Liberal members.

As Samuel was only Deputy Chairman of the Liberal M.P.s, he needed to visit Lloyd George to seek authority from the senior man for the names of Liberals who should be included. Lloyd George was too ill to take office himself, but well enough to discuss the Liberal appointments with Samuel.

The only first-hand account of what there transpired seems to be that of Viscount Samuel.[1] This account reports that Lloyd George 'fully concurred in every step that I was taking. But when it came to appointments in the Ministry, Lloyd George, not being willing to let bygones be bygones, raised strong objections to one or two of my suggestions for junior posts. As he was my leader and I was acting only as his deputy, I could not insist; these exclusions gave rise to difficulties afterwards.'

How much may we read into this? Simon, Hutchison, and Brown had obviously disabled themselves from any claim on preferment through the Liberal Party by formally resigning the whip several weeks earlier. But there were a number of Liberal M.P.s of considerable ability who could reasonably expect a post in a National Government, but who were known to be on bad terms with Lloyd George, who were also excluded. Runciman, Collins,[2] and Hore-Belisha are three obvious examples. It may well be that this exclusion played a major part in driving them out of the Liberal Party a few weeks later.

The new Cabinet of ten included four Labour men, four Conserva-

[1] Viscount Samuel, *Memoirs*, p. 205.
[2] See Crewe to Samuel, 27 August 1931. Samuel papers A/78, fol. 50.

tives and two Liberals – the last-named being Sir Herbert Samuel as Home Secretary (the office he had held under Asquith) and the Marquis of Reading (formerly Sir Rufus Isaacs) as Foreign Secretary. Several other Liberals took Ministerial office – Sir Donald Maclean was appointed President of the Board of Education, the Marquis of Lothian Chancellor of the Duchy of Lancaster, Sir John Tudor Walters Paymaster-General, Sir Archibald Sinclair Secretary for Scotland, and the Marquis of Crewe Secretary for War. There were also a number of Liberal junior Ministers – including Gwilym Lloyd George, whose father approved the appointment.

On 28 August, a gathering of Liberal M.P.s, peers, and candidates established, for a brief moment, the semblance of complete reunion. The leading Liberals in the Government spoke; while messages of support for the decision were read from both Lloyd George and Simon.

*   *   *

The crisis rapidly passed out of its acute phase. A large tiding-over loan was quickly raised. Parliament was summoned, and gave its vote of confidence to the new Government. The Conservatives and the Liberals supported the Government, and so did twelve Labour M.P.s, while five deliberately abstained. The overwhelming majority of Labour M.P.s voted against it, but the Government secured a majority of sixty.

Yet the brief meeting of Parliament in September sufficed to show that the Liberal Party was not truly reunited. On 11 September, Runciman told the House of Commons that he did not believe that a tariff would balance the budget; but that he was willing to support an embargo on luxury imports. Five days later, Sir John Simon staked his claim to be included in a Government of an overtly Protectionist character, by indicating his view that Britain was 'forced in the circumstances to abandon in this emergency the system of free imports'.

*   *   *

Just after the Government was formed, MacDonald had declared that it was established in order to effect the economies which were necessary to set the country on its feet; and that, once this was done, the Parties would resume their freedom of action and make their separate appeals to the nation. MacDonald's views on the subject were endorsed exactly by the first Lord Hailsham from the Conservative side. We do not need either to credit the Conservatives with altruism or to charge them with hypocrisy. They had every reason to believe that they would win the election whenever it came.

As for the Liberals, they had no reason whatever to desire an election before the Government broke up. This applied no less to men like Simon who were moving towards the Conservatives than it applied to the men who had followed Lloyd George; for Lloyd George's opponents had been omitted from the National Government, but might well hope for office in a post-election Conservative administration. On 23 September, a gathering attended by fifty of the Liberal M.P.s requested Samuel to convey to MacDonald their strong opposition to a dissolution of Parliament.

But the Conservatives gradually came to the conclusion that an early General Election was to their advantage, and the Prime Minister began to waver.[1] On 4 October, Samuel visited Lloyd George, who set the maximum possible pressure on him to resist a dissolution.[2] On the next day MacDonald himself visited Lloyd George at Churt. After the visit, Lloyd George telephoned Samuel, urging him to stand firm against an election, whatever happened.[3]

The same evening, the Cabinet decided otherwise. Samuel and Reading resisted the decision,[4] but did not resign when it was taken.

But Samuel was not utterly beaten. From that fateful Cabinet meeting, he extracted one concession of substance. The Conservatives sought a joint declaration by the participants in the Government on which they would fight the election. Such a declaration would presumably have included a paragraph favouring Protection. Samuel resisted this utterly, and apparently carried the point against the whole Cabinet. His own account[5] says that, 'I found myself without a single supporter', which seems to imply that even the Liberal Lord Reading would not back him. But Samuel's intransigence succeeded. It was agreed that the Prime Minister should issue

[1] Samuel to Lloyd George, 25 September 1931. Lloyd George papers G/17/9/16.
[2] Samuel, *Memoirs*, p. 210.
[3] Frank Owen, *Tempestuous Journey*, p. 719.
[4] Samuel to Lloyd George, 6 October 1931. Samuel papers. A/81, fol. 86.
[5] Samuel, *op. cit.*, p. 211.

a general statement in his own name to which all Ministers could assent, while the Parties should make their separate appeals to the electorate. No one was better qualified to make a general statement to which men of incompatible opinions could assent than Ramsay MacDonald, who was well known for his unmatched ability to make impressive-sounding pronouncements which were of uncertain meaning. On 6 October, MacDonald formally asked the King for a dissolution, and went to the country as head of the National Government. Polling day was to be 27 October – which was only three weeks ahead.

Lloyd George was furious. He told the Liberal M.P.s who visited him soon afterwards, 'You have sold every pass that we held!'[1] On 8 October, the two members of his family who held junior office in the Government – Gwilym Lloyd George and Goronwy Owen – both resigned. The decision of Gwilym Lloyd George at any rate was taken independently of his father.[2] Contact between Lloyd George and the other leading Liberals was not completely broken; Samuel still tried to include Lloyd George in the Liberal declarations. The election manifesto was much modified to satisfy Lloyd George's criticisms, and Samuel attempted to persuade him to sign it.[3]

*   *   *

But Samuel was not only faced with the determined opposition of the Lloyd George family. He was also confronted with a renewed and much more extensive revolt from Simon and his allies. The speech which Simon delivered on 15 September exerted a great influence on those Liberal M.P.s who were already predisposed to seek some accommodation with the Conservatives. On 21 September, twenty-two Liberal M.P.s signed a Memorial to MacDonald – who was already for all practical purposes a prisoner of the Conservatives – indicating their determination 'to support the Prime Minister in

[1] Frank Owen, *op. cit.*, p. 720.
[2] The late Viscount Tenby (Gwilym Lloyd George) informed the present author that he indicated his decision to resign on the night of 7 October. At Sinclair's request, he agreed to sleep on the matter. On the following morning he telephoned his father, who suggested that the draft resignation should first be shown to him. Only when his draft was shown did the elder man indicate that he concurred with his son's decision.
[3] Samuel to Lloyd George, 9 October 1931. Lloyd George papers G/17/9/17.

whatever measures he and the majority of his Cabinet colleagues may think necessary to maintain the financial stability of the country and restore the balance of trade'.[1]

The Simonite revolt continued. On 5 October, at the very moment when the Cabinet was taking its fateful decision about the General Election, Simon and his associates were also meeting. Twenty-one of these M.P.s carried unanimously a resolution to establish 'a body to give firm support to the Prime Minister as the head of a National Government and for the purpose of fighting the General Election'. The body thus constituted became known as the Liberal National Group, and a number of other Liberal M.P.s soon joined as well.

The Liberal National meeting was held, it will be recalled, *before* the Cabinet decision about an early election was known. The Cabinet was known to be divided, with the Liberals strongly opposed. No doubt the Simonites hoped that once the decision in favour of the election was definitely taken, Samuel and his associates would resign from the Government. In order to preserve the façade of a true all-Party National Government, it would be necessary for some ostensible Liberals to be included to replace these men, and in those circumstances the Simonites could have walked straight into the Cabinet room, while Samuel and his allies went into opposition. The Samuelite group could be paralleled closely by Simonites with equally impressive records of public and of Liberal service who had been omitted from the Government.

Although its immediate object failed, as Samuel did not resign, the new group remained in existence. On 13 October, it was announced that negotiations between them and the Conservatives had made good progress, and that many of the M.P.s who had joined the Liberal Nationals and were prepared to support the Government 'and all that it implies' would not have Conservative opponents.

Lloyd George, whose health had by now much improved, stated his position in his election broadcast of 15 October. Discounting the possibility of a majority Labour Government, he argued that the danger was 'all in the direction of Protection', and declared that, 'I should use my vote to avoid that calamity.' However keen the differences between the Lloyd Georgeites and the official leadership of the Liberal Party, they were differences of tactics and not of

[1] *The Times*, 22 September 1931.

principle. Both groups agreed that Free Trade must be defended; the operative question between them was whether the defence should take place within the Cabinet room or outside it. The gap was a real one; but it was also one which time must heal. The fundamental division lay between both of them on the one hand, and the Simonites on the other; for the Simonites had manifestly repudiated Free Trade altogether, and had also declared against all freedom and independence of Liberal action. At that moment, however, the division between Samuelites and Lloyd Georgeites appeared to be sharper. Thus, Major Gwilym Lloyd George not only encountered criticism from his Pembrokeshire constituents who regretted his resignation from the Government; he once told the present author that Samuel's stock message of support was sent to his opponent.

But the boundaries between the three Liberal groups were obscure – and today it is still not always easy to classify a Liberal M.P. or candidate who stood in that election. Five of the M.P.s who were seeking election may be recognized as members of Lloyd George's 'family group'.[1] A few other candidates adopted a similar position, including the celebrated novelist Edgar Wallace. The majority could be regarded as Samuelites who were prepared to support the Government for the time being, but who would not countenance any interference with Free Trade. A smaller group, consisting largely but not entirely of M.P.s, were Simonites.

The fifty-nine M.P.s who had been elected in 1929 as Liberals were all still alive and in the House at the time of the dissolution. They divided as follows:

Twenty-four fought as 'official' Liberals.
Twenty-six fought as Liberal Nationals.
Five adhered to Lloyd George's 'family group'.
Two did not contest the 1931 election.
One (Jowitt) had joined the Labour Party, but stood in 1931 as a National Labour candidate.
One (C. R. Dudgeon) adhered at first to the Liberal Nationals, but eventually defended his seat as a 'New Party' candidate.

There were about 125–30 candidates who were supporting either

[1] David, Gwilym, and Megan Lloyd George; Goronwy Owen; Frank Owen.

the Samuelite or the Lloyd George wing, and about 40–45 who should be considered Liberal Nationals. Thus, on the most sanguine possible view, the Liberals could not hope to be more than a very junior partner in the Government.

It frequently required a great deal of subtlety for an elector with no more than a candidate's election address in his hands to decide whether the candidate should be classified as a Liberal or a Liberal National. The cynic may observe that the candidates who declared themselves unambiguously as orthodox Liberals were often either people whose election was more or less certain, or people whose chances were hopeless. A cursory survey of the election addresses of the various Liberals and nominal Liberals who went to the poll indicates that the use of the words 'National' and 'Liberal' was very loose. Sir Herbert Samuel himself is described in his Darwen address as 'the Liberal and National candidate', while in Dewsbury the staunch Free Trader Walter Rea, who never had any connection with the Simonites, is simply called the 'Liberal National Candidate'.

Alec Glassey in East Dorset was a Samuelite who had taken junior office in the Government. At first the Conservatives in his constituency decided not to oppose him, and a number actually signed his nomination papers. But this decision was soon reversed, and the Conservative whom Glassey had defeated in 1929 was adopted against him. Describing himself as 'THE National Government Candidate', Glassey declared in his address that, 'If I am elected I am prepared to abide by and support the actions of the National Government in all matters.'

E. A. Strauss of North Southwark was one of the four M.P.s[1] whose names appear on both Liberal and Liberal National lists. He had narrowly lost his seat to Labour in 1929, and in 1931 was approached by his Conservative opponent, who offered to stand down if Strauss would write a suitable letter to the local Conservatives. Strauss suggested that the Conservative should draft the letter. When it was written, Strauss took it to Liberal Headquarters, in order to be satisfied that there was no suggestion that he was improperly surrendering his sound Liberal views. On receiving an assurance, Strauss sent if off. The Conservative did not run, and Strauss was elected. Later, when the Liberals and Liberal Nationals began to

[1] The others were Walter Runciman, Edgar Granville, and Duncan Millar.

act differently in the House of Commons, Strauss worked with the Liberal Nationals; but there was no indication at the time of the election that he would do so.[1]

Most of the Simonites were successful in buying off Conservative opposition. Anomalously, two had a Conservative but no Labour candidate against them – T. B. W. Ramsay in the Western Isles, and R. M. Kedward in Ashford. A strange situation arose in Heywood and Radcliffe, where Colonel England, who had joined the Simonites, decided not to defend his seat. A Conservative had already appeared in the field when the decision was taken; as a result, the seat was not defended by even a nominal Liberal.

*　　*　　*

The National Government's majority was the largest ever: 500 seats over the whole Opposition. Seventy-two M.P.s included the word 'Liberal' in their designation. Four were opponents of the Government, while the remainder were divided nearly evenly into Samuelites and Simonites. The official representatives of the Labour Party were down to forty-six.

The Samuelite group held seventeen of its twenty-four seats, lost seven, and gained sixteen more. Twelve of the successful defences, and fourteen of the gains, occurred in places where no Conservative stood. The Lloyd George group returned four of their five M.P.s – Frank Owen being defeated in a straight fight with a Conservative at Hereford. R. M. Kedward was the only Simonite defender who lost his seat.

In an attempt to draw together the ostensible Liberals from all three groups, a decision was taken on 30 October to issue the whip to all M.P.s 'whose candidatures received the approval of their local Associations' – which would have included both Simon and Lloyd George. The Simonites, however, decided not to accept the Liberal whip – placing themselves under the Government whip as such, and not the whip of any Party. As the 'official' Liberal Party was still at this stage supporting the Government, this indicates that the Liberal Nationals regarded themselves as a wholly separate group, in spite of their Liberal origins and the fact that they were supporting the same Government and the same measures in Parliament. There

[1] Information from the late H. J. Glanville, J.P.

could be little doubt that this was a bid for recognition when the Government should be reconstituted, and a clear notice to the Conservatives that all Liberal antecedents might henceforth be ignored.

*   *   *

When the Liberal M.P.s met on 5 November, a letter was read from Lloyd George, in which he declined to stand again for the Liberal leadership, indicating that he was 'completely at variance with the disastrous course into which the Party has been guided'.[1]

Sir Herbert Samuel was unanimously elected Chairman of the Liberal M.P.s. The Lloyd George group, although technically independent of the Samuelites, behaved in the division lobbies in a manner almost indistinguishable from the 'official' sector of the Party.

Neither the Samuelites nor the Simonites were anxious to emphasize their differences. The Simonites held their seats by compounding the Liberal and Conservative votes; if they declared their new position too abruptly, they would lose vital support in their own constituencies. Perhaps most of them had no idea in 1931 that they were sundering themselves for ever from the body of the Liberal Party, for a Lloyd Georgeite spectator at one of their early Conferences reported that they were 'a body of genuine Liberals anxious to preserve the Liberal Party as a separate entity. They regard co-operation with the Conservatives in a 'National' Government as the only effective way to that end under existing circumstances.'[2]

The Samuelites may have been whistling to keep up their spirits, or they may have recalled the Liberal Imperialist split and the split over the Coalition. For whatever reason, they convinced themselves that the Liberal Nationals would eventually rejoin their ranks, and they continued in that assumption for years. The *Liberal Year Books* did not distinguish the biographies of Liberals and Liberal Nationals before 1936, and continued right down to 1939 to list the Liberal

---

[1] See also his letter to Sir Herbert Lewis, 31 December 1931. Lloyd George papers G/12/1/20.
[2] Notes on conversation by A. H. Henderson-Livesey with (?) A. J. Sylvester. Lloyd George papers G/12/3/1.

National bodies among the 'Principal Organizations of the Liberal Party'.

*   *   *

On 5 November – the very day on which the Liberal Nationals as a body refused the Liberal whip – the Government was reconstituted. The composition of the new Ministry gave warning of things to come. The ten offices in the old Cabinet were held by four Labour members, four Conservatives, and two Liberals. The new Cabinet of twenty consisted of eleven Conservatives, four National Labour members, three Liberals, and two Liberal Nationals.

The Liberal members of the Cabinet were Sir Herbert Samuel (Home Secretary), Sir Donald Maclean (President of the Board of Education), and Sir Archibald Sinclair (Secretary of State for Scotland). Of the Liberal Nationals, Sir John Simon was Foreign Secretary and Walter Runciman President of the Board of Trade.

The overwhelming Conservative majority in Parliament made it obvious that the battle for Free Trade would be an excessively difficult one. Samuel and his friends were in an incomparably worse position than they had been before the election. In September, their presence within the Government had seemed like a guarantee that there would be no tampering with Free Trade so long as the Government lasted; but by November they were already expendable. Should Samuelites be replaced by Simonites, the politically informed would know that the Government was no longer National but Tory; but the public as a whole would neither know nor care what had happened.

Among the erstwhile Labour supporters of the National Government, the cause of Free Trade was also gravely weakened. Snowden had not defended his seat at the General Election. Being out of the House of Commons, he could not remain Chancellor of the Exchequer. He went to the Lords as a Viscount, and took the office of Lord Privy Seal; but in the new post he had no special *locus standi* in economic matters.

Almost at once, the Protectionists began to tighten the screw. The first measure was the Abnormal Importations Bill, which sought to authorize the Treasury to impose duties of up to 100 per cent

R

ad valorem on goods entering the country in abnormal quantities in anticipation of tariffs. The Minister in charge of the Bill was Runciman. As with McKenna sixteen years earlier, his strong personal reputation as a Free Trader made it peculiarly difficult for Free Traders to resist.[1]

The appeal which the Protectionists made during the election for Free Trade votes had turned on one thing: that no final decision should be taken on the fiscal question, except in the light of an impartial enquiry. This did not materialize. What did materialize, however, was a very far from impartial Cabinet Committee on the balance of trade, which worked through the Christmas recess, and finally decided by a majority in favour of a general 10 per cent tariff on a wide range of goods, with a later increase on 'non-essential' goods. Predictably, the Conservative members, Neville Chamberlain and Cunliffe-Lister, both supported the recommendations. The Liberal Nationals, Simon and Runciman, supported it as a 'temporary' expedient. (Repressive measures are usually described as 'temporary'. Life, also, is temporary.) Samuel for the Liberals, and Snowden for the National Labour group, both refused to accept the tariffs. When the matter came before the Cabinet on 21 January 1932, the majority decision was inevitable, but four Free Trade Ministers – Snowden, Samuel, Maclean, and Sinclair – dissented immovably from the majority decision. Everyone expected the Free Traders to leave the Government; but this clean break was temporarily avoided by the so-called 'agreement to differ', by which the Cabinet agreed that these Ministers might urge their views on the floor of the House, and in the division lobbies, yet share in the general responsibilities for other Government decisions, and remain in office. On the Second Reading division of the Import Duties Bill, which enshrined the majority view, thirty-one Liberals voted against it and two more were paired against it – but of course the Bill passed just the same.

One of the Members usually listed as Liberal Nationals – A. C. Curry, of Bishop Auckland – voted against the Bill as well; but two M.P.s who had been regarded as Liberals without qualification – Dr J. Hunter of Dumfriesshire and J. A. Leckie of Walsall – voted with the Government. In future critical divisions, Curry voted with

[1] *Liberal Magazine*, 1931, p. 549, is very illuminating about contemporary Liberal doubts, and also about attitudes to Runciman.

the Liberals, while Hunter and Leckie[1] voted with the Liberal Nationals. In some divisions on the clauses of the Bill, however, the voting was less sharp. Thus, on 24 February, an amendment was moved to exclude food from the list of taxable commodities. The 'official' Liberals who voted all supported the amendment; while the Liberal Nationals split into ten voting with the Liberals and nine voting with the Government.

*   *   *

As time went on, the Liberal rank-and-file became increasingly restive about the presence of the Liberal Ministers in the Government. At the N.L.F. meeting in Clacton in April 1932, amid the usual obeisances which a political Party makes to the wisdom and judgement of its leaders (especially when it has the gravest doubts on the subject), a neatly worded resolution was carried which declared 'the independence of the Liberal Party as a whole and its freedom from any obligation to support the policy of the present Government'.

While the Liberal Ministers yet remained in the Government, even the Liberal Nationals could scarcely declare their new allegiance too openly. This was illustrated in the by-election in North Cornwall which followed the death of Sir Donald Maclean in June 1932.

Maclean had had a small majority over a Conservative, and the Labour vote was microscopic. At the by-election, Sir Francis Acland was advanced in the Liberal interest, and had a straight fight against the Conservative. The Liberal National executive did not dare come out openly against Acland, but confined itself to expressing 'regret that the Liberal candidate did not share their view that support, without reservation, of the National Government is vital in the present political situation'.[2] In the event, Acland was returned, with a very slightly increased majority.

*   *   *

Although the process of extracting the Liberal Ministers from the Government has been compared, not wholly unfairly, with that of

---

[1] Leckie's attitude is remarkable. On 31 October 1931, he had written to Samuel, 'I am one of *yours*, not Simon's.' Samuel papers A/82, fol. 27.

[2] *The Times*, 30 June 1932.

pulling kittens by their tails from a jug of cream, the break was bound to come. The agreements which were reached at the Imperial Economic Conference in Ottawa in the late summer of 1932 were more than the Free Trade Ministers could stand. Ten Liberals, and also Snowden, resigned from the Government; and Runciman, still a Free Trader at heart, very nearly resigned with them.

A somewhat ambiguous passage in the official biography of George V seems to imply that the King himself tried to persuade the 'elder statesmen' of the Liberal Party – Lord Reading, Lord Crewe, and Lord Grey – to exert their influence on the Liberal Ministers, to dissuade them from resignation.[1] But instead they wrote a letter to the Press approving the decision (29 September). For some of them at any rate this represented a comparatively recent change of mind.[2]

Runciman was further disturbed by the 'elder statesmen', but was not dislodged from the Government.[3]

For the time being, the Liberals continued to sit on Government benches, in spite of the growing qualms which they felt about the direction which the Government was taking. Several of the Samuelites were apparently wondering whether they should cross the floor very early in 1933, and the suggestion was made that Lloyd George should urge them to do so. But in fact he made no active move in that direction,[4] although one M.P., Major H. L. Nathan of NE. Bethnal Green, moved to the Opposition in February of that year.

The Conference of the N.L.F. at Scarborough in May bluntly told the Liberal M.P.s that their proper place was on the Opposition benches. It seems that the M.P.s had decided by July that they must eventually comply.[5] After dragging their feet for a while, they acceded to the demands of their followers. On 16 November, Sir Herbert Samuel made a broadcast speech which took the form of a wide-fronted attack on the Government's record since Ottawa, and

---

[1] Sir Harold Nicolson, *King George V*, p. 496.

[2] See Grey to Runciman, 21(?) June 1932, Runciman papers. Crewe to Samuel, 25 January 1932, Samuel papers A/87, fol. 4. Grey to Samuel, 27 January 1932 (copy), *ibid.*, fol. 6. Lothian to Samuel, February 1932 (copy), *ibid.*, fol. 8.

[3] Compare Snowden to Samuel, 23 August 1932. Samuel papers A/98, fol. 2.

[4] Memorandum of T. F. Tweed to Lloyd George, 1 February 1933. Lloyd George papers G/20/2/63.

[5] Sinclair to Samuel, 18 July 1933. Samuel papers A/95, fols. 1–5.

announced the belated decision of the Liberal M.P.s to cross the
floor. Yet Samuel was not able to take with him all of those men who
had been elected as 'straight' Liberals in 1931, or even those who
had voted against the Government in the crucial divisions of 1932.
Not only did Hunter and Leckie remain on the Government side
of the House – from their voting behaviour it was obvious that they
would – but so also did William Mabane of Huddersfield, William
McKeag of Durham, Robert Bernays of Bristol North, and J. P.
Maclay of Paisley.[1] Bernays seems to have been willing, against his
own judgement, to follow Samuel, but had trouble from his local
Liberal Association, who 'do not mind how much I criticise and vote
against the Government – but . . . contend that except on some great
issue I ought to do so from the Government side of the House'.[2]
This may suggest that Samuel could have appealed more convincing-
ly to Liberals if he had moved from full support of the Government
to full opposition in one step instead of three: but in view of the
attitude of the 'elder statesmen' and some of the M.P.s it is doubtful
whether he had much alternative.

*   *   *

The chronic financial difficulties of the Liberal Party showed no
improvement in the early 1930s. Just after the 1931 General Election, Sir Archibald Sinclair told Samuel that, 'unless certain steps
are taken immediately we shall be unable to maintain the present
structure of the Party – apart from any question of enlarging and
strengthening it'. The Parliamentary organization of the Party had
recently been running at £3,000 a year, of which slightly less than
a third had been provided by the Liberal Central Association, and
the remainder by the Lloyd George Fund trustees – whose contribution would presumably cease.[3] Further light on the financial situation was cast by Harcourt Johnstone, who was one of the Whips,
and for the remainder of his life one of the most important 'backstage
figures' in the Liberal Party. Mr T. D. Nudds, who was in a good

---

[1] *The Times*, 17 December 1933, mentions the other three, but omits Maclay.
See McKeag to Samuel, 20 November 1933; Leckie to Samuel, 20 November
1933; Maclay to Samuel, 18 November 1933. Samuel papers A/95, fols. 39, 43, 46.
[2] Bernays to Samuel, 'Friday night' (? 19 November 1933) and 'Friday night'
(? 26 November 1933). Samuel papers A/95, fols. 41, 51.
[3] Sinclair to Samuel, 3 November 1931. Samuel papers A/84, fol. 10.

position to observe Johnstone's work, has described him to the present author as 'an aristocrat to his finger-tips, but a radical of the first water', a combination by no means unknown in the Liberal Party either before or since. Johnstone concluded that:

> 'The minimum income on which the Party as at present constituted can survive is £10,000 p.a. – that is, £4,500 for the Central Organization, £3,000 for the L[iberal] P[ublication]D[epartment] and £2,500 for necessary assistance to district Federations and constituencies. In addition a minimum sum of £20,000 must be raised as an election fund. Towards this the Party has an income of approximately £1,000 p.a. and the nucleus of an election fund amounting to approximately £4,500. Moreover these are the very minimum figures. . . .'[1]

So straitened were finances that Johnstone went on to observe that, 'I myself was compelled last week to give the L.C.A. a cheque for £100 to meet the ordinary expenses of charwomen's wages etc.' How, and to what extent, the Liberal Party contrived to meet this problem is obscure, although a fair guess would be that Harcourt Johnstone himself, and some friends on whom he could call, helped a very great deal. The death in 1933 of Viscount Cowdray, who had been a major contributor for years, made the position even worse.[2] The immediate result, however, was that the Liberal Party was in no position to contest by-elections on a large scale, to give much financial help to local and Federation organizations which needed it, or to amass any substantial fund towards the forthcoming General Election.

*   *   *

The gulf between the Liberals and Liberal Nationals continued to grow, and was not confined to the whipping arrangements in the House of Commons. Even before the Liberal Ministers had left the Government, an extra-Parliamentary body called the Liberal National Council was formed (11 July 1932). In April 1933, the Liberal Nationals decided to establish Area Committees in various

---

[1] Johnstone to Samuel, 30 November 1931. Samuel papers A/84, fols. 24–42.
[2] Sinclair to Samuel, 14 October 1933, Samuel papers A/95, fol. 8.

parts of the country.[1] Yet long, long after the vital and irrevocable steps had been taken on the floor of Parliament and in the country, vestiges of the old unity persisted, and frequently caused utter confusion to the outsider. The National Liberal Federation did not disaffiliate constituency organizations which supported Liberal National M.P.s, and it may well be that some of them remained within its ranks right until the N.L.F. itself was dissolved in 1936.[2] In some places, such as Luton, the Liberal National organizations continued to call themselves 'Liberal Associations' until well after the Second World War.

Runciman in particular showed great reluctance to sever his links with the Liberal Party. He was re-elected a Vice-President of the Liberal Council as late as March 1934 – although apparently without his approval. Indeed, he continued to make impeccably Liberal speeches throughout most of the 1930s, and was obviously very far from happy with his new associates.

*   *   *

One general fact seems to emerge through the murk and confusion of the period. The split did not occur because Liberals disagreed fundamentally among themselves as to what measures were necessary for the country. If they had formed a Parliamentary majority in 1929, there is nothing to suggest that they would have been any less united than any other Party in dealing with the problems of the day. They had a policy of great vision, and it is most probable that they would have co-operated in applying that policy.

No. The disruption came from an entirely different cause. The Liberals were a comparatively small third party in 1929. They allowed themselves to be torn to pieces because most of their leading men did not ask themselves so much the question, 'What is the Liberal answer to this particular current problem?', but instead the

[1] *The Times*, 12 April 1933.
[2] Thus, Mr Tom Dale, Liberal candidate for Harwich on three recent occasions, informs the author that the Liberal Association in Harwich, which supported P. J. Pybus as a Liberal, continued to support him as a Liberal National, and remained affiliated to the N.L.F. at least until 1934 or 1935. Unfortunately the Annual Reports published by the N.L.F. do not list affiliated constituency Associations, and the N.L.F. Minutes seem to have been lost or destroyed in one of the rather frequent moves of Liberal Headquarters.

question, 'Would I prefer a Labour Government or a Conservative Government?' In Parliament and in the nation, the Liberal Party inevitably split three ways: into those with a marked preference for one, those with a marked preference for the other, and those who were substantially indifferent to both of them. If the Liberal Party had been, or could possibly be, a disciplined army at all levels: the leadership, the M.P.s, the constituency activists, and the voters – then there would have been a considerable argument for periodically making and breaking alliances with other Parties to achieve particular objectives. But it was nothing of the sort. In 1929, there can have been few informed Liberals who felt wholehearted confidence in any of the available leaders; and three or four years later there seemed even less cause for trusting the judgement of anyone.

13

Between the Millstones

The real enemy of the Third Reich is Liberalism.
ADOLF HITLER
Quoted in Sir Archibald Sinclair's
broadcast, 12 July 1945.

There is no man alive who is sufficiently good to rule the life
of the man next door to him.
SIR RHYS HOPKIN MORRIS, M.P.

Down to August 1931, there was a powerful argument for the view
that the Liberal Party was exerting, and would continue to exert,
a profound effect on British politics, even though the prospect of a
Liberal administration being formed in the foreseeable future was
exceedingly small.

It was not unreasonable to contend that the continued existence
of the Liberal Party had been of major importance in preserving
Free Trade throughout the 1920s. In the summer of 1931 it even
appeared that the Liberal Party was in the process of compelling
a reluctant Labour Government to adopt Liberal policies to deal
with unemployment, and to apply measures of electoral reform which
would remove from the Liberals the 'third party squeeze' which had
done them so much harm in the past.

Yet by the late autumn of 1933 the Liberals were a pathetic
remnant. Not one of the three groups into which they were divided
had much prospect of becoming politically effective. The Liberal
Nationals – however Liberal the opinions which some of them still
held – had become Conservatives for all practical purposes, and it
would be exceedingly difficult to point to a single legislative measure
in which they influenced National Government policy in a distinc-
tively Liberal direction throughout the long and wretched history

of that administration. The Samuelites would have made some real impression if they had left the Government and crossed to the Opposition when MacDonald broke his promise about an early election, or even when a general tariff was adopted in 1932. The expedient of 'agreement to differ' did them no credit, and the fact that the N.L.F. was compelled first to pull them out of the Government and then to make them cross the floor added nothing to their calibre as statesmen. As for Lloyd George, he declined rapidly, both politically and personally. He seems to have become a self-indulgent and rather embittered man. His last, hopeless crusade, the 'Council of Action' of the 1930s, secured some impressive-sounding adherents, but at no time showed real hope of achieving any positive political objectives.

Outside the Conservative Party, there were in 1933 three sizeable groups in the House of Commons, each with between thirty and fifty seats: the Samuelite Liberals, the Liberal Nationals, and the Labour Party. If the Samuelites could form an alliance with either of the others, there was at least a prospect that they might establish a substantial and important bloc in Parliament, and some possibility that they could eventually become a possible alternative Government.

Samuel seems at first to have envisaged a reunion with the Liberal Nationals, declaring his aim to be 'to gather together all Liberals', and promising that, 'there can be no heresy hunt, no excommunications'.[1] The same view was taken up editorially in *Liberal Magazine*: '. . . with one or two exceptions, the Liberal Nationals are bound in the course of time to reunite with the normal Liberal Party.'[2] Yet it was obvious that the National Government had complete control of the political situation, and was likely to retain that control for a very long time. It is remarkable that the Liberals were able to persuade themselves that the Liberal Nationals, who had not even made some sort of perfunctory protest at the abandonment of Free Trade, would dislodge themselves from their offices in the National Government in order to join Samuel in the wilderness.

There had only been one occasion, before Samuel crossed the floor, on which the Liberals and Liberal Nationals had collided at the polls. This was not an experience which the Liberals would

[1] Speech at Paisley, 9 December 1933. *Liberal Magazine*, 1934, p. 1.
[2] *Ibid.*, p. 5.

be anxious to repeat. East Fife had been Asquith's seat before 1918. The Liberal M.P., J. Duncan Millar, went Liberal National, and was unopposed in 1931. When he died a year or so later, the Liberal Association received, but resisted, blandishments to support a genuine Liberal. Instead, they put forward a Liberal National, Henderson Stewart. A young Liberal, David Keir, was set up against him, with support from Liberal Headquarters. The Conservatives did not contest the seat, but Labour and two 'freak' candidates did. Keir ran fourth, while Stewart held the seat with an overall majority. After East Fife, the Liberals were most unwilling to confront the Liberal Nationals in their own constituencies, or to establish genuine Liberal Associations in rivalry with the organizations which were supporting Liberal National M.P.s.

In Scotland even more than England, the line between Liberals and Liberal Nationals remained blurred for several years. Thus, when D. M. Cowan, Liberal M.P. for the Scottish Universities, died at the end of 1933, he was succeeded (14 March 1934) by G. A. Morrison, who is described in contemporary accounts as a 'Liberal'. But Morrison supported the National Government, and was re-elected in 1935 as a Liberal National.

Dr Joseph Hunter is described in the poll records of 1931 as Liberal, not Liberal National, M.P. for Dumfriesshire; but he voted regularly with the Government thereafter, and became organizer of the Liberal National Party in 1934. He died suddenly in July 1935. The Constituency Liberal Association showed no inclination to promote a genuine Liberal to defend the vacancy, but unanimously adopted Sir Henry Fildes, a Liberal National. With a small dissident minority, the local Conservatives also adopted Fildes, who was returned, in a straight fight with Labour, by a substantial margin. The Liberals allowed his constituency to lie fallow for years.

The second possible strategy for the Liberals was to work for some kind of alliance with the Labour Party. For a couple of years after the 1931 General Election, there were few more signs of any improvement in Labour's stock than there was of the Liberals'. Even so, Sinclair was quoting, with apparent agreement, the view that, 'progressives are more and more beginning to look to the Labour Party as the only possible alternative to the present Government.'[1] The idea of a Liberal–Labour alliance was pressed hard in the *News*

[1] Sinclair to Samuel, 14 October 1933. Samuel papers A/95, fol. 9.

Chronicle. This newspaper had been formed in 1930 by the fusion of the *Daily News* and the *Daily Chronicle*, and, although officially Liberal, exhibited throughout its life much tenderness for Labour. Whatever the advantages of an alliance from the Liberals' point of view, Labour's fortunes improved suddenly and substantially in 1934, and the proposal was firmly repudiated by both sides. One Liberal M.P., H. L. Nathan of NE. Bethnal Green, joined the Labour Party (July 1934). He was vigorously denounced by his local Liberal Association.

More alarming to the Liberals than the defection of one man was the reverse which they encountered soon afterwards in another London constituency of a rather similar kind. Frank Briant had been in and out of Parliament as Liberal M.P. for North Lambeth since 1918. He was much loved locally for his social work in this working-class constituency, and in 1931 recaptured the seat in a straight fight with Labour. In 1934 he died, and the ensuing by-election gave the seat to Labour with a huge majority.

*   *   *

The next General Election was in 1935, and the Liberals faced it in a woeful state of unpreparedness. Only 161 candidates were fielded, against 579 supporters of the Government (of whom no fewer than 515 were avowed Conservatives), and 552 Labour candidates. The Liberals could blame the shortage of candidates largely on their desperate poverty; but it is remarkable that they showed little inclination to advance candidates against Liberal Nationals. Only in two places – Oldham and Denbigh – did the two parties collide.

The Liberals lost still more ground, and were reduced to twenty-one seats. Sir Herbert Samuel was defeated rather narrowly by a Conservative at Darwen. Two other Liberal ex-Ministers lost their seats: Sir Walter Rea, who ran third at Dewsbury, and Isaac Foot, who was turned out at Bodmin. Harcourt Johnstone was heavily defeated in South Shields, and E. L. Mallalieu, who had secured an impressive victory in Colne Valley in 1931, was also beaten. Only two gains were made, and both of them occurred in remote rural constituencies with a strong radical tradition which Labour did not contest: Barnstaple, won by Richard Acland, and North Cumberland, where the victor was Wilfrid Roberts. Only six candidates had successfully withstood the combined challenge from Labour and National Government candidates, and three of these six came from rural parts of Wales. A third of the Liberal M.P.s had majorities of less than 1,000.

By 1935, the Liberal Nationals had established a complete concordat with the Conservatives, and were nowhere opposed by them. Their results were closely similar to those of the Conservatives, from whom they were already indistinguishable in Parliamentary behaviour.

On one matter, the 1935 General Election marked an improvement in Liberal relationships. In the previous Parliament, the Lloyd George 'family group' – particularly the head of that group – had been rather aloof from the ordinary activities of the Liberal Party. But after the 1935 General Election, Lloyd George was persuaded to preside over the first meeting of the M.P.s, although he was unwilling to stand for the Chairmanship of the Parliamentary Party. On Lloyd George's proposal, Sir Archibald Sinclair was elected (26 November 1935). Although Sinclair had been Chief Whip in 1930–1, and had held office in the National Government from 1931–2, he was not well known in the country as a whole when he became Chairman. Yet by the outbreak of war in 1939, his name was a household word. He was held in wide respect far outside the range of his own Party; but on the Liberals he impressed his own character and personality to a very great extent.

There was only one Liberal M.P. left in London – Sir Percy Harris, who sat for SW. Bethnal Green. When the news of Harris's election came through, Simon literally jumped on his hat. Harris was appointed Chief Whip and Chairman of the L.C.A. But one is left with the impression that Sinclair did not repose complete confidence in him, for, at Sinclair's special request, Harcourt Johnstone remained in charge of the L.C.A. office.[1]

Not all was lost, but what was held was precarious. There was scarcely such a thing anywhere as a safe Liberal constituency. The Liberal M.P.s could hardly look forward to the next election with anything but gloomy foreboding.

*   *   *

[1] Sir Percy Harris, *Forty years in and out of Parliament*, p. 151.

Organization again came under review. In the middle of 1936, a special Convention was held, which established a new body, the Liberal Party Organization (L.P.O.) This incorporated all Liberal bodies except the L.C.A., which was kept in existence for essentially financial reasons. The old N.L.F. was wound up.[1]

The chief permanent official of the new L.P.O. was W. R. Davies, who had been Secretary of the N.L.F. since 1931, and who was to remain in office until his retirement in 1955. W. R. Davies, like his cousin R. H. Davies, played a major part in keeping the Liberal Party alive in times of great trouble. Whatever one may think of the political leaders of the Liberal Party, it is impossible to feel anything but admiration for the professional workers, throughout the whole of our period of study.

*   *   *

The first by-election result after the 1935 General Election was appalling. In the traditionally Liberal area of Ross & Cromarty, the Liberal ran fourth, with only 738 votes. No more by-elections were contested by the Liberals for more than a year, but when they returned to the fray there were some signs of improvement.

Runciman's elevation to the peerage led to a by-election in St Ives in the middle of 1937. Isaac Foot, the Liberal candidate, was only 210 votes behind the Liberal National defender in a straight fight. A fortnight later, the Liberals missed capturing North Dorset by less than 600 votes. Vernon Bartlett, whose sympathies were Liberal, but who stood as an Independent Progressive, captured Bridgwater in November 1938. When the death of Sir Francis Acland caused a by-election in North Cornwall, the constituency was held with a slightly increased vote, in spite of the intervention of J. A. Spender, the distinguished Liberal journalist, who objected to the attacks which Sir Archibald Sinclair made on the Prime Minister. In other places the Liberal advances were perceptible, and in several the Liberal was second in a triangular contest.

*   *   *

[1] For a criticism of the situation before this reorganization, see *Westminster Newsletter*, April 1936.

Although two Liberal M.P.s crossed the floor to the Liberal Nationals
– R. H. Bernays in 1936, and Herbert Holdsworth in 1938 – there
were still certain indications that the Liberal Nationals were not
wholly satisfied with their current position, and might still envisage
ultimate reunion.

In May 1936, Baldwin made a speech to the Conservative Private
Members' Committee. This was variously reported in the Press, but
he seems to have drawn a parallel between the Liberal Nationals
and the old Liberal Unionists; and, according to one report at least,
he implied that the Conservative and Liberal National Parties
would eventually join. This was too much even for the Liberal
Nationals, and the June 1936 issue of the *Liberal National Magazine*
firmly repudiated the suggestion.

An obscure pamphlet, *Twenty Liberal National Points of Policy*,
was published in January 1938. Apart from item 3 – 'the continuance
of the National Government' – there was little that Liberals would
dissent from, and much that they would applaud, one item even
being 'the removal of the maximum number of restrictions on
foreign trade'. In February this document was discussed in the House
of Commons, where two Liberal National M.P.s indicated their
support; but it was then suddenly withdrawn from circulation in
circumstances indicative of high embarrassment among Liberal
National officials.[1] Of all the leading Liberal National figures, the
one who showed most sign of genuine and continuing Liberalism
was Viscount Runciman. In the spring of 1938, he declared that 'we
have to fall back on pure, simple, strong Liberalism in order to save
this country from disaster.'[2]

*   *   *

The Liberal Party may properly claim to have shown an appreciation of the menace of European Fascism, and a frank acceptance of
distasteful measures in order to combat it, long before any other
Party. For this the main credit must go to Sir Archibald Sinclair.
As far back as February 1936 – when Italy had already marched
against Abyssinia, but long before Nazi Germany was widely seen
as a major challenge – he declared that 'the only possible justifica-

---

[1] *Liberal Magazine*, 1938, pp. 113–14.
[2] *Newcastle Journal*, 1 April 1938.

tion of any measure of rearmament would be that it forms part of a policy which aims at increasing collective security.' With profoundly accurate foreboding, he went on to say that, 'The tree of Protection and economic nationalism is in flower. Unless we cut it down it will bear fruit after its kind, and the fruit will be war.'[1] Sinclair continued throughout the 1930s to preach a policy, not of alliances, but of collective security. In 1937, for example, he told the Liberal Summer School that 'I want to make friends with Germany and Italy, but not by bargains at other people's expense. . . . For example, I should be strongly opposed to purchasing the friendship of Italy by recognizing the conquest of Abyssinia. . . .'[2] In sharp contrast with the Labour Party, which could not be brought to accept the need for rearmament right down to the outbreak of war, the Liberals, under Sinclair's guidance, evinced early signs of a willingness to face the unpalatable needs of the situation. At a time when they could win no popularity but only blame thereby, the Liberals backed increased Defence estimates.[3]

Yet there was something of a division of generations among the Liberals. Viscount Runciman, whose continuing ideological – though not practical – Liberalism we have noted, was Neville Chamberlain's emissary to Czechoslovakia, in 1938, and the author of the report which paved the way to the Munich settlement. It is only just to note, however, that the report was generally acclaimed by Press and public at the time, and that Runciman was himself an ailing man, and had been so for two years.[4] There is real tragedy that such a man should disappear from our story, and from public life, with ribald Sudeten Nazis singing:

> *Wir brauchen keinen Weihnachtsman,*
> *Wir haben unseren Runciman!*

> We need no Father Christmas,
> We have our Runciman![5]

[1] Speech at National Liberal Club, 12 February 1936. *Liberal Magazine*, 1936 speakers' notes, p. 6.

[2] *Liberal Magazine*, 1937, p. 376.

[3] As in the divisions of 15 and 16 March 1937. *Liberal Magazine*, 1937, p. 189.

[4] One of the symptoms of his illness is indicated in Runciman's letter to Samuel, 19 September 1938. Samuel papers A/110, fol. 26.

[5] Information from Mr W. Glanville Brown.

The Munich settlement also divided the Liberal M.P.s, fourteen voting with the Opposition and four with the Government. The Liberal Party Organization Council, however, took a very strong line of opposition to appeasement[1] and this seems to have been characteristic of most of the Liberals in the country. The Liberal M.P.s nevertheless showed a sharp division over the introduction of conscription early in 1939, six voting in favour and seven against.[2]

No Liberals of prominence opposed the declaration of war on Germany in September 1939, and the inclusion of Winston Churchill and Anthony Eden in the Government was welcomed. But neither of the Opposition Parties could feel confidence in the leadership of Neville Chamberlain, and for that reason Sir Archibald Sinclair and Clement Attlee did not join the Government. One Liberal, however, accepted junior office on the outbreak of war – Gwilym Lloyd George, who was appointed Parliamentary Secretary to the Board of Trade.

In the middle of September 1939, some Conservative and Liberal National M.P.s who no longer felt confidence in Chamberlain began to meet, and to examine political questions frequently and very critically. The Chairman and major personality of the group was Clement Davies. He had been elected as Liberal M.P. for Montgomeryshire in 1929, but defended his seat in 1931 and 1935 as a Liberal National. He resigned from the Liberal Nationals in November 1939, and sat for a time as an Independent, eventually rejoining the Liberals in February 1942. Lord Boothby (then Robert Boothby) was Secretary of the group, and has expressed to the present author the view that Clement Davies was one of the two men who were to play the most vital part in bringing about the eventual downfall of Chamberlain's Government, and installing Churchill.[3]

In May 1940 the administration came under attack in the great debate on the fall of Norway. When the Prime Minister concluded his defending speech with the words, 'I call on my friends to support us in the Lobby tonight', this drew from Lloyd George his last memorable and devastating speech, with its crushing peroration:

---

[1] *Liberal Magazine,* 1938, p. 497.
[2] 27 April 1939. *Liberal Magazine,* 1939, p. 246.
[3] See also Robert Boothby, *I fight to live,* pp. 195, 218, 219.

s

'The Prime Minister . . . has appealed for sacrifice. . . . I say solemnly that the Prime Minister should give an example of sacrifice, because there is nothing which can contribute more to victory in this war than that he should sacrifice the seals of office.'

The Government won the division which followed. It could scarcely do otherwise in a Parliament where it had a nominal majority of well over two hundred; but that majority was cut to eighty-one and thirty-nine of its normal supporters voted in Opposition lobbies.[1]

During the two days of doubt and confusion which followed the crucial division of 8 May, Clement Davies established contact with the leaders of the Labour Party who were preparing for their Conference in Bournemouth, and repeatedly insisted that Churchill was the man for the Premiership. When the news of the German invasion of the Low Countries came through, Chamberlain deliberated for a moment whether the changed circumstances made it necessary for him to remain. His closest colleague, Sir Kingsley Wood, insisted that the very reverse was the case, and this seems finally to have decided Chamberlain to resign. On the same day, 10 May 1940, Winston Churchill received the King's commission to form a Government.

The Liberal and Labour Parties indicated their willingness to serve under Churchill. An Inner War Cabinet of five was established. This did not include any Liberals, but did include two members of the Labour Party. Some resentment was felt among the Liberals at the exclusion of Sir Archibald Sinclair; but, as Secretary of State for Air, he played a major part throughout the war, and was frequently present at Cabinet meetings. Churchill was unable to persuade David Lloyd George to accept office, although he certainly tried. There were some rather surprising inclusions and omissions among the Liberals,[2] and it is noteworthy that Sir Percy Harris, the Chief Whip, knew nothing of these appointments until he read them in the Press.

With Sir Archibald Sinclair in charge of one of the most important functions of the war, it was obviously impossible for him to perform

[1] For the Government: Conservatives 252; Liberal Nationals 20; National Labour 4; Liberals 2 (Gwilym Lloyd George and J. P. Maclay); Others 5. Against the Government: Labour 142; Conservatives 33; Liberals 15; Liberal Nationals 4 (H. W. Butcher, L. Hore-Belisha, F. Medlicott, Henderson Stewart); Others 6 (including Clement Davies and Vernon Bartlett).

[2] Sir Percy Harris, *op. cit.*, pp. 150–1.

in an active manner the full duties of Chairman of the Liberal M.P.s. Therefore, Sir Percy Harris became Deputy Chairman, and performed for the rest of the war many of the Chairman's functions.

Sir Percy Harris had a very difficult task indeed.[1] Most of the ablest M.P.s became members of the Government, and did not always take kindly to criticism. The fact that the Liberal Parliamentary Party maintained a high prestige was very largely due to Harris. No orator, and in no ordinary sense a natural leader, he did his duty because it was his duty, and he did it admirably, under great difficulties. It was to a very large extent the personal feat of Sir Percy Harris that the poor and slum-ridden constituency of SW. Bethnal Green remained Liberal a decade after any other in London.

* * *

In the middle of the war, a profound change came over British politics. It is extremely difficult to measure the change, because an agreement concluded between the three Parties at the outbreak of war prevented them from opposing each other when by-elections took place. It is no less difficult to understand why it happened at that particular moment. Certainly a violent swing against the Conservatives took place about 1941 or 1942 – and it does not seem to be attributable to the conscious propaganda of any politicians or political parties.

In this mid-war period, the Liberals received a very important recruit – Sir William Beveridge. He had been associated with some of the economic work promoted by Lloyd George, but had never belonged to any political party. In June 1941 he was selected to preside over an Inter-Departmental Committee to examine all aspects of social insurance. In the following year, this Committee produced the celebrated 'Beveridge Report', which proposed a great extension and rationalization of the social services. There were many back-benchers, both Liberal and Labour, who considered that the Government's reception of the Report had not been sufficiently enthusiastic, and most of the Liberal and Labour M.P.s who did not belong to the administration took part in a rather spectacular

[1] *Ibid.*, pp. 154–5.

'revolt'. In spite of a strong appeal by their leaders in the Government, 119 M.P.s, of whom nine were Liberals, supported a critical amendment.[1]

*   *   *

The relationship between the Liberals and the Liberal Nationals came under very serious review during the war. When Churchill formed his Coalition Government in May 1940, Sir John Simon became Lord Chancellor, and took a peerage. The leadership of the Liberal Nationals devolved upon Ernest Brown; but his Party showed early signs of melting away. We have noted that Clement Davies resigned from the Liberal Nationals as far back as November 1939. In February 1942, he was followed by three more Liberal National M.P.s – Leslie Hore-Belisha, Sir Henry Morris-Jones, and Edgar Granville. In the following month, Sir Murdoch Macdonald withdrew from the Liberal National group in Parliament, without, however, resigning from the Party.[2]

There was serious interest in the achievement of complete fusion of the two Parties. In July 1943, Ernest Brown offered to inaugurate discussions, and this offer was gladly taken up by Sir Archibald Sinclair.[3] It is evident that this was a genuine attempt on both sides to secure reunion, and no mere propaganda gesture. But on 29 October Ernest Brown expressed the view that, 'the continuance of a National Government after the War was most vital'.[4]

'. . . Continuance of a National Government.' There was the rub. Sinclair was emphatic in his assertions in favour of complete independence, and the popular organs of the Liberal Party took the same line with even more vehemence.[5] These incompatible attitudes really foredoomed the negotiations, but they continued nevertheless for a further year, until they finally collapsed on 20 November 1944,

[1] *The Times*, 19 February 1943. The Liberal 'rebels' were Clement Davies, D. O. Evans, David Ll. George, Megan Ll. George, George Grey, Prof. Gruffydd, Sir Percy Harris, T. L. Horabin, Wilfrid Roberts.

[2] Morris-Jones returned to the Liberal Nationals in March 1943; Granville joined the Liberals in April 1945; Hore-Belisha eventually joined the Conservatives.

[3] *The Times*, 9 July 1943.

[4] *Ibid.*, 1 November 1943.

[5] As in the Liberal Party Organization Council declaration of March 1944.

when correspondence was published. The length of these discussions is remarkable, for the Liberal Party's attitude on independence can never have been in doubt. One may only suppose that the Liberal Nationals were at one point contemplating the termination of their association with the Conservatives.

Other Liberals began to move in other directions. Sir Richard Acland, M.P. for Barnstaple, began making speeches which were inconsistent with Liberal views, even on the broadest possible interpretation of the word 'Liberal'. Pressure was set on Sir Percy Harris to withdraw the whip from Acland.[1] Harris was willing to remonstrate, but would not take this ultimate step. In 1941, Acland established a movement known as the Forward March, which, in the following year, amalgamated with another organization to form a rather evanescent socialist body known as Common Wealth, of which Acland became effectively the leader. He resigned from the Liberals in September 1942. Common Wealth advanced a number of candidates in by-elections, and a few of these candidates were elected.

The opinions of Sir Richard Acland were not widely shared in the Liberal Party, but a considerably larger measure of Liberal support was given to a body formed in 1941 which was originally known as the Liberal Action Group, and later as Radical Action.[2] Broadly, the members were Liberals who were unhappy about the electoral truce, who became increasingly critical of the Government, although they were not committed to any particular 'line' as a term of their membership.

Many influential Liberals belonged at one time to the Group. The Chairman was Lancelot Spicer, and the Treasurer at one stage was Philip Fothergill, who later became a very important figure indeed in the Party. Several M.P.s were also associated.[3] Radical Action was very critical of the talks between members of the Liberal and Liberal National Parties. It also became less concerned to emphasize the traditional Liberal belief in economic freedom; and when this happened such noted libertarians as Philip Fothergill became less prominent in the Group's activities.

[1] Sir Percy Harris, op. cit., p. 142.

[2] The author is much indebted to Mr Lancelot Spicer for most of the information here published about Radical Action.

[3] Including, at various times, Clement Davies, George Grey, T. L. Horabin, Wilfrid Roberts, Professor Gruffydd, Megan Lloyd George, and Sir William Beveridge. Vernon Bartlett was also a supporter.

The economic and social ideas of Radical Action were in no sense original; they were general currency in the early forties. But the Group's emphasis on the need for profound reorganization as an essential condition of Liberal revival may well have played a vital part in stimulating the renewed interest in establishing an effective electoral machine which was so characteristic of the Liberal Party in the second part of the decade.

*   *   *

The problems, and the temptations, of the Party Truce, which so troubled Radical Action, proved unsettling to the Liberal Party as a whole in the later stages of the war. Like both other Parties, the Liberals naturally rejoiced at the opportunity of returning M.P.s without the hazard of a serious contest when their own constituencies fell vacant. Such personalities as Sir William Beveridge, Harcourt Johnstone, George Grey, and Air Vice Marshal Bennett were thus at various stages of the war enabled to assume their places on the Liberal benches in the House of Commons. But during the later phases of the war, some most improbable candidates seemed to be finding their way into the House through the manifest desire of a large section of the electorate to 'get the Tory out' at almost any price; and Liberals began to feel that a candidate standing under their own label would almost certainly have been returned. An unsuccessful attempt was made at the 1941 Assembly to raise the question of renouncing the Truce,[1] and another attempt was made at a meeting of the Liberal Party Organization Council in 1942.[2]

The point was driven home in two by-elections where known Liberals, compelled to fight as Independents, polled strongly. At Darwen, Honor Balfour came very close to capturing Sir Herbert Samuel's old seat in December 1943. She complained of neglect by the newspapers; noting the youthfulness of the Conservative candidate, she declared that she had to fight not only the boy Prescott but also the Press boycott. In February 1944, Mrs Corbett-Ashby, also fighting as an Independent, secured a very substantial vote at Bury St Edmunds. Lady Violet Bonham-Carter, daughter

[1] J. S. Rasmussen, *The Liberal Party*, pp. 108–9.
[2] *Ibid.*, p. 109.

of Asquith and President of the L.P.O., urged that the three Parties should abrogate the Truce; but her suggestion was not followed. The Liberals were unwilling to act alone in the matter, although there is no doubt that the agreement concluded at the outbreak of war between the three Parties permitted unilateral renunciation by any of them.[1]

*   *   *

The last phase of the war saw the retirement and death of the most famous Liberal statesman of the century. David Lloyd George was warned by his advisers that he would have great difficulty in holding the constituency of Caernarvon Boroughs at the next General Election. He accepted an Earldom – apparently in order to be in a position to advise on the Peace Treaties. But in fact he died on 26 March 1945, before he could even take his seat in the Lords. In a memorable oration, Winston Churchill described his old friend as 'the greatest Welshman since the Tudors'. Of that assessment, at least, there can be no doubt.

*   *   *

The withdrawal of the Labour members from the Government in May 1945, at the end of the European war, made a General Election inevitable. A 'caretaker' Government was formed until this election could be held; but as the Liberal Party was determined to fight as an independent body, the principal Liberal Ministers could not continue in office. The administration, therefore, was composed mainly of Conservatives and other 'Nationals'. But Gwilym Lloyd George, though still a Liberal, remained in office as Minister of Fuel and Power.

The Liberal Party could not fight the General Election on as broad a front as it had hoped, although this was a good deal broader than it had been in 1931 or 1935. For 640 seats, the Liberal Party fielded 307 candidates, while the Labour Party and the various 'Nationals'. each fought more than 600. In all Parties, there was a high proportion of new candidates, but among the Liberals this was

[1] R. B. McCallum and Alison Readman, *The British General Election of 1945*, p. 2.

particularly marked. No fewer than 87 per cent of the Liberal candidates were standing for the first time.[1]

Almost two and a quarter million votes were cast for the Liberals, against twelve million for Labour and ten million for the various 'Nationals'. But although the Liberal poll was far higher than at any election since 1929, only twelve M.P.s were returned.

The mortality was peculiarly heavy among the Leaders. Sir Archibald Sinclair was defeated in Caithness & Sutherland in an agonizingly close 'triple marginal' result – fewer than seventy votes separating the three candidates. The Liberal Party, regarding Sir Archibald's seat as safe, had deployed him widely in speaking for other candidates. The Chief Whip and Deputy Chairman, Sir Percy Harris, was defeated in SW. Bethnal Green. Sir William Beveridge met a similar fate in Berwick-upon-Tweed. With the exception of Gwilym Lloyd George, all the Liberal M.P.s who had ever held Government office were defeated: Dingle Foot at Dundee; Goronwy Owen in Caernarvonshire; James de Rothschild in the Isle of Ely, and Graham White in Birkenhead East. So were well-known figures like Sir Geoffrey Mander and Air Vice-Marshal Bennett.

Only seven Liberal M.P.s who had sat in the old House were returned, while two other Liberals successfully defended old Liberal seats whose M.P.s were retiring. Three Liberal gains were recorded, two of them being won in straight fights against Conservatives. One surprising victory was that of Rhys Hopkin Morris in Carmarthenshire – for, fighting on a traditional libertarian platform, he took a seat from Labour.

In most other places which had been Liberal in 1935, the Liberal was far behind. Mark Bonham-Carter, son of Lady Violet, secured a good second place in Barnstaple – Sir Richard Acland's constituency; but the Liberal in Holdsworth's old seat of South Bradford ran third; and in Paisley, which had been (ostensibly) a Liberal seat down to the dissolution, the Liberal forfeited her deposit. Bernays's old seat of Bristol North was not contested at all. Caernarvon Boroughs, which Lloyd George had captured from the Conservatives in a famous by-election in 1890, and had held for nearly fifty-five years, was one of the few Conservative gains in the election.

*   *   *

[1] Rasmussen, *op. cit.*, p. 11.

CLEMENT DAVIES (1884–1962)

One of the unknown great men of modern times, 'Clem' played a very large part in bringing down Chamberlain in 1940, and later inspired the Liberals at one of the most desolate periods of their history.

(copyright of the Ministry of Food, supplied by the Liberal Party Organization.)

(*photographs by courtesy of Associated Newspapers Limited.*)

ORPINGTON, 1962

'THE ORPINGTON MAN'

Eric Lubbock (1928–   ) was the hero of the amazing Orpington by-election
of 1962. In the picture above he is seen with Jo Grimond, whose
immediate comment on the almost unbelievable result was – 'My God!'

(photograph by courtesy of Syndication International

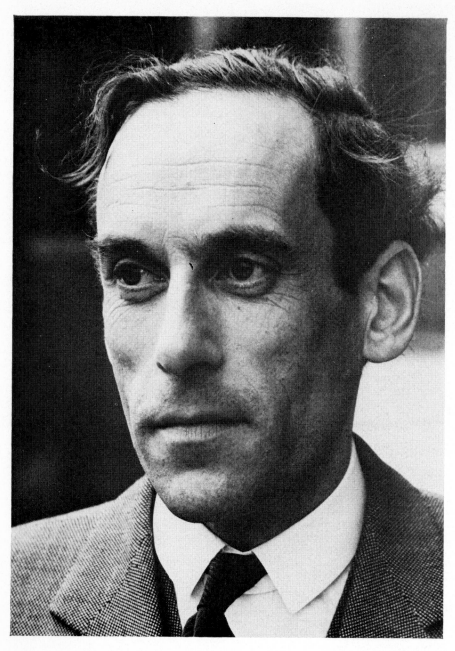

JEREMY THORPE (1929–)

The heir to Gladstone. The party is smaller; the issues have changed, and there is a new problem. Can the Liberals again become a party of the masses?

(photograph by courtesy of the Popperfoto Library.)

The first problem which confronted the Liberals after the 1945 General Election was the need to elect a sessional Chairman for the M.P.s. At first this seemed likely to be only a temporary appointment. The Conservative who defeated Sinclair so narrowly had promised that, if elected, he would resign on the defeat of Japan. The Liberals, and everyone else, anticipated that the promise would be honoured; and the Liberals had reasonable hopes that Sinclair would recapture the seat in the by-election which would ensue. In fact the M.P. did not honour his promise, and Sinclair did not return to the House.

In any case an appointment had to be made. Sir Archibald Sinclair and some of his closest associates met to discuss the question.[1] Sinclair and Sir Percy Harris first approached Gwilym Lloyd George, but he refused, largely because he could not afford the incidental expenses which the office would entail.[2] He was also offered – and also refused – the Chairmanship of the Liberal National Party about the same time.[3] When the new House met, he was offered a place on the Opposition front bench by Winston Churchill. Gwilym Lloyd George replied that he would only sit as a Liberal. Churchill's reply was characteristic: 'And what the hell else should you sit as?' But Liberals soon came to the conclusion that he was effectively supporting the Conservatives.

Thus the selection of the Chairman was left to the Liberal M.P.s, without the benefit of the advice of senior members of the Party. The remaining M.P.s knew little of each other's capabilities, and several of them had not even met before the election.[4] They adopted the remarkable expedient of asking each member to withdraw in turn, while the others discussed his suitability. At least one of the M.P.s who was well qualified for the office, Hopkin Morris, refused to allow his name to be considered in this manner.[5] But at last a selection was made, and on 2 August they were able to announce that Clement Davies had been chosen Chairman and T. L. Horabin Chief Whip. Whatever could be said of Clement Davies's Liberal National past, his Liberalism in the new office to which he was so

---

[1] *The Times*, 31 July 1945.
[2] Information from the late Gwilym Lloyd George (Viscount Tenby).
[3] Obituary in *The Guardian*, 15 February 1967.
[4] Rasmussen, *op. cit.*, p. 40.
[5] Information from the late Sir Rhys Hopkin Morris.

unexpectedly called was impeccable, and he rapidly grew in stature in the Party.

*   *   *

In the 1945 General Election and its immediate aftermath, local workers in the Liberal cause constantly reported that large numbers of voters were saying, 'I am really a Liberal, but I am voting Conservative [or Labour] because the Liberals are too weak' – or for some other related reason, like 'to get the Socialists out', 'to keep the Tories out', or 'because the Liberals are so split'. Thus, most active Liberals became convinced that if the Liberal Party could improve its organization substantially, a political chain-reaction would be set up, by which these 'Liberals-but' (as they were usually called) would be scooped into the Party by the million.

The Liberal reorganization after 1945 was a very different thing from that of ten years earlier, and the Liberal Assembly of 1946 was held in an atmosphere almost of religious revivalism. Several personalities achieved prominence on that occasion, and continued to influence its activities for a number of years. Philip Fothergill, Vice-Chairman of the Reconstruction Committee, was a friendly, thoroughly accessible little man with a keen sense of humour, always willing to help Liberals, however undistinguished or inexperienced. If there is one man to whom, more than any other, the credit should be given for keeping the Liberal Party alive and fighting at a time when it could well have fallen to pieces, that man was Philip Fothergill.

Another man of a very different stamp was Edward Martell. One must not discount his services to Liberalism in the late 1940s because of the astounding political adventures on which he was later to embark. Although a man with the makings of a dictator, he supplied the Liberals with a ceaseless flow of ideas, and a great infusion of enthusiasm. His judgement often proved wildly wrong, and many of his ideas failed – some disastrously – but some were, and are to this day, of great value to the Liberal Party.

Both Fothergill and Martell gave great attention to the question of securing broadly based finance for the Liberal Party. In the previous ten years, the annual income of Headquarters had never reached £15,000, and had sometimes been as low as half that figure. A serious political party could not long be maintained on such meagre finance. The Liberal Party therefore launched the 'Foundation Fund' at the 1946 Assembly. The instigators of the Fund sought to raise substantial sums by a series of devices, some of them quite ingenious. Public appeals were made at rallies all over the country. Bonds, based on individual promises to pay or collect £50 a year for the next five years, were launched. Liberals were invited to make compacts for smaller sums, to make bequests to the Party, and so on. The most original method of all, and potentially the most important, was what was first called *Liberal Newscard*, but was continued as *Liberal News*. This was not intended as 'value for money', but as a means of collecting weekly contributions – originally threepence – through newsagents. On the current hypothesis that there were millions of people yearning for the Liberal Party to return, and who would scarcely notice threepence a week, the scheme seemed sound enough.

Nor was finance the only department in which the Liberal Party underwent a substantial revival during 1946 and the early part of 1947. Plans were set out, explaining to the Liberal enthusiast how to build up a Liberal Association from nothing, and to bring it to massive fighting strength, from which a Liberal victory could be anticipated. The new enthusiasm swept the Liberal Party at all levels. Constituency Associations were set up in places which had been derelict for many years. By the 1947 Assembly, Philip Fothergill was able to report that 500 constituency Liberal Associations existed, as against only 200 a year before.[1] The Liberal Party was certainly receiving a very large influx of support from young and youngish people with much energy, imagination, and idealism. This far more than compensated for their relative failure to reclaim the support of older Liberals whose assistance had lapsed in the 1920s or 1930s.

1946 was an important and exciting year for the Liberal Party. On 7 March, two Liberals were returned to the London County Council for SW. Bethnal Green – Sir Percy Harris and Edward Martell. The Party Assembly in May was described by a veteran Liberal leader as the finest for forty years. In August, the Liberal Party Executive adopted a plan designed to secure a Liberal majority Government at the next General Election – '600 candidates, backed by 600 live Associations'. In November, the Rotherhithe

[1] Rasmussen, *op. cit.*, p. 15.

by-election showed that a determined campaign, even in a constituency with no recent Liberal tradition, could deliver encouraging results.

*   *   *

There were some people who belonged to the Liberal Party at the end of the war who held opinions so close to the Labour Party's that it is extremely difficult to understand why they did not join the larger body in preference to the smaller. It was highly embarrassing for the Liberal Party that one of those people was the Chief Whip, T. L. Horabin.

After some public protest at the opinions he expressed, Horabin resigned his post in the spring of 1946, and some eighteen months later was received into his natural home, the Labour Party. Yet he did not afford the electors of North Cornwall the opportunity of deciding whether they wished him to continue as their representative under his new colours. Frank Byers, who was appointed Horabin's successor, was a man of incomparably higher calibre. He was still in his very early thirties, a forceful, dynamic, clear-minded man, whose occasional brusqueness was readily forgiven as the product of his enthusiasm. His devotion to Liberalism was paramount, and he was respected and admired throughout the Party.

Although there were one or two other M.P.s who held views not wholly different from those of Horabin, the Labour Party soon declared its intention in future to oppose all Liberal M.P.s. But neither the Conservatives nor the Liberal Nationals were equally obdurate.

In the immediate aftermath of the war, there were many people to whom it seemed that the Conservatives had sustained a blow so severe that they might never form the Government again. In these circumstances, an extraordinary movement appeared, which at one stage seemed likely to affect the whole political history of Britain to a profound extent.[1] It was to centre on a pamphlet called *Design for Freedom*. The role of the movement was generally misunderstood at the time, and the misunderstanding has persisted to this day.

---

[1] The present author is indebted to the late Mr David Goldblatt for discussions on the matter, and also for allowing him to read and quote from an unpublished manuscript account of the episode.

On 21 September 1945, a letter appeared in *The Spectator* over the signature of Quintin Hogg, who was generally regarded as one of the ablest and most promising of the younger Conservative M.P.s. This letter indicated that there was a 'Tory Reform Group' thirty or forty strong in the House of Commons, whose views on policy showed 'no striking difference from the Liberals'; and claimed that, 'if only the Liberals would come and help . . . we would, together, capture the Conservative Party'.

In February 1946, four of the 'Tory Reformers' (not including Mr Hogg), and four Liberals, headed by a former candidate, David Goldblatt, met privately. One of the Conservatives soon withdrew, but the remaining seven men agreed to draw up a statement for signature, and in the meantime to keep both Liberal and Conservative Headquarters informed of developments.

The pamphlet *Design for Freedom* was ready for signature in the late autumn of 1946. By then, the respective Party Headquarters had begun to define their views. The Liberals, inspired in particular by Edward Martell (such are the vagaries of politics!), were hostile. The Conservatives were still uncommitted. By January 1947, the document was in proof, but had not yet been published. Over fifty Conservatives were signatories. The list was an impressive one, including such names as D. Heathcote Amory, Quintin Hogg, Selwyn Lloyd, Reginald Maudling, Hugh Molson, Oliver Poole, and Peter Thorneycroft – four of them future Chancellors of the Exchequer. There were also nearly fifty Liberals, most of them recent candidates, headed by David Goldblatt.

Conservative leaders began to get anxious. An acrimonious meeting was held, at which the signatories were called upon to retract. Thorneycroft, as their spokesman, refused to do so, since the master copy had already been signed. There was at least the possibility that the Conservative leadership might be forced to apply disciplinary measures which would drive the signatories irretrievably out of their Party.

On 15 February, just before the pamphlet was published, Clement Davies spoke at Colwyn Bay, and there condemned the publication. One of the Liberal M.P.s, Emrys Roberts, called it 'the greatest act of sabotage to the Liberal Party since 1931'. A moderately phrased letter was sent from Liberal Headquarters to all constituencies, not dissenting from the contents of *Design for Freedom*, but reaffirming

independence, and, by implication, advising Liberals to have
nothing to do with the movement. David Goldblatt thus described
the *dénouement*:

'Dispirited Tories who, a few days earlier, had wondered on their
future, were amazed at the official public reaction of Liberal
H.Q. They deemed it profitless to compromise themselves for a
cause which was so ham-handedly managed. . . . Within a week or
so the two sides moved away each from the other. Two further
pamphlets were issued, but since they had not been strained
through the sieve of joint authorship they represented nothing.
The affair was over.'

*   *   *

While the strange manœuvres of the *Design for Freedom* movement
were in operation, there was a good deal of further rethinking about
the relationship between the Liberal Party and the Liberal Nationals.
However close the resemblance between the Liberal Nationals and
the Conservatives in the division lobbies, the two Parties had their
quite separate organizations at local and national levels. At the 1945
General Election only thirteen Liberal National M.P.s had been
returned. In some places, the Liberal Nationals entered discussion
with the Liberals. There was interest in the prospect of reunion of
the organizations in Devon and Cornwall.[1] In Scotland, discussions
reached an advanced stage, and a draft statement setting out a basis
for fusion was issued jointly by the Scottish Liberal Party and the
Scottish Liberal National Association in October 1946.[2] But these
negotiations later broke down, as also did the principal English
negotiations. In London the story was different, for the Liberal
Nationals in the area actually reunited with the London Liberal
Party.[3] As there were no Liberal National M.P.s remaining in
London, this did not affect the Parliamentary position.

*   *   *

In the course of 1947, there were still plenty of signs of a sharp
decline in Liberal fortunes, and this decline affected greatly the

[1] *The Times*, 18 March 1946.
[2] *Ibid.*, 28 October 1946.
[3] *Liberal News*, 5 July 1946.

relations between the Liberals and other Parties. This probably explains both the speedy termination of the 'reunion' negotiations and the developing coolness of the Conservative 'Designers'. In 1946, as we have seen, the Liberals sought to establish themselves as a credible alternative Government, and the calibre of the leadership remained remarkably high for such a small Party. But the wave of enthusiasm in 1946–7 tempted Liberals to say and do things which they very soon came to regret. 'We can govern Britain' was one of the theme-slogans, and this was to look pretty fatuous a year or two later. In an attempt to prove that the Liberal revival had really come, Liberals began to fight by-elections in hopeless places, and often with little or no organization. Thus, in the latter half of 1947, the Liberals contested five of the six by-election vacancies, and forfeited their deposits in all but one of them. The ultimate horror was the disaster of Camlachie (Glasgow) on 29 February 1948; in a six-cornered contest, the Liberal finished sixth. A further lost deposit with Air Vice-Marshal Bennett as the candidate in the much more promising territory of North Croydon (11 March) confirmed that the frost had set in, and from then onwards the Liberals were far more reluctant to contest by-elections.

Yet the Conservatives could scarcely doubt that their best hope of electoral victory in the tangible future lay in attracting Liberal votes. Both Winston Churchill and the Conservative Chairman, Lord Woolton, worked hard to develop a Liberal-sounding appeal. By April 1947, Lord Woolton was proclaiming the overriding need for people who saw the dangers of socialism to unite, and argued that this meant supporting the Conservative Party, since only they had a chance of forming a non-socialist Government.[1] This theme was taken up with more and more vigour by Conservative speakers down to the 1950 General Election. Large-scale defections from the Liberals were inevitable. The truly remarkable thing was that they were not more numerous still. But for the inspiring leadership of Clement Davies, Frank Byers, Philip Fothergill, and a few others, the Liberal Party might well have collapsed.

The relationship between the Conservatives and the Liberal Nationals was at last regularized, through what became known as the Woolton–Teviot agreement. This was concluded between Lord Woolton and Lord Teviot, his opposite number in the Liberal

[1] *The Times*, 28 April 1947.

Nationals, on 9 May 1947.[1] This agreement provided for the union of the two Parties at the constituency level, and the adoption of candidates who might be recommended by either Headquarters. A couple of years later, the arrangement was extended to make definitive provision governing the titles of candidates supported by these 'combined associations'. Early in 1950, a joint statement was issued by Churchill, for the Conservatives, and Lord Rosebery (son of the former Prime Minister), for the Liberal Nationals,[2] urging that they should be described as 'Liberal-Conservatives' or 'Liberal-Unionists', prefixing this title by the word 'National' when a genuine Liberal was in the field. Liberal Headquarters declared that every one of the candidates so designated was controlled by the Conservative Party, and had no connection whatever with the Liberals. They also considered the possibility of legal action; but on this matter Counsel's opinion was adverse.

Although the informed section of the electorate knew perfectly well that candidates standing under such labels[3] – felicitously described by Fothergill as 'liquorice allsorts' – were committed to vote with the Conservative Party in Parliament, and many of them had not even the remote and tenuous connection with historical Liberalism which the Liberal Nationals could claim, yet many people were doubtless confused.

The Conservatives seem to have exceeded all ordinary political bounds in their ruthless determination to arrogate the name 'Liberal' for their own supporters. In a public letter to Winston Churchill,[4] Clement Davies provided some startling examples of the way in which this was done.

'(i) In November 1948, a meeting was held in Dunstable in private, with only invited persons present. The prospective Liberal candidate and some members of the local Liberal Association were refused admittance to the meeting, which set up the 'United Conservative and Liberal Association'.

[1] *The Times*, 10 May 1947.
[2] *The Times*, 24 January 1950.
[3] At the 1950 General Election, there were seven 'Conservative and Liberal', twenty-one 'Conservative and National Liberal', six 'National Liberal', fourteen 'National Liberal and Conservative', and five 'Liberal and Conservative' candidates. To complicate matters yet further, in Scotland the word 'Unionist' was used instead of 'Conservative'.
[4] *The Times*, 24 January 1950.

'(ii) In December 1948, a meeting was held in Kirriemuir to consider a merger between the local Liberal and Unionist Associations. A handful of Unionists attended; no Liberals were present. The merger was approved by no single Liberal.

'(iii) In February last, a meeting was held in North Angus, attended by some 400 Conservatives and three Liberals, steps having been taken deliberately to exclude Liberals in general. The three present were asked to leave when they voiced their objection. The formation of a Liberal-Unionist Association was approved – but by no single Liberal.

'(iv) In March last all Liberals and Conservatives "interested" were invited to attend a meeting of the "Torrington Division United Liberal and Conservative Association (Bideford Area)." The Chairman, Secretary and some members of the Bideford and District Liberal Association were "interested" enough to attend, but too interested to be allowed to remain. They were informed in reply to a question that "Liberal" had been incorporated in the title by the convenors as the result of a decision taken at an earlier meeting which was attended by no Liberals. On rising to protest, the Secretary of the Liberal Association was told that she could remain silent or leave the hall. She left with some 20 other Liberals. . . .'

Churchill returned a bantering reply, but did not confute any of the substantive charges. Indeed, it seems that the only person with a current title to the word 'Liberal' who stood under a combined label was Major Gwilym Lloyd George, from whom the Liberal whip had been withdrawn about 1946, and who unsuccessfully defended Pembrokeshire as a 'Liberal and Conservative' candidate.

The arrangements of 1947 led inevitably to the final extinction of the Liberal National Party, although the process was prolonged, and the organization was not finally wound up until 1968.

Only in one place was there any operative understanding between Liberals and Conservatives. This was Huddersfield, where the Labour M.P. for the old undivided Borough opted for the new East constituency. The Liberals chose Donald Wade as candidate for the West, and the Conservatives adopted a candidate for the East. It was generally assumed that if the Conservatives 'invaded' the West,

T

the Liberals would 'invade' the East, and *vice versa*; but there was no pact, and either Party could have advanced a candidate in the other Division without fearing an accusation of dishonour from the other.[1]

There was an attempt to secure an arrangement in the two Dundee constituencies. The local Liberals and Conservatives agreed that the Liberals should not stand in either constituency at the forthcoming General Election; but if the Conservatives failed in either or both, then at the following election the Conservatives would stand down in that place and leave the Liberal a straight fight against Labour. This arrangement was torpedoed by the Headquarters of the Liberal Party, who contrived a candidate for Dundee West, in the teeth of the opposition of the local Liberals.

*   *   *

The next General Election was held on 23 February 1950, and was a peculiarly open one. There had been a profound revision of constituency boundaries. The number of seats was reduced from 640 to 625, and only eighty constituencies were completely unchanged. The University seats, the business vote, and the few remaining two-member constituencies, were all abolished.

The effect of the Liberals was hard to predict. Long before 1950, a Liberal victory was inconceivable; nevertheless, it was certain that the Liberals would receive a lot of votes, and no one knew how those votes would otherwise have been partitioned.

As in several of the elections of the twenties, three-cornered contests were the rule and not the exception. With considerable difficulty, the Liberal Party scraped together 475 candidates; but it was impossible to conceal the fact that some of these were last-minute adoptions in constituencies with virtually no organization, and certainly no prospect of anything but a derisory result. Some of the last-minute candidates were obviously unsuitable people with little political knowledge, who had only accepted candidature after great pressure had been exerted upon them. The overwhelming majority of the candidates who stood in 1950 were well capable of standing comparison with those of any other Party; but the remainder proved a great liability.

[1] See *Liberal News*, 27 January 1950.

Several of the 'veterans' who had lost their seats in 1945 were persuaded to stand again. Sir Geoffrey Mander had joined the Labour Party,[1] and Sir William Beveridge had accepted a peerage, but most of the other 'notables' stood. Sir Archibald Sinclair fought in Caithness and Sutherland, Sir Percy Harris in Bethnal Green, Graham White in Bebington.

Not least of the difficulties which the Liberals faced in a very 'open' election was the uncertainty over deposits. A field of 475 candidates meant a stake of £70,000. This problem was eventually overcome by insurance; at the end of January 1950 it was announed that Lloyd's had underwritten all Liberal deposits after the first fifty, up to a total of 250, for £5,000. This figure indicates that the underwriters did not anticipate many more than eighty lost deposits.

It seems likely that some senior members of the Liberal Party were far from happy about the decision to contest the election on such a broad front – and, in particular, to set forward unsuitable candidates in places with hardly a semblance of organization. These people refrained from making any public statements which could damage the Party, but their silence was often eloquent enough. Winston Churchill drew attention to the fact that neither Sir Archibald Sinclair nor Lady Violet Bonham-Carter was delivering an election broadcast for the Liberal Party – and actually offered Lady Violet one of the twenty-minute broadcasts which had been allocated to the Conservatives.[2] Obviously she could not accept; but the offer caused some embarrassment, and her absence from the very long list of Liberal candidates was also an inevitable subject of adverse comment. She did, however, speak in support of several Liberal candidates.[3]

*   *   *

The Labour Party secured a very narrow overall majority, the Liberal Party another disaster. All of the three Liberal M.P.s who

---

[1] It is said that a poem in *Liberal News* which appeared at the time of Sir Geoffrey's secession may have prevented him securing a peerage:

'Geoffrey, Geoffrey Mander,
Whither will you wander?
Left turn? Right turn?
To the Upper Chamber?'

[2] H. G. Nicholas, *The British General Election of 1950*, pp. 86–7.
[3] *Liberal News*, 17 February 1950.

had had straight fights with the Conservatives in 1945 now had Labour opponents as well, and all were defeated. The loss of Frank Byers was particularly serious. Another Liberal seat was lost through the abolition of the University seats. For its losses the Liberal Party received few gains. Not one of the old leaders who had been defeated in 1945 was able to return to the House. The only victories to cheer the Liberals were two gains from the Conservatives – Orkney & Zetland, which was taken by Jo Grimond, and Roxburgh & Selkirk, which elected A. J. F. Macdonald – plus the new constituency of Huddersfield West, which returned Donald Wade. Well over two and a half million votes had produced only nine Liberal M.P.s.

No fewer than 319 out of the 475 candidates forfeited their deposits. It will be noted that these figures were far greater than the underwriters of Lloyd's had anticipated a few weeks previously. There can be no doubt that the election 'turned sour' on the Liberals shortly before polling day.[1]

There was much speculation, both before and after the election, about the effect of the massive Liberal 'intervention' on the relative positions of the other two Parties.[2] A careful analysis of the votes cast has shown that 'no likely division of the Liberal vote would have produced what is normally regarded as a decisive Parliamentary majority'.

Techniques of public opinion sampling had reached a point of sufficient accuracy by 1950 for it to be possible to say roughly where the votes of the different Parties came from.[3] The Liberals showed a remarkably even distribution whether the population was divided according to social class, sex, or age. This pattern has persisted to the present day.

*   *   *

The tiny majority of the Labour Government made it likely that another General Election would follow very quickly. Therefore the Liberals would have no time to engage in major reconstruction; but it was certain that the Liberals would be unable to contest the next

[1] The present author, whose deposit was one of the 319, was assured by the experienced Labour agent, immediately before the counting of the votes, that he had secured about 8,000 votes. In fact he received just over half of that figure.

[2] Discussed in Nicholas, op. cit., p. 300 seq.

[3] B.I.P.O. polls tabulated in H. G. Nicholas, op. cit., p. 303.

election with anything like as many candidates as they had fielded in 1950. Even though many of the constituency Associations kept in fairly good heart, most of them could not hope to raise the several hundred pounds which would be necessary to support a candidate with an election campaign, and to guarantee his very vulnerable deposit. Liberal Headquarters would not be able to render much financial assistance.

The remarkable thing about the Liberal Party after 1950 is how few prominent members joined other Parties. Large numbers of people lapsed into inactivity; but the general organization of the Liberal Party continued – at Headquarters, in the Federations, and in most of those constituencies which had 'real' Associations in the first place. The machine was weakened, but it did not collapse.

* * *

In the immediate post-election period, it became evident that the tactical aim of the Conservative leadership was not so much the destruction of the Liberal Party as the establishment of some kind of arrangement whereby the Liberal Party – or such Liberals as were prepared to co-operate – would be brought into alliance with the Conservative Party, while in name at least the Liberal Party would continue to exist. On 29 April, Lord Woolton told the Conservatives that he did not know 'of any practical issues on which Liberals and Conservatives are not agreed'.[1]

There was some indication that Conservative back-benchers were very far from agreeing with their Party's Chairman;[2] while, from the Liberal side, Clement Davies found it necessary to make a public statement that there was 'no intention of compromising the independence of the Liberal Party'.[3]

Although the official leadership might declare itself opposed to any alliance, there was no doubt that some Liberals were showing marked signs of preference for one or other of the opposing Parties. On 6 November 1950, the Conservative Opposition moved a critical amendment to the Address on the subject of housing. Three of the nine Liberal M.P.s voted with the Government, four with the

[1] *The Times*, 1 May 1950.
[2] *The Times*, 3 May 1950.
[3] *Idem.*

Opposition, and two were unavoidably absent. This was an extreme case, but it gave rise to much ridicule.

*   *   *

When the next election came, on 25 October 1951, the Liberals could muster only a very small front of candidates – 109 in all – against a nearly complete field contested by the other two Parties. The Liberals could not offer, even theoretically, an alternative Government. Their highest aim was, in Philip Fothergill's word, a 'bridgehead'. The 'veterans' who had stood in 1950 in a vain attempt to regain their old constituencies did not stand again.

The Conservatives adopted tactics towards the Liberals remarkably similar to those which they had employed as far back as 1924. The M.P.s who were particularly unacceptable were all opposed. In the other cases, the Conservatives only stood against those M.P.s whom they considered they had some chance of replacing. Clement Davies, Hopkin Morris, Donald Wade, and Roderic Bowen were all left without Conservative opponents, while Lady Megan Lloyd George and Emrys Roberts were opposed, even though the Conservatives had no hope of winning their constituencies.

Except in Huddersfield, where the understanding reached in 1950 continued, there is no reason to think that the Conservative decision not to oppose existing Liberal M.P.s was the result of any bilateral arrangement whatever, at either the local or the national level. In 1951, however, a 'pact' was made in Bolton. In 1950, each of the two Bolton seats had been represented by a Labour M.P., and each of those M.P.s had a narrow majority in a three-cornered contest, with the Liberal polling well. In 1951, there was an agreement under which the Conservatives did not oppose the Liberal, Arthur Holt, in Bolton West, and the Liberal did not oppose the Conservative in Bolton East. A number of Liberals had felt some qualms over Huddersfield, but concern over Bolton was much stronger and much more general.

In one other constituency, very special conditions applied. This was Colne Valley, which had had a very long and turbulent political history, but which regularly recorded a high Liberal vote. The Liberal candidate was Lady Violet Bonham-Carter. Not only did the Conservatives refrain from opposing her, but in addition Winston Churchill himself visited the constituency and spoke in her support, in order to secure the positive adherence of local Conservatives to her cause. There was a considerable furore in the Liberal Party, but it is now clear that her Liberalism was wholly uncompromised, and those (including the author) who suspected her of 'going Tory' gravely misjudged her.

* * *

In place of a tiny Labour majority, the 1951 General Election produced a Conservative majority which was not much larger, while the Liberal results were even worse than they had been in 1950. Only five of the Liberal M.P.s who had sat in the old House were returned – and four of these had had no Conservative opponent. The only gain was Bolton West, which many Liberals regarded as a dubious blessing. Against this were four losses: Merioneth, which had been held since 1868; Anglesey, where Lady Megan Lloyd George was defeated;[1] Eye, which even the adaptable Edgar Granville could hold no longer; and the 'freak' 1950 gain of Roxburgh & Selkirk. A glance at the election figures shows that the Liberals would have been reduced to three seats at the most if the Conservatives had opposed all their candidates.

Not only did the Liberals suffer a loss in their representation, and the massive fall in total votes which was inevitable with a greatly reduced field of candidates, but in nearly all constituencies the Liberal poll was considerably lower even than in 1950. Only two substantial increases were recorded: Orkney & Zetland, where the Liberal poll rose from 47 per cent to 58 per cent, and Paisley, where it rose from 8 per cent to 14 per cent. In both of these places it is likely that personal factors played a large part. In others, the Liberal vote slumped fearfully: in Bebington, and in Caithness & Sutherland, where a more or less unknown candidate followed a veteran with a long record of Parliamentary service, the Liberal vote was halved.

And so, on Friday 26 October 1951, when Winston Churchill again accepted the King's commission to form a Government, it truly seemed that the Liberal Party was finished. Even the staunch old *Manchester Guardian* almost lost hope:[2]

[1] Both Anglesey and Merioneth were gains by Labour. One prominent Anglesey Conservative commented that this was a swing to the right!

[2] *Manchester Guardian*, 27 October 1951.

'It is hard to see in this depressing picture much ground for building up a country-wide political party on the old model. Unless there is some change in the Conservative Party or some break-up in the Labour Party, the Liberal Party can look forward only to further attrition and further losses to the two major parties.'

PUNCH, OR THE LONDON CHARIVARI.—NOVEMBER 6, 1935

COUNCIL OF FACTION.

"THREE WISE MEN OF GOTHAM
WENT TO SEA IN A BOWL.
IF THE BOWL HAD BEEN STRONGER
MY TALE HAD BEEN LONGER."—*Old Nursery Rhyme.*

[To commemorate the triple alliance—on the microphone—of Sir HERBERT SAMUEL, Lord SNOWDEN and Mr. DAVID LLOYD GEORGE.]

14

New Directions

Toryism has always been a form of paternal socialism.

HAROLD MACMILLAN

(*Interview in* The Star, *25 June 1936*)

Free Trade is death to guaranteed prices and assured markets. If I believed the opposite I would change sides and be a protectionist.

SIR RONALD WALKER, *sometime President, Liberal Party Organization, in debate on agriculture at the Liberal Assembly, Ilfracombe, April 1953.*

Just after the 1951 General Election, the Conservatives fired what might have proved the deadliest shaft of all. Winston Churchill, now established as Prime Minister, offered Clement Davies the Ministry of Education. Clement Davies consulted the leading Liberals, including Lord Samuel, Lady Violet Bonham-Carter, Philip Fothergill, and Frank Byers. They were unanimous in recommending him to refuse. Their advice was loyally (although perhaps regretfully) accepted,[1] even though Clement Davies must have realized that this would be the last occasion in his life when an offer of Ministerial office would be made to him. If he had accepted, the Liberal Party might well have broken to pieces.

It remained almost touch-and-go whether the Liberal Party could survive as a serious political Party with a national organization. Its weakness was not only signalled by the bad results which most candidates had secured in 1950 and the even worse results of 1951. The measure of despair is the fact that two-thirds of the candidates who fought in 1951 never stood again.[2]

[1] *Liberal News*, 1 November 1951.   [2] J. S. Rasmussen, *The Liberal Party*, p. 20.

Nor was the financial outlook any more encouraging. The annual accounts of the Party, which in 1949 were balancing at over £50,000, stood at less than half that figure in 1952. The 'Assembly Appeal', which was the major financial event of the year, had raised £10,000 in 1948, but only a quarter as much in the early 1950s. By 1956, the income of the Party was below £17,000.[1] Most local organizations were also in desperate financial straits.

*   *   *

Most of the recommendations of the Reconstruction Committee had been set into effect, with or without modifications, in 1946. There was one notable exception. The Report to the Party had suggested that 'a Director of the Party be appointed, at a commensurate salary. He shall be the Principal Executive Officer, will act as chief agent, and will be the "dynamo" of the whole national machinery.'[2] Why steps were not taken at the time to implement this proposal does not seem to have been disclosed; but after the 1951 Election, six Liberals guaranteed the salary of such an official, without drawing on the desperately low finances of the Party. The proposal to make an appointment was taken at the Liberal Convention held in December 1951.[3] In October 1952, Mr H. F. P. Harris, a man who hitherto had been almost unknown in the Liberal Party, was appointed. He commenced duties in March 1953. Slowly, but definitely, the Liberals in the constituencies responded to the new sense of direction and the limited but realistic aims which Harris brought to the Party.

Mr W. R. Davies, who had been Secretary of the Liberal Party Organization since its inception, and Secretary of the N.L.F. before that, thoroughly approved of the idea as a reinforcement of the small Headquarters staff. He co-operated loyally with Harris for two years, but eventually resigned, after forty-seven years' service, in 1955.

*   *   *

In April 1955, Sir Winston Churchill retired from the Premiership, and his successor Sir Anthony Eden decided to hold an election

[1] J. S. Rasmussen, *The Liberal Party*, pp. 15, 19, 24, 90 fn.
[2] *Coats off for the future!*, p. 35.
[3] *The Times*, 17 December 1951. *Liberal News*, 21 December 1951.

almost immediately. The line-up of candidates was very similar to that of 1951, the Conservatives and Labour both fighting nearly every seat, and the Liberals contesting 110 – just one more than in 1951.

The campaign was one of the quietest of modern times. There were very few issues which stirred the people at large. This reduction of the political temperature may have operated in favour of the Liberals, for it reduced the force of the 'third party squeeze'.

The Government broke with precedent by improving its position, and securing an overall majority of sixty. Thus it was no longer vulnerable to the accidents of casual illness, faulty whipping arrangements, minor rebellions, or adverse by-elections.

The Liberals more or less broke even. No seats were gained or lost. The secession of two ex-M.P.s to the Labour Party in the previous few years[1] seems to have produced no ripple on the surface. Indeed, the unwonted Parliamentary unity may have done much more good than the loss of important names did harm. The Liberal percentage of the poll increased marginally;[2] 14·7 per cent was the average vote in 1951, 15·1 per cent in 1955; sixty-six deposits were forfeited in 1951, sixty in 1955. In a few places, there was a substantial improvement – North Devon (where Jeremy Thorpe stood) and North Cornwall (where Edwin Malindine became candidate) being notable examples. Small as this improvement was, it was the first General Election since 1929 when any overall improvement whatever could be recognized.

* * *

The retirement of Winston Churchill from the Conservative leadership, and of Clement Attlee from the Labour leadership, led to a certain movement for the replacement of Clement Davies by a younger Chairman of the Liberal M.P.s. This movement was not perceptible among the rank-and-file of the Party, who were well satisfied, but was noticeable among some of the more senior members. At the 1956 Assembly, to the real sorrow of many delegates, Clement

[1] Edgar Granville (*The Times*, 8 January 1952) and Lady Megan Lloyd George (April 1955). Dingle Foot was supporting the Labour Party, but did not actually join until July 1956.
[2] D. E. Butler, *The British General Election of 1955*, p. 199.

Davies resigned his office. *The Times* justly commented on his leadership, 'No leader could have prevented [the] numerical decline [of the Liberal M.P.s]; a less devoted leader than Mr Clement Davies might have failed to prevent it turning into a rout.'[1]

The choice of a successor was predetermined. One of the five remaining Liberal M.P.s, Sir Rhys Hopkin Morris, was Deputy Chairman of Ways and Means, which debarred him from active Party work. Two others, Donald Wade and Arthur Holt, could not hope to hold their seats if the Conservatives chose to oppose them, and dependence of this kind would be highly embarrassing for the Liberal Party. A fourth M.P., Roderic Bowen, was too busy with his legal practice. This only left one man: Jo Grimond, the Chief Whip. On 5 November 1956 he was therefore elected Chairman of the Liberal M.P.s.

* * *

The so-called 'Suez' expedition against Egypt at the close of 1956 redounded substantially to the benefit of the Liberal Party. A considerable section of middle-class opinion which had been supporting the Conservatives for years was profoundly shocked, and in some cases this shock was so intense that the people concerned detached themselves wholly from the Conservatives. More serious for the Government than the actual defections which occurred was the fact that Liberal-minded voters were now much less willing than before to believe that the Conservative Party had been 'Liberalized'.

While the risings in Hungary and other parts of Eastern Europe and the Middle East crisis were both at their height, the Liberal Party suffered the great loss of Sir Rhys Hopkin Morris, M.P. for Carmarthenshire, who died on 22 November 1956. *The Times* regarded 'his whole life [as] a plea for the liberty of the individual', and spoke of his 'absolute integrity'. The present author recalls Hopkin Morris as one of the finest and purest exponents of Liberalism whom he has ever known or heard.

Perhaps no one would have been able to hold Carmarthenshire after Hopkin Morris; but the circumstances of the election were peculiarly unfortunate for the Liberal Party. Lady Megan Lloyd George was selected as the Labour candidate. The Liberal defender

[1] *The Times*, 1 October 1956.

was obviously anxious for Conservative votes, and took a line remarkably close to the Conservatives. This caused some embarrassment among the Liberals, but he received official support. In an extremely high poll, the Labour Party's new convert won the seat by a 3,000 majority. The Liberal Party's representation was thus reduced to five – the lowest figure ever.

Yet in spite of this depressing event, the very slow, but general, advance of the Liberal Party continued. In those by-elections which the Liberals fought, their vote steadily rose. At South Edinburgh, North Dorset, Gloucester, and Ipswich, the Liberal vote rose substantially. In Rochdale, in February 1958, the Liberal secured an impressive second place, and the Conservative fell to a bad third.

Then, on 21 March 1958, Mark Bonham-Carter secured for the Liberals the sensational gain of Torrington, which was won from the Government by an extremely narrow margin. This was the first Liberal by-election gain since 1929, and was greeted with wild enthusiasm. There was much dramatic irony about the event. A victory by Asquith's grandson at Torrington atoned for the loss of Carmarthen to Lloyd George's daughter a year earlier. There were also further depths to the irony, for the Torrington vacancy was caused by the succession of the younger George Lambert to the peerage of his father and namesake, who had joined the Liberal Nationals in 1931.

From the Torrington by-election down to the General Election, the Liberals made no further gains, but they continued to score very substantial votes wherever they fought. Even finance began to improve; by the end of 1957, accounts balanced at over £24,000.[1]

Yet none of these advances could compensate for the loss of Philip Fothergill, who died at the age of fifty-two on 31 January 1959. It has not been – perhaps it never will be – possible fully to assess his contribution to the Liberal cause, for so much of his work was necessarily done behind the scenes, and he never sat in Parliament. In the opinion which the present author holds, but cannot prove, Fothergill was the most powerful single force of cohesion in the Liberal Party for the last dozen years of his life. We who have had the privilege of knowing him held him in very

[1] Rasmussen, *op. cit.*, p. 24.

high affection, and had repeated occasion to be grateful for his kindness and help. Jo Grimond wrote of him as '. . . father confessor and favourite uncle, old family nurse, friend for a pleasant evening and purveyor of good ideas, with his heart firmly fixed in native integrity and his judgment never in doubt'.[1] Philip Fothergill lived long enough to see the Liberal Party, to which he had given so much, already beginning to recover. By the time of his death, at least there was no danger of speedy extinction, and there was a real hope of substantial advance.

*   *   *

In September 1959, the Prime Minister, Harold Macmillan, announced the dissolution of Parliament and a new General Election. The Liberals had undoubtedly made important progress in several directions. They had nearly twice as many candidates as four years earlier – 216 against 110 – and most of their constituency organizations were considerably improved. The Torrington victory, and the other good by-election results, had brought a good deal of encouragement. On the other hand, the Liberals' fundamental weakness still lay in the fact that they were obviously incapable of forming a Government. To a lesser extent, they suffered from an uncertain public image; a Gallup Poll earlier in the year had disclosed that 59 per cent of the people did not know what the Liberal policy was – and this included almost half of those who proposed to vote Liberal.[2]

The 1959 General Election brought the Conservative overall majority to 100 and the Liberals still only had six seats. The by-election gain of Torrington was wiped out, and Carmarthen was not regained; but Jeremy Thorpe secured a great personal triumph by capturing North Devon, though with a tiny majority. The constituency is contiguous with Torrington, and the by-election victory almost certainly played a vital part in the result.

Whereas only one Liberal M.P. had been returned in 1955 against both Conservative and Labour opposition, three were so returned in 1959. There were half a dozen places where the Liberal stood within striking distance of victory, and in twenty-seven the Liberal

[1] *Liberal News*, 5 February 1959.
[2] D. E. Butler and Richard Rose, *The British General Election of 1959*, p. 33.

ran second. The loss of deposits was much less grievous than in the preceding General Election: 55 out of 216, compared with 60 out of 110 in 1955.

The effect of the Liberals on the relative positions of the other two Parties was negligible. After a careful and detailed analysis, Butler and Rose, in their study of the 1959 General Election, conclude:[1] 'Apart from the seats which Liberals won, their decision on whether to stand or not can only have determined the issue in half a dozen constituencies at most.'

Yet while the Liberals had no more seats than they had had at the two preceding General Elections, there could be no doubt that their morale was far higher, organization incomparably better, and on any assessment their prospects were a good deal brighter than in the immediate aftermath of either of the other two General Elections. Very slowly, very gradually, the Liberal Party was building up; and the discerning observer in the autumn of 1959 could recognize that this improvement had already been in operation for perhaps six years.

*   *   *

The Liberal Party, as it stood at the General Election of 1959, was recognizably the full and legitimate heir of the Liberal tradition. The nadir had passed. The Liberals were no longer desperately struggling for survival, as they had been eight years earlier. They were now fighting for recognition, and – ultimately – for power. Yet almost immediately the whole future was cast in doubt.

Just one day after the election, Jo Grimond made the startling announcement that, 'I am hopeful that the result will be the creation of a new progressive movement.'[2] On the following day, he gave an interview to the *Observer* in which he developed this rather cryptic remark further.[3]

'I would like to see the radical side of politics – the Liberals and most of the Labour Party – make a new appeal to people to take a more active part in all sorts of real political issues. . . . There

[1] *Ibid.*, p. 234.
[2] The *Guardian*, 10 October 1959.
[3] The *Observer*, 11 October 1959.

must be a bridge between socialism and the Liberal policy of co-ownership in industry through a type of syndicalism coupled with a non-conformist outlook such as was propounded on many issues by George Orwell.'

Jo Grimond also stood on record with the opinion that, unless the 'progressives', the 'radicals', got together, 'the Left may be in opposition for years and years'.

The full implication of these statements was – and is – far from clear; but the explanation which Grimond gave to *The Times* on the same night as the *Observer* interview appeared hardly resolved the confusion: 'I really mean nothing more than I have been saying on the subject for some time. . . . I am not talking about any immediate coalition, and I am merely speaking for myself. . . .'[1] It is difficult to see how a man occupying the principal office in a political party can ever fail to implicate others when he makes public pronouncements on political questions, and there was a considerable degree of apprehension and concern among the rank and file of the Liberal Party. Yet, for the time being, the matter blew over. Perhaps everyone who in other circumstances might have made a fuss was too exhausted after the General Election. Perhaps they were satisfied that reciprocity from the Labour side was out of the question, and therefore that there was no need to worry.

* * *

The next surprising development arose in an entirely different field. During the General Election, a Campaign Committee had been established, of which Frank Byers was Chairman. After the election it was decided that a similar body should continue in existence, 'to give continual thrust and direction to our affairs'.[2] This body[3] rapidly began to exercise most sweeping powers in a matter which was apparently within the normal functions of the Council or the Executive. Two days after the Committee had been established, Byers saw H. F. P. Harris, the General Director, and, after a stormy

[1] See also *Liberal News*, 15 October 1959.
[2] L.P.O. Council, 12 December 1959. *The Times*, 14 December 1959.
[3] It consisted of Frank Byers (Chairman), Mark Bonham-Carter, Arthur Holt, M.P., Jeremy Thorpe, M.P., and Richard Wainwright. *Liberal News*, 17 December 1959.

interview, Harris agreed to discuss terms of resignation.[1] The L.P.O. Council and Executive ratified the reorganization, but most members knew nothing of what had transpired. The circumstances of Harris's departure led to the resignation of Reginald Smith, editor of *Liberal News*. As the facts gradually leaked out, *The Times* wrote that, 'Mr Smith is not alone in the Liberal Party in regretting the decision . . . and the manner in which it was done. So far it would appear that only a small minority oppose the change, though many are unhappy about the circumstances.'[2]

New problems were soon posed over the Liberal Party's attitude to the proposal that Britain should join the European Economic Community – the 'Common Market'. The nature of the Liberal dilemma may only be seen in its context.

At all times, the Liberal Party has pressed for the removal of trade barriers, and after 1945 this attitude was signalled by a specific demand for the removal of such barriers in Europe. In the early 1950s, the official Liberal view was to support some kind of British association with the developing economic units of Western Europe, such as the Coal and Steel Community – although a substantial number of Liberals opposed this view, arguing that such organs would lead to the development of cartels rather than to the liberalization of trade. While discussions were proceeding for the formation of the Common Market, and also for the formation of the European Free Trade Association (EFTA), an article was carried in *Liberal News* (1 February 1957). This was stated to have been 'prepared after discussion among those chiefly responsible for guiding Party opinion, and . . . with the endorsement of . . . Mr Jo Grimond.' This article declared that:

'Liberals support the proposals that the United Kingdom should join THE FREE TRADE AREA – NOT THE CUSTOMS UNION. The more countries are committed to lowering tariffs while still free to fix the level of their tariffs against countries outside the Common Market, the more likely it is that tariffs all round will be low, so that trade will be increased.'

This statement obviously favoured membership of an organization

[1] Press Conference, 29 February 1960.
[2] *The Times*, 15 January 1960.

U

like EFTA, while it was equally inconsistent with membership of the E.E.C.

But on 24 July 1960, a statement in favour of Britain initiating negotiations to join the E.E.C. was sponsored jointly by an influential all-Party group of M.P.s, including Jo Grimond, Clement Davies, Arthur Holt, and Jeremy Thorpe. On the same day a pamphlet with the appropriate title *New Directions* was published by a committee working under Jo Grimond, and this also emphasized the argument for Britain joining the E.E.C.

On 29 September 1960, the matter was considered at the Liberal Party's Annual Assembly at Eastbourne. A resolution was carried urging the Government 'to start consultations with other members of the Commonwealth and of the European Free Trade Area with a view to the entry of the United Kingdom and other countries into the Common Market'. Thus, the Liberal Party was in no way committed to accept British membership if the terms offered were oppressive, while it was bound to consider the views of countries with which Britain had special economic links.

The Llandudno Assembly of 1962 was by far the most publicized Liberal Assembly of recent times, and it carried a resolution in favour of Britain joining the Common Market, which made no reference to EFTA or the Commonwealth, and expressed no reservations about conditions which might prove unacceptable. The Liberal Party suffered some important losses as a result of the rigour with which the Common Market was pressed. One former M.P., Air Vice-Marshal Bennett, resigned from the Party altogether. Oliver Smedley, a former Vice-President of the Party, resigned his candidature. Several other anti-Market candidates dropped off, although some remained in the Liberal Party.

Liberal opinion in the country was very far from united. A Gallup Poll in October 1962 indicated the division of a category consisting overwhelmingly of Liberals into 42 per cent approving, 32 per cent disapproving, and 26 per cent 'don't knows'.[1] More recent polls have shown that the proportion of Liberal voters opposing entry

---

[1] Poll carried out 12–20 October 1962. It includes what are technically known as 'incliners'. Both other Parties were largely split.

[2] Thus, the National Opinion Poll published in the *Daily Mail*, 27 October 1970, showed those disapproving of Britain joining the Common Market ranged between 55 per cent and 67 per cent in the three Parties, while those approving ranged from 22 per cent to 28 per cent.

to the Common Market has risen from a substantial minority to a large majority.[2] There were signs that the Common Market issue might have produced intolerable strains in all three Parties. But this was prevented – or perhaps postponed – by the collapse of the negotiations at the beginning of 1963.

* * *

Whether any of these matters produced a substantial effect on the electoral fortunes of the Liberal Party one way or the other is very doubtful. It is even more doubtful whether much effect was produced by another development which would have been of climacteric importance a few decades earlier. This was the sudden demise of two great, and putatively Liberal, newspapers on 17 October 1960. The *News Chronicle*, with a daily sale of well over a million, was widely (although wrongly) considered to be the authoritative voice of Liberalism. It was also regarded as the fairest and most responsible of the 'popular' newspapers, and this view was by no means confined to Liberals. Its companion the *Star* had the second largest circulation of the three London evening newspapers, and was read extensively throughout South-East England. Its Liberalism was a good deal more shadowy even than that of the *News Chronicle*; there was no London evening newspaper of officially Labour complexion, and the *Star* was in truth more Labour than Liberal. Nevertheless it was usually possible for Liberals to secure some sort of platform in the *Star*.

The Liberal leadership realized that the *News Chronicle* was in difficulties. Just after publication ceased, Mark Bonham-Carter said in a television interview that Liberals had tried without success to make contact with the *News Chronicle* for some months. A good deal of ill-feeling was generated in the Liberal Party by the circumstances of the final demise of the *News Chronicle* – not least because the proprietor, Laurence Cadbury, was a noted Liberal, and many Liberals felt that a good deal more effort could have been made to summon timely help to rescue the paper. Neither the public, nor the staff of the newspapers, received more than a few hours' notice. But in the circumstances of 1960 the loss of two newspapers was more than compensated by the gain of numerous personalities on the new medium of television, who frequently evinced sympathy for the Liberal Party, and in a number of cases became Parliamentary candidates.

* * *

In the period immediately after the 1959 General Election, it appeared that the Labour defeat might be turning into a rout. The Government captured the marginal constituency of Brighouse & Spenborough in March 1960, with a majority of 666, which some might call Apocalyptic. The Labour Party was – or seemed to be – deeply split on a variety of issues, ranging from nationalization to nuclear disarmament. In this climate, a considerable number of people who in the past would have been more likely to support the Labour Party were entering the Liberal Party. Jo Grimond and most of the other leading figures presented a highly attractive 'image' – young (as politicians go); sincere; genuinely concerned about social problems if somewhat vague about the necessary remedies; empirical. By early 1960, the Liberals were scoring good votes in by-elections, while the leadership of the Party was well respected outside, and immensely popular within.

In November 1960, long before this Liberal revival had acquired its full momentum, a by-election occurred in Bolton East. Liberals repudiated the tacit arrangement with the Conservatives by which they left that seat unfought in return for a straight fight against Labour in the West side of the town, and fielded no less a candidate than Frank Byers. The Conservatives held the seat, and Byers – although he polled substantially – ran third. This made Conservative intervention in Bolton West and also in Huddersfield West inevitable at the next General Election.

At Asquith's old seat of Paisley, in April 1961, the Liberals did much better, and John Bannerman brought them well within 2,000 votes of victory. By February 1962, the Liberals had climbed into second place in no fewer than eight by-elections in diverse constituencies where they had been third in 1959. On 13 March 1962, in the most impressive result thus far, the Liberal candidate at Blackpool North, Harry Hague, came within 1,000 of triumph. On the following day, two more constituencies polled. At Middlesbrough East, Labour inevitably held the seat, but the Liberal ran a comfortable second, and the Conservative barely saved his deposit.

But the sensation – one of the biggest by-election sensations of the twentieth century – was Orpington.[1] The constituency was regarded as impregnably Conservative. Just before the poll, *The Times*

[1] Discussed in Donald Newby's pamphlet, *The Orpington Story*, 1962.

'attempted with confidence' the prediction that the Conservatives would win.[1]

Victory of any kind for the Liberals would have seemed almost miraculous, but the victory which ensued was utterly staggering, and was treated as major news not only in Britain but internationally. The Liberal, Eric Lubbock, was returned with a majority of nearly 8,000 votes over the Conservative, and an overall majority over both other Parties combined. The Labour candidate forfeited his deposit.[2] Nor could the other Parties console themselves by arguing that the high position of the Liberal was due to a low poll. The poll was exceptionally high for a by-election – over 80 per cent, and therefore well within the range which is common at a General Election. Making all allowances for alterations of the register, it seems clear that something like ten thousand people who had voted for the Conservative candidate in Orpington in 1959 voted Liberal two and a half years later.

Clement Davies, whose patient courage in the desolate years had played such a large part in keeping the Liberal Party in existence, lived just long enough to see the first certain fruits of his efforts. He died on 23 March, only nine days after Orpington had polled.

The Liberals, who were compelled to defend his Montgomeryshire constituency, would have feared defeat a year or so earlier. But this time, with Emlyn Hooson as their candidate, they secured an overall majority in a four-cornered contest.

The general story of the by-elections and local elections was similar everywhere. When the English Boroughs polled in May, one-third of the Liberals who stood were returned – sometimes to their own amazement, and occasionally to their own consternation. With twice as many candidates as they had fielded three years earlier, the Liberals captured twelve times as many seats. In many of these places, the Liberal organization was sketchy in the extreme.[3] Even in Northern Ireland – desolate territory for the Liberals for

---

[1] *The Times*, 13 March 1962.

[2] Orpington, 14 March 1962   Eric Lubbock (Lib.) 22,846 (9,092)
   (1959 in brackets)   P. Goldman (Con.) 14,991 (24,303)
                            A. Jenkinson (Lab.) 5,350 (9,543)

[3] In the Borough and U.D.C. elections of May 1962, Liberals gained 553, held 138, and lost 19. Of the gains, 389 were from Conservatives, 68 from Independents, 93 from Labour, and 3 new seats. See *Liberal News*, 19 May 1962.

three-quarters of a century – there were signs of Liberal progress. As early as 24 November 1961, Sheelagh Murnaghan had been returned to the Stormont Parliament as Liberal M.P. for Queen's University, Belfast. It was a notable triumph both for the candidate and her Party.

Public Opinion Polls confirmed the story of the great rise in Liberal support. In the middle of 1961, the Gallup Poll was recording[1] that 14–15 per cent of the electors would vote Liberal 'if there were a General Election tomorrow'. By November, the figure stood at 20 per cent, and by late April 1962 it was no less than 26 per cent. The National Opinion Poll published in the *Daily Mail* was even more encouraging; on 28 March 1962, in answer to a similar question, it actually recorded that the Liberals were marginally in front of both of the other Parties.[2] The 'Orpington tide' continued to run for some time. Although no further seats were gained, the Liberals came second in another eight places in the remainder of 1962 and in 1963. In three of these places, they ran within two thousand votes of victory.

*   *   *

Yet the Liberals had some cause for restraint in their jubilations. Those who were active in the elections of the period will recall that there was not much knowledge of – still less enthusiasm for – any particular Liberal policies, either new or old. After the spring of 1962, Liberal support gradually fell off. Lacking the money and organization of their rivals – above all, lacking the permanent salaried officials in the constituencies – the Liberals could not take full advantage of the tide in their favour. Tempted by the sudden improvement in their fortunes, the Liberals made the situation much worse by overstraining their resources – notably, in acquiring new and much more expensive Headquarters, which were soon to prove a millstone round their necks. As the Labour Party gradually composed its differences, and even the Conservative morale improved, the Liberals were driven remorselessly back.

[1] Excluding 'don't knows' and non-voters.
[2] *Daily Mail*, 28 March 1962. This gave: Liberals 30 per cent, Labour 29·9 per cent, Conservatives 29·2 per cent.

Clear signs of the decline were to be seen in the Public Opinion Polls well before the end of 1962. By September the intending Liberal voters were down to 17·5 per cent. As the General Election approached, the decline became increasingly rapid; by June 1964, they were as few as 9 per cent. The by-elections confirmed the story. For a long time, the Liberals still seemed to be advancing, because the standard of reference was their performance in 1959, not their performance in the spring of 1962. But after the gain of Orpington and the retention of Montgomeryshire, no more Liberal M.P.s emerged. By-elections occurred later in 1962 in Chippenham and West Derbyshire. Both of these would have been captured on Orpington 'form', and a second win was badly needed to revive the Orpington enthusiasm in the constituencies.

The 1963 results were a good deal less satisfactory than those of the previous year. The local elections of May 1963 rather obscured the reality of this decline, for the seats which came up for contest were those which had last been fought in 1960. The Liberals gained many more seats than they lost; but there had been a marked decline by comparison with the position twelve months earlier. By the end of 1963 and the beginning of 1964, the Liberal by-election votes were very poor indeed, and the earlier impetus had been almost entirely lost. In December 1963, Sudbury & Woodbridge actually recorded a poorer vote than at the previous General Election.

A series of troubles beset the Conservative Government, and culminated in the displacement of Harold Macmillan by Sir Alec Douglas-Home in the autumn of 1963. Adverse public reactions caused the General Election to be postponed until almost the latest date which was constitutionally possible – 15 October 1964. By this time the Liberal Party was far past its best, while the Labour Party and to some extent the Conservative Party had largely recovered their morale. As on all recent occasions, the Conservative and Labour Parties contested practically every constituency in the United Kingdom. For the first time since 1950, the Liberals contested more than half – 365 out of 630. They even began to take Northern Ireland seriously – which they had not done since 1929 – and fought four seats out of twelve.[1] For the first time, every single Liberal candidate had to face opposition from both other

[1] One seat – South Belfast – had been contested in 1959.

Parties.[1] In particular, the arrangements at Bolton and Huddersfield were abrogated.

The election campaign, like most in recent years, was a quiet one. Attendances at meetings declined still further, and television played by far the leading part as a medium for political debate. Although the Liberals were allowed fewer programmes than the other two Parties, by general consent they acquitted themselves well on television, and this almost certainly turned to their advantage on polling day. Jo Grimond proved quite outstandingly successful in that medium. One commentator went so far as to describe him later as 'the possessor of probably the best television image in the country'.[2]

Discounting the Speaker, the Labour Party secured an overall majority of five, and on 16 October Sir Alec Douglas-Home resigned, and was succeeded by Harold Wilson. The Liberals made an overall improvement in their representation for the first time since 1929, and brought their total to nine. The Bolton and Huddersfield seats, inevitably were lost; the surprising thing was that Huddersfield West was missed by fewer than 1,300 votes. Against these two losses, the Liberals gained four seats – three in the far north of Scotland and one in Cornwall. To the considerable surprise of many observers, the Liberals retained their by-election gain of Orpington. In three other places, the Liberals were very close to victory.

*   *   *

The Liberal Party received a considerable fillip from the by-election in Roxburgh, Selkirk & Peebles on 23 March 1965. The Liberal candidate, David Steel, who had come close to victory in 1964, this time captured the seat with a convincing majority, while the Labour candidate forfeited his deposit. For the first time since 1950, the Liberal Party was in double figures in the House of Commons. Roxburgh, indeed seemed to be part of a pattern which could be seen in several by-elections about the same time. In Conservative

---

[1] Sir Harry Hylton-Foster defended the Cities of London & Westminster as 'The Speaker', although he had formerly sat there as a Conservative. The Liberal and Labour Parties both decided to oppose him.

[2] Sir Colin Coote, *Daily Telegraph*, 31 January 1967.

'He needs me'
(Harold Wilson and Jo Grimond)

(The Guardian)

seats, the Party which had been third in 1964 lost support heavily, while the Party which had been second improved its position. It seemed as if there were many voters who had opposed the Conservatives, but were largely indifferent to the relative claims of Liberals and Labour, and who therefore voted for the locally stronger challenger.[1]

Apparently impressed by these results, and by the mild behaviour of the Labour Government, Jo Grimond gave an interview to the *Guardian* in June 1965. This interview was reported under the grossly misleading headline, 'Coalition offer to Labour by Mr Grimond' – which was firmly repudiated by Grimond himself.[2] Nevertheless Grimond did indicate that he would be prepared to contemplate coming to terms with Labour if there could be 'a serious agreement on long-term policies'. It is difficult to see what effect Grimond sought to produce, or how he imagined that this statement would assist. There was much alarm among Liberals, and the sharpness of their reaction seems both to have pained and surprised Grimond. If he sought to bring Party advantage to the Liberals by inclining to Labour in a balance-of-power situation, it is difficult to see why he thought that he would succeed with ten M.P.s, when Lloyd George had failed with fifty-eight, and Asquith had failed with a quarter of the House of Commons. If he sought some fundamental realignment of British politics, then he palpably misjudged completely the temper of active workers in both the Liberal and Labour Parties. A few brief conversations with constituency officers of the Liberal Party, or others in frequent contact with ordinary voters, would have sufficed to assure him that his plans, whatever they were, were simply 'not on'.

*   *   *

The next General Election was held on 31 March 1966. The Party lists were very similar to those of seventeen months earlier. The Conservative and Labour Parties again fought practically every constituency. The Liberals fought fewer than in 1964 – 311 instead of

---

[1] The Liberal, who had been second in 1964, improved his position in East Grinstead (February 1965) and Roxburgh (March). The Labour candidate, who had been second, improved his position at the Liberal expense in Altrincham & Sale (February), Salisbury (February), and Saffron Walden (March).

[2] Letter in the *Guardian*, 25 June 1965.

365.[1] Again, all of the British candidates faced both Labour and Conservative opposition – but this time none of the three Liberals who fought in Northern Ireland had a Labour opponent.

The Labour Government substantially increased its majority, securing this time ninety-seven seats more than all the other voting M.P.s together. The Liberal representation again rose – this time to twelve. Two seats were lost, and four gained. Both the gains and the losses were interesting, and perhaps significant. Cardiganshire, which had been consistently Liberal since the middle of the nineteenth century, fell to Labour. It was widely considered that the decision of Roderic Bowen to take the office of Deputy Chairman of Ways & Means not long before the election played a large part in bringing about his defeat. The loss of Caithness & Sutherland is more difficult to interpret, for George Mackie was defeated by a Labour candidate in a constituency where an examination of recent figures would suggest that the main threat came from the Conservatives.[2] The gains were even more interesting. Two 'Celtic fringe' constituencies were won, both from the Conservatives: North Cornwall, where the Liberal and Conservative votes have been fairly close for three-quarters of a century,[3] and, more surprisingly, West Aberdeenshire, which seems to have been largely a personal triumph for James Davidson. The other two gains were in the North of England. Colne Valley, which Richard Wainwright captured in the Liberal interest, was the only Labour loss in the whole election, and a comparison with the 1964 figures suggests that the principal cause of this victory was the transfer of former Conservative votes to the Liberal. The remaining gain was Cheadle, a constituency with an enormous electorate, which has been called 'Manchester's Orpington'. Like Orpington (which the Liberals again retained), Cheadle is essentially a residential suburban constituency on the outer fringe of a great city. Apart from the actual gains and losses, the 1966 General Election afforded the Liberals cause both for pleasure and for concern. The Liberal vote, on the whole, diminished by

---

[1] Eighty-seven constituencies fought by the Liberals in 1964 had no Liberal candidate in 1966. Thirty-three constituencies were fought in 1966 where there had been no Liberal candidate in 1964.

[2] D. E. Butler and Anthony King, *The British General Election of 1966*, pp. 227–32, gives a detailed examination of Caithness & Sutherland.

[3] The pre-1918 North-East Cornwall corresponds roughly with the modern North Cornwall.

comparison with 1964, and the aggregate was nearly three-quarters of a million down. This loss is partly, but not entirely, explained by the reduced number of candidates.[1] Yet the Liberals had withstood, with fair success, the most potent and deadly weapon which is used against them – the 'squeeze' which applies when the House of Commons is closely divided between the other two Parties, and voters become inclined to ignore the Liberals in their eagerness to defeat one of the two larger Parties. Nor was the Liberal Party behoven to the kind offices of either of the other Parties, nor to electoral arrangements of any kind, for a single one of its twelve seats.

* * *

On 17 January 1967, Jo Grimond resigned the Chairmanship of the Liberal M.P.s. Grimond explained his decision at the time by saying, 'If I had remained leader it would have been necessary to continue until the next General Election, which would mean another four or five years. I therefore felt it was necessary to make the change now so that the new leader will have plenty of time to prepare for the next election.' To some, however, this withdrawal looked something like a confession of failure. Grimond, at fifty-three, could hardly be considered too old to remain in office for a lot more than four or five years. There is a certain amount of evidence that Grimond was suffering a considerable strain on his health; but journalists were quick to remember that in 1957 he had said, 'In the next ten years it is a question of get on or get out.'[2] It was a striking coincidence that he resigned a little under ten years later. Grimond had been an immense electoral asset; but whether his true *métier* was ever that of the leader of any political Party is doubtful, and whether a Party which followed his lead closely would be a truly Liberal Party is more so. Any Parliament would probably benefit from the existence of a dozen or twenty cross-benchers of Grimond's type: people whose political judgement is sometimes extraordinarily faulty and even naïve, but who at times perceive important political truths with quite exceptional clarity. It is hard

---

[1] From the figures given in the Appendix to Butler and King, *op. cit.*, pp. 313–25, the Liberal percentage poll rose in twenty-nine constituencies and fell in 278 constituencies fought in both elections.

[2] *Liberal News*, 27 September 1957.

to dissent from Paul Johnson's comment at the time of Grimond's retirement:[1] 'I don't think I have ever heard him say anything, in public or private, which is not sensible, true, rational and decent. Even the most malicious political gossips have never accused him of a mean or underhand or even merely devious act. He has supported many unpopular causes simply because he felt them to be right.'

No clear successor to Grimond had 'emerged' at the time of his resignation. Jeremy Thorpe was the best known of the M.P.s, both for his television appearances and for his activity in the ordinary work of the Party. As Treasurer of the L.P.O. at the time of Grimond's retirement, Thorpe had very substantially reduced the chronic bank overdraft. But there were some Liberals to whom he was by no means wholly acceptable, and there were other strong claimants among the M.P.s, who decided to appoint a successor by ballot among themselves on the very next day. This inevitably meant that there was no opportunity of ascertaining the general views of Liberals outside Parliament. On the first count, Jeremy Thorpe secured six votes, Emlyn Hooson and Eric Lubbock three each. Both of the others then withdrew, and on the second count Thorpe was elected with unanimity.[2]

The changes in the House of Commons were soon followed by parallel changes in the Lords. Lord Rea resigned the Liberal leadership in that House for reasons of health in March 1967, and was succeeded by Lord Byers – as Frank Byers had now become. Thirty-nine Liberal peers were eligible to vote, and Byers secured twelve votes to nine cast for Lord Wade (until recently Donald Wade). Some significance may attach to Lord Byers's appointment of Lord Gladwyn as his Deputy. Gladwyn had had a distinguished diplomatic career, but had only been prominent in the Liberal Party for a very short time, and was known as a particularly strong advocate of British entry to the Common Market.

While the sharp divisions on leadership in both Houses of Parliament seemed to suggest that some Liberals were not wholly satisfied with the directions in which they were being led, the late 1960s produced one event very auspicious for Liberalism. The Ladywood Division of Birmingham was captured by a Liberal on 26 June 1969.

[1] *New Statesman*, 20 January 1967.
[2] The *Guardian*'s analysis of the M.P.s' voting (19 January 1967) was unauthorized, but does not seem to have been controverted.

This was widely regarded as a personal victory for the candidate, Wallace Lawler, who had acquired much respect for his achievements as a local councillor – and not as indicative of a real movement towards the Liberal Party on national questions.

* * *

The euphoria did not last. The 1970 General Election brought 332 Liberal candidates to the contest – rather more than there had been in 1966. By common consent, the moment of the election had been chosen by Harold Wilson, the Labour Prime Minister, because the indications of the Public Opinion Polls and the local elections had been favourable to the Labour Government. The prediction of most commentators was that Labour would again be returned, although perhaps with a diminished majority. On this view, most of the Liberal M.P.s who were defending their seats, and some of the candidates who had come a close second to a Conservative in 1966, could be reasonably sanguine. But events went completely against the predictions. The Government lost heavily, and the Conservatives secured an overall majority of thirty. Some argued that the cause of the apparent swing to the Conservatives was differential Labour abstentions; but this view has been subjected to a critical analysis,[1] and it now seems that a higher poll would probably have resulted in an even larger Conservative majority.

As on all past occasions when there was a strong swing to the Conservatives from a Labour Government, the Liberal results were disastrous. There had been thirteen M.P.s at the dissolution. Only six of them were returned: Jeremy Thorpe in North Devon, Jo Grimond in Orkney & Zetland, John Pardoe in North Cornwall, David Steel in Roxburgh, Selkirk & Peebles, Russell Johnstone in Inverness-shire, and Emlyn Hooson in Montgomeryshire. All except Russell Johnstone suffered reductions in their majorities, and none of the six seats may be counted safe. Five of the other seven defenders came within two thousand votes of success, and so also did the Liberal who was seeking to regain Cardiganshire, but there were not many other places where the Liberal ran at all close to victory. This gloomy situation could be attributed in part to the adverse effect of the swing to the Conservatives, and in part to the existence of a

[1] The *Observer*, 21 June 1970.

small and very noisy band of young 'Liberals' whose opinions and attitudes bore no relation to the views of any substantial section of the Party – but who alarmed a number of potential Liberal voters. The Party's official commitment to the unpopular policy of support for British entry to the European Common Market may also have done damage which was of critical importance in certain constituencies.

Yet none of these explanations is of itself sufficient. For more than ten years, the Liberal Party had been led in new directions. After this long and sometimes exciting journey, it was back, in the summer of 1970, where it had been a dozen years earlier.

15

Retrospect and Prospect

'Reflections upon the Divisions in the Liberal Party.'
title of a pamphlet by ROBERT MCMURRAY
published in 1860.

Heckler: Liberalism is dead!
R. Hopkin Morris M.P.: Yes – and look at Europe!
Exchange during the North Croydon by-election, 1948.

It is most difficult to draw together the strands of the story of an institution which is still alive. It is rather like summarizing the life of a man whose career is not over. Today, as at most other moments in the last forty-five years, there are voices which cry that the Liberal Party will shortly be interred, and other voices which cry with no less insistence that it is more firmly established than it has been for a very long time. It is truly extraordinary that both points of view have been arguable for so long. The Liberal vote in the country is not very much stronger, or weaker, than it was in 1950, in 1935, or in 1924. In most constituencies, a Liberal candidate will run third in a triangular contest, but his vote will nearly always reach four figures, and not infrequently five. He is not often within striking distance of victory, but his vote is far stronger than that of other 'third parties' (except for the Nationalist parties in the 'Celtic fringe'), or of independents, who seldom register a thousand votes. There are but six Liberal M.P.s today, yet only seven of the Liberals of 1924 had been returned in triangular contests, and a glance at the election figures does not suggest that many more of the Liberals of 1924 would have been capable of withstanding opposition from both other Parties together.

x

For forty years, the Liberal Party has had no large funds. Business-men seeking a knighthood, or an insurance policy against socialism, have looked elsewhere. Trade Unions and co-operative societies seeking special favours have paid their money to others. In finance as in physical effort the Liberal Party has been kept in existence by people with nothing to gain and much to lose by so doing. Few have had even the prospect of a seat in Parliament, while the prospects of a place in the Government have been remote indeed. Yet at no stage has the Liberal Party lacked men and women of front-bench calibre, and at most points a Liberal commissioned by his Sovereign could have produced from his own Party a Ministry not noticeably inferior to that which any other Party could form. Whatever view one may hold of the value of the Liberal Party, it is impossible to regard as less than sublime the devotion which has been rendered to it by so many people at so many levels in the last thirty or forty years. We have already had cause to consider most of the politicians of note; but there have been the professional workers like W. R. Davies and T. D. Nudds; the 'backroom boys' like Harcourt Johnstone and Major-General W. H. Grey; and constituency workers in every part of the land who could so easily have secured recognition in any other interest.

It is sometimes argued that the decline of the Liberal Party was historically inevitable. The burden of proof must lie on the shoulders of the person who maintains such a point of view; and this apparently simple explanation does not seem tenable when the situation at the time of the most rapid Liberal collapse is examined in some detail. What evidently damaged the Liberal Party most was not questions of policy but questions of strategy. Should they continue the coalition with the Conservatives after 1918? Should they set a Labour Government in office in January 1924, and should they defeat it in October? Should they bend Liberalism to sustain Labour in 1929–31, and should they bend Liberalism to sustain the National Govern-ment after Labour had collapsed?

Matters like these split the Liberal Party into warring groups which could never again feel confidence in the leadership of men from the opposition faction. No one could really believe in Liberal Reunion in 1923, when people could remember, a couple of years earlier, hearing Lloyd George Liberals telling their followers to vote for a Conservative against an Asquithian – and Asquithian

Liberals telling their followers to vote for a Labour man against a Lloyd Georgeite. It was not that there were any perceptible differences of policy between Asquith and Lloyd George in 1923, but that personal confidence had been irretrievably broken. Paradoxically, the Liberal Party suffered largely because of the exceptional capacity of the Liberals on the two sides of the House in 1919–22. Lloyd George completely overshadowed his Conservative allies; while first Maclean and then Asquith equally completely overshadowed the Labour section of the Opposition. If the Liberals on either side had been nonentities, then the polarization of Liberal opinion and the long-term damage to the Party would have been much less.

On the two occasions when the Liberals found themselves holding the balance of power, a new and unnecessary division arose. Instead of judging each issue which arose in the light of Liberal principles, whether the consequence was that the Government stood or fell, they preferred to attempt the fatal choice between Conservative and Labour Governments. Inevitably, the Liberal Party in Parliament split, and Liberals in the country were demoralized. It is almost unbelievable that Grimond should have shown signs of making the same disastrous error in 1965, and the Liberals were only saved from a further split by the fact that Labour treated his kite-flying with contempt.

Indeed, this is but one of many examples of the strange failure of the Liberal Party to take proper measure of the Labour Party and its predecessor. At best, it was divisive of the forces of change; at worst, it served notice to working men that they should seek a different champion from the Liberal Party. The Liberal Whips of the late nineteenth century very rightly encouraged the election of working men who would sit as Liberals; the Liberal Whips of the early twentieth century made a disastrous and culpable error in encouraging the election of working-class M.P.s who would refuse the Liberal whip.

The error persisted long after the 1906 Election. No Headquarters encouragement was given to the Liberal miners who did not wish to join the Labour Party in 1908. When local Liberals insisted on attacking Labour seats – at Hanley in 1912, or at NE. Derbyshire in 1914 – they received little help in the combat.

The Trade Union Act of 1913 was perhaps the most disastrous measure which the Liberals could possibly have set upon the Statute

Book. If they had merely restored the law to where most people thought it stood before Osborne's case, and authorized Trade Unions to use what funds they wished for politics, without keeping their political funds separate, then Henderson would have found no treasure-chest awaiting the Labour Party at the end of the war; for the competing claims of industrial action and the benefit funds would have been too strong for him to secure more than nominal contributions.

After 1918, the Liberal Party continued to delude itself about the Labour Party. When the Labour M.P.s refused to renew their alliance with the Liberals at the beginning of 1919, the signs were clear enough; yet in 1923–4 the Liberals decided to establish in office a Labour Party which had sworn to blot them out of existence.

Thus was Labour allowed to grow and establish itself, and to cultivate the myth that socialist policies represented the true interests of the workers. And today, more than half a century on from the last Liberal Government, the country has seen only one Labour Government in whose achievements Labour supporters themselves seem to feel much pride. The real beneficiary of the efforts which the Labour Party made, and the encouragement which the Liberals gave them, has not been the workers, and has not been socialism. The real beneficiary has been the Conservative Party.

*　　*　　*

Policy differences have played little part in the Liberal decline. The Liberal Party, like every party of change, is, and always has been, a coalition of people with diverse opinions and aspirations. It is not difficult to show that the ideas existing within any party of change derive from different, and often antagonistic, theories of political philosophy. This makes life difficult for the leaders of such a party, particularly when it is in office, but one must go back to 1886 to find any important breakaway resulting from what a Liberal Government did, or attempted to do. Some Liberals criticized the behaviour of the Government between 1905 and 1915, but only four M.P.s seceded from the Party. One of these was a rogue, and two of the other three were complete nonentities.[1] Even in the division

---

[1] The rogue was Horatio Bottomley. The nonentities were Leslie Renton and Sir John Rees. The fourth M.P. was Harold Cox.

lobbies, Liberals exhibited a degree of cohesion when their Party was in office which was greater than that of the other two Parties.[1] Nor did they even encounter insuperable difficulties with wealthy subscribers while the Liberal Party was conducting the most impressive social revolution of modern times. J. A. Spender noted how the Master of Elibank 'soothed the rich Liberals who were uneasy about Lloyd George's Limehouse speech, and got large cheques out of them to be used for their own despoiling.'[2]

*   *   *

While we may attempt some explanations of the Liberal decline in the decade before 1924, it is much more difficult to explain the Liberal Party's persistence since then, for this is at variance with the usual rule that an institution must either advance or retrogress, and can never stand still. After the last subvention from the Lloyd George fund was received in 1931, the Liberal Party was thrown wholly on its own resources. Some individuals were able to give considerable sums. Most of that money seems to have been paid with pure altruism, often anonymously, and with no possible prospect of reward or recognition. These contributions have on several occasions rescued the Liberal Party from imminent disaster; but although they have seemed large to Liberal treasurers, they have represented what for both other Parties was a negligible sum. The Liberal Party has contrived to exist, and to maintain a national organization, on sums which are less than some constituency Conservative Associations receive.

At the local level, the story has been similar. In the remote past, there were plenty of rich men who would 'buy out' a constituency for the sake of a seat in Parliament, or in order to maintain some tangible objective like Free Trade. But as the M.P.s were defeated, the large subscriptions vanished, and local people were thrown on local resources alone. It has been the efforts of local volunteers which have produced the Liberal advance into new territories, and have compensated for the loss of old Liberal seats which were often paid for by rich men.

[1] Samuel Beer, *Modern British Politics*, pp. 122–3.
[2] J. A. Spender, *Journalism and Politics*; quoted in A. C. Murray, *Master and Brother*, p. 34.

Thus sheer altruism in the provision of money and effort seems to be the great characteristic of modern Liberal survival and revival. No small part has been played by the intelligent and imaginative use of slender resources. The Liberals have shown great skill in using small sums of money to the best effect, but much less skill in developing methods of increasing substantially the amount of money available.

In certain places, local feeling and local problems have undoubtedly played a large part in restoring the Liberal Party in recent years. The Scottish Highlands recorded a series of victories in the 1960s, and the fact that two of these constituencies were lost in 1970 may perhaps be due to the intervention of Scottish Nationalist candidates who presented Liberal devolutionary policies in a more extreme form, rather than to any substantial increase in the appeal of the two larger Parties. There have also been a number of Liberal victories in South-West England in recent years, although there again some recession occurred in 1970. Though these were areas of historic Liberal strength, both of them were for a time completely without Liberal representation. The modern revival seems to be due not primarily to a resuscitation of interest among 'lapsed' Liberals, but to a feeling in the remote areas that the big Parties are neglecting them, and are indifferent to their special needs and problems. It is more difficult to explain why there has been no corresponding advance, but only a continued decline, in Wales. Even less easy to understand is the Liberal advance in places like Orpington and Cheadle. The fact that these constituencies were both rather narrowly lost by the Liberals in 1970 does not derogate from the interest of their original capture, and a number of other middle-class dormitory constituencies on the fringe of great towns continue to exhibit a Liberal vote well above the national average. More astonishing still is the short-lived Liberal tenure of a constituency in Birmingham – a town on which the Liberals could make no impact in the *annus mirabilis* 1906. Yet in the same year every seat but one in Wales was Liberal; while the Liberals only hold a single Welsh seat.

A possible, but by no means completely satisfactory, hypothesis is that the Liberal persistence has been due to different things at different times. Down to 1939, the main factor was the memories of ageing people who had formed their political attitudes in the Liberal heyday, plus a considerable influx of much younger people who were attracted by the Liberal social policies set forward in the late 1920s. These groups were augmented at the end of the Second World War by the influx of further young people who considered the Conservatives deficient in social conscience, but were repelled from Labour by its strong class bias and collectivist mentality. Since the early or middle 1950s, there has been a gradual diminution of apparent policy differences between the two larger Parties – which has reduced the pressure to vote *against* the more distasteful of those Parties, and has also encouraged people who despair of securing much interest for their personal or local problems from either great Party to look to the Liberals.

*   *   *

These factors may give a partial explanation of the Liberal persistence. They do not explain, however, the occasional periods of Liberal upsurge: the times when sanguine Liberals have really believed that a breakthrough had been achieved, while independent and even hostile commentators have treated the Liberals as serious aspirants for power. There was the upswing of the late 1920s; the much smaller revival just before the Second World War; the revival of the 'Martell' period, about 1946; the 'Torrington' revival in 1957–8; the strange, heady 'Orpington' revival which reached its peak in the early part of 1962. These various upsurges have certain features in common. Every one has occurred at a time when the Government has been losing support rapidly, but the larger Opposition Party was for some reason unable to occupy the vacant space in the political field.

In the late 1920s, the Conservative Government was becoming unpopular, through its failure to tackle unemployment and other social problems; while the Labour Party, although strongly entrenched in the industrial constituencies, had scarcely begun to establish a serious organization in the rural areas. The much smaller revival of the late 1930s corresponds with a period when the National Government had begun to arouse increasing alarm on both patriotic and social grounds, while the Labour Party had still not fully recovered from the shattering blow of 1931. The revival of the late 1940s belonged to a time when the Labour Government was producing both disappointment and alarm, while many voters still feared that the return of the Conservatives would also mean the return of the dole queues. The two more recent revivals both seem to be due to the inability of the Labour Opposition to show either the flexibility or the imagination to capture dissident ex-Conservative votes.

It may be argued that these revivals have all taken place for negative reasons. That is probably true; but it is no less true that most political swings take place for negative reasons. Far more enthusiasm can always be generated for putting out Party A than for putting in Party B. But why have the Liberals failed to capitalize their initial advantages on all of these occasions?

The failure of the late 1920s is the only one which seems to be attributable to any objections to the Liberals, and these centred on the personality of Lloyd George. He was indispensable to the Liberals, both for funds and for leadership; but he was more widely and deeply distrusted as a man than anyone else in the whole field of British politics. Whether he deserved that mistrust is, and will remain, a cause of debate; but the fact that he was believed to have misled the nation in 1918 is much more important than whether he really did so or not.

The failure of all the more recent revivals seems to be due primarily to the Liberal weakness in finance and – even more so – organization. The Orpington period illustrated this more impressively than the other brief revivals, but we may recognize similar features in all of them. What the Liberals needed desperately was a few more by-election victories in the immediate aftermath of Orpington. A glance at the by-election figures shows clearly that there were several places where this could have happened, and probably would have happened, if the constituency organization had been in proper fettle.

The real weakness of Liberal organization in recent years has lain in its complete dependence on voluntary workers at the constituency level. Waves of enthusiasm come and go, and casual considerations like some change in the personal circumstances of an active local Liberal, or the disaffection of one or two individuals, or even someone moving house – all of these have repeatedly caused promising Liberal organizations to collapse, or to fade into relative inactivity. Thus, when favourable circumstances have suddenly occurred, the Liberals have usually lacked a substantial team of trained and experienced workers who could take advantage of the situation. If the Liberal Party is to revive on a sound and permanent basis, the overriding problem is not how to strengthen the Head-quarters organization but how to strengthen the constituency organizations. This means, above all, that cadres of local salaried workers must be built up, whose remuneration is fully commensurate with what they could receive in outside employment, and who are paid out of income, not out of capital. That this state of affairs is desirable is hardly a matter of dispute; but, in the author's view, it is the most important organizational objective of all. Spectacular by-elections are soon forgotten; but the gradual establishment, week by week and year by year, of a really efficient political machine of this kind is of permanent value.

The Liberal Party has often planned carefully for an election two or three years ahead, but since the First World War it has never really looked beyond the oncoming General Election. As a result, it has never been able to maintain itself adequately after defeats – despite the high morale of its supporters and candidates. Nor has it been able to follow up its occasional victories.

The difference between six M.P.s and ten, twenty, or even thirty, is of no substantial importance to the modern Liberal Party, because thirty M.P.s are not much more likely to get their way in the House of Commons than six are. But what is of gigantic importance is the difference between fifty and five hundred well-organized constitu-encies in determining whether the Liberals will be able to derive long-term advantages from one of those casual improvements in their fortune which occur from time to time. If the constituency organizations had been strong enough to enable the Liberals to follow up Orpington or even Torrington with a run of several by-election victories, the whole of British politics might well have been transformed to the Liberals' advantage.

* * *

The question of Liberal survival is not unrelated to an issue which has repeatedly perplexed the Liberal Party in the last fifty years: for what purpose is the Party in existence at all?

Before 1914, there was no doubt about the answer. The Liberal Party existed in order to secure the return of a Liberal majority to

Parliament, and a Liberal Ministry which could be expected to pursue policies broadly consistent with the wishes of the Liberal rank-and-file.

The 'Coupon' Election of 1918, and its aftermath, threw this objective into doubt. Did the Liberal Party exist to maintain, and perhaps to influence, the Coalition, or did it exist to destroy the Coalition and to replace it by a Government of a different kind? Most Liberal M.P.s gave one answer to that question; most of the Liberal rank-and-file gave another. Even the question of what the Liberals might propose to set in place of the Coalition was not answered with certainty. At the beginning, the answer would probably have been 'a Liberal Government'. But by the end, many Liberals would have preferred any Government, whether Liberal, Labour, Conservative, or some mixture of the three, to a Lloyd George administration. 'Wee Frees' who began by attacking the Coalition for being too Tory ended up by welcoming the purely Conservative administration of Bonar Law in preference to the Coalition. No less remarkable is the fact that many of the Liberals who had fought hardest against Lloyd George's Coalition (in which the Liberals were at least on something approaching parity with the Conservatives) should eventually disappear without trace amid the huge Conservative majority of the National Government to which they were completely dispensable.

The real weakness of the Lloyd George Coalition was of the very nature of all truly coalition arrangements. It is noteworthy that before the Coalition fell the Conservatives were almost as ready to damn it for being too Liberal as the Liberals were to damn it for being too Conservative. In any political party, the mainspring of activity is – almost by definition – the enthusiasts; and it is the enthusiasts who are most easily disgruntled by those compromises with the traditional 'enemy' which a coalition necessarily entails. The behaviour of many Coalition Liberal M.P.s brings this out strongly. They gave what we must presume to be sincere support to the Coalition in 1918; yet as soon as the Coalition obliged them to vote for many Conservative measures, they began to demur, and many of them were obviously only 'brought to heel' by the growing awareness that they could only hold their own constituencies by 'buying off the Danes'.

The Liberal reunion of 1923 seemed, for a very brief space, to restore to the Liberal Party its old objective of a Liberal Government; but when the fatal decision was taken to support the Labour Party in office, this goal was again forgotten. In the remainder of the 1920s, the Liberals seemed to oscillate between the old answer, 'a Liberal Government', and a new answer – 'to maintain enough Liberal M.P.s to ensure that no Government, whether Conservative or Labour, is able to pursue a positively illiberal policy'. Asquith made what was really this point in his famous announcement of 18 December 1923, when he declared: 'What was the main plank of the Tory platform? Protection. What was the main plank of the Labour platform? The Capital Levy with its socialist adjuncts and accessories. Both have been rejected and repudiated with over-whelming emphasis by the voice of the country. . . .'[1]

The vast majority which the National Government secured in 1931, and the fact that no Opposition could possibly hope to wear that majority down for a very, very long time, brought a new uncertainty of Liberal objective. This objective was further obscured because the Liberal transfer from Government to Opposition was so protracted, and the main stages in the process did not correspond with the moments at which the Liberals could have departed on a recognizable matter of principle. Men who had simply 'agreed to differ' over the abandonment of Free Trade could scarcely show reason why they were unable to swallow the Ottawa agreements as well; while the actual moment selected for crossing the floor showed no sense of political timing at all.

Yet by the middle 1930s, when Sinclair succeeded Samuel, the old goal of a Liberal Government, remote and improbable though it might appear, had been restored. The preamble of the Constitution which the new Liberal Party Organization adopted in 1936 began with the words: 'The Liberal Party exists to build a Liberal Common-wealth in which every citizen shall possess liberty, property and security and none shall be enslaved by poverty, ignorance or unemployment. . . .'

This general objective remained with the Liberal Party for the next twenty years or more. It was only in 1959 that Jo Grimond began to hint at a different objective – some sort of new alliance, whose members would presumably be drawn for the most part from the Labour Party. Those who know the Liberal Party will not

[1] *Liberal Magazine*, 1924, p. 19.

dissent from the view that if anything of the kind had been brought about it would have shattered the whole organization.

*   *   *

Since 1960, an entirely new problem has beset the Liberal Party. Unlike the old issues which pared people from the periphery of the Liberal Party, this has caused the bitterest doubts among 'hardcore' Liberals. That is the growing fear that the Liberal Party has been moving rapidly away from traditional Liberalism in very recent years.

The threads which have run through the Liberal Party for the whole period of our present study have been those of liberty, particularly economic liberty, and those of social justice. Although some Liberals have given primacy to one of these objectives over the other, yet to most they have been indivisible and inter-dependent.

In the 1960s, there were some signs that the Liberal Party had been reducing its emphasis on both of these causes. Economic liberty had been discounted, Free Trade neglected, and participation in the European Economic Community had been emphasized. Tenderness was shown towards a degree of mandatory government planning which did violence not only to the libertarian tradition, but even to the doctrines associated with the 'Yellow Book' era, which emphasized so firmly that the State should only intervene in order to increase the quantum of liberty in the community. Such ideas as retrenchment of public spending, and sound money, were largely ignored. The taxation of land values had not been relegated as completely as some Liberal economic doctrines, but it had been set into a minor place.

A remarkable, and not wholly unjust, criticism of the Liberal Party appeared in *The Times*, before the 'Orpington' impetus had quite spent itself:[1]

'There is a fly-paper quality about Liberal policy exercises; ideas which happen to be buzzing around at the time tend to get stuck on. This makes the proposals in the present case difficult to square one with another. Restore to Parliament the power and

[1] *The Times*, 10 September 1963.

respect it once had. Good; but that means, supposing it could be done, that Parliament would cease to be a compliant instrument of the Government or majority party, and that individual members would be able to act once more in fluid combinations of interests and views in order to restrain, overthrow or force the hand of the Government; and that, however nice a prospect, is not the surest way of achieving smooth, purposive, centralized five-year planning with all targets hit, which is another Liberal ambition – unless, of course, the professional planners were to carry on regardless of the politicians, an arrangement ruled out elsewhere in the statement of policy. Nor would elected regional councils enjoying the benefits of devolution facilitate the task of the central planners – unless in such matters as land use, communications, industrial and educational development they were to be allowed to do nothing except in conformity with central policy, in which case why go to the bother of setting them up in the first place?'

This critical editorial throws considerable light on the approaches to new policy matters which have characterized the Liberal Party in the 1960s. Liberals have been 'undoctrinaire' in the sense that they have brought freshness and originality to political questions, and have not sought to make the facts fit preconceived theories; but they have often failed to apply their minds sufficiently to the question of how these various policies integrate with each other – still less what relationship they bear to underlying Liberal principles. It is not difficult, for example, to devise a policy for agriculture which might be expected to confer benefits on that particular occupation; but it is politically inevitable that if special treatment is granted, other industries will press irresistibly for favours for themselves, and the net effect on agriculture is more likely to be harmful than beneficial.

* * *

There is a common, but erroneous, view that the issues of politics today are marginal and blurred. The current questions on which a British Government has the choice between two or more radically different courses are as numerous as they have been at most stages in our national history, and the human consequences of those decisions will not be less momentous. Yet the old ideas of 'right' and 'left' in politics are becoming unrecognizable. Is it 'right wing' or 'left wing' to advocate entry to the Common Market, or to urge disengagement East of Suez, or to plead for more regional autonomy? These new questions cut right across the old alignments, and make the popular jargon of politics largely meaningless.

The real political differences of our own time have become more the difference *within* Parties than the differences *between* the leaderships of the various Parties. The Party managers in all Parties have acquired a degree of control which once would have seemed impossible; and to those Party managers the important thing is not so much the advancement of what their Party is supposed to stand for as the preservation and prosperity of their Party as a social institution. All Parties have tended to refrain from taking bold and distinctive attitudes – and it seems that part, at any rate, of the reason is a determination to avoid antagonizing any substantial body of supporters or interests within the Party, and to play for uncommitted votes in the centre ground of politics.[1] It is at least arguable that the second aim conflicts with the first, for the determinant of modern elections may not be so much how floating voters float as how many committed voters bother to turn out to the polling stations; it may be more important to raise the morale of supporters than to avoid frightening off waverers.

In this context, we note that the issues on which Liberals did battle fifty, or even a hundred, years ago are largely still with us. It is sometimes doubtful whether the great Liberal figures of the past would recognize all of the modern apologists as their lawful successors; while, conversely, we find that views which bear a remarkable resemblance to historical Liberalism are often propounded by people who would certainly not call themselves Liberals. It is possible today to argue Free Trade in almost any circles, and to secure a more sympathetic and attentive audience than at any time since the early 1930s. It is almost a commonplace to point out that public money is being squandered on a scale which would have been impossible a very few years ago, and with a frivolous irresponsibility which would have made an eighteenth-century Bourbon or a

[1] See Anthony Downs, *An economic theory of democracy*: E. G. West, *Economics, Education and the Politician* (I.E.A., Hobart paper 42, pp. 14–19).

nineteenth-century Romanov blush for shame. Innumerable people, many of them quite simple and humble, are very conscious that this process is going on, and are very anxious to see it stopped – but they find no political body which is giving adequate expression to their just anger, and their just demands for rectification. The present seems a peculiarly appropriate moment to raise the old Liberal cry of 'Peace, Retrenchment, and Reform'.

Thus historical Liberalism is more widely acceptable today than it has been for a very long time, yet it receives remarkably little expression at the centre of politics. It is very commonly said that Liberalism has infected all Parties. In some respects this is true; but in many matters – particularly in economic fields – it is more correct to say that all three Parties are far less Liberal in the traditional sense of the term than they were a few decades ago.

That the philosophy and the ideas of Liberalism will eventually be enshrined again in a great political movement is scarcely a matter for doubt. The operative question for modern Liberals is whether their own Party is still firm enough in the pristine faith which it maintained so desperately in the bleak years when the cause seemed hopeless. If that faith has been lost, then the Liberal Party will have no future, and deserve none; but if it yet remains, then the Liberal Party need have no fear of what may lie ahead.

Biographical Notes

ACLAND, Francis (1874–1939). Succeeded Baronet 1926. M.P. Richmond (Yorks) 1906–10; NW. Cornwall (Camborne) 1910–22; Tiverton 1923–4; N. Cornwall 1932–9. Financial Secretary War Office 1908–10; Under Secretary Foreign Affairs 1911–15; Financial Secretary Treasury 1915; Secretary Board of Agriculture 1915–16. Heir and successor Richard Acland.

ADDISON, Viscount (1869–1951). Christopher Addison, 1st Baron 1937, 1st Viscount 1945. M.P. Hoxton 1910–22; Swindon (Labour) 1929–31, 1934–5. Minister Munitions 1916–17; Minister in charge of Reconstruction 1917; President Local Government Board 1919; Minister of Health 1919–21; Minister without Portfolio 1921; also in office 1929–31, 1945–51.

ASQUITH, Baroness (1887–1969). (Helen) Violet Asquith; Lady Bonham-Carter 1915; Lady Violet Bonham-Carter 1925; Baroness Asquith (Life Peeress) 1964. Daughter of 1st Earl of Oxford and Asquith. President Women's Liberal Federation 1923–5, 1939–45. President Liberal Party Organization 1945–7. Governor B.B.C. 1941–6.

ASQUITH, Herbert Henry. See Oxford and Asquith, Earl of.

ASQUITH, 'Margot' (Emma Alice Margaret). See Oxford and Asquith, Countess of.

BEAUCHAMP, Earl (1872–1938). William Lygon, succeeded as 7th Earl 1891. 1st Commissioner Works 1910–14; Lord President of Council 1910 and 1914; Liberal Leader House of Lords 1924–31. Heir and successor, Viscount Elmley.

BENN, William Wedgwood. See Stansgate, Viscount.

BEVERIDGE, Lord (1879–1963). William Henry Beveridge. K.C.B. 1919; 1st Baron 1946. M.P. Berwick-upon-Tweed 1944–5. Director L.S.E. 1919–37; Master University College Oxford 1937–45; Vice-Chancellor University of London 1926–8; Chairman Interdepartmental Committee on Social and Allied Services 1941–2, and author of 'Beveridge Report'.

BIRRELL, Augustine (1850–1933). M.P. West Fife 1889–1900; North

Bristol 1906–18. President Board of Education 1905–7; Chief Secretary Ireland 1907–16.

BONHAM-CARTER, Lady (Helen) Violet. See Asquith, Baroness.

BONHAM-CARTER, Mark Raymond (1922–   ). M.P. Torrington 1958–9. Chairman Race Relations Board 1966–70; Community Relations Commission 1970–   . Son of Baroness Asquith, grandson of Lord Oxford.

BRIANT, Frank (1865–1934). M.P. North Lambeth 1918–29; 1931–4.

BROWN, (Alfred) Ernest (1881–1962). M.P. Rugby 1923–4; Leith 1927–31 and (Liberal National) 1941–5. Ministerial office 1931–45. Leader Liberal National Party 1940–5.

BRYCE, Viscount (1838–1922). James Bryce, 1st Viscount 1914. M.P. Tower Hamlets 1880–5, South Aberdeen 1885–1907. Chief Secretary Ireland 1905–7. Ambassador Extraordinary to U.S. 1907–13. O.M., F.R.S. Historian of the Holy Roman Empire.

BURNS, John (1858–1943). Lib-Lab M.P. Battersea 1892–1918. President Local Government Board 1905–14; President Board of Trade 1914.

BYERS, Lord (1915–   ). (Charles) Frank Byers. Life Peer 1964. M.P. North Dorset 1945–50. Chief Whip 1946–50. Chairman Liberal Central Association 1946–52; Chairman Liberal Party 1965–7. Liberal Leader House of Lords 1967–   .

CAMPBELL-BANNERMAN, Henry (1836–1908). Assumed extra name 'Bannerman' 1872. G.C.B. 1895. M.P. Stirling Burghs 1868–1908. Financial Secretary War Office 1871–4, 1880–2. Secretary to Admiralty 1882–4; Chief Secretary Ireland 1884–5; Secretary War 1886, 1892–5. Prime Minister 1905–8.

CHAMBERLAIN, Joseph (1836–1914). M.P. Birmingham 1876–85; West Birmingham 1885–6 and (Liberal Unionist) 1886–1914. President Board of Trade 1880–5; President Local Government Board 1886; Secretary Colonies (Unionist) 1895–1903.

CHURCHILL, Winston Leonard Spencer (1874–1965). K.G. 1953. M.P. (Conservative) Oldham 1900–4; (Liberal) Oldham 1904–5; NW. Manchester 1906–8; Dundee 1908–22; (Conservative) Epping 1924–45 and Woodford 1945–64. Under Secretary Colonies 1905–8; President Board of Trade 1908–10; Home Secretary 1910–11; First Lord Admiralty 1911–15; Chancellor of Duchy of Lancaster 1915; Minister of Munitions 1917–19; Minister of Supply 1919; Secretary War 1919–21; Secretary Colonies 1921–2; (Conservative) Chancellor of Exchequer 1924–9; First Lord of Admiralty 1939–40; Prime Minister 1940–5 and 1951–5.

(1875–1936). Godfrey COLLINS, K.B.E. 1919. M.P. Greenock 1910–31 and

(Liberal National) 1931–6. Parliamentary Private Secretary to Secretary War 1910–14; and to Liberal Chief Whip 1915. Liberal Chief Whip 1924–6.

COWDRAY, Viscount (1856–1933). Weetman Dickenson Pearson, 1st Viscount Cowdray 1916. Chairman Air Board 1917. Noted engineer.

CREWE, Marquis of (1858–1945). Robert Offley Ashburton Crewe-Milnes, succeeded as Baron Houghton 1885; created Earl of Crewe 1895, Marquis of Crewe 1911. Lord Lieutenant Ireland 1892–5; Lord President of Council 1905–8, 1915–16; Lord Privy Seal 1908, 1912–15; Secretary Colonies 1908–10; Secretary India 1910–15; President Board of Education 1916; Chairman London County Council 1917; Ambassador to Paris 1922–8; Secretary War 1931; Liberal Leader House of Lords 1908–23 and 1936–44. 2nd wife Lady Margaret Primrose, daughter of Earl of Rosebery.

DAVIES, (Edward) Clement (1884–1962). M.P. Montgomery 1929–31 and (Liberal National) 1931–9 and (Independent) 1939–42 and (Liberal) 1942–62. Chairman of Liberal M.P.s 1945–56.

DAVIES, Richard Humphrey (1872–   ). Worked at Liberal Headquarters 1895–1926. Private Secretary to successive Liberal Chief Whips 1899–1916; Clerk to Parliamentary Recruiting Committee 1914–16; Secretary Liberal Central Association 1917–26; Hon. Secretary Museum of Welsh Antiquities Bangor 1929–48. C.B.

DAVIES, William Robert (1891–   ). Worked at Liberal Headquarters 1908–55. Assistant Secretary National Liberal Federation 1926–30; Joint Secretary 1930–1; Secretary 1931–6; Secretary Liberal Party Organization 1936–55.

DEVONSHIRE, 8th Duke of (1833–1908). Spencer Compton (Cavendish). Lord Cavendish 1834–58; Marquis of Hartington 1858–91; succeeded as Duke of Devonshire 1891. M.P. N. Lancashire 1857–68; Radnor 1869–80; NE. Lancashire 1880–5; Rossendale 1885–6 and (Liberal Unionist) 1886–91. Under Secretary War 1863–6; Secretary War 1866; Postmaster-General 1868–71; Chief Secretary Ireland 1871–4; Secretary India 1880–2; Secretary War 1882–4. (Unionist) President of Council 1895–1903; President Board of Education 1900–2.

EDGE, William (1880–1948). Knighted 1922; 1st Baronet 1937. M.P. Bolton 1916–22 and (National Liberal) 1922–3; (Liberal) Bosworth 1927–31 and (Liberal National) 1931–45. Joint Lord Treasury 1919–22; a National Liberal Whip 1922–3.

ELIBANK, Master of. See Murray, Lord.

ELLIS, Thomas Edward (1859–1899). M.P. Merioneth 1886–99. Liberal Chief Whip 1894–9; Patronage Secretary Treasury 1894–5.

FOTHERGILL, (Charles) Philip (1906–1959). Joint Treasurer Liberal Party Organization 1954–9; Chairman Executive Liberal Party Organization 1946–9, 1952–4; President 1950–2; Vice-President 1952–5; President United Kingdom Alliance 1952–9.

FOWLER, Henry Hartley. See Wolverhampton, Viscount.

GAINFORD, Lord (1860–1943). Joseph Albert Pease, 1st Baron Gainford 1917. M.P. Tyneside 1892–1900; Saffron Walden 1901–10; Rotherham 1910–16. A junior Liberal Whip 1897–1905; Junior Lord of Treasury 1905–8; Parliamentary Secretary Treasury 1908–10; Chancellor Duchy of Lancaster 1910–11; President Board of Education 1911–15; Postmaster General 1916; Chairman B.B.C. 1922–6; President Federation of British Industries 1927–8.

GEAKE, Charles (1867–1919). Secretary Liberal Publication Department 1894–1919; Editor *Liberal Magazine, Liberal Year Book, Liberal Monthly.* Editorial Staff *Westminster Gazette* 1896–1919.

GEORGE, David Lloyd. See Lloyd George, Earl.

GLADSTONE, Viscount (1854–1930). Herbert John Gladstone, 1st Viscount 1910. Fourth son of William Ewart Gladstone. M.P. West Leeds 1880–1910. Private secretary to father 1880–1; a Lord of Treasury 1881–5; Financial Secretary War Office 1886; Under Secretary Home 1892–4; First Commissioner Works 1894–5; Chief Whip 1899–1906; Home Secretary 1905–10; Governor-General and High Commissioner South Africa 1910–14. Played a major part in Liberal organization 1919–24.

GLADSTONE, William Ewart (1809–1898). M.P. (Tory) Newark 1832–46; (first Tory then Liberal) Oxford University 1847–65; (Liberal) South Lancashire 1865–8; Greenwich 1868–79; Midlothian 1879–95. Under Secretary Colonies 1835–41; Vice-President Board of Trade and Master of Mint 1841–3; President Board of Trade 1843–5; Colonial Secretary 1845–6; High Commissioner Ionian Islands 1858–9; Chancellor of Exchequer 1852–5; 1859–66; 1868–74; 1880–2; Leader House of Commons 1865–6; Prime Minister 1868–74, 1880–5, 1886, 1892–4; Lord Privy Seal 1886, 1892–4.

GREENWOOD, Viscount (1870–1948). Hamar Greenwood, 1st Baronet 1915; 1st Baron 1929; 1st Viscount 1937. M.P. York 1906–10; (Conservative) East Walthamstow 1924–9. Under Secretary Home 1919; Secretary Department Overseas Trade (B.o.T.) 1919–20; Chief Secretary Ireland 1920–2; Treasurer Conservative Party 1933–8.

GREY, Viscount (1862–1933). Edward Grey, succeeded Baronet 1882; 1st Viscount 1916. M.P. Berwick-upon-Tweed 1885–1916; Foreign Secretary 1905–16; Temporary Ambassador to U.S. 1919; President Liberal Council 1927–33.

GRIMOND, Joseph (1913–   ). M.P. Orkney & Zetland 1950–   ; Chairman Liberal M.P.s 1956–67; Chief Whip 1950–6.

GUEST, Frederick Edward (1875–1937). M.P. Dorset E. 1911–22; Stroud 1923–4; Bristol N. 1924–9. M.P. (Conservative) Plymouth (Drake) 1931–7. Parliamentary Secretary to Treasury and Coalition Liberal Chief Whip 1917–21. Secretary Air 1921–2.

GULLAND, John William (1864–1920). M.P. Dumfries Burghs 1906–18; Scottish Whip and Junior Lord Treasury 1909–15; Parliamentary Secretary Treasury 1915–16; Chief Whip 1915–19.

HALDANE, Viscount (1856–1928). Richard Burdon Haldane. 1st Viscount 1911. M.P. Haddingtonshire 1885–1911; Secretary War 1905–12; Lord Chancellor 1912–15, and (Labour) 1924. F.R.S., O.M.

HARCOURT, Viscount (1863–1922). Lewis ('Lulu' or 'Loulou') Harcourt, 1st Viscount 1916. M.P. Rossendale 1904–16. First Commissioner Works 1905–10 and 1915–16; Secretary Colonies 1910–15. Son of Sir William Harcourt.

HARCOURT, William George Granville Venables Vernon (1827–1904). Knighted 1873. M.P. Oxford 1868–80; Derby 1880–95; West Monmouthshire 1895–1904. Solicitor-General 1873–4; Home Secretary 1880–5; Chancellor of Exchequer 1886 and 1892–5; Chairman of Liberal M.P.s 1895–8. Grandson of an Archbishop of York.

HARMSWORTH, Lord (1869–1948). Cecil Bisshopp Harmsworth. 1st Baron 1939. M.P. Droitwich 1906–10, Luton 1911–22. Under Secretary Home 1915; Under Secretary Foreign 1919–22. Younger brother of Lords Northcliffe and Rothermere.

HARRIS, Percy Alfred (1876–1952). 1st Baronet 1931. M.P. Harborough 1916–18; SW. Bethnal Green 1922–45. London County Councillor SW. Bethnal Green 1907–34 and 1946–52. Liberal Whip Chief 1935–45; Deputy Chairman Liberal M.P.s 1940–5.

HARTINGTON, Marquis of. See Devonshire, 8th Duke of.

HERBERT, Jesse (1851–1916). Knighted 1911. Political Secretary Liberal Chief Whip; Honorary Treasurer Liberal Central Association 1908–16. Sometime Professor of International Law, Canton.

HOGGE, James Myles (1873–1928). M.P. East Edinburgh 1912–24. Joint Chief Whip 1919–23.

HOLT, Arthur Frederick (1914–   ). M.P. Bolton W. 1951–64. Chief Whip 1962–3.

HORABIN, Thomas Lewis (1896–1956). M.P. North Cornwall 1939–47 and (Labour) 1947–50. Chief Whip 1945–6.

HORE-BELISHA, Lord (1895–1957). Leslie Hore-Belisha, 1st Baron 1954. M.P. Devonport 1923–31 and (Liberal National) 1931–42 and (Independent) 1942–5. Various offices 1931–40 and 1945. Belisha Beacons named after him.

HOWARD, Geoffrey William Algernon (1877–1935). M.P. Eskdale 1906–10; Westbury 1911–18; Luton 1923–4. Parliamentary Private Secretary to Prime Minister 1910. Junior Lord of Treasury 1915–16; played a large part in Liberal organization 1919–26.

HUDSON, Robert Arundell (1864–1927). Knighted 1906. Secretary National Liberal Federation 1893–1922; Hon Secretary Liberal Central Association 1893–1927. His second wife was the widow of Lord Northcliffe.

HUTCHISON, Lord (1873–1950). Robert Hutchison. K.C.M.G. 1919. 1st Baron 1932. M.P. (National Liberal) Kirkcaldy 1922–3; (Liberal) Montrose 1924–31 and (Liberal National) 1931–2. Scottish National Liberal Whip 1923; a Liberal Whip 1924–6; Chief Whip 1926–30. In office 1935–8. Major-General.

ILLINGWORTH, Percy Holden (1869–1915). M.P. Shipley 1906–15. Junior Lord of Treasury 1910–12; Parliamentary Secretary Treasury and Liberal Chief Whip 1912–15.

ISAACS, Rufus Daniel. See Reading, Marquis of.

JOHNSTONE, Harcourt (1895–1945). M.P. East Willesden 1923–4; South Shields 1931–5; Middlesbrough West 1940–5. Secretary Board of Overseas Trade 1940–5.

JONES, Henry Haydn (1863–1950). M.P. Merioneth 1910–45.

JONES, Leif(child). See Rhayader, Lord.

JOWITT, Earl (1885–1957). William Allen Jowitt. Knighted 1929. 1st. Baron 1945; 1st Viscount 1947; 1st Earl 1951. M.P. Preston 1922–4 and 1929 and (Labour, then National Labour) 1929–31 and (Labour) 1939–45. Minister 1929–31, 1940–51.

KENNET, Lord (1879–1960). Edward Hilton Young. G.B.E. 1927. 1st Lord Kennet 1935. M.P. Norwich 1915–22 and (National Liberal) 1922–3 and (Liberal) 1924–5 and (Conservative) 1925–9; M.P. (Conservative) Sevenoaks 1929–35. Financial Secretary Treasury 1921–2; also in office 1931–5.

KIMBERLEY, 1st Earl (1826–1902). John Wodehouse, succeeded Baron Wodehouse 1846, created 1st Earl of Kimberley 1866. Ministerial office 1852–6, 1859–61, 1868–74, 1880–2; Secretary India 1882–6 and 1892–4; Foreign Secretary 1894–5. Leader of Liberal Peers 1891–4 and 1896–1902.

LAMBERT, Viscount (1866–1958) George Lambert, 1st Viscount 1945. M.P. South Molton 1891–1924, 1929–31 and (Liberal National) 1931–45. Civil Lord Admiralty 1905–15. Chairman 'unofficial' (effectively, Coalition) Liberal M.P.s 1919–22.

LLOYD-GEORGE, Earl (1863–1945). David Lloyd George, 1st Earl 1945. M.P. Caernarvon Boroughs 1890–1945 (1922–3 as National Liberal; 1931–5 as Independent Liberal). President Board of Trade 1905–8; Chancellor of Exchequer 1908–15; Minister of Munitions 1915–16; Secretary War 1916; Prime Minister 1916–22. Chairman Liberal M.P.s 1924–31.

LLOYD GEORGE, Gwilym. See Tenby, Viscount.

LLOYD GEORGE, Megan (1902–1966), Lady Megan Lloyd George 1945. M.P. Anglesey 1929–51 and (Labour) Carmarthen 1957–66. Daughter of Earl Lloyd-George.

LUBBOCK, Eric Reginald (1928–   ). M.P. Orpington 1962–70, Liberal Chief Whip 1963–70. Heir Presumptive to Lord Avebury.

McCURDY, Charles Albert (1870–1941). M.P. Northampton 1910–22 and (National Liberal) 1922–3. Parliamentary Secretary Ministry Food 1919–20; Food Controller 1920–1; Joint Parliamentary Secretary Treasury and Coalition Liberal Chief Whip 1921–2.

McKENNA, Reginald (1863–1943). M.P. North Monmouthshire 1895–1918. Financial Secretary Treasury 1905–7; President Board of Education 1907–8; First Lord Admiralty 1908–11; Home Secretary 1911–15; Chancellor of Exchequer 1915–16. Later Chairman Midland Bank.

MACLEAN, Donald (1864–1932). K.B.E. 1917. M.P. Bath 1906–10; Peebles & Selkirk 1910–18; Peebles & S. Midlothian 1918–22; North Cornwall 1929–32. Deputy Chairman Committee House of Commons 1911–18; Chairman Liberal M.P.s 1919–22; President Board of Education 1931–2.

MARCHAMLEY, Lord (1855–1945) George Whiteley, 1st Baron Marchamley 1908. M.P. (Conservative) Stockport 1893–1900; (Liberal) Pudsey 1900–8. Patronage Secretary Treasury and Chief Whip 1905–8.

MARTELL, Edward Drewett (1909–   ). London County Council, SW. Bethnal Green 1946–9. Deputy Chairman Liberal Central Association 1950–1.

MASTERMAN, Charles Frederick Gurney (1873–1927). M.P. West Ham

North 1906–11; SW. Bethnal Green 1911–14; Rusholme (Manchester) 1923–4. Secretary Local Government Board 1908–9; Under Secretary Home 1909–12; Financial Secretary Treasury 1912–14; Chancellor Duchy of Lancaster 1914–15.

MELCHETT, Lord (1868–1930). Alfred Moritz Mond, 1st Baronet 1910; Baron Melchett 1928. M.P. Chester 1906–10; Swansea 1910–23; Carmarthen 1924–8 (Conservative 1925–8); First Commissioner Works 1916–21; Minister of Health 1921–2. D.Sc., F.R.S.

MOND, Alfred Moritz. See Melchett, Lord.

MORLEY, Viscount (1838–1923). John Morley. 1st Viscount 1908. M.P. Newcastle-upon-Tyne 1883–95; Montrose Burghs 1896–1908. Chief Secretary Ireland 1886, 1892–5; Secretary India 1905–10; Lord President of Council 1910–14. O.M.

MORRIS, Rhys Hopkin (1888–1956). Knighted 1954. M.P. Cardiganshire 1923–32; Carmarthenshire 1945–56. Deputy Chairman Ways & Means 1951–6; Metropolitan Magistrate 1932–6.

MUIR, Ramsay (1872–1941). M.P. Rochdale 1923–4. Chairman Organization Committee Liberal Party 1930–1; Chairman National Liberal Federation 1931–3; President 1933–6; Professor Modern History Liverpool 1906–13, Manchester 1913–21.

MURRAY, Lord (1870–1920). Alexander William Charles Oliphant Murray, Master of Elibank; 1st Baron Murray 1912. Heir to, but predeceased, 1st Viscount and 10th Baron Elibank. M.P. Midlothian 1900–5; Peebles & Selkirk 1906–10; Midlothian 1910–12. Scottish Liberal Whip 1906–10; Under Secretary India 1909–10; Parliamentary Secretary Treasury and Liberal Chief Whip 1910–12.

NUDDS, Thomas David (1905–   ). Worked at Liberal Headquarters 1920–68; Secretary Liberal Central Association 1949–68, now Honorary Secretary.

OWEN, Goronwy (1881–1963). Knighted 1944. M.P. Caernarvonshire 1923–45. Welsh Liberal Whip 1926–31; Chief Whip Sept.–Oct. 1931.

OXFORD AND ASQUITH, Earl of (1852–1928). Herbert Henry Asquith, 1st Earl of Oxford and Asquith 1925. M.P. East Fife 1886–1918; Paisley 1920–4. Home Secretary 1892–5; Chancellor of Exchequer 1905–8; Prime Minister 1908–16; Secretary War 1914; Leader of Liberal Party 1908–26; Leader of Opposition 1920–2.

OXFORD AND ASQUITH, Countess of (1864–1945), 'Margot' (Emma Alice Margaret) Asquith, née Tennant; Countess of Oxford and Asquith 1925. Married H. H. Asquith 1894 (his second marriage).

PEASE, Joseph Albert. See Gainford, Lord.

PHILLIPPS, (Henry) Vivian (1870–1955). M.P. West Edinburgh 1922–4. Private Secretary to H. H. Asquith 1917–22; Chief Whip 1923–4; Chairman Organizing Committee Liberal Million Fighting Fund 1925–7.

PRINGLE, William Mather Rutherford (1874–1928). M.P. NW. Lanarkshire 1910–18; Penistone 1922–4.

REA, 1st Lord (1873–1948) Walter Russell Rea, 1st Baronet 1935; 1st Baron 1937. M.P. Scarborough 1906–18; N. Bradford 1923–4; Dewsbury 1931–5. A Liberal Whip 1915–16 and 1924; Chief Whip 1931–5; Comptroller of Household 1921–2. Son of Russell Rea; father of 2nd Lord Rea.

REA, 2nd Lord (1900–   ) Phillip Russell Rea; succeeded father 1948. Liberal Chief Whip, House of Lords 1950–5; Liberal Leader House of Lords 1955–67. President Liberal Party Organization 1955.

READING, Marquis of (1860–1935). Rufus Daniel Isaacs. Knighted 1910; 1st Baron 1914; 1st Viscount 1916; 1st Earl 1917; 1st Marquis 1926. M.P. Reading 1904–13. Solicitor-General 1910; Attorney-General 1910–13; Lord Chief Justice 1913–21; High Commissioner and Special Ambassador U.S.A. 1918; Viceroy and Governor-General India 1921–6; Foreign Secretary 1931; Liberal Leader House of Lords 1931–6.

RHAYADER, Lord (1862–1939). Leifchild (usually known as Leif) Jones. 1st Baron Rhayader 1932. M.P. N. Westmorland 1905–10; Rushcliffe 1910–18; Camborne 1923–4 and 1929–31. President Liberal Council 1934–7; sometime President United Kingdom Alliance.

RIPON, 1st Marquis (1827–1909). George Frederick Samuel Robinson. Son of Viscount Goderich, the Prime Minister. M.P. 1852–9. Succeeded father as Earl of Ripon and uncle as Earl de Grey 1859; Marquis 1871. In Cabinet 1863–6, 1868–73, 1886; Secretary Colonies 1892–5; Lord Privy Seal and Liberal Leader in Lords 1905–8. Roman Catholic convert.

ROSEBERY, Earl of (1847–1929). Archibald Philip Primrose, succeeded as 5th Earl of Rosebery 1868. Under Secretary Home 1881–3; Lord Privy Seal 1885; Chief Commissioner Works 1885; Foreign Secretary 1886 and 1892–4; Prime Minister and Lord President of Council 1894–5; Chairman London County Council 1889–90, 1892. Married Hannah, heiress of Baron Meyer de Rothschild. President Liberal League 1902–9.

RUNCIMAN, 1st Lord (1847–1937). Walter Runciman. Baronet 1906; 1st Baron 1933. M.P. Hartlepool 1914–18. Shipowner.

RUNCIMAN, 1st Viscount, 2nd Baron (1870–1949). Walter Runciman jr. 1st Viscount Runciman 1937; succeeded as 2nd Baron 1937. M.P. Oldham 1899–1900; Dewsbury 1902–18; Swansea West 1924–9; St Ives

1929–31 and (Liberal National) 1931–7. Parliamentary Secretary Local Government Board 1905–7; Financial Secretary Treasury 1907–8; President Board Education 1908–11; President Board Agriculture 1911–14; President Board of Trade 1914–16 and (Liberal National) 1931–7; Head of mission to Czechoslovakia 1938; Lord President of Council 1938–9.

SAMUEL, Viscount (1870–1963). Herbert Louis Samuel. G.B.E. 1920; G.C.B. 1926; 1st Viscount 1937. M.P. Cleveland 1902–18; Darwen 1929–35. Under Secretary Home 1905–9; Chancellor Duchy of Lancaster 1909–10; Postmaster-General 1910–14; President Local Government Board 1914–15; Chancellor Duchy of Lancaster 1915–16; Home Secretary 1916 and 1931–2. High Commissioner Palestine 1920–5. Chairman Liberal Organization Committee 1927–9; Deputy Chairman Liberal M.P.s 1929–31; Chairman 1931–5; Liberal Leader House of Lords 1944–55.

SIMON, Lord, of Wythenshawe (1879–1960). Ernest Darwin Simon, 1st Baron 1947. M.P. Withington 1923–4, 1929–31. Parliamentary Secretary Ministry of Health 1931; Lord Mayor of Manchester 1921; Chairman B.B.C. 1947–52. Joined Labour Party ca. 1945. Not related to Viscount Simon.

SIMON, Viscount (1873–1954). John Allesbrook Simon. Knighted 1910. 1st Viscount 1940. M.P. Walthamstow 1906–18; Spen Valley 1922–31 and (Liberal National) 1931–40. Solicitor-General 1910–13; Attorney-General 1913–15; Home Secretary 1915–16; (Liberal National) Foreign Secretary 1931–5; Home Secretary and Deputy Leader House of Commons 1935–7; Chancellor of Exchequer 1937–40; Lord Chancellor 1940–5. Leader Liberal National Party until 1940.

SINCLAIR, Sir Archibald. See Thurso, Viscount.

SPENCER, 5th Earl (1835–1910). John Poyntz Spencer. Succeeded Earl Spencer 1857. Viceroy Ireland 1869–74, 1882–5; Ministerial office 1880–3, 1886; 1st Lord Admiralty 1892–5. Leader Liberal Peers 1902–5.

SPENDER, John Alfred (1862–1942). Assistant Editor *Westminster Gazette* 1893–6; Editor 1896–1922. Biographer of Campbell-Bannerman and (with Cyril Asquith) of Lord Oxford and Asquith.

STANSGATE, Viscount (1877–1960). William Wedgwood Benn, 1st Viscount Stansgate 1941. M.P. St George's 1906–18; Leith 1918–27; (Labour) Aberdeen N. 1928–31 and Gorton (Manchester) 1937–41. Junior Lord of Treasury 1910–15; Joined Labour Party 1927, held office 1929–31 and 1945–6.

STEEL, David Martin Scott (1938–). M.P. Roxburgh, Selkirk &

Peebles 1965– . Assistant Secretary Scottish Liberal Party 1962–4; Scottish Liberal Whip 1967–70; Chief Whip 1970– . Sponsor of Private Member's Bill on abortion law, 1966–7.

STRABOLGI, Lord (1886–1953). Joseph Montague Kenworthy. Succeeded Lord Strabolgi 1934. M.P. Central Hull 1919–26 and (Labour) 1926–31. Labour Chief Whip House of Lords 1938–42.

TENBY, Viscount (1894–1967). Gwilym Lloyd George, 1st Viscount Tenby 1957. M.P. Pembrokeshire 1922–4, 1929–50 (as Independent Liberal 1931–5; Liberal whip withdrawn ca. 1946); Parliamentary Secretary Board of Trade 1931 and 1939–41; Parliamentary Secretary Ministry of Food 1941–2; Minister of Fuel 1942–5; held office also 1951–7.

THORNE, George Rennie (1853–1934). M.P. Wolverhampton East 1908–29. Joint Chief Whip 1919–23.

THORPE, (John) Jeremy (1929–   ). M.P. North Devon 1959– . Chairman Liberal M.P.s 1967– ; Privy Councillor 1967. Son and grandson of Conservative M.P.s.

THURSO, Viscount (1890–1970). Archibald Henry Macdonald Sinclair. Succeeded Baronet 1912; 1st Viscount Thurso 1952. M.P. Caithness & Sutherland 1922–45. Chief Whip 1930–1; Secretary Scotland 1931–2; Secretary Air 1940–5; Chairman Liberal M.P.s 1935–45.

WADE, Lord (1904–   ). Donald Wade. M.P. Huddersfield West 1950–64. Chief Whip 1956–62; Deputy Chairman Liberal M.P.s 1962–4; Life Peer 1965.

WEDGWOOD, Lord (1872–1943). Josiah Clement Wedgwood, 1st Baron 1942. M.P. Newcastle-under-Lyme 1906–19 and (Labour) 1919–42. Labour Chancellor Duchy of Lancaster 1924. Mayor Newcastle-under-Lyme 1930–2.

WHITELEY, George. See Marchamley, Lord.

WOLVERHAMPTON, Viscount (1830–1911). Henry Hartley Fowler, 1st Viscount Wolverhampton 1908. M.P. Wolverhampton 1880–1908. Under Secretary Home 1884–5; Financial Secretary Treasury 1886; President Local Government Board 1892–4; Secretary India 1894–5; Chancellor Duchy of Lancaster 1905–8; Lord President of Council 1908–10.

YOUNG, Edward Hilton. See Kennet, Lord.

Bibliography

1. Private Papers
Acland papers (Sir Richard Acland)
Asquith papers (Bodleian Library, Oxford)
Burns papers (British Museum)
Campbell-Bannerman papers (British Museum)
Elibank papers (National Library of Scotland)
Fisher papers (Bodleian Library)
W. E. Gladstone papers (British Museum)
Viscount (Herbert) Gladstone papers (British Museum)
Haldane papers (National Library of Scotland)
Bonar Law papers (Beaverbrook Library)
Lloyd George papers (Beaverbrook Library)
McKenna papers (Churchill College, Cambridge)
Rosebery papers (National Library of Scotland)
Runciman papers (seen when in the possession of Sir Steven Runciman; now at
   University of Newcastle-upon-Tyne)
Samuel papers (House of Lords Record Office)

It is likely that useful and important material will also be found in three sets of
papers which the author has not yet been able to consult: the Maclean papers
(which are in the process of being deposited at the Bodleian Library); the
Simon papers (Viscount Simon) and the Sinclair papers (Dowager Viscountess
Thurso).

2. Periodicals, etc.
The most useful daily newspapers in this work have been: *The Times* (whole
period); *Manchester Guardian* (since 1959, *The Guardian*) (whole period); *Daily
Chronicle* (to 1930); *Daily News* (to 1930); *Westminster Gazette* (to 1928) and *News
Chronicle* (1930-60), but numerous other newspapers have been consulted as
well.
   Several Liberal Party productions have proved invaluable. *Liberal Magazine*,
especially in the period down to about 1941, is most useful as a source of
general history as well as Liberal history. *Liberal News* (1946 onwards) has
appeared as a weekly, and recently as a fortnightly, Party paper. The *Liberal
Year Books* (1905-39) give an immense amount of current information, and
also poll lists and biographies of Liberal M.P.s. The bound volumes of *Liberal
Pamphlets and Leaflets* (1893-1929) give some very important sidelights on the
political battle as it was being fought. Several other periodical publications have
appeared from time to time; among these should be mentioned *The Liberal*

Agent, Liberal Monthly, Westminster Newsletter, and an earlier series of *Liberal News* which existed in the 1930s. Of the Liberal 'heresies', the Liberal League produced a number of pamphlets; the Coalition Liberals produced *Lloyd George Liberal Magazine* (1920–3), and the Liberal Nationals produced *Liberal National Magazine* and, more recently, *New Horizon.*

There have been innumerable publications by individuals and bodies of Liberal persuasion. *New Outlook* is a useful platform for the discussion of current issues of politics and political philosophy, and contains some articles of serious historical interest. Unfortunately Beatrice Hill's *Liberal Forward* recently expired. A large number of election addresses from candidates of all Parties are kept in the Gladstone Library at the National Liberal Club, and have been extensively consulted. Among non-Liberal publications, frequent use has been made of the official *Parliamentary Debates,* especially those of the House of Commons; of *Dod's Parliamentary Companion,* the *Reformer's Year Books,* the *Constitutional Year Books,* the *Annual Register, Keesing's Contemporary Archives, Who's Who* and various issues of *Who was Who.*

3. Books

Addison, Christopher (Viscount): *Four and a half years* (2 vols, 1934)
    Politics from Within, 1911–1918 (2 vols, 1924)
Bassett, R: *Nineteen thirty-one* (1958)
Bealey, F., and Pelling, H.: *Labour and Politics 1900–1906* (1958)
Beaverbrook, Lord: *Decline and Fall of Lloyd George* (1963)
    Politicians and the War (2 vols, 1928)
Beer, Samuel: *Modern British Politics* (1965)
Blake, Robert: *The Conservative Party from Peel to Churchill* (1970)
Bonham-Carter, Lady Violet (Lady Asquith): *Winston Churchill as I knew him* (1965)
Churchill, Sir Winston: *The World Crisis* (5 vols, 1923–9)
Cole, G. D. H.: *British Working Class Politics, 1832–1914* (1941)
    History of the Labour Party from 1914 (1948)
Cross, Colin: *The Liberals in power, 1905–1914* (1963)
Cruikshank, R. J.: *The Liberal Party* (1948)
Dangerfield, George: *The strange death of Liberal England, 1910–1914* (1935)
Ensor, Sir Robert: *England 1870–1914* (1936)
Fyfe, Hamilton: *The British Liberal Party* (1928)
Gardiner, A. G.: *Life of Sir William Harcourt* (1923)
Geake, Charles, and Gould, F. Carruthers: *John Bull's Adventures in the Fiscal Wonderland* (1904)
George, Henry: *Progress and Poverty* (1879, etc.)
    Protection or Free Trade (1886, etc.)
Gregory, Roy: *The Miners and British Politics 1906–1914* (1968)
Halévy, Elie: *Imperialism and the Rise of Labour 1895–1905* (1926, etc.)
    The Rule of Democracy 1905–1914 (1932, etc.)
Hanham, H. J.: *Elections and Party Management* (1959)
Harris, Sir Percy: *Forty years in and out of Parliament* (c. 1947)
Hazlehurst, Cameron: *Politicians at War, July 1914–May 1915* (1971)
Hobhouse, L. T.: *Liberalism* (1911)
James, R. R.: *Rosebery* (1963)

Jenkins, Roy: *Asquith* (1964)
   Mr. Balfour's Poodle (1954)
Jennings, Sir Ivor: *Party Politics* (3 vols, 1961–3)
Jones, T.: *Lloyd George* (1951)
Kinnear, Michael: *The British Voter: an atlas and survey since 1885* (1968)
(Liberal Publication Department): *The Government's Record 1906–1913* (1913)
Lloyd George, David (Earl Lloyd-George): *War Memoirs* (6 vols, 1933–6; later edn. in 2 vols)
Lloyd George, Frances (Countess Lloyd-George): *The Years that are Past* (1967)
Lloyd George inquiries:
   Britain's Industrial Future ('Yellow Book') (1928)
   Coal and Power (1924)
   Land and the Nation ('Green Book') (1925)
   Towns and the Land ('Brown Book') (1925)
Lynam, R.: *The First Labour Government* (1957)
McCallum, R. B.: *The Liberal Party from Earl Grey to Asquith* (1963)
McKenzie, Robert: *British Political Parties* (2nd edn, 1963)
Magnus, Philip: *Gladstone* (1954)
Mallet, Sir Charles: *Herbert Gladstone: a memoir* (1932)
Morley, Viscount: *Life of Gladstone* (2 vol edn, 1908)
   Memorandum on Resignation, August 1914 (1928)
Mowat, C. Loch: *Britain between the Wars, 1918–1940* (1963)
Murray, A. C.: *Master and Brother* (1945)
Nicholson, Harold: *King George V* (1953)
The 'Nuffield Monographs' on the General Elections: 1945 (R. B. McCallum and Alison Redman); 1950 (H. G. Nicholas); 1951 (D. E. Butler); 1955 (D. E. Butler); 1959 (D. E. Butler and Richard Rose); 1964 (D. E. Butler and Anthony King) and 1966 (D. E. Butler and Anthony King)
Ostrogorski, M.: *Democracy and the Organization of Political Parties* (1902)
Owen, Frank: *Tempestuous Journey: Lloyd George, his life and times* (1954)
Oxford and Asquith, Earl of: *Memories and Reflections* (1928)
   The Genesis of the War (1923)
   The Paisley Policy (1920)
Pelling, Henry: *Short History of the Labour Party* (1961)
Phillipps, Vivian: *My days and ways* (private circulation, c. 1943)
Poirier, Philip: *The advent of the Labour Party* (1958)
Rasmussen, J. S.: *The Liberal Party* (1965)
Rowland, Peter: *The last Liberal Governments: the Promised Land 1905–1910* (1968)
Samuel, Viscount: *Memoirs* (1945)
Skidelsky, Robert: *Politicians and the Slump: The Labour Government of 1929–1931* (1967)
Slessor, Sir Henry: *A History of the Liberal Party* (1944)
Snowden, Viscount: *Autobiography* (1934)
Sommer, Dudley: *Haldane of Cloan* (1960)
Spender, J. A.: *Life of Sir Henry Campbell-Bannerman* (2 vols, 1923)
   Sir Robert Hudson (1930)
Spender, J. A., and Asquith, Cyril: *Life of Lord Oxford and Asquith* (2 vols, 1932)
Stansky, Peter: *Ambitions and Strategies: the struggle for the leadership of the Liberal Party in the 1890s* (1964)
Sylvester, A. J.: *The Real Lloyd George* (1947)

Taylor, A. J. P.: *English History 1914–1945* (1965)
Taylor, A. J. P. (editor): *Lloyd George: twelve essays* (1971)
Thomson, Malcolm: *David Lloyd George* (1948)
Watkins, Alan: *The Liberal Dilemma* (1966)
Watson, R. Spence: *The National Liberal Federation 1877–1906* (1907)
Wilson, Trevor: *The Downfall of the Liberal Party, 1914–1935* (1966)

Index

Abbey 177
Aberavon 164
Aberdeenshire 141, 242
Abingdon Street 182n, 183
Abnormal Importation Bill/Act 1931 225
Abrahams, William 83
Abyssinia 239–40
Acland, Sir A. H. D. 33
Acland, Sir Francis 32–3, 128n, 130, 133, 142, 170, 227, 238, 303
Acland, Sir Richard 236, 245, 248, 303
Adamson, William 140–1, 152
Addison, Christopher (Viscount) 104–5, 111, 116, 147–8, 164, 303
Adult suffrage 55
Agents 11
Agriculture 3, 299
Allard, William 26, 28, 43n, 79
Alsace 112
Alstead, R. 180n
Altrincham & Sale 281n
Amory, D. Heathcote 283
Anglesey 170, 263
Anglicans, *see* England, Church of
Antrim 34
Area Federations 15, 62, 134, 149, 230, 261
Armenia 19
Armistice 110, 118–19
Arnold, Sydney 128n
Appeasement 241
Ashford 223
Asquith, Baroness, *see* Bonham-Carter, Lady Violet
Asquith, H. H. (1st Earl of Oxford and Asquith); Asquithians 12, 19n, 20–3, 26–7, 30–3, 36, 40–51, 55–60, 63, 85, 88, 91–124, 128–51, 154–57, 161–4, 167–76, 181–201, 206, 212–13, 217, 247, 269, 276, 281, 288–9, 296–7, 304, 310, 311–12
Asquith, 'Margot' (Countess of Oxford and Asquith) 21, 102, 161, 199, 310
Atlantic Monthly 103n

Attercliffe 80, 82
Attlee, Clement (Earl) 165, 241, 267
Avon, Earl of, *see* Eden, Anthony
Aylesbury 173
Ayr 151

Baldwin, Stanley (Earl) 132, 170, 173, 176, 187–8, 204–6, 216, 239
Balfour, A. J. (Earl), 26, 29, 30–1, 34, 38, 52, 83, 101, 117, 146, 160
Balfour, Honor 246
Banbury 110
Bangor 207n
Banks, Mitchell 180n
Bannerman, John (Lord) 276
Baptists 6
Barnard Castle 71–3
Barnby, Lord 129n
Barnes, G. N. 120
Barnes, Harry 144
Barrand, A. R. 144
Bartlett, Vernon 238, 242n, 245n
Barton, Sir William 142, 154
Battersea 193
Baxter, Frank 16
Beaconsfield, Earl of, *see* Disraeli, Benjamin
Beauchamp, 7th Earl 94–5, 195
Beaufort, Duke of 42
Beaumont, Hubert 71–3
Beaverbrook, Lord 93, 106
Bebington 259, 263
Belfast 279n
Belgium 93–4, 112
Bell, Richard 67, 75
Belper 89
Benn, William Wedgwood (Viscount Stansgate) 97, 128n, 130, 134, 136, 138, 142, 157, 189, 195n, 196n, 202, 303
Bennett, A.V.-M. Donald 246, 248, 255, 274
Berkeley, R. C. 180n
Bernays, R. H. 229, 239, 248

z

Berwick & Haddington 163

Berwick-upon-Tweed 248

Bethnal Green 4n, 53, 89, 164, 186n, 205, 228, 236–7, 243, 248, 251, 259

Beveridge, Sir William (Lord); Beveridge Report 243, 245n, 246, 248, 259, 303

Bideford 257

Birkenhead 248

Birkenhead, Lord (Frederick, Edwin Smith) 146, 160, 166

Birmingham 1, 4, 5, 12–14, 34, 40n, 142, 172, 284, 292,

Birrell, Augustine 33, 38, 55n, 58, 61n, 100–1, 303–4

Bishop Auckland 226

'Black and Tans' 150

Blackpool 173, 276

Blake, Sir Francis 128n, 133

Blindell, James 203

Bliss, Barbara 197n, 198n

Blyth 123

Bodmin 30, 236

Boer War 23–6, 29, 67, 115

Bolshevism 185

Bolton 262–3, 276, 280

Bonham-Carter, Mark 248, 269, 275, 304

Bonham-Carter, Lady Violet (Baroness Asquith) 47–8, 105, 114n, 198, 246–8, 259, 262–3, 265, 303–4

Boothby, Robert (Lord) 241

Bosworth 202

Bottomley, Horatio 290n

Bourbons 300

Bournemouth 242

Bow & Bromley 84n, 164

Bowen, Roderic 262, 268, 282

Bradford 149, 172, 248

Bramsdon, Sir Thomas 128n

Briant, Frank 128n, 133, 189, 196n, 205, 236, 304

Bridgwater 238

Brigg 37

Brighouse 276

Bristol 129n, 186, 229, 248

Britain's Industrial Future, see 'Yellow Book'

Broadhurst, H. 65

Brown, Ernest 202, 214, 216, 244–5, 304

'Brown Book' 191, 203

Bryce, James (Lord) 15, 21, 33, 304

Buckingham Palace Conference 60–1

Buckmaster, Lord 112, 195n

Budgets (1906–8) 36; (1909) 40–7, 52, 56, 86; (1915) 99, 100; (1919) 142; (1931) 312–15

Burns, John 33, 66n, 94–5, 304

Burt, Thomas 65, 82, 90

Bury St Edmunds 246

Butcher, Sir H. W. 242n

Buxton, C. R. 145n

Buxton, Lord 55n, 195n

Buxton, Noel 130, 165

Byers, Frank (Lord) 252, 255, 260, 265, 272, 276, 284, 304

Byles, W. P. 76n

Cadbury, George 68

Cadbury, Laurence 275

Caernarvon 247–8

Caithness & Sutherland 164, 248, 259, 263, 282

Camberwell 144, 147

Cambridge, Duke of 21

Camlachie 255

Campaign Committee 272

Campbell, J. R.; Campbell case 178–80, 183

Campbell-Bannerman, Sir Henry 12n, 14, 20n 21–33, 37–40, 68–70, 74, 77, 93, 148, 304

Capital Levy 297

Cardiganshire 173, 282, 285

'Caretaker Government' 247

Carlton Club 160–1

Carmarthenshire 203, 248, 268–70

Carson, Sir Edward (Lord) 59, 60

Catlow, Alderman 70

Cecil, Lord (Hugh) 30n, 50; (Robert) 61n, 157–9

'Centre Party' 146, 158, 166–7

Chamberlain, Sir Austen 141, 156, 159, 160

Chamberlain, Joseph 4, 6, 12, 13, 24, 29, 40, 74, 304

Chamberlain, Neville 226, 238, 240–2

Cheadle 282, 292

Cheshire 76

Chester-le-Street 78

Chesterfield 27, 87, 124

Chief Whip, see Whip

Chippenham 279

Churchill, Sir Winston, 25 30, 33, 40, 42, 55n, 57, 99, 105, 107, 110, 128, 146, 147, 161, 164, 167, 171, 173–7, 241–4, 247, 249, 255–9, 262–7, 304

Churt 183, 218

Cirencester 42n

Clacton 227

Clitheroe 69, 70, 73

Clynes, J. R. 175–6, 179

Coal, see Miners

Coal Bill/Act 1930 209–10

Coal and Power 191

Coalition; proposals (1910) 48; (1915) 98, 99, 109; (1916) 106–7, 113, 118; (1918–22) 119–65, 167, 207, 296; (1940) 242, 244

Coalition Committee 146

Coalition Liberal Organization (National Liberals) 140, 149, 150, 156, 190, 200

Cobden, Richard 6, 119

Cocoa 100

Collective Security 240

Collins, Sir Godfrey 128n, 136–9, 189, 190n, 194–7, 211n, 216, 241, 304–5

Colne Valley 37, 80, 82, 84, 164, 236, 262, 282

Colonies 32

Colwyn Bay 253

Common Market (European) 273–5, 284, 298, 300

Common Wealth 245

Communists 178–9, 185

Concentration Camps 25

Congregationalists 6

Conscription 100–1, 111, 117, 212, 241

Conservatives, *passim*

Constitutional Conference 48

Constitutional Year Book 165

Co-operative Societies and Party 67, 144–5

Co-ownership 272

Corbett-Ashby, Mrs 246

Cornwall 172, 205–6, 238, 252, 254, 267, 280, 282, 285

Cory, Sir Clifford 176n

Cotton 111

'Council of Action' 234

'Coupon' 120–6, 129n, 132–3, 154, 162

Coventry 130

Cowan, D. M. 196n, 235

Cowdray, Lord (Weetman Pearson) 158, 181n, 195n, 230, 305

Cox, Harold 40–1, 290n

Cozens-Hardy, Lord 128n

Craig, H. J. 123

Crewe 89n

Crewe, Marquis of 48–50, 139, 158, 216–17, 228, 305

Cromer, Lord 50

Crooks, Will 71, 78

Cruisers 178

Cunliffe-Lister, Sir Philip 226

Curragh 59, 96

Curran, Peter 37, 79

Curry, A. C. 226

Czar, *see* Nicholas II

Czechoslovakia 240

Daily Chronicle 29, 115, 116, 125, 167–8, 200, 236

Daily Mail 6, 278

Daily News 24, 29, 68, 71–3, 115, 125, 141, 236

Daily Telegraph 112

Dale, Tom 231n

Dalmeny 32

Dalmeny, Viscount, *see* Rosebery, 6th Earl

Dalziel, Sir Henry 116

Darwen 206, 222, 236, 246

Davidson, James 280

Davies, Clement 209, 241–2, 244, 245n, 249–50, 253–7, 261–2, 265–8, 274, 277, 305

Davies, David 189, 196n

Davies, Sir John 200

Davies, R. Humphrey 11n, 14–17, 22, 54n, 62, 65n, 78n, 159n, 198, 238, 305

Davies, W. R. 238, 266, 288, 305

Defence estimates 240

Denbigh 236

Deposit 130, 145, 255, 259–261, 271, 277

Derby 9n, 68, 125

Derby, Lord 49, 100, 147, 174n

Derbyshire 80–2, 87–9, 125, 279, 289

Design for Freedom 252–5

Devolution 299–300

Devon 15, 45n, 49, 172, 254, 267, 270, 285

Devonport 186n

Devonshire, 8th Duke of (Marquis of Hartington) 305

'Diehards' 50–1, 160

Dilke, Sir Charles 93

Director, *see* General Director

Disraeli, Benjamin (Earl of Beaconsfield) 110, 154

Dissenters, *see* Nonconformists

Doctors 54

Dominion Home Rule 151

Donald, Robert 116

Dorset 164, 222, 238, 269

'Double-whipping' 169

Dower, E. L. G. 249

Dreadnoughts 92

Drink, *see* Temperance

Dublin 34, 61, 101

Dudgeon, C. R. 169, 221

Duma 93

Dumfriesshire 226, 235

Dundee 35n, 75, 164, 248, 258

Dunstable 256

Durham 45n, 71, 75, 89, 165, 229

East End, *see* London
East Grinstead 281
East Ham South 120, 163
Eastbourne 274
Eastwood, Alderman 87–8
Eddisbury 203
Eden, Anthony (Earl of Avon) 241, 266
Edge, Sir William 190n, 200, 209n, 211n,
    305
Edinburgh 23n, 92, 137, 145, 172, 269
Edinburgh Evening News 116
Education 6, 13, 25, 29, 36, 38–9, 172,
    189
Edward VII, King 42, 48–9, 93
Edwards, Clem 120
Edwards, Enoch 86
Edwards, J. H. 176n, 196n
Egypt 268
Electoral Reform 212–13, 233
Elibank, Master of (Lord Murray) 33,
    46n, 48n, 50n, 53–4, 62, 69, 77n,
    98, 117–18, 139, 291, 310
Elland 60, 130, 152
Ellis, Thomas E. 16–19, 21–2, 306
Emerson, William 71n
Empire, *see* Imperialism
England 9, 34, 39, 45, 48–9, 76–7, 80,
    149, 169, 213, 254, 275, 277, 282, 292
England, Church of 6
England, Lt. Col. A. 176n, 196n, 223
English Universities 202
Entente cordiale 91–2
Entwistle, C. F. 128n, 192
Epping 177
Estate Duties 41
European Economic Community, *see*
    Common Market
European Free Trade Area (EFTA)
    273–4
Euripides 64, 108
Evans, D. O. 244n
Evans, Ernest 150n
Ex-servicemen 200
Eye 263

Fabian Society 29
Fairfax, Col. Bryan 143–4
Farquhar, Earl 161
Fascism 239
Featherstone 21
Federations, *see* Area Federations
Fenby, T. D. 196
Fenwick, Charles 82n, 90
Ferens, T. R. 181n
Fife 49, 84, 123, 129, 235
Fildes, Sir Henry 200, 235

Finances, Liberal 10–12, 14, 17, 22, 28,
    68, 74, 127–8, 134–5, 140n, 141, 159,
    179–84, 190–2, 197–200, 203–4,
    229–30, 250–1, 259–61, 266, 269,
    284, 288, 291–2, 294; *see* also
    Lloyd George Fund
Finney, S. 86
Fisher, H. A. L. 147, 196
'Five cruisers' 178
'Flappers' 204
Foot, Sir Dingle 248, 267
Foot, Isaac 186, 236, 238
Forrest, Walter 196n
Forteviot, Lord 181n
Forward March 245
Fothergill, C. Philip 245, 250–1, 255–6,
    262, 265, 269–70, 306
Foundation Fund 251
Fowler, Sir Henry (Viscount
    Wolverhampton) 20–1, 26–7, 33, 313
France 91–4, 112
France, Gerald 143–4
Franchise 10, 55–6, 125, *see* also Reform
    Acts
Fraser, Sir Malcolm 156
Free Trade (also Protection, Tariffs,
    Tariff Reform etc.) 5, 18, 29–30, 32,
    34, 36, 40, 42, 46, 56, 71n, 74, 99,
    110, 154, 170–1, 174, 177, 189,
    212–221, 225–6, 228, 233–4, 239–40,
    265, 273, 291, 297–8, 300
Free Trade Union (now Free Trade
    League) 30, 198
Freeman-Thomas, F. 28n, 30n, 39n, 43n
'Fusion' 146–7, 149

Gainford, Lord 306
Galloway 169
Gallup Polls 270–1, 274, 278
'Garden Suburb' 140
Gardiner, A. G. 112n, 115
Gardiner, James 128n
Gateshead 82–3
Geake, Charles 15–16, 139, 306
General Director 266, 272–3
General Elections (1874) 12, 65; (1892)
    66; (1895) 9, 19; (1900) 4, 25;
    (1906) 28, 34–5, 38, 82, 84, 211;
    (Jan. 1910) 45, 82–4; (Dec. 1910)
    48–9, 84; (1918) 108, 118–32, 143,
    148, 157, 207, 296; (1922) 161–6,
    168; (1923) 170–1; (1924) 180–7,
    191, 206, 287; (1929) 188, 200,
    203–8; (1931) 218–22, 235–6; (1935)
    230, 236–8; (1945) 247–50, 254;
    (1950) 251, 255, 258–60; (1951) 260,

General Elections *continued*
  262–6; (1955) 266–7; (1959) 270–2,
  276; (1964) 279–281; (1966) 281–2;
  (1970) 285, 292
General Strike 193–4, 197n
George V, King 48–51, 55, 60, 93, 96,
  103–4, 119, 175, 212, 216, 219, 228
George VI, King 242
George, Henry 3–4, 41, 56, 64
Germany 3, 23, 61, 92–4, 102, 105, 113,
  119, 142, 239–40, 242
Gladstone, Henry (Lord Gladstone of
  Hawarden) 22
Gladstone, Herbert (Viscount Gladstone)
  12n, 14, 16, 22, 25n, 26–33, 62n,
  68–74, 76, 78, 134n, 139n, 140, 165n,
  167–8, 169n, 181–3, 194, 197, 204,
  306
Gladstone, William Ewart 6, 7, 12–13, 16,
  18–20, 22, 65, 69, 94, 306
Gladwyn, Lord 284
Glanville, H. J. (senior) 128n, 133;
  (junior) 233
Glasgow 43, 165, 172, 255
Glasgow Herald 125
Glassey, Alec 222
Glendinning, Robert 34
Gloucester 172, 269
Goldblatt, David 252n, 253–4
Goldman, P. 227n
Gorton 35n
Govan 25n
Government of Ireland Bills/Act 58, 96
Graham, W. 158
Granville, Edgar 244, 263, 267
Gray, Milner 214n
Grayson, Victor 37, 80, 84
Greece 160
'Green Book' 191, 203
Greenock 139
Greenwood, Sir Hamar (Viscount) 142,
  173, 306
Grey, Sir Edward (Viscount 19, 23–8,)
  31–3, 48, 55, 93–4, 100, 113, 157–8,
  169, 195n, 198, 228, 307
Grey, George 244n, 245n, 246
Grey, Maj.-Gen. W. H. 288
Griffiths, Kingsley 202
Grimond, Jo 260, 268, 270–6, 281,
  283–5, 289, 297, 307
Gruffydd, Professor 244n, 245n
Guardian 271, 281, 284n, *see* also *Manchester
  Guardian*
Guest, F. E. 109–10, 113, 116–19, 121–3,
  126, 129n, 133, 134n, 138, 141n, 142,
  144, 146, 155, 164, 169, 171, 173,

181, 190, 196, 204–5, 208, 307
Guest, O. 146

Hague, Harry 276
Haig, Sir Douglas (Earl) 107
Hailsham, Lord (1st Viscount) 218; (2nd
  Viscount) *see* Hogg, Quintin
Haldane (Viscount) 21n, 23, 24n, 26, 29,
  31–3, 95, 99, 151, 176, 307
Halifax 60, 202
Hall, Fred 83, 89
Hallamshire 89
Halsbury, Earl of 50–1
Hamilton, Sir Robert 196n
Hancock, J. G. 81, 88–9
Hanley 40n, 56–7, 86–7, 130, 289
Harbison, T. J. S. 180n
Harborough 124
Harcourt, Lewis (Viscount) 8, 42, 50,
  55n, 94, 113, 307
Harcourt, Sir William 7–9, 18–21, 25–7,
  31, 307
Hardie, J. Keir 56n, 66–7, 76n, 78, 83
Harmsworth, Alfred, *see* Northcliffe, Lord
Harmsworth, Cecil (Lord) 69, 106, 109,
  115, 122, 307
Harmsworth, Harold, *see* Rothermere,
  Lord
Harper, Sir Edward 41n
Harris, H. F. P. 266, 272–3
Harris, Sir Percy 124, 162, 180n, 189n,
  196n, 209n, 237, 242–5, 248–9, 251,
  259, 307
Harrow 158
Hartshorn, Vernon 210
Harvey, W. E. 88–9
Harwich 231n
Haslam, James 87–8
Hastings 35n
Hastings, Sir Patrick 179
Henderson, Arthur 71–3, 75, 96, 99, 104,
  120, 129, 158, 164, 173, 176, 179, 290
Henderson, H. D. 201
Henderson-Livesey 224n
Herbert, Lt.-Col. A. 122
Herbert, Sir Jesse 15, 48, 62, 68, 72–4,
  76–8, 96, 139, 307
Hereford 223
Hesiod 166
Hewart, Sir Gordon 113 146, 156
Heywood & Radcliffe 223
Hillary, A. E. 180n
Hitler, Adolf 233
Hoare, Sir Samuel (Viscount
  Templewood) 114
Hobhouse, Sir Charles 55n, 129, 130

Hodge, Col. 180n
Hogbin, H. C. 176n, 193
Hogg, Quintin (2nd Viscount Hailsham)
    253
Hogge, J. M. 122, 128n, 133, 137–40, 142,
    145, 168–9, 180n, 186, 307
Holdsworth, Herbert 238, 248
Holland-with-Boston 203
Holmes, J. S. 128n
Holt, Arthur 262, 268, 274, 308
Home Counties 15, 26, 45n
Home Rule, see Ireland
Hooson, Emlyn 277, 284–5
Horabin, T. L. 244n, 245n, 249, 252, 308
Hore-Belisha, Leslie (Lord) 192, 213, 216,
    242n, 244, 308
Houghton-le-Spring 89
Howard, Geoffrey 130, 134n, 140, 168,
    181, 195n, 308
Howard, S. G. 128n
Howth 61
Huddersfield 82n, 229, 257–8, 260, 262,
    276, 280
Hudson, Sir Robert 14–18, 31n, 63, 96,
    108, 139–40, 197–8, 308
Hudson, Walter 38
Hughes, Collingwood 180n
Hughes, S. Leigh 79
Hull 141, 172, 191, 202
Hungary 268
Hutchison, Sir Robert (Lord) 190n, 198,
    209, 211, 214, 216, 308

Ilfracombe 265
Illingworth, Percy 57, 62–3, 91, 97, 308
Imperial Economic Conference 228
Imperial Preference 142
Imperialism 5, 20, 23, 25–6, 32, 33, 65
Import Duties Bill/Act 226, 234
Income Tax 41
Independent Labour Party (I.L.P.) 66,
    68, 75, 78–9, 81–2, 96, 136
Independent Nationalists, see O'Brien,
    William
India 11
Industrial disputes, see Trade Unions
Insurance Collectors 54
Invernesshire 285
Ipswich 34, 269
Ireland, Irish Party, Irish Nationalism,
    etc. 4, 6, 8, 9, 13, 20, 22, 25, 27,
    30–5, 38n, 39, 45–9, 55n, 56n, 57–61,
    78–9, 95–6, 99–101, 107, 111, 114–17,
    121–2, 128, 150–1, 156, 173, 177,
    277–9, 282
Isaacs, Sir Rufus, see Reading, Marquis of

Isle of Ely 248
Italy 239, 240

James, Lord (of Hereford) 30n
Japan 249
Jarrow 37, 79, 80, 82–3
Jenkins, John 78
Jenkins, Roy 105
Jenkins, W. A. 176n
Jenkinson, A. 277n
Jennings, Sir Ivor 199n, 200n
Jews 53
John, E. T. 130
Johnson, Paul 284
Johnson, William 88
Johnstone, Harcourt 170, 229, 230,
    236–7, 246, 288, 308
Johnstone, Russell 285
Jones, H. Haydn 128n, 308
Jones, Leif (child) (Lord Rhayader) 209n,
    311
Jowett, F. W. 56n
Jowitt, Sir William (Lord) 180n, 208,
    221, 308

Kay, R. N. 176n
Kedward, R. M. 211n, 223
Keir, David 235
Kellaway, F. G. 148
Kennet, Lord, see Young, E. Hilton
Kenworthy, J. M. (10th Lord Strabolgi)
    141, 180n, 197, 202, 313
Kenyon, Barnet 87–8, 124–5
Kerr, Philip, see Lothian, Marquis of
'Key Industries' 154
Keynes, Lord 181
Kiley, J. D. 128n, 133
Kilmarnock 173
Kilmuir, Lord, see Maxwell-Fyfe, David
Kimberley, Lord 19, 26, 309
King, J. 145n
King's Norton 4–5
Kirriemuir 257
Kitchener, Earl 96, 101
Knollys, Lord 44n, 47, 50, 51n

Labouchère, H. 26
Labour Leader 82
Labour Party, passim
Labour Representation Committee 2, 34,
    37–9, 67–78, 84
Ladywood 284
Lambert, George (1st Viscount) 128n,
    130, 136, 138, 186, 211n, 269, 309;
    (2nd Viscount) 269
Lambert, R. C. 145n

Lambert North 186n, 205, 236
Lanarkshire 35n, 69, 83, 89n
Lancashire 4, 34, 45n, 69–70, 74, 76, 80, 162, 174
Lancaster 202
Land; land problem; land value taxation; land taxes, etc. 3–4, 13, 39, 41–2, 56–7, 86, 145, 150, 163, 172, 189, 191–3, 214, 298
Land and Nation League 192, 200
Land and the Nation, see 'Green Book'
Lansbury, George 164
Lansdowne, Marquis of 50, 101–2, 112
Law, A. Bonar 52, 54n, 58–60, 85, 96, 98, 101–6, 113, 117–19, 121, 124, 143–7, 156, 159–61, 170, 296
Lawler, Wallace 284–5
Lawson, Sir Wilfrid 24
Layton, Sir William (Lord) 201
Leamington, 148
Leckie, J. A. 226–7, 229
Leeds 57, 74, 172
Lees-Smith, H. C. 145n
Lehmann, R. C. 29
Leicestershire 80, 173
Leith 89n, 202
Leviticus 36
Lewis, Sir Herbert 163, 224
Leyton 141 155
Liberal
　Action Group 245
　Associations 10–13, and passim
　Central Association 11–17, 65, 127–8, 169, 198, 229, 230, 237–8
　Clubs 17, 70
　Council 198, 203–4
　Imperial Council 26, 28, 68
　Industrial Inquiry 201
　-Labour, see 'Lib-Labs'
　Land Conference 192–3
　League 27–8, 31, 34, 43, 68, 79
　Magazine 15, 87, 89, 150, 158, 167, 198, 234
　Million Fund 190–1, 197, 200
　National Magazine 239
　Nationals 156, 211n, 220–7, 230–41, 244–5, 249, 252–7, 269
　News 251, 259n, 273
　Newscard 251
　Party Convention 190
　Party Organization 238, 241, 244n, 246–7, 265, 273, 284, 297
　Publications Department 15, 17, 128, 230
　Reconstruction Committee 250, 266
　Registration Association 11

Shadow Cabinet 193–6
Summer Schools 191, 201, 240
Unionists 4, 9, 13, 34, 52, 239
Year Books 15, 133, 224
'Lib-Labs' 45, 65, 68, 70, 75–6, 78, 80–3, 87, 89, 92, 93n
Limehouse 42–3, 165
Lincolnshire 186
Lincolnshire, Marquis of 195n
Linlithgowshire 202
Liquor taxes, see Budget (1909)
'Liquorice Allsorts' 256
Liverpool 4, 19, 20, 34, 46, 172, 193
Liverpool Post 125
Livingstone, Mackenzie 189, 196n, 208
Llandudno 274
Lloyd, Selwyn 253
Lloyd George, David (1st Earl Lloyd-George) 1–3, 26, 29, 33, 36, 40–5, 48, 53–7, 61, 88, 93–4, 96, 99, 101, 103–51, 155–6, 159–62, 166–70, 174, 181–205, 208–24, 228, 234, 237, 241–4, 247–8, 281, 288–9, 296, 309
Lloyd George, Frances (Dowager Countess), see Stephenson, Frances
Lloyd George Fund 116, 159–61, 168, 171, 180–4, 191–2, 197–200, 203, 209, 229, 291
Lloyd George, Gwilym (Viscount Tenby) 217, 219, 221, 232, 241–2, 247–9, 257, 313
Lloyd George Liberal Magazine 150, 171
Lloyd George, Lady Megan 221n, 244n, 245n, 262–3, 267–9, 309
Lloyd Georgette Organization 109–11
Lloyd's 259–60
Lloyd's Weekly News 116
Local elections 277, 279, 285
London 4, 34, 45n, 62, 71, 172, 174, 202, 205, 254
London County Council 251
Long, Walter 34, 101
Lords, House of 6, 8 13, 37–59, 64, 84, 96, 139, 169, 170, 214
Loreburn, Earl, see Reid, Sir Robert
Lorraine 112
Lothian, Marquis of 112, 210, 217, 228n
Lough, Thomas 110n
Louth 152, 155
Lubbock, Eric 227, 284, 309
Lucy, Sir Henry 26
Ludlow 170
Luton 231

Mabane, William 229
McCallum, Sir John 123, 128n, 138, 144

Macaulay, Lord 188
Maclean, Sir Donald 128n, 129n, 135–40,
    142, 144–5, 148, 151, 158, 164–5,
    168, 173, 181, 183, 190n, 194, 195n,
    206, 209n, 211n, 217, 225–7, 289, 309
McCurdy, C. A. 142, 155, 173, 190n,
    195n, 200, 308
Macdonald, Alexander 65
Macdonald, Archibald J. F. 260
MacDonald, James Ramsay 56n, 73,
    75–6, 95–6, 129, 164, 175–80, 208
    210, 214–20, 234
Macdonald, John A. M. 128n
MacDonald, Sir Murdoch 176n, 196n,
    211n, 244
McKeag, William 229
McKenna, Reginald; McKenna Duties
    33, 61n, 99, 100, 101n, 112
Mackie, George, 282
Maclay, J. P. 229, 242
Macmillan, Harold, 265, 270, 279
McMurray, Robert 287
Macnamara, T. J. 144, 147, 186, 195n
MacPherson, Ian 195n
Maidstone 35n
Malindine, Edwin 267
Mallalieu, E. L. 236
Manchester 23n, 34, 57, 83, 143, 162,
    172–3, 199, 213, 282
Manchester Guardian 115, 125, 134, 151
    263–4, *see* also *Guardian*
Mander, Sir Geoffrey 209n, 248, 259
Mansion House 93
Marchamley, Lord (George Whiteley)
    159, 309
'Marconi Scandal' 53–4
Marshall, Sir Arthur, 130, 168–9
Martell, E. D. 250, 252–3, 293, 309
Mason, D. M. 130
Massingham, H. W. 29
Masterman, C. F. G. 53–4, 63, 173, 186,
    195n, 309–10
Masterman, Mr Lucy 63
Maudling, Reginald 253
Maurice, Sir Frederick; Maurice Debate
    113–16, 122
Maurice, Nancy 114n
Maxwell-Fyfe, David (Lord Kilmuir) 204
May, Sir George; May Committee 215
Medlicott, Sir Frank 252n
Melchett, Lord, *see* Mond, Sir Alfred
Memorial (Suffrage 1911) 55; (Land
    Taxing 1911) 56, 87; (National
    Government 1931) 219–20
Merchant Shipping Act 1907, 36
Merioneth 186n, 263

Merthyr Tydfil 67, 83
Methodists 6
Middlesbrough 72n, 202, 276
Millar, Sir J. Duncan 209n, 222n, 235
Miners; Miners' Federation; Mines 45,
    61, 65, 67, 76, 80–3, 86–9, 107, 154,
    193, 199, 289
Mitchell, Rosslyn 185
Moslon, Hugh 253
Mond, Sir Alfred (1st Lord Melchett)
    155, 170, 173–4, 183, 192, 196, 203,
    310
Money Bills 47
Monmouthshire 9n
Montagu, Edwin 104, 111
Montgomeryshire 241, 277, 279, 285
Montrose 9n, 84
Moreing, A. H. 129n
Morgan, W. Pritchard 67
Morley, Arnold 14
Morley, John (Viscount) 7, 9, 20–1, 23,
    26, 33, 46, 93–5, 212, 310
Morpeth 123
Morris, Sir R. Hopkin 173, 186, 196n,
    233, 248–9, 262, 268, 287, 310
Morris-Jones, Sir Henry 244
Morrison, G. A. 235
Mosley, Sir Oswald 146, 158
Muir, Ramsay, 173, 186, 201, 209n, 213n,
    310
Munich 240–1
Munitions 99, 104
Murnaghan, Sheelagh 278
Murray, A. C. 144
Murray, Dr D. 129n
Murray, Professor Gilbert 157
Murray, Lord, *see* Elibank, Master of

Nash, Vincent 44n, 47n, 50n
Nathan, Lord 228, 236
National
    Anti-Gambling League 137
    Democratic Party 120–1, 123, 129n,
        144, 162
    Government 216–25, 233–9, 244, 288,
        293, 296–7
    Insurance Bill, Act 1911, 54
    Liberal Club 17
    Liberal Federation 12–17, 27, 37, 55,
        57, 71, 127–8, 134, 142, 148–9, 182,
        197–9, 201, 208n, 213, 231, 234, 238,
    Liberals (Lloyd George), *see* Coalition
        Liberals
    Liberals (Simon), *see* Liberal Nationals
    Opinion Polls 278
    Reform Union 26

Union (Conservatives) 5, 143
Volunteers (Ireland) 61
Nationalists, Irish, see Ireland
Nationalization 276
Naval Conference 210
Navy 7, 92, 178
Naylor, T. E. 158
Nazis 239–40
Negotiated Peace 91
Neilson, Francis 91
Newcastle-upon-Tyne 9n, 43, 61, 65,
    70–1, 172–3
Newcastle Programme 13, 27
New Directions 274
New Party 221
Newport 160
News Chronicle 235–6, 275
Nicholas II, Czar 93
Nigeria 102
Nonconformists 6, 8, 9, 29, 36, 38, 151
Norfolk 130, 165
Norman, Sir Henry 138
Normanton 83, 89
Northcliffe, Lord 15, 107, 109, 130
Northern Echo 71, 125
    Ireland 58, 277–9, 282
    Liberal Federation 15, 71n, 72–3
Northumberland 45n
Norway 241
Norwich 75
Nottingham 172
Nuclear Disarmament 276
Nudds, T. D. 229, 288, 310
Nuneaton 88

O' Brien, William; Independent
    Nationalists 46–7
Observer 271–2, 285
O'Connor,T. P. 46, 180n
Old Age Pensions 40–1, 172
Oldham 25, 30, 89n, 236
Old Queen Street 197n
O'Neill, J. J. 180n
Orange Lodges 61n
Organization and Election Committee
    181
Orkney & Zetland 260, 263, 285
Orpington 276–82, 292–5, 298
Orwell, George 272
Opposition Leadership 140–1, 163
Osborne case 84–5, 290
Ottawa 228–9, 297
Outhwaite, R. L. 56–7, 86–7, 89, 130,
    145n
Outvoters 11
Owen, Frank 199n, 221n, 223

Owen, Sir Goronwy 219, 221n, 248, 310
Oxford 158, 164, 178, 201
Oxford & Asquith, Countess of, see
    Asquith, 'Margot'
    1st Earl of, see Asquith, H. H.
Oxfordshire 172

Pacifism 36, 94–6, 115, 145
Paisley 123, 137, 145, 185–6, 229, 234n,
    248, 263, 276
Palestine 199
Pall Mall Gazette 62
Palmer, Sir Charles 79
Pardoe, John 285
Parliament Bill/Act 47–59, 84
    Street 16
Parliamentary Recruiting Committee 96
Parliamentary (Patronage) Secretary to
    Treasury 16–17, 109–10
Parmoor, Lord 176
Partington, Oswald 43
'Party Truce' 96, 110, 243, 246–7
Patents 36
Paul, St 208
Payment of M.P.s 84
'Peace, Retrenchment and Reform' 301
Pease, Sir Joseph 71
Pease, Joseph A. (Lord Gainford) 55n,
    94, 306
Peebles and S. Midlothian 164
Pembrokeshire 221, 257
Penistone 164
Perks, R. W. 27n
Phillipps, Vivian 161, 168–9, 174n, 177,
    182, 186, 189–91, 195n, 197, 203,
    207n, 321
'Phylacteries' 27
Pickersgill, E. H. 53
Panning 299
Plural Voting 55–6, 58n
Pointer, J. 81
Police Recruiting 95
Ponsonby, A. A. W. H. 145n, 165
Poole, Oliver 253
Poplar 89n
Preece, Percy 95n
Prerogative 47, 49
Presbyterians 34, 137
Prescott, S. 246
Preston 42n
Primitive Methodists 6
Primrose, Neil 43, 109, 110
Pringle, W. M. R. 122, 137, 192, 195n,
    311
Prohibitionists 164

Proportional Representation, *see* Electoral
 Reform
Protection, *see* Free Trade
Public Opionion Polls 260, 270, 271, 274,
 278–9, 285
Pybus, P. J. 231n

Quelch, Harry 69

Radical Action 245–6
 Group 189, 196–7
Raffan, P. W. 133
Railwaymen 61
Ramsay, T. B. W. 223
Rea, Sir Walter (1st Lord) 130, 222, 236,
 311;
Rea, Sir Philip(2nd Lord) 284, 311
Reading, Marquis of (Sir Rufus Isaacs)
 53–4, 217–18, 228, 311
Rearmament 240
Recessions, *see* Trade Recessions
'Recording Angel' 15
Red Cross 96, 139
Redmond, John 46–7, 101
Reed 70
Rees, Sir Beddoe 176n, 196
Rees, Sir John 290n
Rees, J. Tudor 129n
Reform Acts (1832) 23, 49; (1867) 10, 55;
 (1884) 10, 55; (1918) 125
 Club 108
Regionalism 299, 300
Reid, Sir Robert (Earl Loreburn) 26, 33,
 112
Religion 5–6
'Relugas Compact' 31
Rendall, Athelstan 180n
Renton, Leslie 290n
Representation of the People Act 1918
 125
Retrenchment 298, 301
Reunion, Liberal 166–70
Rhodes, Cecil 14, 23
Rhodes, Sir Edward 162
Rhondda 83
Rhondda, Viscount, *see* Thomas, D. A.
Riga 185
Ripon, Marquis of 65, 311
Roberts, Emrys 253, 262
Roberts, George H. 120
Roberts, Wilfred 237, 244n, 245n
Robinson, Sir T. 176n, 196n
Robinson, W. E. 176n
Rochdale 173, 269
Romanovs 301

Rosebery, 5th Earl 7–8, 16, 18–20, 23–4,
 26–32, 37, 39–40, 43–4, 47–8, 51, 66,
 79, 91–3, 109, 199, 311
Rosebery, 6th Earl (Viscount Dalmeny)
 44, 256
Ross & Cromarty 238
Rotherhithe 251–2
Rothschild, James de 248
Rowntree, Seebohm 210
Roxburghshire, etc. 260, 263, 280, 285
Runciman, Hilda (Viscountess) 202, 205
Runciman, Sir Walter (1st Baron) 181n
Runciman, Walter (2nd Baron, 1st
 Viscount) 33, 42, 55, 60, 62n, 69, 94,
 95n, 100, 101n, 106, 115, 122n,
 128–30, 135, 139, 145, 157–8, 171,
 189, 195n, 196–7 199, 200, 205,
 209n, 211n, 212, 216–17, 222n,
 225–8, 232, 238–40, 311–12
Rusholme 173
Russia 92–3, 180, 185
Rutherford, A. V. 145n

Safeguarding of Industries Act 154
Saffron Walden 281n
St Davids, Lord 166, 170n, 200–1
St Ives 202, 205, 238
'Sale of Honours' 159–60
Salford 76n, 162
Salisbury 281n
Salisbury, 3rd Marquis of 7, 9, 157
Salisbury, 4th Marquis of 146
Salvidge, Sir A. 174n
Samuel, Sir Herbert (Viscount) 33, 55n,
 94, 106, 129, 130, 152, 199–202, 206,
 211, 215–29, 234–6, 246, 265, 297,
 312
Scarborough 228
Schnadhorst, Francis 12n, 14, 16
Schools, *see* Education
'Schopenhauer' 23
Scotland 9, 34, 39, 45, 67, 75–7, 80–1,
 137, 149, 169, 181, 192n, 235, 254,
 280, 292
Scott, C. P. 115–16, 151, 168, 175
Scottish
 Land Bills 39
 Liberals 77, 192n
 Nationalists 292
 Universities 235
 Workers' Parliamentary Elections
  Committee 67, 69
 Workers' Representation Committee
  67, 75–7
Scrymgeour, E. A. 164
Scurr, John 88–9

Seaham 165

Second Preference Voting, *see* Electoral Reform

Seely, J. E. B. 30, 55n, 59, 186

Selborne, Earl of 51

Servants' Tax Registers' League 52

Sex equality 172

Shackleton, David 69–70, 75

Sheffield 80, 82, 169, 172

Shipley 63

Shipping 107

Shops Bill 53

Shoreditch 4n, 164

Simon, E. D. (Lord Simon of Wythenshawe) 209n, 312

Simon, Sir John (Viscount) 94–5, 100, 129, 143–4, 156, 158, 164, 168, 170, 175, 186, 189, 193, 195n, 196, 198, 204, 208, 211–27, 237, 312

Sinclair, Sir Archibald (Viscount Thurso) 164, 209, 211, 217, 219n, 225–6, 228n, 229, 230n, 233, 235–45, 248–9, 259, 297, 312

Sinn Fein 128

Slessor, Sir Henry 176–7

Slump, *see* Trade Recession

Smallholdings 13

Smedley, Oliver 274

Smillie, R. 69, 83

Smith, F. E., *see* Birkenhead, Earl

Smith, Reginald 273

Smithfield 53

Snowden, Philip (Viscount) 75, 129, 164, 177, 210, 213–15, 225–6, 228

Social Democratic Federation 69

Socialists, Socialism 4, 37, 43, 66, 69, 76–7, 79–81, 137, 149, 169, 181, 192n, 235, 254, 280, 292

Somerset 172

Sound Money 298

South Africa 22, *see* also Boer War

South Molton 186

South Shields 236

Southwark 158, 202, 222

Sowerby Bridge 60

Speaker, The 55, 166

Spears, General 176n

Spectator 14, 253

Spen Valley 143–4, 147–8, 164, 186, 204–5, 212

Spencer, Earl 7, 18, 22, 31

Spender, J. A. 31, 115, 238, 291, 312

Spero, Dr 180n

Spicer, Sir Albert 54

Spicer, Lancelot 245

Spirits 41, 46–7

Stamfordham, Lord 98

Stamp Duties 41

Stansgage, Viscount, *see* Benn, W. W.

Star 34, 125, 265, 275

Steel, David 280–1, 285, 312–13

Steel-Maitland, Sir Arthur 158

Stephenson, Frances (Dowager Countess Lloyd-George) 107, 114n

Stephenson, H. K. 169

Stepney 4

Stewart, J. Henderson 235, 242n

Stirling 25, 30, 37

Stirrock, J. B. 176n

Stockport 145–6

Storey, Samuel 71n, 72–3

Stormont 278

Strabolgi, 10th Lord, *see* Kenworthy, J.M.

Strauss, E. A. 222–3

Stroud 173

Stuart-Wortley, C. B. 55n

Sudbury & Woodbridge 279

Sudetens 240

'Suez' 268–9, 300

Suffolk 34

Suffragettes, *see* Women's Suffrage

Surtax, Supertax 31

Suspensory Bill, Act 1914 96

Sutherland, Sir William 150, 168n

Swansea 186n, 205

Swindon 57

Syndicalism 61

Talbot, Lord Edmund 109

Tariffs, Tariff Reform, *see* Free Trade

'Tartan Book' 192n

Tavistock 205

Taylor, Alan J. P. 85, 105

Taylor, Austin 34

Taylor, J. W. 78, 82

Tea 100

Television 275

Temperance 6, 13, 41, 164

Templewood, Viscount, *see* Hoare, Sir Samuel

Tenby, Viscount, *see* Lloyd George, Gwilym

Tennant, H. J. 129

Territorials 95

Teviot, Lord 255–6

Thomas, D. A. (Viscount Rhondda) 67

Thomas, J. H. 210

Thomas, Sir R. 176n

Thompson, T. 129n

Thompson, W. T. 189

Thornborough, F. C. 122–3

Thorne, G. R. 129n, 136, 139, 142, 168, 189 213, 313
Thorneycroft, Peter (Lord) 253
Thorpe, Jeremy 267, 270, 274, 284–5, 313
Thurso, Viscount, *see* Sinclair, Sir Archibald
Tillett, Ben 83
The Times 81, 83n, 86–8, 103–4, 129–30, 162, 199, 268, 272–3, 276–7, 298–9
Tiverton 170
Tobacco 41
Torrington 257, 269, 270, 293, 295
Tort 38
'Tory Reform Group' 253
Tower Hamlets 4n
Towns and the Land, see 'Brown Book'
Trade disputes, Trade Unions, etc. 29, 36, 38, 65, 61, 66–71, 79, 84–6, 120, 288, 290
Trade Disputes Act 1906, 38, 79
Trade recessions 36, 79
Trade Union Labour Group 78, 82
Trade Unions Act 1913, 84–6, 289
Trevelyan, Sir Charles 60–1, 95, 130, 145n, 152, 165
'Triple Alliance' 61
Truro 30
Tudors 247
Turkey 19, 160
Tweed, T. F. 197n, 199, 228n
Tweedsmouth, Lord 21n
'Twelve Apostles' 195–6
Twenty Liberal National Points of Policy 239
Tynemouth 123
Tyneside 9

Ulster 34, 57–61, 101, 117
Unemployment 54, 154, 170–1, 201, 203–4, 210, 214–15, 233, 293–4
Unionist Free Traders 30, 34
Unionists, *see also* Conservatives, Liberal Unionists 4, 5, 7–10, 15, 17, and *passim*
Unitarians 6
United Free Church of Scotland 137
United States of America 3
Universities 34, 55, 258, 260
Utrecht, Treaty of 49

Versailles 142
Victoria, Queen 9, 20–2

Wade, Donald (Lord) 260, 262, 268, 284, 313
Wadsworth, John 89
Wainwright, Richard 282

'Wait and see' 47–8
Wales, Welsh Church, Welsh Party, etc. 9, 13, 34, 36, 45, 48, 53, 57, 67, 76–7, 80, 96, 120, 134, 149, 164, 166, 237, 247, 289, 292
Walker, Sir Ronald 209n, 265
Wallace, Edgar 221
Walsall 226
Walters, Sir J. Tudor 217
Walthamstow 186, 211
Walton, Sir Lawson 38
War Committees 102–3
Ward, John 189n
Ward, W. Dudley 123n, 138n
Watson, R. Spence 9n, 10n
We can conquer unemployment 201, 203–4
Webb, Beatrice 120, 152
Webb, Sidney (Lord Passfield) 27, 120, 165
Webster, William, 77n
Wedgwood, Josiah (Lord) 136, 145n, 150, 313
'Wee Frees' 137, *see* also Asquithians
Welsh Liberal Federation 149
    National Liberal Federation 149, 150
Wesleyan Methodists 6
West Ham 4n, 66
West Riding 9, 60, 89
Westbury 202
Western Counties 45n
    Isles 186n, 223
    National Liberal Organization 190
Westminster 4, 58, 177
Westminster Gazette 115, 125
Westminster Hall 50
Weston-super-Mare 197
Wheatley, John 177
Whigs 7, 23, 152
Whips, Party 11, 12, 15, 16, 62, 69, 70, 73, 90, 109, 127, 130, 134, 140, 149, 159, 168, 169, 181, 186, 200, 223, 257; *see* also under names of individual Whips.
White, C. F. 129n
White, Graham 248, 259
Whiteley, George, *see* Marchamley, Lord
Whitley, J. H. 97, 165, 189n
Whittaker, Sir Thomas 143
Widnes 164
Wilhelm II, Kaiser 95, 207n
Willesden 170
Willey, F. V. (Lord Barnby) 129n
William IV, King 49
Williams, Aneurin 129n
Williams, C. P. 196n
Williams, Penry 129n

Wilson, E. 77n
Wilson, Harold 285
Wilson, J. Havelock 66, 72n, 129n
Wilson, J. W. 129n
Wilson Trevor 121n
Wiltshire 172
Wimborne, Viscount 110
Wintingham, Mrs Margaret 180n, 190n
Wisbech 110
Wolverhampton 186n
Wolverhampton, Viscount, *see* Fowler,
    Sir Henry
Women's Suffrage 54–5, 61
Wood, A. D. 77n
Wood, Sir Kingsley 242
Wood, T. McKinnon 55n, 94, 129

Woolton, Lord; Woolton-Teviot
    Agreement 255–6, 261
Woolwich 71, 73
Workers' Weekly 178–9

'Yellow Book' 201, 203, 298
Yorkshire 9, 45n, 60, 74, 89, 186
Yorkshire Evening News 116
Young, E. Hilton (Lord Kennet) 129n,
    136, 173, 193, 196, 308
Young Liberals 286
Younger, Sir George (Viscount) 122, 144,
    156, 163, 166

Zimmerman, L. W. 83
Zinoviev, Gregor; Zinoviev Letter 185–6